Information and Communications Technology Law in Ireland

Information and Communications Technology Law in Ireland

By

Dr Rónán Kennedy

BComm, HDipSysAnal, LLB, BL, LLM,
PGCertTLHE, PhD, HDipAcPrac

Dr Maria Helen Murphy

BCL, LLM, PhD

Published by
Clarus Press Ltd,
Griffith Campus,
South Circular Road,
Dublin 8.

Typeset by
DataPage International,
Dublin,
Ireland

Printed by
Sprint Print,
Dublin

ISBN
978-1-905536-96-2

Do Shíomha, as na miongháirí go léir
Rónán Kennedy

For David and the rest of my wonderful family
Maria Helen Murphy

Preface

A key motivation for this book was to produce an accessible and up-to-date text that would demystify the relationship between law and technology. We intend *Information and Communications Technology Law in Ireland* to be a key text for undergraduate and post-graduate law students. The book has particular relevance for those studying IT Law, but will also be of benefit to those studying Intellectual Property Law, Information Privacy Law, Cybercrime, Online Regulation, Media Law, and other subjects. Furthermore, it is also expected that the book will be of interest to those studying in fields as broad as information technology and systems, computer science, and business – areas where the interaction between ICT and law has significant implications.

The broad range of topics covered in this book – and the wide range of students it is designed to be of aid to – demonstrates the entanglement of technology with all aspects of modern life. This book illustrates how many common themes arise in the legal topics discussed and recognises that continuous change in the law is likely in light of ongoing technological and societal development. Indeed, some aspects of the law were reformed as the text was being written. We are pleased to have covered many recent developments including the General Data Protection Regulation, the Criminal Justice (Offences Relating to Information Systems) Act 2017, and crypto-currencies. We aim to deliver a practical, accessible, and critical text that will provide students with a solid grounding in ICT Law. We hope that the "Further Reading" sections included at the end of each chapter will enable students to explore topics of interest in greater depth, whether in preparing for examinations or researching for essays.

Finally, we would like to thank all those who contributed to the production of this book. In particular, we would like to express our thanks to David McCartney and Marsha Swan at Clarus Press for their hard work and expert guidance, and our sincere gratitude to our busy colleagues who have given the time and effort to read draft chapters while busy with other work. Many thanks to Eamonn Barrett, Robert Clark, Caterina Gardiner, Alisdair Gillespie, Willie Golden, Padraic Kenna, Paul Lambert, David Mangan, Maeve McDonagh, Kevin Moore, Sandra Murphy, and Fidelma White for your thoughtful comments. It is much appreciated. Any errors that remain are, of course, our responsibility. Rónán would also like to note his appreciation for Liam O'Malley, for encouraging his interest in this area of law when it was a much smaller field, and to Fiona for giving him the time to write. Maria would like to thank David and the rest of her family for their unending support. We are both grateful for the support of our colleagues at the National University of Ireland Galway and Maynooth University.

Rónán Kennedy
Berkeley, California

Maria Helen Murphy
Maynooth, Ireland

September 2017

About the Authors

Dr Rónán Kennedy

Dr Rónán Kennedy researches and teaches environmental law, information technology law, and the intersections between these. He has a background in information technology and information systems, having spent much of the 1990s working as a programmer, analyst and webmaster. He has organised conferences and workshops on the use of information technology for environmental regulation, algorithmic governance, and blockchain and sustainable communities. He also has an interest in legal research and writing and is one of the editors of *OSCOLA Ireland*. He posts about these and other topics at https://twitter.com/ronanmkennedy.

He worked as Executive Legal Officer to the Chief Justice of Ireland, Mr Justice Ronan Keane, from 2000 to 2004. During this time, he was editor of "The Supreme Court of Ireland: A History", first editor of the *Judicial Studies Institute Journal* from 2001 to 2003, and was involved in a number of initiatives to expand the use of information technology in the courts. Before coming to the Law Faculty in NUI Galway, he taught environmental law and public international law in the University of Limerick. He was the co-ordinator of the LLM in Law, Technology and Governance from 2008 to 2014 and was Associate Head for Development and Promotion for the School from April 2009 to April 2010.

Dr Kennedy holds a degree in commerce and a higher diploma in systems analysis from University College Galway, an LLB with first class honours from the National University of Ireland, Galway, an LLM from New York University and a PhD from University College London. He also studied for the degree of Barrister-at-Law in the King's Inns and was called to the Bar of Ireland in 2003. He was a visiting PhD student in the Tilburg Institute for Law and Technology in 2010, and a Visiting Scholar at the School of Law at the University of California at Berkeley in 2017.

Dr Maria Helen Murphy

Dr Maria Helen Murphy is a Lecturer in Law at Maynooth University. Dr Murphy lectures Information Privacy Law and Information Technology Law at the postgraduate level, and lectures Media Law and Civil Liberties at the undergraduate level. Dr Murphy also serves as a Subject and Programme External Examiner for the University of Hertfordshire Law Department. Previously, she lectured at the Dublin Institute of Technology.

Dr Murphy researches in the areas of privacy law, surveillance, information technology law, and human rights. Dr Murphy is particularly interested in addressing the challenges to privacy in the digital age and in 2015 she co-organised a British and Irish Law Education and Technology Association funded event, 'Privacy: Gathering insights from lawyers and technologists'. Dr Murphy posts about privacy, data protection, and technology law on her Twitter page at https://twitter.com/maria_h_murphy.

In addition to completing her Irish Research Council funded PhD at University College Cork in 2013, Dr Murphy holds a *magna cum laude* LLM degree from Temple University (Philadelphia), and a First Class Honours BCL (International) degree from UCC.

Table of Contents

Detailed Table of Contents

Table of Cases

Australia

Court of Justice of the European Union

European Court of Human Rights

France

Ireland

Singapore

United Kingdom

United States of America

Table of Legislation

Secondary Legislation

France

United Kingdom

United States of America

European Union

International Conventions

PART 1

Contextualising ICT and Law

CHAPTER 1
Contextualising ICT and Law

'The web is more a social creation than a technical one. I designed it for a social effect – to help people work together – and not as a technical toy. The ultimate goal of the Web is to support and improve our weblike existence in the world. We clump into families, associations, and companies. We develop trust across the miles and distrust around the corner.'[1]

ICT: An Overview

[01] It is sometimes said that technology is anything invented after you are born. For most students reading this textbook, therefore, information and communications technology (ICT) does not seem to be a technology – it is simply something that is there, like roads, refrigerators, and agriculture. However, each of these are technologies: they were all invented; they were successfully disseminated and adopted; and they have each become very important social, cultural, and economic phenomena. ICT is no different.

[02] The online databases that you search in the library, the laptop on which you type your essays, and the smartphone through which you communicate with friends and family are all part of a complex collection of interconnected and very sophisticated technologies which have developed in a comparatively short period. In that time, they have become a very important element in modern business, culture, and government. Some technologies and companies have been very successful; others have had brief periods of dominance only to fade from view (for example, the Bebo and MySpace social networks, the web browser Netscape, or the mobile phone company Nokia).

---

[1] Tim Berners-Lee, *Weaving the Web* (HarperCollins 2000) 123.

[1–03]   This textbook considers the relationship between law and ICT: both the way in which the development of ICT is shaped by legal rules, and the way in which ICT is changing the way in which law is developed and implemented. Specific legal regimes, such as intellectual property, defamation, or data protection, have played an important part in creating constraints and rewards for technology entrepreneurs. Many battles for dominance in a digital marketplace have been won or lost in a courtroom rather than in the minds of consumers. Similarly, as the law is fundamentally about working with words, the use of ICT to manage, search, and consider the large volumes of text which a lawyer must marshal and master has become an important element in the day-to-day work of many practitioners. Recent advances in machine learning and so-called artificial intelligence suggest that ICT may create the conditions for radical changes in the ways in which lawyers operate.

How ICT Works

[1–04]   Before considering the steadily expanding body of law that surrounds ICT, it is essential to have a good grasp of the functioning of the technology. There was a time when a 'computer' was an easily identifiable device, large enough to fill a room; then smaller, but still requiring a dedicated desk; now it is often small enough to fit in a pocket or to be embedded in a larger device, such as a weighing scales.

[1–05]   However, all of these devices share common elements. First, there are *micro-chips*: very tightly integrated electronic circuits etched into silicon wafers. Second, they work with *binary data* – sequences of zeros and ones. Third, they follow *stored programs*. All of which is a technical way of saying that no matter what they look like – a desktop computer with screen and keyboard, a tablet with a touch-screen, or an invisible embedded chip in a car ignition – they all work in the same way.

[1–06]   This means that despite the frequent use of labels such as 'intelligent' and 'smart' to describe ICT devices, they are, in fact, machines with quite limited abilities. Much of the way in which they function has to be painstakingly planned in advance, and relies on years of engineering experience. They store all of their information in what are known as *bits* (a binary digit, either zero or one) and *bytes* (a grouped sequence of bits, usually eight, which represents a number, usually from 0 to 255). For a computer to be able to process information – sights, sounds, colours, tastes, smells – it needs to be converted to a numeric representation and ultimately to bits. Finally, any processing that they carry out must be determined in advance, by writing *software* which sets out very detailed instructions for the machine to follow. (There is, at the time of writing, significant and rapid development of what is called 'big data', 'artificial intelligence' or 'machine learning', sometimes subsumed under the shorthand label of 'the algorithm'. This involves approaches to rule development in which the human programmers write programs which allow the computer system to learn from data and amend its own decision-making processes. This is significantly extending the capabilities of computers to carry out tasks which were, until recently, thought to be only feasible for humans. We will briefly consider what this means for legal practice and the future of ICT law in the last two chapters.)

[1–07]   How, then, have such tightly constrained machines become so powerful and important, and why do we perceive them as being intelligent and flexible? Digital computers are examples of what computer scientists call *Turing machines*, after a famous thought experiment conducted by the English mathematician Alan Turing in the early development of computer

4

technology. He imagined a logic device which could follow instructions and was able to show that this was infinitely re-programmable. Digital computers are therefore both very tightly constrained by the limits of hardware design and electronic engineering, and very malleable. This adaptability and flexibility gives them great power, but can also be a source of important legal issues, particularly in the criminal law, as they can be used for fraud and other illegal purposes.

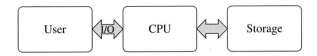

Figure 1   *Basic Computer Architecture*

All computers have a *Central Processing Unit* (CPU), some means of *input/output (I/O)*   **[1–08]** (traditionally a keyboard and display, augmented by printers, scanners, and networking), and some means of *storage* (traditionally temporary storage in fast random-access memory or RAM, and long-term storage in a hard disk). As ICT becomes more mobile and more embedded, the nature of the input/output devices and the types of storage are changing rapidly, with the development of touch-sensitive screens, solid-state hard disks, and the 'Internet of Things' (IoT), where computers are a hidden part of many small devices.

Figure 2   *The Internet of Things*

The IoT involves four main elements: **[1–09]**

1. sensors, to allow an object to detect its physical environment;
2. communicative chips (such as the RFID chips mentioned above) to allow the object to communicate what it has detected and receive back instructions;
3. computers (or servers), which can aggregate and process the data coming from these objects and return commands; and
4. the internet, to connect the objects with the servers.[2]

---

[2] Nick Westbrook and Mark Taylor, 'The Internet of Things' (2013) 19 Computer and Telecommunications Law Review 244, 244–245 citing Michael Chui, Markus Löffler, and Roger Roberts, 'The Internet of Things' 2010(2) McKinsey Quarterly 1.

This also raises legal issues, as rapid market development leads to conflicts over intellectual property and the proliferation of computing throughout the infrastructure of modern life creates privacy problems and opportunities for deceit.

How ICT is Developed

[1–10]   With the often rapid pace of technological development and the obscure terminology used by specialists, you might believe that technology develops by itself, without human intervention, and that it is a pristine artefact, free from human influence. The reality is quite different: ICT is developed through the intense application of human thought, often over long periods of time. It usually requires teams of engineers, systems analysts, and programmers. They will rarely start from nothing but instead will rely on existing standards, already-constructed systems, and general know-how as a way of saving time and effort. (This will often generate legal issues, as the re-use of intellectual property owned by others, either through copyright or patent, will create a need to negotiate a licence, and the development of standards can raise competition law issues.)

[1–11]   ICT has to be embodied in some physical form – *hardware* – which will therefore have to deal with the limits imposed by the laws of physics. Energy requirements, storage capacity and networked communications all have physical dimensions which need to be taken into account. For a mass market, devices need to be easily reproducible in reliable and consistent ways.

[1–12]   In order to be truly useful, ICT must contain detailed instructions – *software* – which describe exactly how the machine is to respond to particular inputs and what output to produce. Programs tend to grow in complexity, often becoming much larger than the scale of human comprehension. For example, the Linux operating system core is about 15 million lines of code; Facebook roughly 20 million lines; the Windows operating system is in the region of 50 million; and Google about 2 billion lines.[3] As these numbers should make clear, writing software is a very slow, difficult, and error-prone process. It is also one which relies very much on assumptions and implicit understandings, and thus is vulnerable to being affected by biases and prejudices. As more and more of our commercial, social, and regulatory interactions are mediated by software, this is becoming a serious concern.

[1–13]   Software is written in *code*, generally what are known as *high-level languages* (meaning that they are more like human languages than the low-level binary code which the computer really uses). Programming code allows a human to define the steps that a computer should take in order to carry out a task, and how to respond to the various activities of its users. It is very similar to a recipe in a cookery book. The process is discussed in more detail in [2–09] to [2–11].

Telecoms and the Internet: A Primer

[1–14]   The internet and the World Wide Web, which provide the foundation for the publishing platforms, social networking services, and business-to-business communications that create the context for many of the legal issues and questions that this textbook discusses, can also

---

[3] Cade Metz, 'Google Is 2 Billion Lines of Code–And It's All in One Place' (*Wired*, 16 Sept 2015) <www.wired.com/2015/09/google-2-billion-lines-codeand-one-place/> accessed 13 June 2017.

seem like a magical world – a place of pure thought and of instantaneous transmission of ideas, without boundaries or borders. The reality is more complex and more prosaic.

Internet-connected computers communicate using TCP/IP (Transmission Control Protocol/ Internet Protocol) on a packet switch network. In simple language, that means that everyone who wants to get onto the internet has to agree to communicate using a certain set of rules (a protocol) and that the data is sent from place to place in packets, similar to the way postal services move envelopes from place to place. When you post an envelope, you address it in a certain way and you do not know what path it will take to reach its final destination. If you mis-address it, it will come back to you or get lost in the system. Mixing everyone's letters in together and getting one postman to deliver to one street at a time makes the postal service economical; similarly, the internet is a very cost-effective way of moving information from place to place. [1–15]

The crucial difference between the two methods of communication, and the main reason that there is such interest in the internet, is that it can handle any type of information that a computer can handle, at a much faster speed than the postal service, and all without having to leave your desk. Currently, this means rapid access to mail messages and documents, music, pictures, movie clips, databases of research information, up-to-the-minute statistics, weather forecasts and so on. [1–16]

While it may seem that this occurs somewhere other than in the physical world – in what is often called 'cyberspace' – this transfer of data from person to person also involves moving it from place to place. Perhaps because it is very difficult to identify exactly how and when this occurs (it is much harder to pinpoint which collection of electrons constitute a particular email message than to pinpoint which envelope contains a particular letter), the transfer seems to happen in another dimension. However, it does involve wires, routers, and data storage which are very much part of the real world. [1–17]

It also involves the use of *standards*. In the internet world, these fall into two main categories: commonly agreed and open protocols (often defined in documents called Requests for Comment or RFCs); and closed, proprietary systems (which can be accessed by outsiders through Application Programming Interfaces or APIs). RFCs are essentially public property, whereas APIs are often subject to strong intellectual property rights. Both can give rise to legal issues and problems: RFC-based protocols (such as Simple Mail Transfer Protocol, or SMTP, which is the backbone of most internet email) contain assumptions about the trustworthiness of users which no longer hold true and thus facilitate the problem of spam, while disagreements over access and control of APIs have culminated in lawsuits. [1–18]

A Very Brief History of ICT

The use of technology to store, manage, and manipulate information has a long history, stretching back millennia and perhaps further, with applications in navigation, government, and commerce.[4] The ancient Greeks and Romans possessed devices which could be used to calculate lunar, solar, and stellar calendars. Astrolabes were also common. Various systems [1–19]

---

[4] Abbe Mowshowitz, *The Conquest of Will: Information Processing in Human Affairs* (Addison-Wesley 1976) 24–29.

were developed in order to record numerical information, such as the use of knots, 'tally sticks', calculating rods, and the abacus. The slide rule was an early attempt at devising mechanical aids to mathematical calculations, making it easier for individuals to perform complex operations. Between the 1600s and the 1800s, progressively more complex adding machines were developed, work that culminated in the famous (although never completed) 'difference engine' and 'analytical engine' developed by Charles Babbage, and the electro-mechanical machines developed for the 1890 United States Census by Herman Hollerith.[5] There were also early attempts at telecommunications: some relying on sight, such as the French *télégraphe* (semaphore towers) of the late 1700s, and others on electricity, such as the Morse code and the electrical telegraph. [6] During this period, bureaucracy developed, largely for the purpose of the record-keeping required by centralised government. A significant element of this was the census, which was increasingly automated.[7] The growth of these administrative processes, both in the public and the private sectors, relied heavily on (and encouraged) the development of sophisticated technology, at first mechanical and later digital.[8]

[1–20] Emergencies, particularly warfare, have been significant drivers for the development of ICT. This was the case even before digital computers, as can be seen from the way in which punched cards came to prominence as a way of dealing with staff shortages and increasing demands for services from His Majesty's Stationery Office in the UK during the First World War.[9] The development of the modern electronic computer has its roots in the need to compute ballistics tables during the Second World War.[10] A certain amount of development took place in the years before the war in the United States, chiefly led by John Atanasoff.[11] During the war years, the Allies' efforts to break German military codes gave rise to the development of a digital device known as the Colossus, while the US military's need for mechanical calculations gave rise to the Harvard Mark One and Mark Two computers, and the Electronic Numerical Integrator And Computer (ENIAC). In contrast, research in Germany led by Konrad Zuse was not significant in the development of this type of technology.[12] This development was need-driven, more the product of external social forces rather than itself a driver of social change.[13]

---

[5] Eric G Swedin and David L Ferro, *Computers: The Life Story of a Technology* (Greenwood Publishing Group 2005) 1–23.

[6] James Gleick, *The Information* (Fourth Estate 2012) 129–36, 140–52.

[7] Abbe Mowshowitz, *The Conquest of Will: Information Processing in Human Affairs* (Addison-Wesley 1976) 29–32.

[8] James R Beniger, *The Control Revolution: Technological and Economic Origins of the Information Society* (Harvard University Press 1986) 390–425.

[9] Jon Agar, *The Government Machine* (MIT Press 2003) 159.

[10] Martin Campbell-Kelly and William Aspray, *Computer: A History of the Information Machine* (Westview Press 2004) 71–85.

[11] Paul N Edwards, 'From "Impact" to Social Process: Computers in Society and Culture' in Sheila Jasanoff and others (eds), *Handbook of Science and Technology Studies* (Sage, Thousand Oaks 1994) 258.

[12] Eric G Swedin and David L Ferro, *Computers: The Life Story of a Technology* (Greenwood Publishing Group 2005) 25–45.

[13] Paul N Edwards, 'From "Impact" to Social Process: Computers in Society and Culture' in Sheila Jasanoff and others (eds), *Handbook of Science and Technology Studies* (Sage, Thousand Oaks 1994) 259.

The design of the new technology was influenced by existing patterns of problem-solving [1–21]
and information-processing in engineering and business, and many of the fundamental features of the design of modern computers, such as the stored program, shared storage of
information and instructions, and the sequential processing of these, were defined in this
early period.[14] This highlights how early design decisions can become difficult to change
as a technology develops.

After the War, computer technology was developed in both the United Kingdom and in the [1–22]
United States of America. Machines became available on a commercial basis in the early
1950s, first the Ferranti Mark One (developed in Manchester) and the UNIVAC (developed in Philadelphia). From early on, these new devices were connected together, first by
teletype machines and then by modems.[15] This period was characterised by the mutual
orientation of the military and engineers towards the development of new applications,
with each group providing ideas for the other to support, either with funding or research
effort. Salient examples include MIT's ambitious Whirlwind computer, which attracted
funding when it was aligned with the Air Force's need for an air defence system and
evolved to run SAGE (Semi-Automated Ground Environment). It was probably of limited
operational application but very significant in the development of computer technology
overall,[16] with IBM's involvement incentivising it to develop new capabilities and begin
to dominate the market.[17]

In the period immediately following World War II, government and military funding con- [1–23]
tinued to be important for the development of computer technology, as both sides in the
Cold War sought for strategic advantage from the better control and management of information, particularly for air defence systems. These early devices used vacuum tubes which
were large, generated significant heat, and were fragile. The invention of the transistor
provided a solution and was significant in assisting with the development of increasingly
widespread applications of computer technology. A thriving commercial sector developed,
targeting both government (particularly defence) and large business.[18] Early applications
included census processing, flight reservation and ticketing, and banking.[19] From the
1950s,[20] government departments were quick to adopt the new 'mainframe' computers,
which could be used to store, manage, and process large quantities of data, and these were
seen as essential to normal operation and new policy initiatives (such as the introduction of
value-added tax in Britain in 1972).[21]

---

[14] Paul E Ceruzzi, *A History of Modern Computing* (2nd edn, MIT Press 2003) 15–16.

[15] Eric G Swedin and David L Ferro, *Computers: The Life Story of a Technology* (Greenwood
Publishing Group 2005) 41–45, 111–12.

[16] Paul N Edwards, 'From "Impact" to Social Process: Computers in Society and Culture' in Sheila
Jasanoff and others (eds), *Handbook of Science and Technology Studies* (Sage, Thousand Oaks 1994) 266.

[17] Paul E Ceruzzi, *A History of Modern Computing* (2nd edn, MIT Press 2003) 52–53.

[18] Eric G Swedin and David L Ferro, *Computers: The Life Story of a Technology* (Greenwood
Publishing Group 2005) 47–57.

[19] Nicholas G Carr, *The Big Switch: Rewiring the World, from Edison to Google* (WW Norton 2008) 48–51.

[20] Helen Margetts, 'The Automated State' (1995) 10 Public Policy and Administration 88, 89.

[21] Christine Bellamy and John A Taylor, *Governing in the Information Age* (Open University Press
1998) 11.

[1–24] Throughout the 1950s, innovations in computer architecture made these tools progressively more powerful.[22] The development of the 'integrated circuit' (or microchip) in the latter part of that decade, which allowed the combination of a variety of components in very close proximity to each other, permitted the construction of much faster, cheaper, and more reliable computer technology. This facilitated the commercial development of ubiquitous personal computer technology, such as electronic calculators. Further development of microchips led to the 'microprocessor', which combined all of the fundamental elements necessary for a computer onto a single chip.[23]

[1–25] On the software side, mathematicians developed methods of programming these devices using notation somewhat closer to human speech and writing than the generally inscrutable binary codes of the machinery and systems for the re-use of common sequences of instructions, culminating in the development of 'high level languages' such as FORTRAN, COBOL, and ALGOL, and 'operating systems' to manage the loading and unloading of the resulting programs.[24] Researchers developed 'time-sharing' systems, which allowed several individuals to use the same computer at the same time. Over time, this gave rise to the UNIX system, which was to be a mainstay of computer networking in the future.[25] The 'mainframe' (large, expensive, and managed by specialists) was supplemented by 'minicomputers' (smaller, cheaper, and more individual).[26] During the 1960s, the foundations of what was later to become the Internet were laid with the development of the ARPANET to connect laboratories doing work for the Pentagon. With the advent of jet airliners, IBM developed a computerised reservation system, known as SABRE, for American Airlines. This was put into use in 1964 and still provides essential services for the travel industry today.[27] The building blocks for the expansion of computing technology into the home, and eventually to mobile devices, were now in place.

[1–26] This diffusion of technology to somewhat unanticipated contexts was highly significant, taking the expensive, complex hardware available only to a limited and technical community and making it affordable for all as personal devices. Calculators and computers became commodities and individuals developed very personal uses for, and relationships with, these new devices.[28] During the 1970s, the availability of microchips led to the development of 'microcomputers' and a burgeoning software industry (and the perennial problem of intellectual property infringement). Apple developed easy-to-use computers, and early spreadsheet applications meant that microcomputers became common in business environments. IBM, who had dominated the market for mainframes, designed their own microcomputer, something which gave this new technology significant legitimacy in the

---

[22] Paul E Ceruzzi, *A History of Modern Computing* (2nd edn, MIT Press 2003) 58–64.
[23] Eric G Swedin and David L Ferro, *Computers: The Life Story of a Technology* (Greenwood Publishing Group 2005) 65–68, 80–83.
[24] Paul E Ceruzzi, *A History of Modern Computing* (2nd edn, MIT Press 2003) 82–100.
[25] Eric G Swedin and David L Ferro, *Computers: The Life Story of a Technology* (Greenwood Publishing Group 2005) 69–71.
[26] Nicholas G Carr, *The Big Switch: Rewiring the World, from Edison to Google* (WW Norton 2008) 52–53.
[27] Eric G Swedin and David L Ferro, *Computers: The Life Story of a Technology* (Greenwood Publishing Group 2005) 111–12, 61.
[28] Paul E Ceruzzi, *A History of Modern Computing* (2nd edn, MIT Press 2003) 207–17.

business market.[29] Microsoft sought to dominate the market for home and small business computing that it saw developing.[30] Also in the commercial sphere, the resulting availability of new information resources throughout all levels of the hierarchy of government made possible significant changes in business processes.[31] Meanwhile, during this same period in the private sector government came to contain 'networks of information systems processing data about individuals, organizations, goods and services, carrying out financial transactions, registering authority and providing management information'.[32]

As computer technology became more widespread, there was an increasing need to connect these new devices together. The open and portable nature of UNIX made it a natural foundation for these efforts.[33] The network control program (NCP) developed for the ARPANET was elaborated into the Transport Control Protocol (TCP) and the Internet Protocol (IP). The new network, which developed into the internet (commonly used by millions worldwide today), grew through a process of bottom-up, open development of standards and tools, largely through the Internet Engineering Task Force (IETF) and the Internet Engineering Steering Group (IESG). Over time, as it became the *de facto* standard, the internet has subsumed into itself the Computer Science Network (CSNET).   **[1–27]**

There were alternative networks of bulletin board systems (BBSs), both hobbyist (FidoNet) and commercial (CompuServe, Prodigy, and America Online), which have dwindled in importance or disappeared entirely as the internet has become dominant. New technologies were laid on top of the basic internet protocols, such as the USENET discussion forums, the Gopher information navigation system, and the Wide Area Information Service and Veronica search protocols. However, these were all absorbed and then supplanted by the World Wide Web (WWW or Web), based on hypertext technology, which made text-based and difficult to use systems much more visually appealing and easy to navigate by ordinary users.[34]   **[1–28]**

Knowing the history of the internet is important as it creates the context for much of the privacy and computer crime problems that this book concerns itself with. It was intended to be an indestructible telecommunications network with sufficient resilience to survive a nuclear strike, and it was designed and built by researchers operating in a culture of openness and sharing. It was not originally intended for commercial use. Therefore, it is easy to connect to, has very few gate-keeping mechanisms, and all communications across it are (normally) open and readable by others on the network.   **[1–29]**

It also underlines the transient nature of ICT systems and protocols, the fact that future developments are never inevitable (despite what present-day evangelists and marketers   **[1–30]**

[29] Eric G Swedin and David L Ferro, *Computers: The Life Story of a Technology* (Greenwood Publishing Group 2005) 85–109.
[30] Nicholas G Carr, *The Big Switch: Rewiring the World, from Edison to Google* (WW Norton 2008) 54.
[31] Christine Bellamy and John A Taylor, *Governing in the Information Age* (Open University Press 1998) 12.
[32] Helen Margetts, 'The Automated State' (1995) 10 Public Policy and Administration 88, 90.
[33] Paul E Ceruzzi, *A History of Modern Computing* (2nd edn, MIT Press 2003) 283–84.
[34] Eric G Swedin and David L Ferro, *Computers: The Life Story of a Technology* (Greenwood Publishing Group 2005) 116–30.

may trumpet), and the importance of law in the history. For example, Gopher is said to be better than the WWW from a technical and structural perspective, and amongst the reasons that it did not succeed was that the University of Minnesota (where it was developed) sought licencing fees for its use.[35]

[1–31] The Web, combined with the growth in availability and speed of bandwidth for long-distance communication, has led to the resurgence of the client-server model of the early years of computer technology and the development of business models for the provision of 'cloud computing' services similar to electricity and water utilities.[36] 'Client-server' arrangements involve a large central system ('server') which stores shared data and application software, making this available to end-users ('clients'), generally using much less powerful computers. This model was common in the early decades of the history of computing but declined during the 1990s as personal computers became cheaper and more powerful. With the widespread availability of fast broadband connections, particularly over wireless and mobile telephone networks, the central servers are now globally distributed and the client devices are often small and mobile smartphones and tablets. Computing power and data reside in an unknown location, colloquially referred to as 'the cloud'. Therefore, a user in Ireland may be interacting with a server located in another jurisdiction, generating interesting legal questions regarding which country's law apply. Indeed, that user is probably interacting with several servers in a variety of locations; for example, someone who sees an ad while reading their morning paper and decides to make a purchase may deal with a newspaper website, advertising companies, an electronic commerce vendor, and a financial institution.

[1–32] These developments have also made it possible for public administrations to make data available both between agencies and with the public in a much more flexible fashion. Knowledge-based systems, or expert systems, can support decision-making by individuals. Multimedia, smart cards and information exchange enable new forms of access to information, the reduction of costs and the removal of barriers between organisations and even jurisdictions.[37] Radical frontiers of potential change therefore open up.[38]

[1–33] As the internet moved into the mainstream, two significant forces emerged. One was labelled 'Web 2.0', denoting a move from one-way to two-way communication and the development of open, dynamic mash ups of data. These are developed in a collaborative fashion in an increasingly 'social' space of rapid entrepreneurial innovation. Prominent failures include Friendster and MySpace and well-known survivors include Facebook, Wikipedia, and Twitter. The second was the increasing mobility of computing devices, assisted by the miniaturisation of electronics technology and the growing availability

---

[35] Scott Carlson, 'How Gopher Nearly Won the Internet' (*Chronicle of Higher Education*, 5 September 2016) </www.chronicle.com/article/How-Gopher-Nearly-Won-the/237682> accessed 13 June 2017; Tim Gihring, 'The Rise and Fall of the Gopher Protocol' (*MinnPost* 2016) <www.minnpost.com/business/2016/08/rise-and-fall-gopher-protocol> accessed 13 June 2017.

[36] Nicholas G Carr, *The Big Switch: Rewiring the World, from Edison to Google* (WW Norton 2008) 58–61.

[37] Christine Bellamy and John A Taylor, *Governing in the Information Age* (Open University Press 1998) 15–18.

[38] Helen Margetts, 'The Automated State' (1995) 10 Public Policy and Administration 88, 91–92.

of broadband.[39] If present trends continue, this will lead to the rise of the 'Internet of Things' and 'Web 3.0', in which many more devices contain micro-processors and are connected together in a dispersed communications network of 'intelligent' devices and sensors.[40]

Law in the Information Society

The Law of the Horse?

While the rapid and widespread adoption of the new technologies outlined above highlights their significance as an important element in modern life, does this justify creating a new area of legal study around them? After all, before the development of the digital computer, there have been many other technologies which have had significant social implications, such as the printing press, the postal service, the telephone, the telegram, the fax machine, and television. A prominent US academic and judge, Frank Easterbrook, mocked attempts to develop what was then generally called 'Cyberlaw' as a distinct body of law, claiming that this made as much sense as talking about 'The Law of the Horse'.[41] Is 'Information Technology Law' (or 'Information and Communications Technology Law' as it is beginning to be called) truly a subject in its own right? When digital technology is part and parcel of so many of our routine interactions – social engagements, education, shopping – does it make sense to try to make sense of these by surveying computers-and-criminal-law, computers-and-tort, computers-and-contract, and so on? As Andrew Murray has argued, although the early days of law-and-computers scholarship and teaching were about 'computer world problems', the growing significance of ICT means that a detailed study of these issues can help us to understand broader questions about topics that are quite important generally, such as freedom of speech, the limits to national laws and jurisdictions, and the need to protect the rule of law.[42]

[1–34]

Regulating Bits rather than Things

Before looking at the detail of particular legal issues that arise in the context of ICT, it is very useful to consider the relationship between law and what is often now called the 'Information Society' (or sometimes the 'Knowledge Economy'). The ICT industry is prone to making grand statements about its importance, and often manages to have these taken seriously or even repeated by politicians, media commentators, and policy-makers. The thoughtful reader should therefore treat all claims about the revolutionary and innovative nature of ICT with a considerable degree of scepticism. When a particular cycle of hype is over, the same social and legal problems often remain, unsolved and sometimes even worsened by the technology which was supposed to remove them.

[1–35]

---

[39] Johnny Ryan, *A History of the Internet and the Digital Future* (Reaktion Books 2010) 137–50, 158–59.

[40] Gianluca Misuraca, 'Futuring E-Government: Governance and Policy Implications for Designing an ICT-Enabled Knowledge Society' in Tomasz Janowski (ed), *Proceedings of the 3rd international conference on theory and practice of electronic governance (iCEGOV '09)* (Association for Computing Machinery 2009) 87.

[41] Frank H Easterbrook, 'Cyberspace and the Law of the Horse' (1996) University of Chicago Legal Forum 207.

[42] Andrew Murray, 'Looking Back at the Law of the Horse: Why Cyberlaw and the Rule of Law are Important' (2013) 10 SCRIPTed 310 <script-ed.org/?p=1157>.

[1–36]   Nonetheless, the smartphone in your pocket, the laptop in your bag, and the ever-increasing reliance on computers as means of delivering essential information and content to you as a student are clear indicators of the ways in which ICT has become a key component of modern life. A great deal of mass media, personal and business communication, commercial activity, and the work of government takes place over digital computing channels. The physical world and online world are increasingly tightly woven together, and it is therefore necessary to consider it as a key element of the complex fabric of our societies.

[1–37]   Law and the information society are also very much woven together. Various aspects of the law, such as intellectual property, form part of the foundation for the development of the ICT industry as we know it today. Other aspects of the law, such as privacy and data protection, limit some types of development and encourage others. Thus, for example, much of the commercial software industry relies on copyright for legal protection and as a means to ensure that users provide it with revenue. Privacy law prevents businesses from gathering too much information about individuals or government from surveilling them without some oversight by a court.

[1–38]   This relationship is often very back-and-forth. New technologies will create new legal questions. If the law changes, technology will often change in response, thus creating more legal questions, in a cyclical fashion. Thus, for example, the availability of affordable home broadband and the development of peer-to-peer file sharing software created significant challenges for the copyright industries, a topic which will be covered in detail in Chapter 2. As legislatures and courts responded to this (because the music and movie industries brought cases and lobbied for changes to the law), technology developers modified their software either to stay within the bounds of what was clearly legal or to try to exploit loopholes.

[1–39]   At times, the relationship will pull in different ways at the same time. While it is true that much of the software industry relies on fees for licence agreements as a source of revenue, the Free, Libre, and Open Source Software movement (also discussed briefly in Chapter 2), has sought to develop an alternative model, in which the software is essentially 'given away', and any income derives from consultancy and other services.

[1–40]   Fundamentally, therefore, the role of law in the information society in resolving social, economic, or political questions is very important but it is by no means the final determinant or always the most important factor. However, the increasing importance of information as a source of value, revenue, and control means that it deserves careful scrutiny.

[1–41]   Many industries are becoming digitised, relying on ICT as a key tool for internal co-ordination and external interaction with consumers. Content industries are 'converging' – moving their traditional means of delivery into a much more flexible online format: broadcast media companies with websites that are similar to a print newspaper, and newspapers with websites that contain significant amounts of audio and video. Social media sites, particularly the dominant players such as Facebook, further blur these traditional distinctions, as one can use Facebook to send messages, read articles, and view videos. In the past, each of these would have required different technologies; now they are all possibilities offered by the same smartphone or tablet screen.

With this convergence, the control of information becomes more important than the control [1–42] of things. The scalability of ICT and the possibility of perfect duplication of content, even over very long distances, creates new markets (such as audio and video streaming) and new problems (such as widespread copyright infringement, or hate speech online). Digital content is no longer scarce, and unlike physical distribution channels, assumptions about rivalrousness and uniqueness no longer apply unless the law creates them. Only one of us can read a particular copy of a book or listen to a particular music compact disc at the same time, but many of us can stream that content online simultaneously, providing the servers are available. Commercial law therefore becomes more about regulating trade in intangible goods and services than physical objects.

The Theory and Practice of ICT Regulation

These developments raise a number of interesting and challenging questions which aca- [1–43] demics, judges, and legislatures have tried to answer and will continue to grapple with for quite some years to come. Should cyberspace be regulated? Can it be regulated, or is the internet too decentralised and anarchic to ever be controlled? Who should be responsible for carrying out the regulatory functions – the government, private organisations, or internet users themselves?

It is often the case that as ICT brings with it new legal questions, we have no choice but [1–44] to apply 'old law', which is often unsatisfactory as it relies on assumptions that no longer hold true. 'New law', supposedly designed for the new technological context, is often no better. The law-making cycle is often not able to keep with the pace of change in ICT and lawmakers may not have a clear understanding of what they are seeking to control, so by the time the law is changed, it is still out of step with the potentials and limits of the digital infrastructure. Sometimes the old law works perfectly well but industry lobbyists seek to change it as it impedes their business models. All claims about the law being out of date or needing to be modernised should be taken with a pinch of salt.

Making law for digital technology is also challenging because there is a need to build in [1–45] flexibility, so that the rules are not too specific to particular technological configurations (although at times very specific rules can be useful). Law reform must also operate with an eye to the international dimension: technologies may be developed or hosted in another jurisdiction; there are often treaties to be taken into account; and having too tight a regula- tory framework in a particular country may be self-defeating as the relevant industry can quickly and easily re-locate.

Over time, scholars have developed a variety of theories of regulation for the internet and [1–46] ICT. In the early years of general use of the internet, strong *cyberlibertarian* arguments were made that cyberspace is unregulable. One such famous statement is that made by John Perry Barlow:

> Governments of the Industrial World, you weary giants of flesh and steel, I come from Cyberspace, the new home of Mind. On behalf of the future, I ask you of the past to leave us alone. You are not welcome among us. You have no sovereignty where we gather.

> We have no elected government, nor are we likely to have one, so I address you with no greater authority than that with which liberty itself always speaks. I declare the global

social space we are building to be naturally independent of the tyrannies you seek to impose on us. You have no moral right to rule us nor do you possess any methods of enforcement we have true reason to fear.[43]

[1–47] Legal academics who espoused this view included David Johnson and David Post. They argued that as internet traffic did not respect national boundaries, and individuals could essentially 'relocate' themselves at will, traditional geographically oriented methods of control would simply not function.[44] The essential argument that was being made was that law was constrained by territorial borders but that the internet was not subject to these limits and therefore could not be controlled. Important cases, such as the controversy over the sale of Nazi memorabilia on Yahoo! (which is considered further in [8–18] to [8–20]), demonstrate that while this may be true for certain types of activity (such as pornography and obscene speech), it is not universally the case. The internet is not a separate 'place', somehow distinct from the 'real world',[45] and can be subject to the jurisdiction of the courts.

[1–48] Another important strand of academic thought on the internet is *cyberpaternalism* – the idea that cyberspace is controlled through design choices made by software and hardware developers (either deliberately or accidentally). Joel Reidenburg pointed out the importance of network infrastructure and technological standards as a means of control, and speculated that we will see the development of a 'Lex Informatica'.[46] This is perhaps summed up by Lawrence Lessig's claim that 'Code is Law';[47] in other words, what is often more important for individual users is not whether or not the law forbids or permits a particular behaviour but whether the computer they are using allows it. If the underlying code on a particular device prevents a user from engaging in an activity that is legal, the end result is even more definite than a rule that bans that activity. The user has no way of doing something that they should be able to do. While this approach has been very influential in the development of academic perspectives on ICT law, it has been criticised as being excessively 'techno-logically deterministic' (in other words, it assumes that humans have no choices, and that particular configurations of technology will always yield the same results, no matter what the context).[48]

[1–49] This perspective has been developed by Andrew Murray into an approach which he calls Network Communitarianism, which sees ICT as offering new opportunities for connection, communication, and co-ordination between individuals.[49] Lessig sees the end user as a 'pathetic dot', at the mercy of external forces (law, social norms, the market, and architecture)

---

[43] John Perry Barlow, 'A Declaration of the Independence of Cyberspace' (*Electronic Frontier Foundation* 1996) <www.eff.org/cyberspace-independence> accessed 13 June 2017.

[44] David R Johnson and David Post, 'Law and Borders: The Rise of Law in Cyberspace' (1996) 48 Stanford Law Review 1367.

[45] Jack Goldsmith, 'Regulation of the Internet: Three Persistent Fallacies' (1997) 73 Chicago-Kent Law Review 1119.

[46] Joel R Reidenberg, 'Governing Networks and Rule-Making in Cyberspace' (1996) 45 Emory Law Journal 911; Joel R Reidenberg, 'Lex Informatica: The Formulation of Information Policy Rules through Technology' (1997) 76 Texas Law Review 553.

[47] Lawrence Lessig, *Code: And Other Laws of Cyberspace* (Version 2.0, Basic Books 2006).

[48] Viktor Mayer-Schonberger, 'Demystifying Lessig' (2008) Wisconsin Law Review 713.

[49] Andrew Murray, *The Regulation of Cyberspace: Control in the Online Environment* (Routledge 2007).

that he or she cannot do much to influence, whereas Murray sees a more symbiotic and communicative process, in which regulation operates within an interconnected matrix of stakeholders. He recommends that regulators work with rather than against the regulated community for the best results.

Governance and ICT
Co-Production of Technology

It should be clear from the discussion in sections 1 and 2 of this chapter that technology does not emerge out of a void but is, in fact, developed by individuals and groups. It therefore arises out of a social context, and so the structure, preferences, and politics of that particular situation will be an important influence on the ways in which technology is developed. In turn, the available technology and the types of actions which it enables or makes more difficult (what are now increasingly called *affordances*) informs, channels and sometimes controls the development of society, the economy, and the political system. Both influence each other in an ongoing and dynamic fashion, which is sometimes known as *co-production*. **[1–50]**

It has already been mentioned that technology is not neutral. It will often contain embedded assumptions and biases about social roles, particularly with regard to gender, race, social class and so on. Scholars have been discussing this for many years. Some have focused on the role of power in decision-making about technology. Langdon Winner, for example, pointed out that the bridges over the roads leading from New York city to the Long Island beaches were too low to allow buses to pass, but high enough for cars, thereby discriminating against low-income (and chiefly black) communities who would be more likely to rely on public transport to make this journey.[50] Others have preferred to provide integrated descriptions of the importance of technology. Bruno Latour has discussed how we should examine technology to determine what social role it plays – in other words, we should ask what human work a particular device replaces. Amongst the examples that he uses is an automatic door-closer. If it did not exist, there would need to be a human being standing at the door to ensure it stays closed.[51] Latour extends this perspective on the role of technology to develop *actor-network theory*, which highlights how individuals or groups will try to enlist technology in their projects and initiatives in such a way that the tool can be understood as a participant in the process, and is sometimes perceived as part of a single actor.[52] For example, an online commerce website will involve assembling a variety of social structures (the core business, suppliers, financial institutions) and technologies (the internet, electronic commerce platforms, financial transaction software) into a system that seems like a unified whole. **[1–51]**

---

[50] Langdon Winner, 'Do Artifacts Have Politics?' in *The Whale and the Reactor: A Search for Limits in an Age of High Technology* (University of Chicago Press 1986) 19–39.

[51] Bruno Latour, 'Where Are the Missing Masses? The Sociology of a Few Mundane Artifacts' in Wiebe E. Bijker and John Law (eds), *Shaping Technology/Building Society: Studies in Sociotechnical Change* (MIT Press 1992) 225–58.

[52] Bruno Latour, *Reassembling the Social: An Introduction to Actor-Network Theory* (Oxford University Press 2005).

[1–52]   The study of the social implications of technology is a large and complex field, and this text-book will not do any more than touch on it very briefly. However, it is very important to bear in mind that all aspects of ICT emerge from a social context which can have significant legal dimensions. For example, [2–49] to [2–99] discusses how peer-to-peer file sharing software was a social phenomenon with important economic consequences that arose because of the capacities which technology provided. That led to legal responses, which in turn led to technologists modifying their development plans in order to accommodate the new rules.

[1–53]   The social context, and the assumptions and biases which they contain, can lead to important choices in the development of ICT, some of which are made unconsciously or without discussion by the developers. Google Image Search has displayed racial and gender biases – labelling pictures of black people as 'gorillas',[53] selecting mug shots when asked to show 'three black teenagers' but selecting happier images when asked to show 'three white teenagers',[54] and under-representing women in searches for career-related keywords.[55] Sometimes the choices made are deliberate. Facebook has been accused of manipulating the news stories which are highlighted in individuals' feeds.[56] Some instances of the social consequences of ICT involve deceit. Volkswagen has admitted installing software in its diesel cars that cheat on emissions tests, something which has led to prosecutions for executives and fines of $4.3 billion.[57] Not all of these issues are confined to the private sector: face-recognition software which is used for criminal investigation is more likely to return false positives on people of colour.[58]

[1–54]   Lawyers should therefore bear in mind that technology will enable and prevent certain types of social, economic or political developments, and what technologies are supported or banned by the law are ultimately political and moral questions (even if they do not present that way in the first instance). This is a key consideration to keep in mind while reading the subsequent chapters.

ICT as a Tool for Governance

[1–55]   'Governance' is a word that has become increasingly popular in recent years,[59] particularly in the wake of the so-called 'credit crunch' and the resulting financial crisis. This usage

---

[53] Jana Kasperkevic, 'Google Says Sorry for Racist Auto-Tag in Photo App' *The Guardian* (London, 1 July 2015).

[54] Elle Hunt, '"Three Black Teenagers": Anger as Google Image Search Shows Police Mugshots' *The Guardian* (London, 9 June 2016).

[55] Emily Cohn, 'Google Image Search Has a Gender Bias Problem' (*The Huffington Post*, 21 April 2015) <www.huffingtonpost.com/2015/04/10/google-image-gender-bias_n_7036414.html> accessed 13 June 2017.

[56] Michael Nunez, 'Former Facebook Workers: We Routinely Suppressed Conservative News' (*Gizmodo*, 9 May 2016) <gizmodo.com/former-facebook-workers-we-routinely-suppressed-conser-1775461006> accessed 13 June 2017.

[57] Megan Geuss, 'DOJ Indicts 6 Volkswagen Executives, Automaker Will Pay $4.3 Billion in Plea Deal' (*Ars Technica*, 11 January 2017) <arstechnica.com/cars/2017/01/vw-group-likely-to-pay-4-3b-plead-guilty-to-criminal-charges-in-diesel-scandal/> accessed 13 June 2017.

[58] Olivia Solon, 'Facial Recognition Database Used by FBI is Out of Control, House Committee Hears' *The Guardian* (London, 27 March 2017).

[59] Andrew Jordan, KW Wurzel, and Anthony Zito, 'The Rise of "New" Policy Instruments in Comparative Perspective: Has Governance Eclipsed Government?' (2005) 53(3) Political Studies 477.

may simply be a passing fashion, but there does seem to be a new model of management of the economy, a move away from the territorial, hierarchical, and controlling structures put in place in the 1930s and 1940s to a paradigm which is more global and pluralist but less interventionist.[60] There is no universally accepted definition of governance,[61] but it could be seen in general terms as 'effective co-ordination when power, information and resources are widely distributed'.[62] One possible definition is as

> ... a process of governing which departs from the traditional model where collectively binding decisions are taken by elected representatives within parliaments and implemented by bureaucrats within public administrations. ...[It] is often described as a process of co-ordination within networks ...[T]he core meaning of governance [is] steering and co-ordination of interdependent (usually collective) actors based on institutionalized rule systems.[63]

This means that power no longer resides solely in the hands of the State (if it ever did), and that we are seeing the rise of a 'post-regulatory state', which tries to involve other actors in managing the economy and society.[64] This leads to a more complex and sophisticated picture of modern regulation, as something which is moving beyond the central control of the State, which does 'less rowing and more steering' and shares that work of steering.[65]   **[1–56]**

This can be connected to the work of Michel Foucault, a prominent French thinker, who highlighted the loss of power of the central sovereign and the rise in importance of alternatives to direct command-and-control of a population. Introna writes about the role of ICT in this indirect exercise of power. According to him, Foucault sees power as a technique that achieves its effects through a disciplinary power (surveillance) and bio-power (control of bodies). Power is exercised through relationships in a network of forces, which control, constrain, manage, and create options for individuals. It is not simply the use of violence or physical force.[66] ICT allows for the measurement of our daily activities, extrapolations about our preferences and choices, and the enabling and disabling of options in response. For example, significant work is being done on 'smart' electricity grids, which develop detailed usage patterns, predict when peak loads may occur, and raise or lower prices in order to smooth out demand.   **[1–57]**

---

[60] Orly Lobel, 'The Renew Deal: The Fall of Regulation and the Rise of Governance in Contemporary Legal Thought' (2004) 89 Minnesota Law Review 262, 344.

[61] Andrew Jordan, KW Wurzel, and Anthony Zito, 'The Rise of "New" Policy Instruments in Comparative Perspective: Has Governance Eclipsed Government?' (2005) 53(3) Political Studies 477, 478.

[62] Gilles Paquet, 'Governance in the Face of Sabotage and Bricolage' (2001) 24(3) Canadian Parliamentary Review 11.

[63] Oliver Treib, Holger Bähr, and Gerda Falkner, 'Modes of Governance: Towards a Conceptual Clarification' (2007) 14 Journal of European Public Policy 1, 3.

[64] Colin Scott, 'Regulation in the Age of Governance: The Rise of the Post-Regulatory State' in Jacint Jordana and David Levi-Faur (eds), *The Politics of Regulation* (Edward Elgar 2004) 147.

[65] Leighton McDonald, 'The Rule of Law in the "New Regulatory State"' (2004) 33 Common Law World Review 197, 199.

[66] Lucas D Introna, *Management, Information and Power* (Macmillan 1997) 124–30.

[1–58]   ICT is used in these types of governance arrangements in a variety of ways. At the most fundamental, they provide essential support services through databases and other administrative systems (often called 'back office') which enable the day-to-day administration of schemes of regulation. They also assist a great deal with information gathering, and many agencies will rely on tools such as geographic information systems, pattern recognition, and predictive modelling in order to determine where resources should be allocated. They are also increasingly used for what is sometimes called 'soft regulation' – the use of media advertising and social media messaging in order to influence perceptions and behaviour, particularly 'naming and shaming' type campaigns.

[1–59]   This is sometimes called *informational governance*: 'the idea that information is fundamentally restructuring processes, institutions and practices of … governance'.[67] This is not the same as *disclosure-based regulation*, which is one of the responses to the perceived inefficiency and ineffectiveness of traditional command-and-control regulation. Often called 'informational regulation', this can be defined as 'government mandated public disclosure of information on the environmental performance of regulated entities'.[68] It has a history that pre-dates digital ICT to US federal securities laws in the 1930s.[69] Much of the promise of the application of ICT to regulation relies on the power of information to change behaviour, whether individual or organisational,[70] which is a 'reflexive' theory of regulation:

> The idea is to employ law not directly in terms of giving specific orders or commands, but indirectly to establish incentives and procedures that encourage institutions to think critically, creatively, and continually about … their activities…[71]

[1–60]   For example, governments have used 'league tables' of, for example, school performance or business environmental performance as a means of 'exclamation and excoriation', or highlighting good and bad performers in health and safety ('naming and faming'/'naming and shaming'),[72] while efforts to deal with political corruption, poor diet and energy efficiency in cars and household appliances have made use of information disclosure techniques.[73] Disclosure requirements have also been used in an effort to deal with the more recently developing problem of large-scale data breaches,[74] with some success.[75]

---

[67] Arthur PJ Mol, *Environmental Reform in the Information Age: The Contours of Informational Governance* (Cambridge University Press 2008) 83.

[68] David W Case, 'Corporate Environmental Reporting as Informational Regulation: A Law and Economics Perspective' (2005) 76 University of Colorado Law Review 379, 380–83.

[69] Mary Graham, *Democracy By Disclosure: The Rise of Technopopulism* (Brookings Institution Press 2002) 1–2.

[70] Arthur PJ Mol, *Environmental Reform in the Information Age: The Contours of Informational Governance* (Cambridge University Press 2008) 114–15.

[71] Eric W Orts, 'A Reflexive Model of Environmental Regulation' (1995) 5 Business Ethics Quarterly 779, 780.

[72] Karen Yeung, 'Government by Publicity Management: Sunlight or Spin?' (2005) Public Law 360, 372–73.

[73] Michael E Kraft, Mark Stephan, and Troy D Abel, *Coming Clean: Information Disclosure and Environmental Performance* (MIT Press 2011) 8.

[74] Paul M Schwartz and Edward J Janger, 'Notification of Data Security Breaches' (2007) 105 Michigan Law Review 913.

[75] Sasha Romanosky, Rahul Telang, and Alessandro Acquisti, 'Do Data Breach Disclosure Laws Reduce Identity Theft?' (2011) 30 Journal of Policy Analysis and Management 256.

Although disclosure-based instruments might seem on the surface to be examples of 'soft law', the reality is that they are used as both 'soft' and 'hard' tools (for example, to help with enforcement and prosecution) in a hybrid mix.[76] This flexibility is often achieved through ICT, which allows for greater transparency (by making available information on interactions between the regulator and the regulated), two-way interaction with the public, and dissemination of emissions data.[77] The widespread availability of networked digital telecommunication systems creates the possibility of new forms of informational regulation. These will increasingly empower individual citizens and will involve interactive, customisable and more quickly updated interfaces. The systems are likely to be increasingly collaborative, with government still playing a key role but somewhat displaced to the position of convener and facilitator. The capacities of ordinary users, information disclosers and regulators will be expanded by these new systems.[78]

[1–61]

Further Reading

- Martin Campbell-Kelly and William Aspray, *Computer: A History of the Information Machine* (Westview Press 2004)
- Nicholas G Carr, *The Big Switch: Rewiring the World, from Edison to Google* (WW Norton 2008)
- Paul E Ceruzzi, *A History of Modern Computing* (2nd edn, MIT Press 2003)
- James Gleick, *The Information* (Fourth Estate 2012)
- Jack Goldsmith and Tim Wu, *Who Controls the Internet?: Illusions of a Borderless World* (Oxford University Press 2006)
- Katie Hafner and Matthew Lyon, *Where Wizards Stay Up Late: The Origins of the Internet* (Simon and Schuster 1998)
- Dan Hunter, *Cyberspace as Place and the Tragedy of the Digital Anti-Commons* (2003) 91 California Law Review 439
- Sheila Jasanoff, *States of Knowledge: The Co-Production of Science and the Social Order* (Routledge 2006)
- Lawrence Lessig, *Code: And Other Laws of Cyberspace, Version 2.0* (Basic Books 2006)
- Evgeny Morozov, *The Net Delusion: How Not to Liberate the World* (Penguin UK 2011)
- Andrew Murray, *The Regulation of Cyberspace: Control in the Online Environment* (Routledge 2007)
- Johnny Ryan, *A History of the Internet and the Digital Future* (Reaktion Books 2010)
- Eric G Swedin and David L Ferro, *Computers: The Life Story of a Technology* (Greenwood Publishing Group 2005)
- Jonathan Zittrain, *The Future of the Internet and How to Stop It* (Allen Lane 2008)

---

[76] Dorit Kerret, 'Don't Judge a Book by its Cover: Use of an Analytic Framework and Empirical Data in Analyzing Environmental Policy Tools' (2012) 42 Environmental Law Reporter 10078.

[77] Dennis D Hirsch, 'Globalization, Information Technology, and Environmental Regulation: An Initial Inquiry' (2001) 20 Virginia Environmental Law Journal 57, 72.

[78] Archon Fung, Mary Graham, and David Weil, *Full Disclosure: The Perils and Promise of Transparency* (Cambridge University Press 2007) 152–58.

PART 2

ICT and Private Law

CHAPTER 2
Copyright Online

> *'Whatever one may say about the workability of traditional copyright principles as we have come to know them in the analog world of hard copy, I have become increasingly convinced that these concepts simply do not work as currently designed when applied to the Internet.'*[1]

Primer on Intellectual Property

Because information and communications technology (ICT) is so fundamentally entwined with the movement and manipulation of units of data, and that data can have a wide range of meaning to individuals (particularly consumers), it is not surprising that a great deal of information technology law concerns the broad field of intellectual property, commonly known by those who work in the field as IP. The scope and coverage of IP law can be quite confusing to the layperson, and sometimes even to the lawyer – it is not uncommon to hear those new to ICT or IP law talk about a copyright on trade dress, or patenting an idea, **[2–01]**

---

[1]   Diane Zimmermann, 'Finding New Paths Through the Internet: Content and Copyright' (2009) 12 Tulane Journal of Technology & Intellectual Property 145, 145.

although this is not possible. It is therefore useful to provide a brief primer on intellectual property at this point. As this book deals with ICT rather than IP law, it is only a cursory overview. If you would like to learn more, it would be best to consult a dedicated IP textbook, such as those mentioned in the 'Further Reading' section at the end of this chapter. If you have already studied intellectual property, you can skip this section.

[2–02] There are three principal forms of intellectual property: copyright, trademarks, and patents, outlined in Table 1. A fourth, trade secrets, will not be considered here as it has not (yet) raised many issues that are specific in ICT (although the importance of proprietary algorithms may change that in the near future). In addition, there are some regimes that are specific to ICT, such as the protection of semi-conductors and the database right. The former is a niche topic and is not considered in this textbook.[2] The latter is considered in detail in [3–39] to [3–58].

	Copyright	Trade mark	Patent
Protects	Expression	Goodwill	Invention
Duration	Life + 70 years (generally)	Indefinite	20 years

Table 1   *Types of Intellectual Property*

[2–03] *Copyright*, in broad terms, protects the expression of an idea in some fixed and reproducible form. It does not protect ideas themselves, but their tangible expression in a medium which can be shared with others. Copyright also protects similar rights, known as 'neighbouring rights', such as the rights of performers to control the fixation and distribution of recordings of performances. In Irish law, the following can be protected by copyright:

- original literary, dramatic, musical or artistic works,
- sound recordings and films,
- broadcasts and cable programmes,
- the typographical arrangement of published editions,
- computer programs, and
- original databases (note that this is not the same as the database right).

[2–04] Copyright, therefore, protects creative work, but the threshold for creativity is relatively low. 'Original' here means 'originating with the author' rather than 'new and entirely creative'. Copyright lasts for a fixed period of time. It runs from the time at which the work is created and expires 50 or 70 years after the death of the creator or author. The copyright holder has the exclusive authority to carry out or to authorise the copying, making available to the public, or the adaptation of the protected work (and copying or making available of the adaptation). Primary infringement consists of undertaking or authorising another

---

[2]   For a discussion of this right, see Denis Kelleher and Karen Murray, *Information Technology Law in Ireland* (2nd edn, Bloomsbury Professional 2007) ch 7; Maeve McDonagh and Mícheál O'Dowd, *Cyber Law in Ireland* (Wolters Kluwer 2015) ch 4.

to undertake any of the rights restricted by copyright. Secondary infringement consists of dealing with an infringing copy, providing the means for making infringing copies, permitting the use of a premises for infringing performances, or permitting the use of an apparatus for infringing performances.

Trademarks protect the associations that consumers have between a supplier or provider and a good or service – what is known in marketing as a 'brand'. In the modern marketplace, the connection between a particular company, what it sells, and its customers are key to the continued survival of a business. Consider the success of major brands (many of whom are in the ICT business), such as Apple, Google, Microsoft, Coca-Cola, and Facebook; or the damage which scandals have caused to the image of large companies such as FIFA and Volkswagen. Trade mark law protects logos, imagery, trade dress or 'get up'; essentially any sign that can be reproduced graphically and differentiates the supplier of a good or service from its competitors. A trade mark can, in theory, last forever; protection is available so long as the company continues to register or use it. **[2–05]**

A trade mark is a distinctive sign of some kind which is used by a business to uniquely identify itself and its products and services to consumers, and to distinguish the business and its products or services from those of other businesses. It is usually a name, word, phrase, logo, symbol, design, image, or a combination of these elements. It is defined in s 6 of the Trade Marks Act 1996 as **[2–06]**

> any sign capable of being represented graphically which is capable of distinguishing goods or services of one undertaking from those of other undertakings[.]

Trademarks will often be registered, but they do not need to be. An unregistered trade mark can still be protected under the common law tort of passing off.

Trade mark infringement arises when a competitor uses a similar mark in circumstances that would confuse the public, cause the public to associate the marks, take advantage of the first trade mark owner's reputation, or would generally be detrimental to the distinctive character of the mark. **[2–07]**

Patents protect inventions with industrial application. If an individual develops a new device or process, they have a choice: they can keep it secret (which may mean that they can use it forever, but if their competitors learn how to re-create it, they have no legal protection); or they can apply for a patent (which means that they have a limited exclusive right to authorise the manufacture or use of the invention, in exchange for fully disclosing how to reproduce it). Patents are time-limited, generally 10 or 20 years, and once they expire, anyone is free to use the invention. **[2–08]**

Software Development in Brief

Before exploring the case law and legislation that surrounds copyright and software, it is useful to set out briefly how software is developed. Computers do not understand human languages – indeed, at their most basic level, they understand only binary digits ('bits'), which are either one or zero, and can perform only simple arithmetic operations on these – adding, subtracting, comparing, and making choices depending on the results of these calculations. However, the power of digital computers emerges from the way in which it is **[2–09]** possible to construct increasingly complex systems of recording information and making decisions from such basic building blocks. (A digital device which is capable of this level of sophistication and flexibility is often known as a 'Turing machine', after the English mathematician who developed much of the basic theory of computing.)

[2–10] At the fundamental level, a computer program is expressed in *machine code* – a sequence of numbers which represent instructions for the computer in a form that it can immediately follow, or execute. Very few humans can read and understand machine code, and it is not an efficient way to develop software (although in the early years, it was all that was available). At a somewhat higher level, programs can be written in *assembly language*, which is a representation of machine code in a form somewhat easier for a human to read. Some specialised programmers will work in assembly; most will not. Assembly must be translated into machine code, by a program called an assembler, for a computer to be able to execute it. Most programmers, however, work in *high-level languages* (such as BASIC, C, or Java), which are (somewhat) understandable by humans as they resemble the formal language of mathematics (or in the case of a language like COBOL, attempt to mimic the description of a business process). High-level language code must be converted to *object code* (a form of machine code) by a program called a compiler before a computer can execute it.

[2–11] Software, therefore, is generally developed in a high-level language by a programmer (or more often nowadays, a team) writing *source code*, which is then processed by a compiler into object code and is distributed to the end user in the latter form. This means that the end-user often does not have direct access to the source code and so cannot modify the software.

Copyright and Source Code

[2–12] One of the first intersections between IP and ICT was with regard to copyright in computer software. In the early years of the computer industry, when all that was available to a very small market of large business and government were mainframes (which were more often leased than bought), software was included in the overall arrangement or developed in-house on an individual ('bespoke') basis, and tussles over ownership did not occur. As the industry moved from mainframe to mini- and then to micro-computers, with consumer markets and much less of an ongoing relationship between the original vendor and the user, ownership and control of software became more important, and a significant market in its own right.

Literal Copying of Software

[2–13] These technical facts have shaped the case law around copyright and software. The initial question, discussed at some length in the United States during the 1970s by the Commission on New Technological Uses of Copyrighted Works, was whether or not a computer program constituted a 'literary work'. Based on the recommendations of CONTU, the US Copyright Act was amended in 1974 to make it clear that source and object code could be protected by copyright.

[2–14] In the UK, in 1983, Sega Enterprises sued for copyright infringement of a successful computer game which it had developed known as *Frogger*. The defendant, Mr Richards, admitted that he had accessed and copied part of the source code for *Frogger*. However, he contended that the only element of the game that involved significant originality was the development of the original idea; much of the creation of the final object code involved what he called 'automatic means'. The judge, however found that

> copyright under the provisions relating to literary works in the Copyright Act 1956 subsists in the assembly code program ... The machine code program derived from it by the operation of part of the system of the computer called the assembler is to be regarded ... as either a reproduction or an adaptation of the assembly code program, and accordingly ... copyright does subsist in the program.[3]

This case, however, was an application for interim relief pending a full trial, and the judgment was relatively short. In a later case, the Australian courts came (initially) to an opposite conclusion, causing some concern in the growing software industry. The case involved a company which was selling computers which advertised that they were compatible with the then-popular Apple II micro-computer. These contained micro-chips known as ROMs (Read-Only Memory, meaning that they could not be modified by the owner) with copies of Apple software which controlled the basic operation of the computer. There was therefore direct copying of Apple object code. **[2–15]**

However, at first instance, the judge in the Federal Court for New South Wales relied on much older cases which held that 'a literary work ... is something which was intended to afford "either information or instruction or pleasure in the form of literary enjoyment"' whereas '[t]he function of a computer programme is to control the sequence of operations carried out by a computer', and decided that therefore no copyright infringement was taking place.[4] This decision was later overturned,[5] but the need to clarify the issue was clear. After lobbying by the software industry, many legislatures amended their jurisdiction's copyright law in order to make clear that computer programs could be protected by copyright. Of particular importance was the EEC's Computer Programs Directive,[6] transposed into Irish law by a statutory instrument in 1993.[7] Section 2 of the Copyright and Related Rights Act 2000 includes computer software within the definition of 'literary work' for the purposes of copyright law in Ireland. **[2–16]**

In an important and similar US case heard around the same time, the Court of Appeal for the Third Circuit held that copyright extended to object code and to a computer's *operating system* (the essential software which every computer must have in order to be useful; modern examples include Microsoft Windows and Apple's macOS). A company named Franklin Computer introduced micro-computers which were compatible with the Apple II. This was achieved by copying Apple's software on ROM chips, something which was obvious because the Franklin chips contained words such as 'Applesoft'. Franklin claimed that it was not practical for it to write software which would be identical to Apple's and that what was contained on the chips was so fundamental to the operation of the computer that it was necessary to duplicate it exactly in order to be compatible. This argument was successful at first instance but on appeal, Apple was able to convince the Court that (particularly following the CONTU recommendations) software was copyrightable whether it was in **[2–17]**

---

3   *Sega Enterprises v Richards* [1983] FSR 73 (Ch) 75.
4   *Apple Computers, Inc v Computer Edge Pty Ltd* [1983] FCA 328.
5   *Apple Computers, Inc v Computer Edge Pty Ltd* 53 ALR 225, [1984] FSR 481 (HCA).
6   Council Directive (EEC) 250/1991 on the legal protection of computer programs [1991] OJ L 122/42.
7   European Communities (Legal Protection of Computer Programs) Regulations 1993, SI 1993/26.

human-readable form or not, and that it did not matter whether it controlled a low- or high-level aspect of the functioning of the computer.

[2–18] These cases, changes in legislation, and the re-orientation of the software industry around control of source code through copyright protection, were to significantly shape the development of the computer industry from then on. Whereas the norm in the 1960s and early 1970s had been that software was open and shared – a social norm that was in keeping with the research environments in which early computers were generally used – that became less and less common as entrepreneurs sought to protect their intellectual property and profit from software code. A counter-response to this trend gave rise to the various movements and organisations which are often labelled as *open source* or *free software*. We will return to these in [2–117] to [2–120].

Non-Literal Copying of Software

[2–19] Infringement of the copyright in computer software may occur even if there is not direct or complete duplication of source or object code. Remember that copyright does not protect an idea, but the expression of an idea. Exactly where the line is drawn between these two can be difficult to discern in practice, and the courts have struggled with this question in the particular context of software, providing tests that are sometimes criticised as confusing and unhelpful. The early US cases, *Whelan Associates v Jaslow*[8] and *Computer Associates v Altai*,[9] which developed an 'abstraction/filtration test', are not generally followed on this side of the Atlantic.

[2–20] Because legitimate businesses know that they cannot engage in direct duplication of software without risking significant liability, and ordinary consumers do not have access to source code, non-literal copying cases tend to involve former employees who rely either on what they take with them from their place of work or their memory of what they worked on. In *Richardson v Flanders*, Mr Richardson, a pharmacist, developed a program called Pharm-Assist for managing stock and labelling but, as he was not trained as a programmer, he engaged others to improve it. He eventually employed Mr Flanders, who re-wrote the program in assembly language for greater speed but retained its general 'look-and-feel'. Pharm-Assist was a success in the UK and was modified for the Irish market. Unfortunately, the relationship between the two parties broke down and Flanders ceased to be an employee. Richardson was asked by a distributor if he would convert the program from its implementation for BBC micro-computers to be suitable for the IBM PC, which was then growing in popularity. He declined but referred the query onto Flanders, who developed ChemTec for the Irish market. This program was in turn offered to Richardson for the UK market, but he declined. It was modified for the UK by Flanders and put on sale there, at which point Richardson sued for copyright infringement. It was clear that no literal copying had taken place but there were similarities between the ways in which Pharm-Assist and ChemTec operated and therefore the judge had to consider whether there was non-literal copying – in other words, was Flanders relying on his memories of the Pharm-Assist program when developing ChemTec? The judge stated:

> whether a part is substantial is to be decided by its quality rather than by its quantity and that where, as here, the complaint is that copyright in a compilation has been infringed,

---

[8] 797 F 2d 1222; 1240 (3d Cir 1986); 479 US 1031 (1987).
[9] 982 F 2d 693 (2d Cir 1992).

it is necessary to take into account such considerations as originality and the distinction between idea and expression in assessing the quality, and hence the substantiality, of any part which is said to have been copied.[10]

After a detailed consideration of the features which were alleged to have been copied, he found that there had been some copying but it was relatively minor.

In *IBCOS v Barclays*,[11] a programmer named Poole wrote a general accounting package. **[2–21]** He licenced it to an agricultural dealer, and then worked with the dealer to modify the software for the agriculture market. This package was called ADS. Poole also set up a company named PK Ltd to market it. Poole later left PK's employment, but before he left, he accepted a restrictive covenant not to sell 'similar comprehensive software' for a period of two years. Poole worked for another company, Highland, but in his spare time, wrote a program named Unicorn, which competed directly with ADS. This was marketed by Highland once the two years had elapsed. Poole later formed his own company to market the software. IBCOS was the successor in title to PK, and alleged that Unicorn infringed the copyright in ADS. After exhaustive examination of the source code to both packages, the judge concluded that there was overwhelming evidence of copying, particularly because there were idiosyncratic mis-spellings, re-use of uncommon features, and other clear similarities between the two programs that could only be explained by direct duplication. It is interesting to note that the judge declined to follow the US case of *Computer Associates v Altai*[12] as he felt that UK law was more inclined to protect particular forms of ideas.

In *Cantor Fitzgerald International v Tradition UK*,[13] a Mr Howard had been managing direc- **[2–22]** tor for the plaintiff (CFI). After he was dismissed from that post, he began to work for Tradition. He recruited programming staff from CFI and obtained source code for CFI's software packages. Tradition developed software with similar functionality, relying on CFI's source code for direct inspiration and as a point of comparison for test purposes. When CFI learnt of this, they sued. Howard and Tradition first denied and then admitted the copying but claimed it was not substantial. After considerable consideration by the trial judge, only 2% of the code was found to have been copied but this was still sufficient for there to be an adverse finding against Tradition.

These principles were applied by the High Court of Ireland in resolving an allegation **[2–23]** of copyright infringement in *Visusoft v Harris*.[14] An important Irish case which deals with allegations of literal and non-literal copying of software, but does not reference the authorities discussed above, is *Koger Inc and Koger (Dublin) Ltd v O'Donnell*.[15] Again, this involved former employees of the plaintiffs (who sold financial fund management software), who established a company which developed a competing product. The plaintiffs claimed that this had used both literal and non-literal copying of their NTAS software package. After considering reports from experts, the Commercial Court

---

[10] [1993] FSR 497 (Ch) 548–49.
[11] [1994] FSR 275 (Ch).
[12] 982 F 2d 693 (2d Cir 1992).
[13] [2000] RPC 95 (Ch).
[14] [2009] IEHC 543.
[15] [2010] IEHC 350.

held that there was no literal copying (indeed, the plaintiff's expert was of this view, and the failure of the plaintiffs to disclose this to the Court was heavily criticised), that the speed by which the defendants' ManTra package was developed was due to the adoption of 'agile development' methods, and that the technical architecture of the two packages was different, with NTAS being solely a visual reference point. It is interesting to note that (unlike the *IBCOS* case considered above) Feeney J did not accept that errors in NTAS were reproduced in ManTra, or if they were, 'that would not demonstrate access to or use of an unauthorised copy'.[16] The decision was appealed to the Supreme Court, on the basis that the plaintiffs should be permitted to argue that there was infringement by copying from memory (rather than by taking an unauthorised copy), but this was not accepted as it would involve arguing a different case on appeal to what had been run at first instance.[17]

Protection Under the Software Directive

[2–24] The Software Directive, or Computer Programs Directive,[18] clarifies certain aspects of the legal protections available to software, and is implemented in Irish law by the Copyright and Related Rights Act 2000 (CRRA). These are to be protected as literary works (Article 1(1)), but this does not include the underlying 'ideas and principles' (Article 1(2)). In Irish law, s 2(1) of the CRRA includes 'computer program' in the definition of literary work, and s 17(1) provides that copyright subsists in such works.

[2–25] Article 1(3) states that:

> A computer program shall be protected if it is original in the sense that it is the author's own intellectual creation. No other criteria shall be applied to determine its eligibility for protection.

This sets the originality requirement for software quite low, particularly in contrast to the position in some civil law jurisdictions, but it is possible that minor revisions to an existing program will not produce a work that is sufficiently original to qualify for new protection. Under Article 5, a lawful user can make backup copies of a program, and under Article 6, can also engage in de-compilation or reverse engineering. This is implemented in Irish law by ss 80 and 81–82 of the CRRA, respectively.

Software Licensing Issues

[2–26] As it is now clear that copyright subsists in computer software, the licensing of access to particular programs has become a lucrative source of revenue for many businesses. Some particular issues surrounding the legal enforceability and transferability of such licences have arisen.

---

[16] [2010] IEHC 350 [86].
[17] [2013] IESC 28.
[18] Council Directive (EEC) 250/1991 on the legal protection of computer programs [1991] OJ L122/42; codified as Parliament and Council Directive (EC) 24/2009 on the legal protection of computer programs [2009] OJ L111/16.

Shrink-Wrap and Click-Wrap Licenses

One question is whether users can indicate their understanding of, and consent to, a licence **[2–27]** by opening packaging or clicking on an initial screen. The courts have taken the view that this type of activity is sufficient for a licence to be binding.

In *Beta v Adobe*,[19] the defendant had ordered software from the plaintiff by telephone. The **[2–28]** software was delivered in a package covered in shrink-wrapped plastic, on which was a label saying, 'Opening the software package indicates your acceptance of these terms and conditions.' The plaintiff sought to reject the software and not pay for it. The defendant argued that the contract had been concluded when the order was placed but the Court held that the contract was not concluded until the delivery took place and the terms and conditions were accepted by the purchaser.

In *ProCD v Zeidenberg*,[20] the plaintiff sold a telephone directory product on CD-ROM. **[2–29]** The defendant purchased a copy of this at the reduced price for non-commercial users. He then created a website which allowed access to the contents of the CD-ROM to the general public. This was a breach of the licence included with the CD and which was displayed in a 'splash screen' when the software it contained was used. The Court held that this was a valid and enforceable licence, as the defendant had the option of returning the software and had no choice but to accept the licence in order to continue to use it. The Irish High Court engaged in a similar analysis in relation to website terms and conditions in *Ryanair v On The Beach Ltd*.[21]

Re-Sale of Licences

In Case C–128/11 *UsedSoft GmbH v Oracle International Corp*,[22] the Court of Justice **[2–30]** of the European Union considered in detail whether or not it was permissible to re-sell 'second-hand' software licenses. Oracle is a well-known and very successful developer of database software. It offered two types of contracts – a perpetual licence to use a particular version of its software, and a maintenance agreement, which provided access to support and updates. UsedSoft obtained and offered for re-sale 'used' licences for Oracle software, claiming that they were still current as there was a maintenance agreement in place for them. Oracle sought to prevent this, obtaining an injunction from the Munich Regional Court, which was eventually appealed to the CJEU. The German Federal Court asked the CJEU whether:

- the right to distribute a copy of a computer program was exhausted under Article 4(2) of the Software Directive (in other words, no longer under the control of the original seller) where the acquirer had made a copy with the rights holder's consent by downloading the program from the internet; and
- an acquirer of the licence was a 'lawful acquirer' within the meaning of Article 5(1) of the Software Directive such that it could rely on the exhaustion rule under Article 4(2) to use the software on its own systems.

---

[19] [1996] FSR 367 (OH).
[20] 86 F 3d 1447 (7th Cir 1996).
[21] [2015] IEHC 11.
[22] ECLI:EU:C:2012:407.

[2–31]   The Court gave Article 4(2) a broad interpretation, holding that a transaction involving a download and the payment of a fee for a perpetual licence amounted to a sale (as a narrower interpretation would allow this article to be easily avoided by simply calling a transaction a 'licence' rather than a 'sale'). Therefore the original vendor of the software can no longer prevent the redistribution of the copy. The form of delivery of the software (download or disk) is not material to the legal analysis. The perpetual licence includes updates and maintenance versions of the software.

[2–32]   However, the CJEU imposed some stringent restrictions on the re-sale right. The original licensee must ensure that all versions of the software are removed from its systems. The vendor may use technological protection measures, such as product keys, to enforce this. A licence for multiple users cannot be broken up into smaller parts and re-sold piecemeal. It seems that these restrictions may make the development of a viable market in second-hand software too challenging.

Interoperability and Reverse Engineering

[2–33]   Software programs do not exist in isolation. They must frequently communicate with each other – sometimes the output from one program is the input to another; or sometimes a new program must open and modify files created by an older (and perhaps more widely used) package. Software users would prefer to avoid having to learn a new set of commands and keystrokes in order to use a new piece of software. Re-training users can be expensive and error-prone. These factors mean that there is often considerable interest in developing software so that it operates in a fashion similar to a competitor. As has been considered above, direct copying or re-use of source code will constitute copyright infringement, but what is somewhat more of a grey area is what can be achieved by *reverse engineering*. This is something that occurs in many fields of commerce, and involves taking a device which is freely available on the market and closely examining it to determine how it operates and how a competing product can be developed. In software, when the intention is to allow one computer program to interface with another, this is generally known as *interoperability*. When the intention is to create a user interface which is similar to another, this is known as *look-and-feel* duplication.

[2–34]   EU policy is to encourage innovation and competition in software. Therefore, Article 6 of the Software Directive[23] permits copying and de-compilation of a computer program where that is done in order to help achieve interoperability. (De-compilation is the use of software to convert machine code back to its original programming code, or some approximation of it, in order to help understand how a program was originally written.) This is implemented in Irish law in s 81 of the Copyright and Related Rights Act 2000.

Key Cases on Reverse Engineering

[2–35]   Before considering the case law on software reverse engineering, it is necessary to briefly examine some important cases from outside this domain. In *LB Plastics v Swish*,[24] LB made

---

[23] Parliament and Council Directive 24/2009 (EC) on the legal protection of computer programs [2009] OJ L111/16.
[24] [1979] RPC 551, [1979] FSR 145 (HL).

plastic knockdown drawers, which could be assembled and dis-assembled and fitted to furniture made by others. After some trial-and-error, Swish produced a system which was interchangeable with LB's. The House of Lords held that this infringed the copyright in LB's design drawings as they were a three-dimensional reproduction.

This would seem to make it difficult, if not impossible, to engage in legal reverse engi-   **[2–36]**
neering. However, in *British Leyland v Armstrong Patents*,[25] the House of Lords created some leeway. British Leyland wanted to prevent aftermarket sales of replacement exhaust pipes for the Morris Marina. (The market for spare parts can be quite lucrative.) Armstrong produced such replacements, thus infringing the drawings, and seemed to be liable for copyright infringement following *LB Plastics*. However, the House of Lords held that con-sumers had a right to carry out repairs to their possessions in the most economical way, and that therefore the sale of the car carried with it a non-derogation which prevented the seller from taking an action to reduce the value of what is sold to the buyer.

This gives some scope for the consumer to maintain an item even if it involves copyright   **[2–37]**
infringement, although the Privy Council did express reservations about the *British Leyland* decision in *Canon KK v Green Cartridge Co.*[26] This case involved the duplication of designs for printer cartridges. The original manufacturer relied upon the income from the purchase of replacement cartridges, and sought to prevent competitors from reverse-engineering its designs and producing cheaper alternatives. The Privy Council regarded *British Leyland* as having gone too far in solving the problem of monopoly rights created by statute and limited it to its particular facts, essentially holding that cheaper printer cartridges did not come within the 'repair' exception to design rights created by the consumer's non-derogation right.

Green v Broadcasting Corporation of New Zealand[27] demonstrates that there are limits to   **[2–38]**
what can be copyrighted. The plaintiff had developed a television show named *Opportunity Knocks* for British broadcasting. A similar show was shown on New Zealand TV; Green claimed that this was a breach of copyright as it used the same title, some common catch-phrases, and the use of a 'clapometer' to measure audience reaction. On appeal, the Privy Council held that the show format was not a dramatic work, so it was not sufficiently coher-ent to be copyrightable.

Copyrightability of the 'Look-and-Feel' of Software

This openness has tended to be applied in cases involving what might be loosely called   **[2–39]**
'inspiration' taken from earlier software packages. The early case law on reverse engineer-ing in software is somewhat less concerned with exact duplication of a particular prod-uct and more with the overall experience of using software, something which is generally described by the somewhat open term 'look-and-feel'.

The *Atari v Philips*[28] case was relatively clear-cut. Atari had developed a computer game   **[2–40]**
known as Pac-Man, involving a character controlled by the player eating pills in a maze and

---

[25] [1986] 1 AC 577, [1986] 1 All ER 850 (HL).
[26] [1997] AC 728, [1997] FSR 817 (PC).
[27] [1989] RPC 700, [1989] UKPC 26.
[28] 672 F 2d 607 (7th Cir, 1982).

being chased by ghosts, which was a great success. Philips developed a competing game, KC Munchkin, which was somewhat too similar. The Court found that there were too many correspondences between the two games – that the 'total concept and feel' of Pac-Man had been captured – and held that there was copyright infringement.

[2–41] The *Apple v Microsoft*[29] case was more complex and much more significant. Apple is well-known for its user interfaces, and in the early years of the computer industry, these proved fertile ground for litigation. Many of the ideas in Apple's graphical user interface (GUI) for the Lisa computer (which preceded the now-famous Macintosh), including the use of a mouse, icons, and a 'desktop' metaphor, in fact came from Xerox's Palo Alto Research Center. However, Apple developed and expanded these, and then licenced elements of its GUI to Microsoft, which included them in Windows 1.0 but then added new elements of its own in Windows 2.0, whereupon Apple sued. Unfortunately for Apple but perhaps more positively for users of software, Apple was unsuccessful because Microsoft was able to show that it had licenced most of the elements in dispute and the others were not copyright-able. The Court felt that 'look-and-feel' was not copyrightable. Microsoft was therefore able to continue to develop and refine the Windows GUI. If Apple had succeeded, they might have been able to claim copyright over most or all of the concepts underlying a GUI, which would have been good for Apple but could have held back innovation in the marketplace.

[2–42] In another case at about the same time period, *Lotus v Borland*,[30] the US courts were even more receptive to restricting the rights of first movers in the software marketplace. Lotus were significant in the early days of the IBM PC, developing a spreadsheet package called 1–2–3 which was very successful. Borland launched a competing product, Quattro Pro, which included a 'compatibility mode' in which it recognised the keystrokes and menu commands used in 1–2–3. This was done in order to capitalise on the familiarity of its target audience with the 1–2–3 command structure and to minimise the amount of re-training required by those moving to Quattro Pro. Lotus claimed that this was copyright infringement, and were successful at first instance, but on appeal, the Court held that the menu system was a 'method of operation' and therefore not copyrightable. The Court also engaged in an economic analysis, claiming that for users to have to re-learn key-strokes and menu commands as they moved from software package would be absurd. This decision was appealed to the US Supreme Court, which upheld the Circuit Court's decision, but by a 4–4 split, with one judge having recused himself. This means that it is technically only law for the First Circuit, not for the entire United States, but it has been generally followed since. The outcome could have been different, which would have significantly changed the pattern of innovation in the micro-computer software industry at a key time, during the transition from command-line and text interfaces to GUIs based around windows and mice.

[2–43] More recent cases from the UK have tended to take a similar approach. In *Navitaire v EasyJet*,[31] the defendant airline wanted to upgrade software named 'OpenRes', which was used for bookings and reservations. It was unable to agree mutually satisfactory terms with

---

[29] 779 F Supp 133 (9th Cir, 1994).

[30] 49 F 3d 807 (1st Cir, 1995).

[31] [2004] EWHC 1725.

the original developers, Navitaire, and used another software house, Bulletproof, instead. Unlike the sequence of cases considered above when discussing non-literal copying, there was no question of Bulletproof having access to the source code of the system developed by Navitaire. However, Bulletproof were asked to develop a system that mirrored the original OpenRes as much as possible. Navitaire sued but the Court held that the new system, 'eRes', was not infringing except in aspects of the screen displays. The latter were copyrightable but the overall 'business logic' of the system was not.

Nova Productions v Mazooma Games[32] involved alleged infringement of a computerised [2–44] game of pool called 'Pocket Money'. The Court held that there could not be infringement of the idea of a pool game and any similarities between the two were obvious elements of such a game which were not copyrightable. It also held that a computer game was not a dramatic work, as it would unfold differently every time, and could not be both a literary and dramatic work at the same time.

Perhaps the most important authority on the question of the copyrightability of the look- [2–45] and-feel of a computer system is a Court of Justice of the European Union case, C–406/10 *SAS v World Programming* (2012).[33] The plaintiff is a very successful developer of business analytics software. The defendant saw an opportunity to provide a cheaper alternative and developed a system which operated in a very similar fashion and offered the possibility of running scripts written in SAS's macro-programming language. The plaintiff sued in order to prevent this, but on a referral from the High Court for England and Wales, the CJEU held that there was no protection for the functionality of a computer system, for programming languages, or for the format of computer data files. (It did hold that World Programming had infringed copyright in a SAS manual, but this is subsidiary to the main holding.)

Following this case, it seems that it will be difficult to prove non-literal infringement in [2–46] the EU, unless there is evidence of access to source code, copying of screen displays, or other direct infringement of the original program. (In Case C–393/09 *BSA v Ministerstvo kultury*,[34] the CJEU held that a GUI is not a form of expression of a computer program but may be copyrightable as a work of graphical art.) The general idea, functioning, and technical details of a system are not protectable, although supporting documentation (such as manuals) may be.

The US may be moving in a different direction. As software and devices become increas- [2–47] ingly interconnected, the copyrightability of Application Programming Interfaces (APIs) becomes more and more important. These provide the 'connecting tissue' between software packages. Interoperability between different programmes is quite important economically, as it creates more network effects, encourages competition, and allows consumers to move from supplier to supplier. An API is somewhat like a library catalogue – it provides a mechanism for programmers to quickly and easily access elements of a hardware or software package. Without knowledge of an API, it is very difficult to write software that interfaces with a new piece of technology. Conversely, knowledge of an API makes that interfacing much easier.

---

[32] [2007] EWCA Civ 219; [2007] RPC 25.

[33] ECLI:EU:C:2012:259.

[34] [2011] ECR I–3787; ECLI:EU:C:2010:816.

[2–48] One important API is the Java programming language, which has become a well-known standard for writing networked applications and one in which many programmers are proficient. It was originally developed by Sun Microsystems, and is now owned by Oracle. Google wanted to use Java as its development environment for the Android mobile platform. It could not agree terms with Oracle and developed its own version instead, which adopted some of the original Java API and also expanded it. In order to complete this work, it needed to duplicate what are known as 'header files', which are similar to the list of entries in a library catalogue. It wrote its own entries, but Oracle claimed that copying the description of the language was copyright infringement. At first instance, the Second Circuit District Court agreed with Google, but on appeal, the Federal Circuit found that Oracle could succeed in this claim because the organisational structure of the API was an original and creative work.[35] In this particular case, the jury eventually found that Google's copying was 'fair use', which is a distinctive feature of American copyright law allowing (in certain limited circumstances) what would otherwise be illegal. However, the question of whether non-literal infringement extends to infrastructural elements such as APIs is still somewhat open in the US.

The 'Filesharing Wars'

[2–49] Since the turn of the century, one aspect of ICT law that has attracted significant media attention, and been a real concern for many members of the public, has been conflicts between the established content industries – first, record labels, then movie studios, and more recently (although not to the same extent) book publishers – and technology entrepreneurs who have developed innovative means of sharing information across the internet. Much of this sharing is, of course, copyright infringement and therefore illegal. Nonetheless, it is a commonplace phenomenon and the interplay between law and technology has been very important in shaping the modern music and movie industry.

[2–50] The duplication of music and movies is not new. Each generation of music-reproduction technology – sheet music, piano players, cassette tapes – has been used for illicit copying and the industry has had to respond to it through a variety of measures, some focused on better enforcement and some on consumer education. Before computer file sharing, the slogan was 'Home taping is killing music.'

[2–51] Nonetheless, computers introduce new potential for this type of activity. Unlike analogue means of duplication, computers make perfect copies each time. A duplicated cassette tape does not sound as clear as the original, and the quality deteriorates as further copies are made. A computer can make copies very quickly, duplicating hours of audio or video in a matter of seconds. Recording a vinyl record to cassette requires an hour or more. A networked computer can share with individuals across the world with minimal effort on the part of the user. Copied cassette tapes must be physically passed or posted from person to person.

[2–52] These advantages have meant that many individuals were quick to participate in online file sharing, even those who would not have gone to the trouble of engaging in home taping. (It has also meant that the culture of the internet generally perceives of music and movies as 'free', something which the industry would very much like to change.) This enthusiastic take-up meant that software developers saw a market opportunity and provided tools and

---

[35] 872 F Supp 2d 974 (ND Cal 2012), 750 F 3d 1339 (Fed Cir 2014).

platforms which they hoped would work within the boundaries of legality and enable them to profit from attracting large volumes of users, chiefly by selling them advertising.

Case Law on Innovation Policy

Before going through the history of file sharing litigation and related legislative reform, it **[2–53]** is worth taking a moment to consider two highly significant cases that predate the computer era. The first is *Sony v Universal Studios*,[36] which is commonly known as the 'Betamax case'. It concerned video-recording technology; Betamax was Sony's alternative to the ultimately-successful VHS standard. This was being used by consumers to record programmes and movies from broadcast television, in many instances removing the advertisements in the process. (This required manually pausing the recording, but only needed to be done once.) Sony explicitly advertised this ability as a possible use for their VCRs. As the broadcast networks depended on advertising revenue, this was of concern to the movie industry; if no one was watching ads, the networks would no longer have money to pay for broadcast rights. They sued, claiming that this home recording was copyright infringement and that Sony were contributorily liable because they provided the device which enabled the infringement. The case found its way to the US Supreme Court, which found that the home recording was legitimate in US copyright law on the grounds of fair use. Significantly, they held that a device which could be used for infringement could be lawfully sold if it was 'capable of substantial noninfringing uses'. This is often called the '*Sony* safe harbour', and enables technology innovators to place their inventions on the market even if they may have illegal as well as legal uses.

Ironically, the video-tape market became a significant source of profit for the movie indus- **[2–54]** try as sales and rentals of tapes became an additional stream of revenue after a film was no longer in theatres. Indeed, some movies are made for that purpose alone, with no intention of playing in traditional cinemas.

As fair use is not part of Irish copyright law, the Irish courts could have come to a different **[2–55]** decision if they had to decide a case similar to *Sony*. However, there is UK case law which indicates that there is considerable scope for innovation in potentially infringing devices here. In *CBS Songs v Amstrad*,[37] the House of Lords came to a similar conclusion to the US Supreme Court, although with different logic. The defendants manufactured electronic devices; amongst their products was a cassette player with two decks, which was capable of duplicating at double-speed, meaning that it was quicker and easier to copy tapes. This could obviously be used for illegal copying, and it was for this reason that the music industry sued Amstrad (whose advertisements had been careful to draw the attention of the public to copyright law), claiming that they were inciting purchasers to break the law. The Court disagreed, holding that the decision to copy was a matter for the individual; Amstrad may be facilitating that illegal act, but it was not inducing it.

In that case, Lord Templeman alluded to the need to reform copyright law to take account **[2–56]** of developments in technology. This need became more urgent through the 2000s and up to the present day. Copyright law came under significant pressure from 1999 on, when the

---

[36] 464 US 417 (1984).
[37] [1988] 2 All ER 484, [1988] AC 1013, [1988] RPC 567, [1988] 2 WLR 1191, [1988] UKHL 15, [1988] 2 FTLR 168.

Napster service was first released. Although it was short-lived, it was very popular and was the first important event in a still-ongoing story of technological change, industry resistance, and legal reform.

Filesharing Terminology

[2–57] Before going through this narrative in detail, some terminology and technology must be defined. Many computer networking applications have a *client-server* architecture (see Figure 1), meaning that there is a central computer (traditionally a mainframe or mini-computer), to which smaller, cheaper devices connect and request information, access to shared resources, and so on.

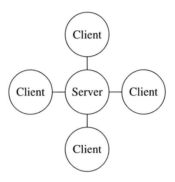

Figure 1   *Client-Server Architecture*

[2–58] Others adopt a *peer-to-peer* (P2P) arrangement (see Figure 2), in which there is no server in the middle but each computer connects to the others as an equal and resources are distributed across the network. This requires some co-ordination and planning in advance, but once established, it is self-organising to a significant extent. It is also important to be aware of the development of audio and video compression technology, chiefly the *MP3 and MP4 file formats*, which enabled music and movies to be shrunk to sizes that could realistically be transmitted. In addition, by the late 1990s, fast, high-capacity *broadband* was becoming increasingly available across the developed world, particularly in universities, where there is a large market for entertainment products.

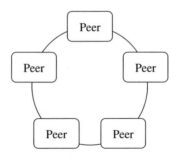

Figure 2   *Peer-to-Peer Architecture*

Digital Music Case Law

There is also some case law relevant to digital music that predates internet filesharing liti- **[2–59]**
gation. As with the *Sony* and *Amstrad* cases above, they demonstrate how tensions between
content providers and technology firms are a recurring pattern, which take place across
generations of reproduction technology and significantly shape the functioning (or dys-
function) of the entertainment marketplace.

Predecessors to the P2P Case Law

The case of *RIAA v Diamond*[38] was an early skirmish in this ongoing struggle. The defen- **[2–60]**
dants manufactured a digital audio player, the Rio. The music industry alleged that this
device did not comply with US legislation, the Audio Home Recording Act of 1992,
because it did not employ a Serial Copyright Management System, which prevented
Digital Audio Tape (DAT) devices from making more than one generation of copies.
(The music industry had argued that this was necessary because digital copies do not
lose quality.) On appeal, the Court of Appeal for the Ninth Circuit held that the Rio's
internal storage hard disk was not a 'digital music recording device' because the device
could store many different types of content. This case indicates that the courts were more
inclined towards innovation.

However, it is clear from *UMG v MP3.com*[39] that there are limits to this. MP3.com pro- **[2–61]**
vided its users with access to their music collection while they were away from home.
Because broadband was not yet widely available, it did this by converting large numbers
of CDs to MP3 format, then making these available to users for playback if they could
prove that they owned a copy of a particular CD by inserting it into their home computer. This meant that ordinary consumers did not have to manually convert and upload
their CDs. The music industry objected to this as unauthorised copying, and the Southern
District of New York agreed, holding that although the copying was being done on behalf
of the consumer, it was nonetheless being carried out by MP3.com and was therefore
unlawful. The significant damages awarded against MP3.com ($53 million) essentially
put it out of business.

Peer-to-Peer Filesharing
The Napster Case

The first generation of filesharing, in the form of Napster, arrived soon after, piggy-backing **[2–62]**
on the technological developments discussed in [2–58], and offering an easy-to-use and rapid
way of sharing music files with other enthusiasts across the world, for free. Unfortunately
for its long-term survival, the content that was thus distributed was largely copyrighted by
others. Originally developed in a university dormitory, and very popular with that particular
demographic, Napster was a peer-to-peer file sharing service that allowed users to search
through, browse, and download from, the music collections of anyone else on the network.
As it achieved global popularity, a vast library was made available. (Its notoriety was driven
to a significant extent by the publicity that developed around the litigation, and the efforts of
some musicians, notably Metallica, to shut it down.)

---

[38] 180 F 3d 1072 (9th Cir 1999).
[39] 92 F Supp 2d 249 (2000).

[2–63] The industry alleged that Napster was contributorily liable for copyright infringement by its users – in other words, file sharing on its network was direct infringement, Napster had both real and constructive knowledge of this, they had the capacity to exercise control, and they were not doing so. Napster argued that the user activity was fair use, as they were either sampling recordings with a view to possible purchase, 'space-shifting' (obtaining digital versions of recordings that they already had in another form), or downloading recordings that artists permitted to be distributed without payment. (With regard to the last of these, it should be noted that some artists, such as the Arctic Monkeys and Wilco, have used this as a deliberate and successful part of their career strategy.) The Court of Appeal for the Ninth Circuit held that the first two of these were not fair use, as the 'sample' became a permanent copy, and the space-shifting necessarily involved sharing the copy with other users. (Napster's software was designed in such a way as to encourage sharing by default.) The last was permissible and could continue.

[2–64] The Court concluded that

> Napster has actual knowledge that specific infringing material is available using its system, that it could block access to the system by suppliers of the infringing material, and that it failed to remove the material.[40]

[2–65] When the case returned to the District Court, Napster was required to put in place measures to police the distribution of copyrighted materials on its network. It did not operate a 'pure' peer-to-peer network; in order to allow searches complete within a reasonable period of time, it maintained an index of files located on individual nodes. This was one of the features that made it attractive; without some form of indexing, a search could take a very long time, as a particular node would have to query every other node in turn until it found the content that a user was looking for. However, it also created a significant legal vulnerability: the music industry was now able to require it to exclude particular artists, albums, and songs from searches. Users began to disguise content by simple mechanisms like substituting the number 1 for the letter i. The judge became impatient and required perfect effectiveness from the filtering mechanism. This, and a settlement for $26 million with the music industry, effectively shut Napster down. (The brand has continued in other forms over the years.)

Responses to Napster

[2–66] Technologists and lawyers watched these developments with keen interest. It was clear that there was a significant potential market of users for peer-to-peer file sharing, if a means could be found of developing a service that was within the parameters of legality and could bring in revenue. A second generation of peer-to-peer filesharing services were launched, such as Gnutella, which had in common the lack of a central index or any effective means of control by the developers. The music industry did not stand by idly and so further legal actions were brought. A number of cases were heard together on appeal to the US Supreme Court in 2005, and that decision was eagerly awaited. When it came,[41] it put an end to any idea that it might be possible to create peer-to-peer soft-

---

[40] *A&M v Napster* 239 F 3d 1004 (2001) 1021.
[41] *MGM v Grokster* 545 US 913 (2005).

ware for illicit distribution that had a viable commercial future. The Court unanimously held that distributing a 'device' (which includes a software program) with the object of promoting copyright infringement is liable for acts of infringement that result. Soon afterwards, the Federal Court of Australia came to a similar conclusion by somewhat different reasoning, holding that Sharman Networks, distributors of the Kazaa filesharing package and originally part of the Grokster litigation in the US, were liable for infringement because they had 'authorised' their users to engage in it.[42] The underlying rationale of both courts was fundamentally the same: these companies depended on advertising for revenue, so they had a vested interest in continuing infringement on their network. If all that was available was out-of-copyright recordings and freebies made available by new, unknown artists, public interest would not be sufficient to make them viable or profitable businesses.

BitTorrent, Trackers and the Pirate Bay

Second generation peer-to-peer software was deliberately designed to operate without a central manager, and so as the businesses that created them closed down, the sharing networks continued to operate. However, the numbers using them dwindled, particularly as the music industry began to aggressively target individuals who had illegally downloaded music. Attention shifted to an alternative means of sharing information, the BitTorrent protocol. This was not developed for sharing music or movies, but was intended as a means for open source software projects that are often lacking in resources, to cheaply and easily make their source code, object files, and other binary files available. In a BitTorrent 'swarm', individuals may have different pieces of a file. As new users join a swarm, they ask for the pieces that they do not have, and as they receive these, they in turn make them available to others. In this way, the swarm makes use of the disk storage and network bandwidth of a distributed group of users without any centralised server or need for co-ordination.   **[2–67]**

From the mid-2000s on, BitTorrent was repurposed for distributing infringing files, but because it was not designed with this in mind, it had two defects from the perspective of illicit copying. First, in order to join a swarm, a user needs a torrent file, which is an entrance or roadmap. These must be obtained from some central repository. Second, a swarm keeps a record of the Internet Protocol (IP) address of every computer that connects to it. It is possible to de-anonymise these addresses, so that one can identify the person who was most likely to be using that device (in an education or commercial context, the user who was logged in; in a domestic context, the person who pays the broadband connection bill). In response to the first issue, there developed a wide range of 'tracker' sites, of which the best known is the Pirate Bay. Its operators were convicted of assisting in copyright infringement by the Swedish courts 2009;[43] other tracker site administrators have similarly been convicted in courts worldwide. Despite these ongoing efforts by the music industry, BitTorrent trackers continue to be widely used. The second defect gave rise to a further series of litigation, which will be considered shortly.   **[2–68]**

---

[42] *Universal v Sharman* [2005] FCA 1242.
[43] Henrik Wistam and Therese Andersson, 'The Pirate Bay Trial' (2009) 15 Computer and Telecommunications Law Review 129.

File Locker Services

[2–69] Also around the mid-2000s, there was an increase in interest in 'file locker' services, such as MegaUpload, Rapidshare, and Depositfiles. These allow users to upload large files and, if desired, share them with others. Like the other services discussed here, these have many legitimate uses. However, they can also be used for illegal sharing, with links circulated by email, social media, or via bulletin boards. The music industry has attempted to shut down many of these, with the most high-profile example being the raid on MegaUpload in 2012. Some services (such as Uploaded.to and BTJunkie) simply shut down in response. Other providers changed their focus to more legitimate offerings, leading to them going out of business. There are, of course, replacements.

USENET

[2–70] Less popular, but nonetheless important, is an increase in interest in USENET. This is an ancient protocol in internet terms, dating to the early years of the network. It is a peer-to-peer distribution mechanism for news articles and discussions; large portions of it are entirely unmanaged and unmoderated. It is possible to distribute large files, such as MP3 or MP4, through USENET, but because the underlying software was designed for short messages that do not contain audio, video, or images, this is cumbersome and tricky. Nonetheless many individuals were able to overcome the technical challenges and engage in file sharing by this method. This has given rise to some case law, as we shall see.

Streaming Services

[2–71] By the beginning of this decade, the marketplace context for file sharing had changed. Much of the case law and controversy discussed above arose because the music industry was unwilling to co-operate with technology firms or to make their products available through online services. By the time it was clear to them that they needed to do this, the balance of power had shifted. Many consumers were used to obtaining music for free. They had also started to use devices such the iPod as a means of transporting and listening to their ever-growing digital music collections. The music (and later the movie) industry had little choice but to collaborate with companies such as Apple and licence their products for purchase and download through online stores.

[2–72] Streaming services, particularly subscription-based options such as Spotify and Netflix, became increasingly popular (and are now becoming a significant primary market, with television shows being developed for first release on these platforms). Services like this allow users to access a variety of types of content from the 'cloud', using a mix of devices, such as desktop computers, mobile phones and tablets, and set-top boxes. These are much easier to use than earlier services, and do not require the user to store and curate a library of digital media. Instead, consumers have instant access to a huge array of music and movies on an on-demand basis. Some of these services are quite legal and operate with the full consent of the relevant rights-holders. Others are not, and rely on charging less than legitimate operators or on advertising as a source of revenue. The failure on the part of the content industry to provide legal and paid services in the early years of internet adoption may have meant that they have lost a significant amount of revenue forever, and that they no longer control the means of distribution as closely as they did in the pre-digital era.

Filesharing Case Law in Ireland

There have been some important file sharing cases in Ireland – indeed, for a while, this **[2–73]** jurisdiction was quite significant in developing the frontiers of digital jurisprudence. The initial approach was to seek what are known as *Norwich Pharmacal* orders, which require an entity who can help to identify a third party who may be engaging in infringement of intellectual property to divulge relevant information to a rights holder. This was a slow and expensive process, and although some settlements were achieved (doubtless leading to difficult conversations between bill-paying parents and music enthusiast teenagers), the investigation and legal costs were far in excess of what was being recouped, and as a strategy to halt illegal filesharing in Ireland, it clearly was not working. The industry therefore decided that it was necessary to enlist Internet service providers (ISPs) in their efforts.

In 2009, the Irish Recorded Music Association (IRMA) sued Eircom, the largest ISP in the **[2–74]** country, in order to force them to implement a graduated response policy (GRS) – what is commonly known as a 'three strikes and you're out', in other words, a sequence of warning letter, restricted internet access, ending in disconnection of service. It is important to note that this process operates in such a way that the music industry does not obtain individual subscriber details. They supply IP addresses at which they allege that infringing conduct took place at a given time; it is for Eircom or another broadband provider to consult its records and determine which subscriber is involved. After eight days at hearing, Eircom settled the case,[44] agreeing to implement such a policy, but only if it was in compliance with data protection law and only if IRMA sought to have other Irish ISPs implement similar rules in order to ensure a 'level playing field'.[45] IRMA went on to apply for, and obtain, court orders blocking access to the Pirate Bay Web site from Eircom's systems. Eircom did not oppose these applications.[46]

At this point, the Data Protection Commissioner (DPC) intervened, as he was concerned **[2–75]** that a three-strikes policy raised privacy questions. However, the Court was not prepared to give him indemnity for his costs and so this issue was argued and decided against the DPC without hearing him. The Court considered three issues in arriving at its decision. The first issue was whether IP addresses are 'personal data' for the purposes of the Data Protection Acts 1988–2003 (DPA), which would require that the protections afforded to such data under that legislation would apply. The judge held that because the music industry had abandoned its previous strategy of seeking *Norwich Pharmacal* orders against ISPs in order to obtain details of individual subscribers whom they suspected of engaging in infringing downloads, they would not come into possession of any personally identifying information.[47]

Second, the DPC was concerned that the processing involved in the disconnection process **[2–76]** (assuming that it involved 'personal data') would be 'unwarranted [under the DPA] … by reason of prejudice to the fundamental rights and freedoms or legitimate interests of the

---

[44] John Kennedy, 'Big Four Music Labels and Eircom in Landmark Piracy Settlement' (*Silicon Republic*, 28 January 2009) <www.siliconrepublic.com/new-media/item/12181-big-four-music-labels-and-e> (accessed 13 June 2017).

[45] *EMI Records (Ireland) Ltd v Eircom PLC* [2010] IEHC 108 [10].

[46] *EMI Records (Ireland) Ltd v Eircom PLC* [2009] IEHC 411.

[47] *EMI Records (Ireland) Ltd v Eircom PLC* [2010] IEHC 108 [25].

data subject'. However, the judge held that copyright was a fundamental right in Irish law, relying on dictum by Keane J in *Phonographic Performance Ireland Ltd v Cody*.[48] On that basis, a three-strikes policy was not unwarranted.[49]

[2–77]   The third issue which the judge considered was whether the processing involved in the three-strikes procedure involved 'sensitive personal data'. Under s 1 of the DPA, 'sensitive personal data' includes:

> personal data as to—...
> (d) the commission or alleged commission of any offense by the data subject, or
> (e) any proceedings for an offense committed or alleged to have been committed by the data subject, the disposal of such proceedings or the sentence of any court in such proceedings.

[2–78]   Section 140 of the CRRA criminalises copyright infringement. However, the judge was '... satisfied that neither the plaintiffs as owners or assignees of valuable copyright, nor Eircom as the Internet service provider, are in any way interested in the detection or prosecution of criminal offences'.[50]

[2–79]   IRMA then moved on to discussions with other ISPs on a three-strikes policy, which became litigation when some were not keen to follow Eircom's lead. UPC, a major broadband provider and part of a large European group, were particularly unhappy with the proposals, and the music industry sued to force them to comply.

[2–80]   Charleton J, who had also heard the *Eircom* litigation, heard this case.[51] He was of the view that because P2P has legitimate, and sometimes important, uses, it is impossible to simply shut it down. These legitimate uses also mean that it would not be proportionate to use packet inspection to throttle P2P transmissions.[52]

[2–81]   The judge was 'not satisfied that the attitude of UPC toward the illegal sharing of copyright material over the Internet is either reasonable or fair'.[53] UPC has a policy of not commenting on filesharing and associated issues, which the judge said was unfair, and he found that 'UPC has no interest in doing anything other than making deceptive noises by reference to its acceptable usage policy.'[54] The judge then reviewed the application of *Norwich Pharmacal*[55] orders (which force a third party to release information on a wrongdoer in a civil case) to filesharing cases. These are not realistic options, as it seems that the costs of three cases brought in Ireland were €680,000, but these only brought in some €80,000 in settlements.[56]

---

[48]   *Phonographic Performance Ireland Ltd v Cody* [1998] 4 IR 504.
[49]   *EMI Records (Ireland) Ltd v Eircom PLC* [2010] IEHC 108 [30]–[35].
[50]   *EMI Records (Ireland) Ltd v Eircom PLC* [2010] IEHC 108 [38]–[41].
[51]   *EMI Records (Ireland) Ltd v UPC Communications Ireland Ltd* [2010] IEHC 377.
[52]   *EMI Records (Ireland) Ltd v UPC Communications Ireland Ltd* [2010] IEHC 377 [29]–[33].
[53]   *EMI Records (Ireland) Ltd v UPC Communications Ireland Ltd* [2010] IEHC 377 [50].
[54]   *EMI Records (Ireland) Ltd v UPC Communications Ireland Ltd* [2010] IEHC 377 [53].
[55]   *Norwich Pharmacal Co & Others v Customs and Excise Commissioners* [1974] AC 133 (HL).
[56]   *EMI Records (Ireland) Ltd v UPC Communications Ireland Ltd* [2010] IEHC 377 [62].

The judge was 'of the view that there are no privacy or data protection implications to detecting unauthorized downloads of copyright material using peer-to-peer technology', because the music industry only has IP addresses rather than full subscriber details.[57]   **[2–82]**

The outcome of the case turned on the application of s 40 of the CRRA. Particularly important were ss 40(3) and 40(4):   **[2–83]**

> (3) Subject to subsection (4), the provision of facilities for enabling the making available to the public of copies of a work shall not of itself constitute an act of making available to the public of copies of the work.
>
> (4) Without prejudice to subsection (3), where a person who provides facilities referred to in that subsection is notified by the owner of the copyright in the work concerned that those facilities are being used to infringe the copyright in that work and that person fails to remove that infringing material as soon as practicable thereafter that person shall also be liable for the infringement.

The judge held that because UPC could prevent infringing material from transiting its network, but could not remove it from the user's home computer, it could not fall into s 40(4). He also held that UPC was a 'mere conduit' in the sense used by the Electronic Commerce Directive, and that while this did require national laws to include the possibility of injunctions against ISPs where infringing material is being made available, it left the form of these procedures to the discretion of national law-makers, a step not yet taken in Ireland. Contrasting the minimal Irish procedures with the UK Digital Economy Act, the French HADOPI legislation, what might emerge from the Belgian *Scarlet v Sabam* case and the US Digital Millennium Copyright Act, he concluded that the Irish legislature needed to intervene 'to protect constitutional rights to copyright and foster the national resource of creativity'.[58]   **[2–84]**

Interestingly, the judge reviewed two of his own previous decisions in filesharing cases, mentioned previously at [2–74] to [2–77]. While he held that his decision regarding the data protection issues involved was still correct, he concluded that he did not have the right to grant an order blocking accessing to the Pirate Bay site and suggested that the parties should consider appealing that case.[59]   **[2–85]**

This latter finding caused significant anxiety for the music industry. The fundamental issue was one which recurs in ICT law – legislation which assumes a particular technological configuration does not function well as new innovations develop. Section 40 assumes a client–server model; it does not fit well with a peer-to-peer architecture. Following lobbying by the industry, including the filing of a lawsuit against the Irish government,[60] a campaign of opposition from civil society groups, and a short debate in Dáil Éireann,[61] a small addition was made to s 40, in order to implement Article 8(3) of the Copyright Directive, which required Member States to 'ensure that rightholders are in a position to apply for   **[2–86]**

---

[57] *EMI Records (Ireland) Ltd v UPC Communications Ireland Ltd* [2010] IEHC 377 [68].

[58] *EMI Records (Ireland) Ltd v UPC Communications Ireland Ltd* [2010] IEHC 377 [131].

[59] *EMI Records (Ireland) Ltd v UPC Communications Ireland Ltd* [2010] IEHC 377 [135] –[137].

[60] See *Sony v UPC Communications Ireland Ltd* [2016] IECA 231 [50].

[61] 753 *Dáil Debates* Cols 264–281.

an injunction against intermediaries whose services are used by a third party to infringe a copyright or related right':[62]

> (5A) (a) The owner of the copyright in a work may, in respect of that work, apply to the High Court for an injunction against an intermediary ...
> (b) In considering an application for an injunction under this subsection, the court shall have due regard to the rights of any person likely to be affected by virtue of the grant of any such injunction and the court shall give such directions (including, where appropriate, a direction requiring a person be notified of the application) as the court considers appropriate in all of the circumstances.

[2–87] This gives wide scope to the courts to grant any injunctions that it thinks fit against ISPs and others. However, the amendment does not provide very much guidance to the courts – it is not clear what is meant by 'due regard', who is 'likely to be affected', or if there is to be any balancing with fundamental rights such as privacy. Under this new section, several injunctions have been granted, blocking access to the Pirate Bay website,[63] and requiring the implementation of a graduated response policy.[64] An NGO, Digital Rights Ireland, sought to be joined to the first such application, to block access to the well-known Pirate Bay website, but this was refused on the grounds that it was not a neutral party and that the case did not raise novel legal issues on which the Court could benefit from external guidance.[65]

[2–88] Meanwhile, in two important cases, the Court of Justice of European Union re-affirmed that, due to the Electronic Commerce Directive, ISPs could not be placed under a general obligation to monitor content on their network in order to deal with copyright infringement.[66]

[2–89] The DPC became involved in filesharing issues again in 2012. Because Eircom did not correctly implement the move to daylight saving time in winter 2010, it incorrectly identified some individuals as having engaging in illegal filesharing when they had not. One of these complained to the DPC, and after investigation, the DPC granted an enforcement order requiring that Eircom cease to operate its graduated response policy. When this order was judicially reviewed before the High Court, Charleton J concluded that the notice was invalid because it failed to give reasons; it was quashed.[67] On appeal to the Supreme Court, the notice was also held to be invalid for the failure to give reasons.[68]

[2–90] The CJEU returned to the question of the remedies available to rightsholders against ISPs in 2014. On a reference from Austria, it held that national courts could, under Article 8(3)

---

[62] European Union (Copyright and Related Rights) Regulations 2012, SI 2012/59.
[63] *EMI Records Ireland Ltd v UPC Communications Ireland Ltd* [2013] IEHC 274.
[64] *Sony Music Entertainment (Ireland) Ltd v UPC Communications Ireland Ltd (No 1)* [2015] IEHC 317; *Sony Music Entertainment (Ireland) Ltd v UPC Communications Ireland Ltd (No 2)* [2015] IEHC 386.
[65] *EMI v UPC* [2013] IEHC 204.
[66] C–70/10 *SABAM v Scarlet Extended* ECLI:EU:C:2011:771; C–360/10 *SABAM v Netlog* ECLI:EU:C:2012:85.
[67] *EMI Records (Ireland) Ltd v The Data Protection Commissioner* [2012] IEHC 264.
[68] *EMI v Data Protection Commissioner* [2013] IESC 34.

of the Information Society Directive,[69] issue an order to an ISP requiring the prohibition of access to a particular website containing infringing content, but need to strike a balance between competing fundamental rights (which include copyrights and related rights, the freedom to conduct a business and the freedom of information of internet users). The ISP can comply with the order by showing it has taken all reasonable measures; it does not need to make 'unbearable sacrifices'.[70]

In 2015, in *Sony v UPC*,[71] the High Court ordered UPC to implement a GRS, which **[2–91]**

> requires UPC to send each relevant subscriber a 'cease and desist' letter upon receipt of notification of the first and second copyright infringement notifications which it receives from the rightholders. On receipt of the third copyright infringement notice, UPC is then required to send the relevant rightsholders a notification that the particular subscriber has been the subject of three such notifications. The rightsholders are then entitled to apply to court for an order terminating the subscriber's internet broadband service. There is a monthly limit of some 2,500 notifications of this kind. ... the rightholders are required to pay 20% of any capital expenditure incurred by UPC with a cap of €940,000 on each such expenditure ...[72]

This was later appealed to the Court of Appeal by UPC, who claimed that it was too detailed **[2–92]** and strayed into policy questions that were inappropriate for a court to consider.[73] The CA had to consider whether s 40(5A) granted sufficient legal authority to the courts to make a GRS order. It held that Article 8(3) (as interpreted by the CJEU) had the effect of 'requiring national courts in appropriate cases to grant injunctions against non-infringing ISPs',[74] which was quite a novel jurisdiction.[75] The CA held that such an order could be granted if it was

(i)   necessary;
(ii) that the costs involved were not excessive or disproportionate and that the order itself should not be unduly complicated;
(iii) that the cost sharing proposals were fair and reasonable;
(iv) that the order respected the fundamental rights of the parties affected, including internet users; and
(v)   that the duration of the proposed injunction and the provisions for review were reasonable.[76]

The Court then reviewed those factors, based on Cregan J's decision in the High Court, and having answered all questions positively, affirmed the original order.

---

[69] Parliament and Council Directive 29/2001 (EC) on the harmonisation of certain aspects of copyright and related rights in the information society [2001] OJ L167/10 (amended by OJ L6/70).
[70] C–314/12 *UPC Telekabel Wien* ECLI:EU:C:2014:192.
[71] [2015] IEHC 317.
[72] [2016] IECA 231 [2]–[3].
[73] [2016] IECA 231 [4].
[74] [2016] IECA 231 [52].
[75] [2016] IECA 231 [53].
[76] [2016] IECA 231 [65].

[2–93] In subsequent litigation, in April 2017, on the application of several major movie and television studios, the High Court granted orders requiring some Internet Service Providers to block access to a number of websites that provided access to infringing 'streams' of content. The applications were unopposed, although one ISP (Eir) sought a cap on the number of websites that might be blocked in the future, something which Cregan J declined to do.[77]

[2–94] In the United Kingdom, the courts granted an order shutting down the Newzbin website, which gave access to illicitly copied material on USENET (a service that has already been discussed above).[78] When this service re-established itself in the Seychelles, the music and movie industry applied for, and were granted, an order requiring British Telecom to use its 'Cleanfeed' monitoring service (which was originally developed to prevent access to child pornography) to block access to this later iteration of Newzbin.[79] It later closed down. The UK courts have also granted orders blocking access to the Pirate Bay website.[80]

[2–95] More recently, they have granted a very interesting temporary injunction to block access to streaming services which were delivering infringing live streams of Premier League matches to UK customers.[81] As noted, these are popular and easy to use, but difficult to shut down as the servers are usually located overseas, the source and nature of the stream is easy to disguise and often only operates for the duration of a particular sporting fixture. The Football Association Premier League (with the support of similar sporting associations), which obtains significant revenue from the broadcast rights to its games, sought an injunction against a number of ISPs to prevent infringing streams. The ISPs did not object; some had purchased the broadcast rights and were keen to halt piracy.[82]

[2–96] The injunction was interesting in a number of ways. First, the servers to be blocked would be identified based on three criteria, one of which remains confidential in order to inhibit attempts at circumvention.[83] The other two are that FAPL (and its appointed contractor)

- must reasonably believe that the server has the sole or predominant purpose of enabling or facilitating access to infringing streams of Premier League match footage; or
- must not know or have reason to believe that the server is being used for any other substantial purpose.[84]

[2–97] Second, the order is only active during the broadcasting of Premier League football matches.[85] Third, the list of target servers is to be re-set each week during the football season.[86]

---

77 Aodhan O Faolain, 'Broadband Providers Ordered to Block Illegal Streaming Sites' *The Irish Times* (Dublin, 3 April 2017).
78 *Twentieth Century Fox v Newzbin Ltd* [2010] EWHC 608 (Ch).
79 *Twentieth Century Fox v BT* [2011] EWHC 1981 (Ch).
80 *Dramatico Entertainment v BSkyB* [2012] EWHC 268 (Ch).
81 *Football Association Premier League v British Telecom* [2017] EWHC 480 (Ch).
82 [2017] EWHC 480 (Ch) [7]
83 [2017] EWHC 480 (Ch) [9] and [21].
84 [2017] EWHC 480 (Ch) [21].
85 [2017] EWHC 480 (Ch) [24].
86 [2017] EWHC 480 (Ch) [25].

Fourth, the order is only active until 22 May 2017, when the season ends. Its effectiveness will be reviewed at that point, and presumably further orders will be sought in future.[87]

The case is also interesting because it is the first UK application of the *GS Media* case, discussed below at [2–112]. However, what is perhaps most interesting about its future application is that the identification of infringing streams depends on supposedly sophisticated technology deployed by the FAPL. It seems that pirates and rights-holders are increasingly in an escalating dynamic of innovation to enable or to detect piracy. **[2–98]**

The CJEU has held that the provider of a free wireless service is not liable for copyright infringement by users, but rights holders can seek injunctions requiring passwords.[88] It has also held that a dynamic IP address is personal data if it can be linked to an individual, and this linking can be done by 'legal means'.[89] This calls into question the finding of Charleton J in the *EMI* case. **[2–99]**

Technological Protection Measures

Many content providers will seek to ensure that the music, movies, software, and other valuable information that they provide to end-users and consumers is protected in some way so that it can only be accessed by those who have legal permission to do so. This will involve the use of serial numbers, passwords, and encryption. These types of access control schemes are known as *digital rights management* (DRM) in the US and as *technological protection measures* (TPM) in Europe. **[2–100]**

In the US, DRM is regulated by the Digital Millennium Copyright Act (DMCA), particularly s 1201, which prohibits circumvention of 'a technological measure that effectively controls access to a work protected' under that law. It has generated a significant body of case law. **[2–101]**

In Europe, TPM are regulated by Directive 2001/29,[90] known both as the Copyright Directive or the Information Society Directive. Article 6 of this requires Member States to 'provide adequate legal protection against the circumvention of any effective technological measures' and also **[2–102]**

> against the manufacture, import, distribution, sale, rental, advertisement for sale or rental, or possession for commercial purposes of devices, products or components or the provision of services which:
> (a) are promoted, advertised or marketed for the purpose of circumvention of, or
> (b) have only a limited commercially significant purpose or use other than to circumvent, or
> (c) are primarily designed, produced, adapted or performed for the purpose of enabling or facilitating the circumvention of,
> any effective technological measures.

---

[87] [2017] EWHC 480 (Ch) [26].
[88] C–484/14 *McFadden v Sony* ECLI:EU:C:2016:689.
[89] C–582/14 *Patrick Breyer v Germany* ECLI:EU:C:2016:779.
[90] Parliament and Council Directive 29/2001 (EC) on the harmonisation of certain aspects of copyright and related rights in the information society [2001] OJ L167/10 (amended by OJ L6/70).

[2–103] However, Member States are also required to ensure that those entitled to an exception or limitation under the Directive (such as private, non-commercial uses, library archives, and museums) are able to benefit from this. Such uses will often involve some means of circumventing the encryption.

[2–104] The Directive is implemented in Irish law by Part VII of the CRRA 2000. Section 370 prohibits the making available of a 'protection-defeating device' or the provision of information of services 'intended to enable or assist persons to circumvent rights protection measures'. Section 371 makes it an offence to receive a broadcast or cable programme to which TPM has been applied with the intention of avoiding paying fees to the provider, with a maximum fine of €1,900. Section 374 clarifies that even though the existence of TPM is protected under Part VII, Chapter 1 does not forbid the carrying out of acts permitted under the CRRA, or 'undertaking any act of circumvention required to effect such permitted acts'. However, this does not require rights holders to provide some means of circumventing TPMs for legal purposes, and does not provide an exemption from Part VII, Chapter 2. The latter prohibits removal or interference with rights management information, with potential prison terms up to five years or a fine of up to €126,000. This means that general TPM cannot be legally circumvented, even to benefit from an exception to copyright law.

[2–105] The Irish courts have been reluctant to grant protection to content simply because it is encrypted. In *News Datacom v Lyons*,[91] the plaintiffs provided encrypted television broadcasts by satellite and sold set-top decoder devices together with a subscription to 'smart cards' which were inserted into the set-top boxes and enabled access to the broadcasts. The defendants sold smart cards which would work with these set-top boxes and also enable access to the broadcast material. The plaintiffs sought an injunction to prevent the sale of the competing cards, alleging that they must have been produced by copying the algorithm used to decrypt the signal. Flood J refused this application, holding that the plaintiffs had not been able to prove that copying was, in fact, taking place, and that there was no scientific basis for this claim. Instead, he held that the fact that the plaintiffs changed their encryption scheme regularly and the defendants were nonetheless able to produce a card which could decrypt this within a short time made copying a highly improbable explanation.

[2–106] The UK courts have taken a similar approach. In *Mars UK v Teknowledge Ltd*,[92] the plaintiff supplied coin discriminating machines, which could automatically identify and authenticate small change. The software used was encrypted to prevent end-users accessing it and modifying the machines. The defendant reverse-engineered the encryption scheme and the coin discrimination software, so that it could re-calibrate the machines. The Court rejected a claim that this was a breach of confidence, holding that if the machine was freely available on the market, the owner had full rights to it, including the possibility of examining and dismantling it to find out how it works.

[2–107] However, where a device is clearly intended to circumvent a legal TPM scheme, the courts are not well disposed towards this type of innovation. In *Sony v Ball*,[93] the High Court of England and Wales held that a chip known as the Messiah2, which tricked a PlayStation 2 games console into believing that a counterfeit CD or DVD (or one imported from another market) contained the necessary embedded codes so that it could be played, was an

---

[91] [1994] 1 ILRM 450 (HC).
[92] [2000] FSR 138 (Ch).
[93] [2004] All ER (D) 334; [2004] EWHC 1738 (Ch).

'infringing article' under the relevant UK legislation, which is similar in scope and intent to Part VII, Chapter 2 of the CRRA 2000.

In Case C–355/12 *Nintendo v PC Box*,[94] the CJEU (on a reference from the Milan District Court) considered a similar 'modchip' device, this time developed for the Nintendo DS and Wii games devices. The defendant here argued that these devices allowed the use of 'home-brew' games developed by programmers not licenced by Nintendo. The Court affirmed the general ideas behind Article 6 of the Copyright Directive but noted that the use of TPMs in videogame consoles must be proportionate, and should not prohibit activities or devices that have a commercially significant purpose or use other than the infringement of copyright. In assessing whether such TPMs are proportionate, national courts should have regard to the purpose of the circumvention devices complained of and the extent to which they are used by third parties for non-infringing as well as infringing purposes. It also pointed out that video games are not solely computer programs but are complex multimedia creations, containing sound and video elements. This may mean that they do not come entirely within the scope of the Software Directive, which means that the re-sale rights identified by the CJEU in the *UsedSoft* case (discussed above) may not apply.

[2–108]

Copyright and Web Linking

An interesting question that has arisen from time to time is whether posting a document to the internet which does not itself contain any infringing content but which links to a location where infringing content can be accessed is a breach of copyright. An early but ultimately inconclusive case is *Shetland Times v Wills*,[95] in which a newspaper was able to obtain an interim interdict (the Scots law equivalent to an interim injunction) preventing a competitor from 'deep-linking' to internal pages on its site. Two factors which were significant in this case – that as it was a preliminary phase of litigation, the pursuer (plaintiff) only need to prove a prima facie case; and that the Court accepted an argument that the website met the statutory definition of 'cable programme service' – mean that it is not good precedent. Case law from civil jurisdictions over the years has been inconsistent, but have tended to favour the linker.[96]

[2–109]

The issue has become increasingly important in European copyright law in recent years, particularly as new technology makes it easier to distribute infringing content in ways that may not generate liability for intermediaries, such as 'tracker' sites for torrent files, indexes of file locker downloads, or streaming services. The key question that has emerged is whether these types of sites are engaged in a 'communication to the public' of an infringing copy, which is prohibited by Article 3 of the Copyright Directive.[97]

[2–110]

The CJEU has held that posting a link to infringing content hosted elsewhere does not constitute 'making available to the public' if no new public is involved.[98] This is also the case if a website 'frames' content that is freely available elsewhere.[99]

[2–111]

---

[94] ECLI:EU:C:2014:25.

[95] [1997] FSR 604 (OH).

[96] Steve Hedley, *The Law of Electronic Commerce and the Internet in the UK and Ireland* (Cavendish 2006) 220–22.

[97] Parliament and Council Directive 29/2001 (EC) on the harmonisation of certain aspects of copyright and related rights in the information society [2001] OJ L167/10 (amended by OJ L6/70).

[98] C–466/12 *Svensson v Retriever Sverige AB* ECLI:EU:C:2014:76

[99] C–348/13 *BestWater International v Mebes* ECLI:EU:C:2014:2315.

[2–112]   However, linking to a work that you know is infringing is itself infringement, particularly if you profit from the link, as this is a communication to the public.[100] More recently, it has held that selling a device (a pre-configured set-top box) which enabled access to websites containing 'streams' of infringing content involved communication to the public of that unauthorised content.[101] The intention to profit from such infringement seems to be an important indicator of liability.

[2–113]   The CJEU has very recently given its judgment in an interesting case, which raised the question of whether a website which does not itself contain any infringing content but indexes metadata about such content, including its location on the internet thus enabling users to upload and download copyrighted material without legal authorisation (such as the Pirate Bay), is engaged in indirect copyright infringement and can therefore be blocked under European law.[102] The Court highlighted the essential role of the site operators in making protected works available to internet users, by making the index easy-to-use, searchable, and up-to-date. The intention of the operators to make these works available to the public, together with the for-profit nature of the site, were also relevant to the finding.

Possible Copyright Law Reform

[2–114]   In 2011, the Minister for Jobs, Enterprise and Innovation established a Copyright Review Committee comprising academics and practitioners with expertise in copyright law and policy. After extensive public consultation, this reported in 2013.[103] While its central focus was on innovation, and its remit extended to copyright as a whole rather than simply the interface between digital technology and copyright, it inevitably included significant discussion of the challenges this raises. The key questions which were referred to it were:

1. Examine the present national copyright legislation and identify any areas that are perceived to create barriers to innovation.
2. Identify solutions for removing these barriers and make recommendations as to how these solutions might be implemented through changes to national legislation.
3. Examine the US style 'fair use' doctrine to see if it would be appropriate in an Irish/EU context.
4. If it transpires that national copyright legislation requires to be amended but cannot be amended (bearing in mind that Irish copyright legislation is bound by the European Communities Directives on copyright and related rights and other international obligations), make recommendations for changes to the EU Directives that will eliminate the barriers to innovation and optimise the balance between protecting creativity and promoting and facilitating innovation.

[2–115]   The report made significant recommendations, including the establishment of a Copyright Council, specialist intellectual property tracks in the courts, and exceptions for innovation,

---

[100] C–160/15 *GS Media v Sanoma* ECLI:EU:C:2016:644.
[101] C–527/15 *Stichting Brien v Filmspeler.nl* ECLI:EU:C:2017:300.
[102] C–610/15 *Stichting Brein v Ziggo* ECLI:EU:C:2017:456.
[103] Department of Jobs, Enterprise and Innovation, 'Copyright Review' (29 October 2013) <www.djei.ie/en/What-We-Do/Innovation-Research-Development/Intellectual-Property/Copyright/Copyright-Review/> accessed 13 June 2017.

fair use, and re-use of very small snippets of text. Amongst the recommendations with a specific focus on ICT were:

- Extending the use of technological protection measures and rights management information
- Introducing exceptions permitted under EU law, including format-shifting
- Extending copyright deposit provisions to digital publications
- The creation of a Digital Copyright Exchange
- The creation of exceptions for text- and data-mining, and digital research and research and computer security
- Clarification that copyright exceptions do not apply to computer programs

In August 2016, the Minister for Jobs, Enterprise and Innovation announced that the government had approved the drafting of a Copyright and Related Rights (Miscellaneous Provisions) Bill 2016.[104] No further information is available on the timetable for this work, and it may be some more years before there is significant reform in Irish copyright law. Meanwhile, the Commission is proposing a Directive on copyright in the digital single market. Its reform proposals aim to make cross-border copyright licensing easier, make re-use of materials easier (particularly in the education market, and using digital tools), greater transparency for remuneration to creators (again with a particular focus on digital content platforms), and more access for persons with disabilities.[105]   **[2–116]**

Free, Libre and Open Source Software

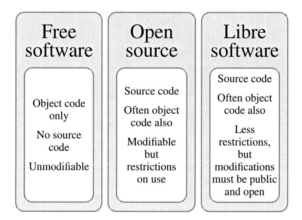

Figure 3   *Types of Free, Libre and Open Source Software*

---

[104] Department of Jobs, Enterprise and Innovation, 'General Scheme of a Copyright Bill approved by Government' (4 August 2016) <www.djei.ie/en/News-And-Events/Department-News/2016/August/04082016a.html> accessed 13 June 2017.

[105] European Commission, 'Proposal for a Directive of the European Parliament and of the Council on Copyright in the Digital Single Market' COM(2016) 593 final.

[2–117]   An important phenomenon in software copyright has been the development of the Free, Libre and Open Source Software (FLOSS) movement, which is really a variety of divergent groups with some common aims but also significant disagreements. One shared goal is to make software as freely available as possible. However, there are a number of significant strands within that general ambit:

- *Free Software*: Making software available in object code form, for free use by anyone, but without source code available (thus preventing modification)
- *Libre Software*: Similar to open source, although with much less limitations on what the end-user may do, although often with a proviso that any changes made must themselves be made available to the public without further restrictions
- *Open Source Software*: Making software available in source code form, often with object code versions also (for convenience) but generally with limitations as modification, re-use, and commercialisation

[2–118]   The most important organisation in the FLOSS world is the Free Software Foundation (headed by Richard Stallman), which has produced a suite of software known as the GNU Operating System. GNU is based on the well-known Unix operating system, and the acronym stands for GNU's Not Unix. Elements of GNU have often been combined with the operating system kernel developed by Linus Torvalds and released for free re-use in the 1990s, to provide a wide range of Unix-based 'distributions' which offer access to a full suite of software at essentially no cost. These are generally known as Linux, or GNU/Linux, and have been very popular both with hobbyists and internet network and system administrators. The FSF is known to take a very strict view on the need for source code to be open and modifiable. The Open Source Initiative is also important and seeks to represent a more pragmatic perspective.

[2–119]   These developments have been underpinned by software licences which allow free re-use, and even modification to the software, but leverage copyright law to impose an obligation that changes must be made available to the public at no charge. This is sometimes called 'viral licensing' or 'copyleft'. There are a wide range of licences; the most common is the GNU Public Licence (GPL), while the Berkeley System Distribution (BSD) is also popular, particularly as it does not require source code redistribution.

[2–120]   The enforceability of these licences has been considered by the courts. There have been a number of successful cases in civil law courts, particularly in Germany.[106] From a common law perspective, in *Jacobsen v Katzer*,[107] the plaintiff had worked on the Java Model Railroad Interface (JMRI) Project, which enabled software control of model trains. It was available under the 'Artistic Licence'. The defendant sold commercial software that used elements of the JMRI in breach of the Artistic Licence. The Court of Appeals for the Federal Circuit held that this was enforceable, which was a significant recognition of the validity of such licences, which had never been tested in court before.

---

[106] Tomasz Rychlicki, 'GPLv3: New Software Licence and New Axiology of Intellectual Property Law' (2008) 30 European Intellectual Property Review 232, 236.
[107] 535 F 3d 1373 (Fed Cir 2008).

Further Reading

- James Boyle, *The Public Domain* (Yale University Press 2008)
- Anna Marie Brennan, 'The Copyrightability of Computer Software in Ireland: The Problem of Non-Literal Copying' (2010) 4 Irish Business Law Quarterly 12
- Robert Clark, *Intellectual Property Law in Ireland* (4th edn, Bloomsbury 2016)
- Robert Clark, 'The Legal Status of Software: Part 1' (2016) 23 Commercial Law Practitioner 48
- Robert Clark, 'The Legal Status of Software: Part 2' (2016) 23 Commercial Law Practitioner 78
- Sinéad Cantillon, 'Property for Free? An Analysis of Music and Copyright in the Digital Age' (2012) 11 Hibernian Law Journal 35
- Paul Edward Geller, 'Beyond the Copyright Crisis: Principles for Change' (2007) 55 Journal of the Copyright Society of the USA 165
- Jane C Ginsburg and Sam Ricketson, 'Inducers and Authorisers: A Comparison of the US Supreme Court's Grokster decision and the Australian Federal Court's KaZaa ruling' (2006) 11 Media & Arts Law Review 1
- Jack Goldsmith and Tim Wu, *Who Controls the Internet?: Illusions of a Borderless World* (Oxford University Press 2006)
- Brian Hallissey, 'Copyright Injunctions, Web-Blocking and Graduated Response Systems' (2016) 34 Irish Law Times 177
- Gerard Kelly, 'A Court-Ordered Graduated Response System in Ireland: The Beginning of the End?' (2016) 11 Journal of Intellectual Property Law & Practice 183
- Rónán Kennedy, 'No Three Strikes for Ireland (Yet): EU Copyright Law and Individual Liability in Recent Internet Filesharing Litigation' (2011) 12 Journal of Internet Law 15
- Sana Khan, 'An Introduction to Open-Source Software for Lawyers' (2016) 23 Commercial Law Practitioner 259
- Peter S Menell, 'An Epitaph for Traditional Copyright Protection of Network Features of Computer Software' (1998) 43 Antitrust Bulletin 651
- Peter S Menell, 'Rise of the API Copyright Dead?: An Updated Epitaph for Copyright Protection of Network and Functional Features of Computer Software' https://papers.ssrn.com/sol3/papers.cfm?abstract_id=2893192
- Kevin T O'Sullivan, 'Irish Digital Rights in Retrograde: The 'Eircom Protocol' and the Normative Framework of European Law' (2013) 36 Dublin University Law Journal 358
- William Patry, *Moral Panics and the Copyright Wars* (Oxford University Press 2009)
- Tomasz Rychlicki, 'GPLv3: New Software Licence and New Axiology of Intellectual Property Law' (2008) 30 European Intellectual Property Review 232
- John Tsai, 'For Better or Worse: Introducing the GNU General Public License Version 3' (2008) 23 Berkeley Technology Law Journal 547

CHAPTER 3
Other Intellectual Property Issues

'[I]ntellectual property casts a protective haze over everything from the words of an email, to the shape of a phone, to the sequence of genes.'[1]

Trademarks Online

In the online environment, trade mark issues generally arise in three particular contexts: the use of confusing domain names, the use of trademarks on trading and auction sites (such as eBay), and the use of a competing mark as an advertising keyword. **[3–01]**

Domain Name Squatting and Typosquatting

Although now most businesses of any appreciable size have a website to promote their business and to communicate with their customers, and part of the process of establishing a brand identity includes registering appropriate domains, this was not always the case. In the early years of commercial use of the internet, some commercial entities were slow to set up websites, creating an opportunity for individuals with fraudulent intent to move first and either try to mislead consumers or to require payment in order to release desirable internet addresses. In order to fully understand this type of behaviour, and the legal responses, it is necessary to explain briefly how the system for managing and recording sites on the internet operates. **[3–02]**

You are probably used to entering website names (such as Facebook.com or Irishstatutebook.ie) into your web browser in order to access information on those sites. Similarly, you will exchange email with addresses that end in @outlook.com or @gmail.com. These addresses identify particular servers and are relatively easy for a human to read and remember. However, underneath these, all internet addresses are a sequence of numbers – four, to be exact, between 1 and 256, and separated by full stops. For example, at the time of writing, Facebook.com is 31.13.65.36, and Irishstatutebook.ie is 89.185.148.47. Obviously, it would **[3–03]**

---

[1] Robin Feldman, 'Intellectual Property Wrongs' (2012–13) 18 Stanford Journal of Law, Business & Finance 251, 251 (citations omitted).

be much more difficult for people to work with these numbers, and therefore the Internet Protocol (IP) networking software uses the more human-friendly system of domain names to map to IP numbers such as the ones mentioned above.

[3–04]   This complexity is managed by the Domain Name System (DNS), which is a very large distributed database that contains tables (essentially lists) of IP names (domains) and the corresponding IP addresses (numbers). As ordinary users type in or otherwise access domain names, these are invisibly translated to numbers and back again by a network of servers which are key to the continued functioning of the internet. When the system was first established, the allocation of names and numbers was managed by the Internet Assigned Number Authority (IANA), who had overall control of the IP address system. The Internet Corporation for Assigned Names and Numbers (ICANN) took over this responsibility in 1998. ICANN allows various 'registries' to handle applications for IP names and addresses.

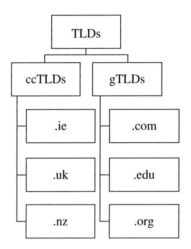

Figure 1   *Structure of Domain Name System*

[3–05]   You will have noticed that domain names end in a relatively limited number of suffixes, such as .com, .ie, or .org. These are known as top-level domains, or TLDs. Some are country-specific, such as .ie, .uk, or .nz (Ireland, the United Kingdom, and New Zealand respectively). These are country-code TLDs, or ccTLDs. Others are not associated with a particular geographic region, such as .com (commercial websites), .org (non-profit), or .edu (educational, chiefly US-based) and are known as generic top-level domains, or gTLDs. However, depending on the registration policies of particular national registries, entities may be registered for a geographic TLD although they have no particular connection to that country or region – for example, .tv (which is the Pacific island nation of Tuvalu) is often used by US-based television companies.

[3–06]   In August 1999, ICANN implemented a Uniform Dispute Resolution Policy (UDRP) based on World Intellectual Property Organisation (WIPO) recommendations. The use of this policy is required by all registrars in the ICANN DNS. In general, the policy is one of 'first-come, first-served', with essentially no advance vetting of use, except for banned words.

This system has given rise to three phenomena which raise legal issues. The first is often known as 'cybersquatting', and consists of registering a domain which is confusingly similar to a trade mark. Generally, the registrant will seek to sell the domain to the trade mark holder for a fee, which can sometimes be substantial. **[3–07]**

The second is known as 'typosquatting' and is similar to cybersquatting, which the difference being that the domain is essentially a common mis-spelling for a trade mark – Mircosoft.com, for example. These domains are usually used to host a website which serves advertising to those who arrive there by accident. Some websites exploit similarities between the roman and other alphabet (particularly the Cyrillic) in order to register domain names that look to the reader to be identical to a known mark, but in fact lead to a different IP address. These are commonly used for spam email advertising. **[3–08]**

The third activity which often occurs online is warehousing of domain names. This tends to be for legitimate purposes, although it can be frustrating for those whose plans it cuts across. Here, a legitimate business will register domain names that are similar to or likely to be confused with its mark, or will register its mark in multiple TLDs simultaneously, often as a way to prevent cybersquatting. Thus, for example, Microsoft.org redirects to Microsoft.com. **[3–09]**

In the Irish context, this type of activity is relatively infrequent. The Irish Domain Name Registry (IEDR) policed registrations for .ie websites relatively carefully in the early years, and although it has somewhat relaxed its policies in recent years, there is still a requirement to prove a connection to Ireland in order to be able to register a domain name. **[3–10]**

In 2000, an individual based in the US registered bertieahern.com and the site was used to serve pornography for a short period of time before it was transferred into the control of the Irish government. In 2006, police.ie, british.ie, look.ie, ipod.ie, adidas.ie, nike.ie and bebo.ie were registered, while in 2007 facebook.ie was similarly registered by entities who were not acting for the trade mark holders. These registrations were subsequently transferred to the rights holders. **[3–11]**

In the Irish courts, trademarks and the DNS arose in the case of *Local Ireland Ltd v Local Ireland-Online Ltd.*[2] The plaintiffs had created a significant online presence around the 'Local Ireland' trade mark, with a wide variety of domain names registered in association with it. The defendants created a business operating under the name 'Local Ireland-Online'. When the plaintiffs commenced legal proceedings, the defendants changed the name to 'Locally Irish'. However, at an interlocutory hearing for a preliminary injunction, McGovern J held that although damages would not be a sufficient remedy for the defendants if they were to succeed at trial, in light of the significant success and considerable investment of the plaintiffs, the balance of convenience favoured the granting of injunctive relief, and so he required the defendants to cease to use 'Local Ireland-Online', 'Locally Irish', or similar phrases, and domain names which contained these phrases. **[3–12]**

---

[2]   [2000] IEHC 67; [2000] 4 IR 567.

[3–13] Bad faith claims can be pursued through the courts, relying on the tort of passing off. In the important *British Telecom v One in a Million* case,[3] the Court found that the registration of domain names associated with a number of well-known UK businesses (such as Marks and Spencer) was done with the intention of re-selling them to the trademarks holders and was thus an instrument of fraud; it required the transfer of the domains to their rightful owners.

[3–14] *Euromarket Designs v Peters*[4] was heard in the UK courts, but involved an Irish-based business which was using the name 'Crate and Barrel', something which was objected to by a US-based company which had built up a significant business around this mark. The High Court declined to find infringement of the trade mark, on the basis that there was no evidence of an intention to trade in the UK.

[3–15] When disputes arise regarding domains within the .ie ccTLD, they can be resolved through the ieUDRP (the Irish version of the UDRP), which is relatively fast and inexpensive. The trade mark owner initiates arbitration by filing a complaint with a panel of three independent experts appointed by the World Intellectual Property Organization. The respondent must submit a written response to the original complaint to the panel within 20 days. A failure to respond will generally favour the complainant, as the panel will make a decision that is based only on the information in the complaint.

[3–16] There are three principal grounds on which one might succeed in an action under the UDRP:

1. The domain name is identical or confusingly similar to a trade mark or service mark in which the complainant has rights
2. The domain name holder has no rights or legitimate interests in the domain name
3. The domain name holder acted in 'bad faith'. This can take a variety of forms, including:
   - The registration was made primarily for the purpose of selling, renting or transferring the registration to the complainant or a competitor for some valuable consideration above the documented costs that directly relate to the domain name ('cybersquatting');
   - The registration was made in order to prevent the complainant from using that domain name, where the respondent has a history of similar conduct;
   - The registration was made with the intention of disrupting the business of a competitor;
   - The registration was made in order to attract users to the respondent's website, by creating a likelihood of confusion with the complainant's trade mark.

[3–17] The respondent does have a number of defences:

- Showing that they either used, or made preparations to use, the domain name or a similar name in connection with a bona fide offering of goods and services;
- That they are commonly known by the domain name, even if they do not have any formally registered trade or service marks;

---

[3] [1999] FSR 1 (CA).
[4] [2001] FSR 20 (Ch).

- They are making a legitimate non-commercial or fair use of the domain name, without intent for commercial gain to misleadingly divert consumers or to tarnish the complainant's trade mark or service mark.

If the panel decides that the registration was in bad faith, it can transfer the domain name to the complainant. The panel can also decide that a complaint was made in bad faith, as occurred in *Driver and Vehicle Licensing Agency v DVL Automation, Inc.*[5] This involved a UK government agency which sought to have transferred to it the domain dvla.com, used by the respondent for its business presence since the mid-1990s. The sole panelist found that the respondent had a legitimate interest in this domain, as it was an abbreviation of its business name, and that the complaint was an attempt to engage in 'reverse domain name hijacking'.   **[3–18]**

Trademarked Goods Online

Issues around trademarks also arise in the context of online selling platforms, particularly the very successful auction and trading site eBay. Many of the items available on this site claim to be well-known (and expensive) brand-name goods. However, they are often counterfeit. This was (and still is) of considerable concern to the trade mark holders, and they argued that eBay should be more proactive in policing the use of trademarks and preventing the sale of counterfeits. eBay had no issue with this in principle, but the work involved in ensuring that only genuine goods are available for sale is considerable and it was not keen on shouldering this burden.   **[3–19]**

The trade mark holders resorted to litigation and were successful in Europe. In 2008, the Tribunal de Grande Instance de Troyes (the French equivalent of the High Court) awarded €20,000 to Hermes International for the sale of four counterfeit bags on the eBay site. eBay's defence had principally rested on the existence of a 'Verified Rights Owner' (VeRO) process whereby mark holders could complain regarding unauthorised use of their intellectual property; Hermes had chosen not to avail of this system. The Court refused to accept an argument that eBay provided sufficient assistance to its users to become an 'editor' of the content that they posted (and thus much more liable for any false statements that they might make). However, the Court held that eBay was performing brokerage activity, bringing together buyers and sellers, and therefore had additional responsibilities. In particular, it needed to ask sellers to provide information (such as serial numbers) to prove that they were selling properly authorised and authenticated merchandise; if they could not do so, to ask that this be stated clearly in the advertisement; and to make the consequence of intellectual property infringement clear to all of its users.   **[3–20]**

Also in 2008 and also in France, several high profile brands, including Louis Vuitton, Christian Dior Couture, and Kenzo were successful in litigation that had commenced in 2004. These cases were heard together in the Tribunal de Commerce de Paris, which found against eBay and awarded damages totalling over €40 million to the plaintiffs. The Court's logic was similar to that in the Hermes case, but the judgment also required that frequent sellers be registered with the ministry for trade and commerce and trade unions.   **[3–21]**

---

[5] Case D2002–0913.

[3–22] These successes are underlined by the CJEU decision in Case C–324/09 *L'Oréal v eBay*.[6] The plaintiff, a well-known vendor of cosmetics and perfumes, sought to prevent the sale of counterfeits on eBay, and the use by eBay of its marks as Google AdWords keywords. The Court held that an online marketplace does not itself 'use' trademarks when providing a service which allows users to post items for sale. However, the marketplace operator plays an active role in the functioning of the site and therefore cannot rely on exemptions from liability (such as the Electronic Commerce Directive). In particular, it cannot rely on such exemptions if it was aware of facts or circumstances on the basis of which a diligent economic operator should have realised that the online offers for sale were unlawful and, once it was aware, failed to act promptly to remove the offers from its site.

[3–23] On the other side of the Atlantic, the courts have sided with the online marketplace providers. The well-known jewellery seller Tiffany's sued eBay, claiming that a large number of counterfeit items bearing its mark were on sale through that site. The Southern District of New York found that any use of Tiffany's marks by eBay was protected fair use, and stated that the burden of policing the use of the mark fell on Tiffany's rather than on eBay.[7] The decision was appealed to the Second Circuit, which also found in eBay's favour.[8] (One issue was sent back to the District Court, which found in eBay's favour on re-hearing.)

Trademarks as Advertising Keywords

[3–24] The use of trademarks in online advertising has also led to litigation. As with other internet-based legal problems, understanding these cases requires an understanding of the technology. A great deal of online advertising takes place on search engines, which will include advertisements on search results pages. You may be familiar with these from your use of services such as Google. The software which manages the search engine will select advertisements based on the words for which you search or which are contained in the pages which are returned. This selection process centres around keywords – for example, searches for 'information technology law' might trigger advertisements for this book, if the publisher has paid for them to be displayed. The search engine will generally allow advertisers to select whatever keywords they want, and will often 'auction' the rights to advertise based on particular phrases, so that if there were multiple textbooks on 'information technology law', search engine users would see adverts for the publisher that was willing to pay the higher price for that particular set of keywords. The advertiser pays only if users click on the link; this type of advertising is often known as 'pay-per-click' or PPC.

[3–25] A trademarks problem arises when a business will pay to have adverts for its goods or services displayed in response to a search for keywords (usually trademarks) associated with its competitors.

[3–26] This was the basis for the referral to the Court of Justice in Case C–236/08 *Google v Louis Vuitton Malletier*[9] to which two other cases raising similar questions were joined. The case

---

6   ECLI:EU:C:2011:474
7   *Tiffany v eBay* 576 F Supp 2d 460 (SDNY 2008).
8   *Tiffany v eBay* 600 F 3d 93 (2d Cir 2010).
9   ECLI:EU:C:2010:159.

centred on Google's AdWords functionality; LV learned that in response to keyword searches for LV trademarks (and for those marks together with phrases such as 'replica' or 'copy'), Google was displaying adverts for counterfeit LV products. It was successful in litigation in the French courts, but the Cour de Cassation (French Supreme Court) stated a number of questions to the CJEU for a preliminary ruling. The other cases were broadly similar. The Court held, first, that while Google was operating in the course of a trade, it was a referencing service provider and therefore not itself using the marks in question; and second, that whether or not Google could benefit from the exemption from liability in Article 14 of the Electronic Commerce Directive (considered further in Chapter 8) depended on whether or not Google's role in the display of advertisements was entirely automatic, technical, and passive.

A similar reference from Austria, C–278/08 *Die BergSpechte Outdoor Reisen v Günter* **[3–27]** *Guni*,[10] raised the follow-on question of whether a trade mark holder could prevent a third party from using the mark (or similar phrases) as advertising keywords in order to display goods or services identical to those for which the mark is registered. The Court held that the important functions of a mark in this context were advertising and indicating origin. Following the *Google* case considered above, the Court considered that this first use was permitted. However, and again following the *Google* case, the Court held that the mark holder could prohibit the use of a mark or related phrases to trigger advertising 'where that ad does not enable an average internet user, or enables that user only with difficulty, to ascertain whether the goods or services referred to therein originate from the proprietor of the trade mark or an undertaking economically connected to it or, on the contrary, originate from a third party'.

In a referral from Germany, Case C–91/09 *Eis.de GmbH v BBY Vertriebsgesellschaft mbH*,[11] **[3–28]** the Court quickly dealt with a similar dispute involving two online vendors of erotic entertainment products, one of which had used the other's trade mark (Bananabay) as an AdWords keyword but did not in fact display the mark in the resulting advertisement. The Court held that this was permitted.

This approach was reiterated in a referral from the Netherlands, Case C–558/08 *Portakabin* **[3–29]** *v Primakabin*,[12] which again involved the use of the plaintiff's trademarks (or near misspellings) as advertising keywords. The defendant sold and leased second-hand mobile buildings, including some of those manufactured and placed on the market by the plaintiff. The Court held that an advertiser can only rely on the defence in Article 6(1) that they can use indications that describe characteristics of the goods or their intended purpose where the use by the third party is 'in accordance with honest practices in industrial or commercial matters'. It also held that a trade mark holder can only prevent an advertiser who is re-selling goods from using a keyword that is the same or similar to the mark if there is a 'legitimate reason', such as if the sale of those other goods risks seriously damaging the image which the owner has created for its mark.

---

[10] ECLI:EU:C:2010:163.
[11] ECLI:EU:C:2010:174.
[12] ECLI:EU:C:2010:416.

[3–30] There is also a referral from the UK, in Case C–323/09 *Interflora Inc v Marks and Spencer plc*.[13] This is part of very long-running litigation between these two well-known businesses, sparked by Marks and Spencer using Interflora's brand as an advertising keyword. The essential issue here was the extent to which internet users might be confused into thinking that Marks & Spencer was part of the Interflora network. Along the same lines as the *Portakabin* case, the Court held that trade mark holders may prevent the use of advertising which does not enable reasonably well-informed and reasonably observant internet users, or enables them only with difficulty, to ascertain whether the goods or services referred to by the advertisement originate from the proprietor of the trade mark. It also held that if there was such confusion in the minds of internet users, there might be trade mark dilution, and if there was no good cause for selecting a mark which was used by a competitor, this could constitute unfair advantage.

[3–31] More recently, the *Louis Vuitton* case has been applied in the UK to somewhat unusual circumstances. Two companies with similar names, Victoria Plum and Victoria Plumbing, are competitors. The latter began to bid for the former's trademarks in pay-per-click advertising, and when it was sued, argued a defence of 'honest concurrent use' against one of the claims. The Court applied the CJEU's test from the *Louis Vuitton* case and found that consumers would be confused or misled by the advertising to think that the goods or services it mentioned originated from Victoria Plum or a business connected to it. Honest concurrent use could apply to the continued use of an existing brand name, but does not extend to using a competitor's trade mark for commercial gain. In addition, advertising that hoped to capitalise on consumer confusion could not be considered 'honest'.[14]

Patents for Software

[3–32] As has been noted at the beginning of this chapter, patents are intended to protect only inventions with some industrial application. IP law does not protect scientific discovery, mathematical methods, or other types of general ideas. It is therefore very difficult or impossible to obtain protection for a particular process, although because these can be very commercially valuable, businesses often try to do so.

[3–33] Section 9 of the Patents Act 1992 makes this clear, setting out what is generally known as a 'three-step test' for patentability and excluding certain types of discovery from the scope of patent law:

> (1) An invention shall be patentable under this Part if it is susceptible of industrial application, is new and involves an inventive step.
> (2) Any of the following in particular shall not be regarded as an invention within the meaning of subsection (1):
>> (a) a discovery, a scientific theory or a mathematical method,
>> (b) an aesthetic creation,
>> (c) a scheme, rule or method for performing a mental act, playing a game or doing business, or a program for a computer,
>> (d) the presentation of information.

---

[13] ECLI:EU:C:2011:604.
[14] [2016] EWHC 2911 (Ch).

This restriction is echoed in the European Patent Convention: **[3–34]**

> 52. European patents shall be granted for any inventions, in all fields of technology, provided that they are new, involve an inventive step and are susceptible of industrial application.
>
> (2) The following in particular shall not be regarded as inventions within the meaning of paragraph 1:
>
>   (a) discoveries, scientific theories and mathematical methods;
>   (b) aesthetic creations;
>   (c) schemes, rules and methods for performing mental acts, playing games or doing business, and programs for computers;
>   (d) presentations of information.

In the United States of America, this topic has been the subject of some high-profile cases.   **[3–35]**
In *Gottschalk v Benson*,[15] the US Supreme Court held that that the method for converting between two different systems for recording numbers (from binary-coded decimals to pure decimals) was an abstract idea and thus not patentable. However, in *Diamond v Diehr*,[16] it held that a process for curing rubber, which relied upon computer calculations to determine when to finish the curing, was patentable. In *State Street Bank v Signature Financial Group*,[17] the Federal Circuit approved a patent for a mechanism to pool the profits from mutual funds to a central hub in a way that avoided income tax and was so complex that it required the assistance of a computer. More recently, however, the Supreme Court has stepped back from this approach and has denied patents to an investment strategy[18] and to an electronic escrow service.[19] It seems, therefore, that in the US, it is possible to obtain a patent for an invention that includes software but not for an abstract or general idea, even if it is implemented in software code.

The European Patent Office does allow a 'computer-implemented invention' (CII) to be   **[3–36]**
patented. It defines these as:

> [an invention] which involves the use of a computer, computer network or other programmable apparatus, where one or more features are realised wholly or partly by means of a computer program.

For a CII to be patentable, it must solve a technical problem in a new and non-obvious manner.   **[3–37]**
There have been proposals to extend the scope of software patenting in Europe, from a conference called to discuss revisions to the EPC in 1998 and from a proposed Directive put forward by the European Commission in 2002. These were not ultimately adopted; the Commission's proposals proved extremely controversial.

---

[15] 409 US 63 (1972).
[16] 450 US 175 (1981).
[17] 149 F 3d 1368 (Fed Cir 1998).
[18] *Bilski v Kappos* 561 US 593 (2010).
[19] *Alice Corp v CLS Bank International* 134 S Ct 2347 (2014).

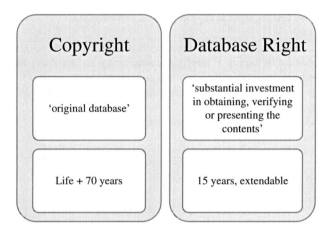

Figure 2 *Legal Protections for Databases*

Legal Protections for Databases

[3–38] One of the more complex aspects of the relationship between ICT and IP law is the legal protections that are available for databases. In its most basic form, a database is a systematic arrangement of information in a way that is easy to manage and manipulate. A simple example that you are probably familiar with is a telephone directory or address book. You have probably also interacted with a database when registering as a student and choosing modules to study: this is now generally handled through online systems which can be quite complex, as they interconnect a variety of databases (for example, student records, class records, and timetables) and apply rules regarding prerequisites, availability of options, and minimum and maximum credit loads. Databases can therefore range from the straightforward to the very complex, and the amount of work involved in developing and maintaining the latter can be substantial. However, the types of database which have tended to be of interest to IP law are in the nature of anthologies of information, newspaper archives, or encyclopaedias.

Database Copyright

[3–39] There are two ways in which a database can be legally protected – under copyright and under a unique right known as the *database right* or the *sui generis* right. First, s 2 of the Copyright and Related Rights Act 2000 includes 'an original database' in the definition of 'work' which can be protected by copyright. This is further defined as a 'database in any form which by reason of the selection or arrangement of its contents constitutes the original intellectual creation of the author'.[20] In *Cambridge University Press v University Tutorial Press*,[21] the Court set a low threshold for originality, requiring only that the work not be copied from some other source. Section 17(3) of the CRRA 2000 limits the scope

---

[20] Parliament and Council Directive (EC) 9/1996 on the legal protection of databases [1996] OJ L77/20, art 3(1).
[21] (1928) 45 RPC 335 (Ch).

of the copyright protection of databases to exclude the contents of the database, meaning that *only* the selection and arrangement of the contents of the database – in other words, its structure – are protected in this way.

In Case C–604/10 *Football DataCo Ltd v Yahoo! UK Ltd*, the CJEU was asked whether the skill and judgment involved in creating a fixture list for a football league could be the basis for a copyright right in the database; in other words, whether 'selection and arrangement' includes adding value to a pre-existing piece of data. The Court held that it did not. **[3–40]**

Database Right

In addition to this copyright right, s 321 of the CRRA 2000 provides that '[a] property right to be known … as the "database right" subsists, … in a database where there has been a substantial investment in obtaining, verifying or presenting the contents of the database'. This is the Irish implementation of Directive 96/9/EC on the Legal Protection of Databases. Under this Directive, a 'database' means 'a collection of independent works, data or other materials arranged in a systematic or methodical way and individually accessible by electronic or other means'.[22] It is more difficult to obtain database right protection than copyright protection – it only applies 'where there has been a substantial investment in obtaining, verifying or presenting the contents of the database'.[23] The database right provides somewhat similar protection to copyright as it gives **[3–41]**

> the owner of the database right … the right to undertake or to authorise others to undertake all or any of the following acts in relation to all or a substantial part of the contents of a database—
> (a) extraction, or
> (b) re-utilisation.[24]

However, the term of the right is, initially at least, shorter than the usual copyright term. Normally, it expires '15 years from the end of the calendar year in which the making of the database was completed'.[25] However, it can be extended, either for re-utilisation of its contents[26] or for sufficient 'substantial change' to the database 'which would result in the database being considered to be a substantial new investment',[27] both of which will give rise to a further 15-year term. In theory, these extensions can continue indefinitely into the future. **[3–42]**

The scope of the right would seem at first glance to be quite broad, but the CJEU has tended to restrict it in its judgments. In 2004, the Court dealt with referrals from a number of Member States that raised similar questions. One involved the British Horseracing Board and William Hill bookmakers;[28] the others involved Fixtures Marketing (which sells **[3–43]**

---

[22] Parliament and Council Directive (EC) 9/1996 on the legal protection of databases [1996] OJ L77/20, art 1 (2).

[23] CRRA 2000, s 321.

[24] CRRA 2000, s 324.

[25] CRRA 2000, s 325(1).

[26] CRRA 2000, s 325(2).

[27] CRRA 2000, s 325(3).

[28] Case C–203/02 *British Horseracing Board v William Hill* ECLI:EU:C:2004:695.

licences to lists of football fixtures in the UK) and various football pools operators.[29] The BHB maintained an extensive database of horses, jockeys, and races, which required considerable investment and expense to create and maintain. The football fixtures list was created by the various leagues within the UK and then collated for distribution by Fixtures Marketing. The bookmakers and pool operators used information from these databases that was available to them from a variety of sources such as newspapers, websites, and other media. They did not have a licence from the BHB or FM to re-use this information.

[3–44]   The key question for the CJEU was whether these databases were subject to database right protection. The Court held that 'investment' in the obtaining of the contents of a database means the allocation of time and effort to locate existing materials and collect them in the database. It does not include putting time into creating new material that makes up the contents of a database. The creator of a database can claim database right protection in circumstances where it also creates the materials which the database contains, but only where obtaining, verifying, and presenting those materials requires substantial investment in quantitative or qualitative terms, which was independent of the resources used to create those materials.

[3–45]   As the football leagues had to create the data regarding football fixtures as part of their routine operation, these materials did not require substantial independent investment. These leagues also had to verify the materials and present them in a particular way, all of which indicated that they were not subject to the database right. The BHB racing information was also not protectable by the database right for similar reasons. In the BHB case, the Court also concluded that the amount reused by the bookmakers was only a small part of the database and therefore not substantial enough to constitute infringement.

[3–46]   In Case C–304/07 *Direct Media Publishing v Albert Ludwig Universität Frieburg*,[30] the CJEU had to deal with a dispute between a university and a commercial publisher. The university ran a project named 'Vocabulary of the Classics', as a part of which it analysed the frequency with which certain poems published between 1730 and 1900 were anthologised. It then published on the internet a list of 'The 1,100 most important poems in German literature between 1730 and 1900'. The publisher created a CD named '1000 Poems Everyone Should Have', which drew heavily on this list. The publisher's list contained 856 poems from the university's list. However, it did not simply copy the list but exercised its own discretion in what to include. The question for the Court was whether 'extraction' would apply in a situation where an individual assessment was conducted, or only where there was simple physical copying. The Court held that conducting an individual assessment did not matter for the question of whether extraction had taken place.

[3–47]   However, there are some cases in which of the Court has been supportive of database rights. In Case C–545/07 *Apis-Hristovich v Lakorda*,[31] the plaintiffs alleged that former employees had re-used without authorisation significant parts of modules of a legal information database

---

[29] Case C–46/02 *Fixtures Marketing Ltd v Oy Veikkaus Ab* ECLI:EU:C:2004:694, Case C–338/02 *Fixtures Marketing Ltd v Svenska Spel AB* ECLI:EU:C:2004:696, Case C–444/02 *Fixtures Marketing Ltd v OPAP* ECLI:EU:C:2004:697.
[30] ECLI:EU:C:2008:552.
[31] ECLI:EU:C:2009:132.

in generating a competing database marketed by the defendant. The defendant's counter-arguments rested largely on the public domain nature of the materials and the significant investment it had put into developing its product, including new functionality. The Court followed *Direct Media* and held that 'extraction' must be interpreted broadly as referring to any unauthorised appropriation of the whole or a part of the contents of a database. The nature, form and purpose of the extraction is not material for the purposes of proving infringement, but the existence of common technical features in both databases might indicate that extraction had occurred. There could be infringement of a sub-part of the database, where that sub-part had required sufficient investment to be subject to the database right; the amount of non-public sources would be relevant to this question, but that most or all of the material came from public sources does not mean that the database is not entitled to protection.

Case C–202/12 *Innoweb BV v Wegener ICT Media BV*[32] involved a dispute regarding what might be called a 'meta search engine'. These types of sites are reasonably common on the internet, and allow a user to enter a search term in one location which is then applied across a number of other websites. In this particular case, searches were for classified advertisements for second-hand cars. The meta search engine, Gaspedaal, performed approximately 100,000 searches per day on a website known as AutoTrack, retrieving approximately 80 per cent of its content, and then aggregating that together with results from other similar sites. The Court held that the provision of such a dedicated search engine, which allows queries to be 'translated' in order to be conducted across other protected databases simultaneously constitutes making available the contents of that database for the purposes of the Database Directive, and is the re-utilisation of a substantial part of the database. **[3–48]**

In Case C–30/14 *Ryanair Ltd v PR Aviation BV*,[33] the CJEU clarified the protections that may be available for databases that do not qualify for Database Directive protection. Ryanair maintains a database of flights, bookings, and prices. Third-party websites 'scrape' this information and aggregate flight data across a range of airlines for consumers. Ryanair objects to this practice and the terms and conditions of its website forbid it. It sued to prevent PR Aviation from engaging in it. The Dutch courts held that the Ryanair database was not subject to protection under the Database Directive, and referred to the CJEU the question of whether this was a lawful use of a database, within the terms of Articles 6 and 8 of the Database Directive, which cannot be derogated by contract. The Court held that if the database was not protected by the Directive, the restrictions in Articles 6 and 8 did not apply. It would seem, therefore, that in certain contexts, a database that is not subject to the Directive could be better protected. **[3–49]**

In Case C–490/14 *Freistaat Bayern v Verlag Esterbauer GmbH*,[34] the Court gave a wide definition to 'independent materials' (and thus to a database). The plaintiff federal government published topographical maps covering the entire state of Bavaria. The defendant publisher had extracted information from these in order to produce its own specialised maps for cyclists, mountain bikers and inline skaters. The Court had to decide whether this information was sufficiently 'independent' in order to constitute a database. It held that it was. **[3–50]**

---

[32] ECLI:EU:C:2013:850.
[33] ECLI:EU:C:2015:10.
[34] ECLI:EU:C:2015:735.

[3–51]   In 2005, the European Commission conducted a review of the Directive.[35] They concluded that the Directive was not stimulating database creation and that CJEU case law was not in line with the Commission's aims. They put forward proposals for changes, but public views on this were mixed and no concrete reforms have yet emerged. However, the Commission has recently launched a consultation on the Directive,[36] which may indicate that reform will occur in the future.

Further Reading

- Alice Blythe, 'Trademarks as Adwords' (2015) 37 European Intellectual Property Review 225
- David Booton, 'The Patentability of Computer-Implemented Inventions in Europe' (2007) 1 Intellectual Property Quarterly 92
- Anna Marie Brennan, 'The Patenting of Software in Ireland: The Pros and Cons' (2011) 18 Commercial Law Practitioner 33
- Estelle Derclaye, *The Legal Protection of Databases: A Comparative Analysis* (Edward Elgar 2008)
- Frazer Hanrahan, 'Software Patents, All or Nothing? A Comparison of the US and EU Approaches' (2006) 6 Hibernian Law Journal 271
- Maurice Schellekens, 'A Database Right in Search Results?: An Intellectual Property Right Reconsidered in Respect of Computer Generated Databases' (2011) 27 Computer Law & Security Review 620

---

[35] European Commission, 'First Evaluation of Directive 96/9/EC on the Legal Protection of Databases' (12 December 2005) <ec.europa.eu/internal_market/copyright/docs/databases/evaluation_report_en.pdf> accessed 13 June 2017.

[36] European Commission, 'Public Consultation on the Database Directive: Application and Impact' (24 May 2017) <ec.europa.eu/info/content/public-consultation-database-directive-application-and-impact-0_en> accessed 13 June 2017.

CHAPTER 4

Commercial Activity Online

'Digitization necessarily disrupts doctrine generated by a world of paper and in-person exchange.'[1]

The internet, and particularly the World Wide Web, have become very significant 'locations' for business over the past two decades. Thirty per cent of businesses in Ireland make electronic sales, the highest proportion in the EU, with 49 per cent of those involving Electronic Data Interchange (EDI).[2] This explosion in 'electronic commerce' has raised some interesting legal questions and led to some changes to the law in order to better accommodate and facilitate this type of transaction while protecting consumers. **[4–01]**

Online Contracts

Validity of Electronic Contracts

The first question which arises with regard to contracts concluded by electronic means is whether or not it is possible to contract electronically. This has never really been in any significant doubt, but s 19 of the Electronic Commerce Act 2000 clarifies that '[a]n electronic contract shall not be denied legal effect, validity or enforceability solely on the grounds that it is wholly or partly in electronic form, or has been concluded wholly or partly by way of an electronic communication', and that the process of negotiating a contract (offer and acceptance, in doctrinal terms) may be conducted through electronic communication. **[4–02]**

---

[1] David Hoffman, 'From Promise to Form: How Contracting Online Changes Consumers' (2016) 91 New York University Law Review 1595, 1600.
[2] Eurostat, 'E-commerce Statistics' (December 2016) <ec.europa.eu/eurostat/statistics-explained/index.php/E-commerce_statistics> accessed 13 June 2017.

Choice of Jurisdiction and Law

[4–03]   Another important question with regard to internet-based contracts is where and when a contract is formed. These will often be conducted across national borders, therefore involving
different jurisdictions (and sometimes quite different legal systems), making it important to
determine exactly where the contract is concluded. The terms and conditions of many online
contracts will often deal explicitly with this issue by specifying which jurisdiction's laws are
to be applied to it, and which courts should resolve disputes that arise under it. Indeed, many
contracts will refer disputes to arbitration rather than to the courts, and some large online
vendors (such as eBay) have developed quite sophisticated systems of alternative dispute
resolution that seek to keep problems away from conventional channels.

[4–04]   The key European legislation relating to jurisdiction is Regulation 1215/2012,[3] commonly
known as 'Brussels I', as it builds on the Brussels Convention of 1968 (although in fact it
replaces an earlier Brussels I regulation, 44/2001). This came into force in January 2015
and deals with the jurisdiction of courts and the recognition and enforcement of judgments
in civil and commercial matters in cross-border disputes within the EU. Under Article
25(1), the agreement of the parties as to which courts should have jurisdiction takes pre-
cedence, unless the agreement itself is null and void under the laws of the chosen Member
State. Otherwise, the default rule is that a person domiciled in a Member State shall be sued
in the courts of that Member State, even if they are not nationals (Article 4). Article 7 does
allow for some types of claims to be brought in another Member State if there is a clear
connection to that jurisdiction: contract (place of performance); tort (place where 'harmful
event occurred or may occur'); civil claim based on criminal proceedings (court where
latter is taking place); civil claim for recovery of cultural object (location of object); claim
relating to branch, agency or other establishment (location of same); trust dispute (domicile
of trust); salvage (court where cargo or freight has been or could have been arrested).

[4–05]   The regulation also contains consumer protection measures. These apply only when a consumer contracts with a business. A consumer is defined as a person concluding a contract
'for a purpose which can be regarded as being outside his trade or profession'. A business is
defined as 'a person who pursues commercial or professional activities in the Member State
of the consumer's domicile or, by any means, directs such activities to that Member State
or to several States including that Member State'. Under s 4 (Articles 17 to 19), a consumer
who enters into a hire purchase agreement, loan to purchase goods, or otherwise contracts
with a business can choose to bring proceedings either in the courts of the domicile of the
business or in the consumer's own domicile. These protections can only be contracted out of
after the dispute has arisen, if the consumer is permitted to bring a claim in a third Member
State, or if both parties are domiciled in the same Member State and the claim can now be
brought in the courts of that jurisdiction.

[4–06]   The meaning of 'directing' in Article 17(1)(c) was discussed in two joined cases, C–585/08
Pammer v Karl Schlütter GmbH & Co KG and C–144/09 *Hotel Alpenhof v Heller.*[4]
These cases involved disputes involving tourism services (a cruise and a hotel booking

---

[3] Parliament and Council Regulation (EU) 1215/2012 on jurisdiction and the recognition and enforcement of judgments in civil and commercial matters [2012] OJ L351/1.
[4] ECLI:EU:C:2010:740.

respectively) where the consumer was located in a different Member State to the business. The CJEU held that simply providing a website that was accessible in another jurisdiction was not sufficient for a business to be regarded as directing activities to a Member State. Instead, national courts should have regard to a range of factors, including the international nature of the activity; mention of itineraries from other Member States to the location of the business; use of a language or a currency other than the language or currency generally used in the Member State where the business is located; and the use of telephone numbers with an international code.[5]

There are additional consumer protection measures in the Unfair Contract Terms Directive.[6] **[4–07]** This legislation has broader application than Brussels I, as it applies to all consumer contracts, rather than only situations where the vendor or service provider 'directs' activities to the Member State in which the consumer is domiciled. A choice of jurisdiction clause which is unfair to the consumer could be set aside under this directive; indeed, Article 6(1) requires Member States 'to ensure that the consumer does not lose the protection granted by this Directive by virtue of the choice of the law of a non-Member country as the law applicable to the contract if the latter has a close connection with the territory of the Member States'.

With regard to the choice of law, the key European legislation is Regulation 593/2008/EC[7] **[4–08]** (commonly known as 'Rome I', because it replaces the Rome Convention on the Law Applicable to Contractual Obligations 1980). The Regulation provides default rules where no explicit choice has been made. These are generally to the benefit of the seller or service provider. Under Article 3(1), the norm is that the law chosen by the parties is what governs a contract, whether that is explicitly stated in the contract or determined from the circumstances. However, under Article 3(3), where all elements relevant to the contract other than the choice of law are located in a country other than that whose laws have been chosen to govern it, the parties cannot contract out of mandatory provisions of the law of that first country.

Where the parties have not specified which laws should apply, Article 4 provides a set of **[4–09]** rules to determine this, as follows:

    (a)   a contract for the sale of goods shall be governed by the law of the country where the seller has his habitual residence;

    (b)   a contract for the provision of services shall be governed by the law of the country where the service provider has his habitual residence;

    (c)   generally, contracts concerning real property shall be governed by the law of the country where the property is situated;

    (d)   however, contracts of tenancy for temporary private use for a period of no more than six consecutive months shall be governed by the law of the country where the landlord has his habitual residence, provided that the tenant is a natural person and has his habitual residence in the same country;

---

[5] Dan JB Svantesson, 'Pammer and Alpenhof – ECJ Decision Creates Further Uncertainty about when E-Businesses "Direct Activities" to a Consumer's State under the Brussels I Regulation' (2011) 27 Computer Law and Security Review 298.

[6] Council Directive (EEC) 93/13 on unfair terms in consumer contracts [1993] OJ L 95/29.

[7] Parliament and Council Regulation (EC) 2008/593 on the law applicable to contractual obligations [2008] OJ L177/6 (Rome I).

(e) a franchise contract shall be governed by the law of the country where the franchisee has his habitual residence;

(f) a distribution contract shall be governed by the law of the country where the distributor has his habitual residence;

(g) a contract for the sale of goods by auction shall be governed by the law of the country where the auction takes place, if such a place can be determined;

(h) a contract concluded in a multi-lateral market for certain types of financial instruments shall be governed by the law that applies to that market.

[4–10] If the application of these rules does not produce a clear outcome, then the contract is governed by the law of the country with which it is most closely connected.

[4–11] Article 6 is a consumer protection measure, to prevent a consumer losing rights that he or she would expect to have under national law. It applies to consumer contracts, defined as 'concluded by a natural person for a purpose which can be regarded as being outside his trade or profession', subject to exceptions such as supply of services abroad, travel, immovable property, and certain financial contracts. The default rule is that the contract is governed by the law of the country of residence of the consumer, where the business

(a) pursues his commercial or professional activities in the country where the consumer has his habitual residence, or

(b) by any means, directs such activities to that country or to several countries including that country,

and the contract falls within the scope of such activities.[8]

'Directing' probably has the same meaning as in Brussels I, and the case law noted above is also likely to be relevant here.

[4–12] Even if the contract specifies another governing law, this cannot deprive the consumer of the protection of mandatory provisions of the law of her habitual residence.[9] In addition, under Article 10, while the norm is that the validity of a contract will be determined by the law of the country chosen, a party who is seeking to establish lack of consent to the contract can rely on the law of the country in which he has his habitual residence if it appears from the circumstances that it would not be reasonable to use the law of the other country.

Contracting and Machines

[4–13] In some instances, contracts can be created automatically, by software programs on both sides of the transaction operating with little or no human intervention. These sometimes take place through Electronic Data Interchange (EDI) or Electronic Funds Transfer (EFT) systems, and also through 'software agents', which are computer programs which search online services, such as auction websites like eBay, automatically buying and selling goods and services. These are generally business-to-business (B2B) transactions, but can also involve consumers. These can raise questions around whether machines can be said to come to agreement, the legal capacity of software agents, and the possibility of 'battle of

---

[8] Regulation 2008/593, art 6(1).

[9] Regulation 2008/593, art 6(2).

the forms' cases, in which the courts must decide which one of a conflicting pair of standard terms should apply to the contract.[10]

However, the principal focus of this section is another type of contracting facilitated by machines, where the contract is negotiated between (on one hand) a human and (on the other hand) a software system acting on behalf of the other party. 'Negotiation' is used here in a limited sense; there is often little scope to deviate from standard terms and conditions drafted well in advance of contracting. **[4–14]**

Validity of Contracts Concluded with a Machine

The common law has (pragmatically) accepted that it is possible to enter into a contract with or through a machine. The key case is *Thornton v Shoe Lane Parking*.[11] Here, the plaintiff took a ticket from a machine at the entrance to a multi-story car park, parked his car and left, and was injured in an accident when he returned. The ticket referred to the conditions of issue on display in the premises, one of which excluded liability for injury. The Court held that the contract was concluded when the plaintiff 'drove up to the entrance and, by the movement of his car, turned the light from red to green, and the ticket was thrust at him'. **[4–15]**

It seems generally accepted that the advertisement of goods and services on a website is an invitation to treat and that the customer makes the offer to buy. The trader can then accept or reject the offer. The contract would be made when the trader acknowledges to the purchaser that his or her offer was accepted, either by direct response on the website or by subsequent e-mail. (As will be discussed in more detail at [4–42] to [4–43], the Electronic Commerce Act 2000 contains provisions that deal with the exact moment at which the contract is to be regarded as concluded.) **[4–16]**

The High Court of Ireland has accepted (although without significant discussion of the point) that use of a website by an automated process constitutes acceptance of its terms and conditions. In two cases involving 'screen scraping',[12] already discussed in [3–39], Ryanair Ltd (a well-known budget airline) sought to prevent travel websites from including its flights in the options available to potential customers. The terms and conditions for the website prohibited the use of 'any automated system or software to extract data from [the] website ... for commercial purposes', unless a licence agreement was in place. Although the cases involved questions of what was the appropriate jurisdiction to hear the case, the High Court raised no issue regarding the validity of the agreement based on the use of software to access the Ryanair website, and cited the *Shoe Lane Parking* case with approval. **[4–17]**

However, the courts will not always side with the consumer. In *Chwee Kin Keong v Digilandmall.com Pte Ltd*,[13] an online computer vendor had mistakenly mispriced printers **[4–18]**

---

[10] See Margaret Jane Radin, 'Humans, Computers and Binding Commitment' (2000) 75 Indiana Law Journal 1125; Tom Allen and Robin Widdison, 'Can Computers Make Contracts?' (2000) 9 Harvard Journal of Law and Technology 25.

[11] [1971] 2 QB 163 (CA Civ).

[12] *Ryanair Ltd v Billingfluege.de GmbH* [2010] IEHC 47 and *Ryanair Ltd v On the Beach* [2013] IEHC 124.

[13] [2005] 1 SLR 502 (CA); [2004] 2 SLR 594.

at a fraction of their value. The Singapore court upheld the validity of the many contracts for purchase placed by consumers (some of whom were informed by friends of the erroneous pricing), finding that there was valid offer, acceptance and consideration. However, it held that the contracts were vitiated by unilateral mistake, as the consumers were aware of the mistake made by the vendor, and this actual knowledge was sufficient grounds for equity to intervene and set aside the contracts as 'sharp practice'. Many online commerce websites will address this issue in their terms and conditions, providing that contracts are only concluded when confirmed by the trader, generally by email or by the dispatch of the goods.[14] Where errors occur, they will often complete the transaction, despite the unprofitable price, in the name of goodwill or perhaps a realisation that they may not have a sympathetic ear in court.[15]

[4–19] A question that is perhaps of more academic than practical interest is whether the so-called 'postal rule' (that a contract concluded by post is not binding until the letter of acceptance reaches the offeror) applies to online communications. This does not arise in practice as it has been dealt with by the Electronic Commerce Act 2000 (considered in more detail below) and is also generally addressed in the terms and conditions for electronic commerce sites. In addition, the courts have not usually extended the postal rule to new forms of communication, such as telex,[16] telephone,[17] or email.[18]

Incorporation of Terms and Conditions

[4–20] Terms and conditions can be incorporated into online contracts in two different ways – either by the website showing them to the user and asking them to click on some link that signifies acceptance ('click-wrap'), or by making them sufficiently prominent on the website and making it clear that continued use of the site constitutes acceptance ('browse-wrap'). This terminology is a reference to so-called 'shrink-wrap' contracts, which take place when the plastic packaging around the disks or manuals for computer software carry a notice specifying that opening this constitutes acceptance of the associated terms and conditions;[19] these are discussed further in [2–27] to [2–29].

[4–21] A relatively early case on this question is *Specht v Netscape*,[20] which involved a plaintiff who sought to avoid an arbitration clause in the terms and conditions for the downloading of a particular software package. These were not obvious on the website and the Court held that they were not binding on the consumer. Similarly, in *Feldman v United Parcel Service Inc*,[21] clicking on a 'print' button was held not to be sufficient to constitute agreement to the terms and conditions for a shipping contract.

---

[14] See Ter Kah Leng, 'Website Pricing Errors, Who Bears the Risk of Mistake?' (2004) 20 Computer Law and Security Report 396; and Benjamin Groebner, 'Oops! The Legal Consequences of and Solutions to Online Pricing Errors' (2004) 1 Shidler Journal of Law, Commerce, and Technology 2.

[15] Robert Clark, *Contract Law in Ireland* (8th edn, Round Hall 2016) 31–33.

[16] *Entores v Miles Far East Corp* [1955] 2 QB 327 (CA) and *Brinkibon v Stahag Stahl und Stahlwarenhandels GmbH* [1983] 2 AC 34 (HL).

[17] *Apple Corps Ltd v Apple Computer Inc* [2004] EWHC 768 (Ch).

[18] *Surrey (UK) v Mazandaran Wood & Paper Industries* [2014] EWHC 3165 (QB).

[19] See *ProCD v Zeidenberg* 86 F 3d 1447 (7th Cir 1996); *Hill v Gateway 2000* 105 F 3d 1147 (7th Cir 1997).

[20] 306 F 3d 17 (2nd Cir, 2002).

[21] WL 800989 (SDNY, 24 March 2008).

However, the courts will accept the validity of click-wrap contracts if there is sufficient oppor- **[4–22]**
tunity to review the terms before the contract is finalised. In *Midasplayer.com Ltd v Watkins*[22]
the plaintiff operated a gaming site and relied on its terms and conditions to prevent the defendant from using cheating software. In *Caspi v Microsoft Network LLC*,[23] the plaintiffs were
unable to bring an action for breach of contract, common law fraud, and consumer fraud in
the New Jersey courts because in order to access the defendant's services, they had to click on
an 'I Agree' button, which made a choice of law and forum in favour of another jurisdiction.
In *AV v iParadigms LLC*,[24] the plaintiffs were high school students who sought to prevent
the operators of the well-known Turnitin anti-plagiarism site from adding their submitted
papers to the database of material used for comparison purposes. The Court held that they had
entered into valid click-wrap contracts, as clicking on an 'I Agree' button was required to use
the site (and to upload required coursework), even though they were minors.

Similarly, in Case C–322/14 *El Majdoub v CarsontheWeb.Deutschland GmbH*,[25] the CJEU **[4–23]**
held that such an arrangement could meet the requirements of the Brussels I regulation (considered in detail in [4–04] to [4–06]). Article 23(1) requires an agreement conferring exclusive jurisdiction to be in writing or evidenced in writing, while Article 23(2) provides that
any communication by electronic means which provides a durable record of the agreement
shall be regarded as equivalent to 'writing'. The dispute concerned the purchase of an electric
car at a bargain price through a website; the seller sought to cancel it before completion on
the basis that the car had been damaged. The purchaser brought a claim in Germany (where
the seller was based) but the seller sought to rely on a jurisdiction clause in the contract
which made it subject to the Belgian courts (where the seller's parent company was based).
The purchaser claimed that the terms and conditions were not explicitly displayed on screen
as part of the purchasing process, but the CJEU held that the fact that they were easily accessible and could be saved or printed was sufficient to comply with Article 23(2).

The validity of browse-wrap agreements may depend on whether the contract is business- **[4–24]**
to-business or business-to-consumer. In business-to-business cases, the courts (particularly
in the US) expect a higher standard of reasonable notice from the trader and evidence of
consent from the consumer. In *Register.com v Verio*,[26] the plaintiff was an internet domain
name registrar which sought to prevent the defendant competitor from extracting the contact information of its customers from WHOIS lookups (a service which the plaintiff was
required to provide by the Internet Corporation for Assigned Names and Numbers as a condition of being a registrar). It included in the results of the WHOIS queries text which for-
bade the use of the data for direct mail, email or telephone solicitation. The Court regarded
this as binding on queries after the first one.

However, in *Defontes v Dell Computers Corp*,[27] the defendant computer vendor sought to **[4–25]**
rely on an arbitration clause in its terms and conditions. One of the locations in which these
were accessible was through a link on the defendant's website. The judge held that this was
'inconspicuously located at the bottom of the webpage' and therefore not incorporated into

---

[22] [2006] EWHC 1551 (Ch).
[23] 732 A 2d 528 (NJ Super 1999).
[24] 544 F Supp 2d 473 (ED Va 2008).
[25] ECLI:EU:C:2015:334.
[26] 356 F 3d 393 (2nd Cir 2004).
[27] WL 253560 (RI Super, 29 January 2014).

the contract. In *Nguyen v Barnes and Noble Inc*,[28] the defendant bookseller also sought to rely on an arbitration clause which was in a 'Terms of Use' document linked to from every page on its website. The Court held that this was not sufficient constructive notice to a 'reasonably prudent user' for incorporation, and indicated that there should be notice to users or a requirement of some 'affirmative action to demonstrate assent'.

[4–26] An issue that may arise with regard to browse-wrap contracts is whether the website operator is providing sufficient consideration for the contract to be binding. In *Ryanair Ltd v Billingfluege.de GmbH*,[29] Hanna J stated

> Ryanair, therefore, must satisfy the Court that they have provided the defendant with consideration. It seems to me that the plaintiff, through their website, offer information for use, subject at all times to their Terms of Use policy, to the users of their website, including the defendants. Although the defendants deny that they use the plaintiff's website and claim that it is the customer or the consumer who does so, it again seems to be that the defendants accept the offer of information made by the plaintiff when they systematically access the Ryanair website though the screen-scraping mechanism. In my view, the provision of information as to flights and prices of flights by Ryanair on their site, subject at all times to their Terms and Conditions, constitutes a sufficient act of consideration for the purposes of making the contract legally binding.

It would seem, therefore, the simple provision of information through a website is sufficient consideration to make a contract binding.

Electronic Signatures

[4–27] Drawing on the United Nations Model Law on Electronic Commerce and hoping to facilitate electronic commerce, the European Union introduced the Electronic Signatures Directive.[30] This was implemented into Irish law by the Electronic Commerce Act 2000 (ECA 2000). The various national approaches to electronic signatures across European Union Member States were not uniform, and there was limited development of this type of document verification in Ireland and Europe.[31] Therefore, the Directive has been replaced by Regulation 910/2014 on electronic identification and trust services for electronic transactions in the internal market (the eIDAS Regulation).[32] However, the Act remains a part of the statutory framework for electronic signatures in this jurisdiction. This section therefore considers both, highlighting the changes introduced by the Regulation as relevant.

---

[28] 763 F 3d 1171 (9th Cir 2014).

[29] [2010] IEHC 47.

[30] Parliament and Council Directive (EC) 1999/93 on a Community framework for electronic signatures [1993] OJ L13/12.

[31] European Commission, 'Electronic Signatures: Legally Recognised but Cross-Border Take-Up too Slow, says Commission' (17 March 2006) <europa.eu/rapid/press-release_IP-06-325_en.htm> accessed 13 June 2017; European Commission, 'Proposal for a Regulation of the European Parliament and of the Council on Electronic Identification and Trust Services for Electronic Transactions in the Internal Market' COM(2012) 238 final.

[32] Parliament and Council Regulation (EU) 2014/910 on Electronic Identification and Trust Services for Electronic Transactions in the Internal Market [2014] OJ L257/73.

The Directive and Act created a framework in which there are two types of electronic sig- **[4–28]** nature, basic and advanced. Documents which are electronically signed can have legal status and are admissible in legal proceedings. There is also a scheme for the accreditation and supervision of certification service providers (which are required for the provision of advanced electronic signatures).

The regulation adds some new elements to this framework. While Member States do not need **[4–29]** to introduce a framework for electronic signatures and providers, if they choose to require an electronic identification means and authentication in order to access public services, they must mutually recognise those provided by other Member States, provided certain conditions are met.[33] The Regulation recognises new technological features, such as electronic time stamps. The framework is extended to cover three types of signatures: basic, advanced, and qualified. It requires Member States to designate a supervisory body for qualified trust service providers,[34] and to provide a 'Trust Mark' for qualified trust services. Under Article 23, those who are on the list of qualified trust service providers maintained under Article 22 can use an EU-managed 'Trust Mark' to indicate what services they provide.

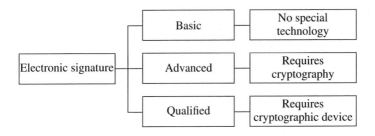

Figure 1 *Types of Electronic Signature*

The ECA 2000 defines an 'electronic signature' as **[4–30]**

> data in electronic form attached to, incorporated in or logically associated with other electronic data and which serves as a method of authenticating the purported originator, and includes an advanced electronic signature[35]

The eIDAS Regulation defines an 'electronic signature' as

> data in electronic form which is attached to or logically associated with other data in electronic form and which is used by the signatory to sign [omitting the authentication requirement].[36]

---

[33] Regulation 2014/910, art 6.
[34] At the time of writing, this is the Irish National Accreditation Board.
[35] Electronic Commerce Act 2000, s 2(1).
[36] Regulation 2014/910, art 3(10).

[4–31] These are relatively open definitions and a simple typed signature at the end of an email message could suffice. For example, in *Hall v Cognos Ltd*,[37] the inclusion of the first names of an employee's line manager and a colleague from personnel at the bottom of email messages approving an expenses claim were held to constitute a signature. However, in *Miles Mehta v J Pereira Fernandes SA*,[38] an automatically inserted email address was not regarded as being sufficient authentication to constitute a signature where the sender's name was not included at the bottom of the message (although the message involved did constitute a sufficient note or memorandum to satisfy the Statute of Frauds 1695).

[4–32] The ECA 2000 also defines an 'advanced electronic signature' as

> an electronic signature—
> (a) uniquely linked to the signatory,
> (b) capable of identifying the signatory,
> (c) created using means that are capable of being maintained by the signatory under his, her or its sole control, and
> (d) linked to the data to which it relates in such a manner that any subsequent change of the data is detectable;[39]

The eIDAS Regulation sets out requirements that an 'advanced electronic signature' must meet, which are broadly similar to the ECA 2000. It must be:

> (a) uniquely linked to the signatory;
> (b) capable of identifying the signatory;
> (c) created using electronic signature creation data that the signatory can, with a high level of confidence, use under his sole control; and
> (d) linked to the data signed therewith in such a way that any subsequent change in the data is detectable.[40]

[4–33] These are much more onerous standards, and meeting them requires the use of cryptographic software, biometrics (such as fingerprints or retina scans), or other sophisticated technology. Advanced electronic signatures are intended for use in the provision of public services (for example, in the filing of tax returns).[41]

[4–34] The Regulation also creates a new category of 'qualified electronic signature', which is 'an advanced electronic signature that is created by a qualified electronic signature creation device, and which is based on a qualified certificate for electronic signatures'.[42] This therefore requires even more complex and sophisticated technology. ('Qualified' here means

---

[37] Hull Industrial Tribunal 1803325/97.
[38] [2006] EWHC 813 (Ch).
[39] Electronic Commerce Act 2000, s 2(1).
[40] Regulation 2014/910, art 26.
[41] Regulation 2014/910, art 27.
[42] Regulation 2014/910, art 3(12).

meeting certain requirements.) These types of signatures are intended to be the electronic equivalent for a traditional manuscript signature.[43]

Under s 9 of the ECA 2000, electronic communications 'shall not be denied legal effect, validity or enforceability solely on the grounds that it is wholly or partly in electronic form, whether as an electronic communication or otherwise'. Section 10 excludes from the purview of ss 12 to 23 (which are described below) certain specific types of laws, including wills, trusts, powers of attorney, real property, making of affidavits, statutory or sworn declarations, or court proceedings. Section 11 also excludes revenue law, securities regulations, criminal evidence, and consumer credit law from the purview of the act as a whole.　**[4–35]**

Section 12 permits the use of electronic means of communication as a way of complying with any legal obligation to provide information 'in writing', making it possible to file forms and other paperwork in digital form. Section 13 permits the use of an electronic signature instead of a written one. Section 14 allows the use of electronic signatures where the signature must be witnessed, but only where both the signature to be witnessed and the signature of the witness are advanced electronic signatures, and the recipient of the signature consents to the use of the electronic signature and, in the case of a public body, that they accept the particular technology and procedures used. Section 16 makes similar provision for the use of advanced electronic signatures to substitute for a seal.　**[4–36]**

Section 15 clarifies that consumer law (considered further below) continues to apply to electronic contracts.　**[4–37]**

Section 17 allows the original form of information to be electronic. This clarification was necessary because the law will sometimes require that information is retained or presented in its original form, but with documents prepared by computer: the original form will consist of electrons stored on a hard disk, which are obviously difficult to present for human inspection.　**[4–38]**

However, s 17(2) imposes several limitations on this flexibility:　**[4–39]**

 (a) if there exists a reliable assurance as to the integrity of the information from the time when it was first generated in its final form, ...

 (b) where it is required or permitted that the information be presented – if the information is capable of being displayed in intelligible form to a person or public body to whom it is to be presented,

 (c) if, at the time the information was generated in its final form, it was reasonable to expect that it would be readily accessible so as to be useable for subsequent reference,

 (d) where the information is required or permitted to be presented to or retained for a public body or for a person acting on behalf of a public body, and the public body consents to the information being presented or retained in electronic form, whether as an electronic communication or otherwise, but requires that it be presented or retained in accordance with particular information technology

---

[43] Regulation 2014/910, art 25(2).

and procedural requirements – if the public body's requirements have been met and those requirements have been made public and are objective, transparent, proportionate and non-discriminatory, and

(e) where the information is required or permitted to be presented to or retained for a person who is neither a public body nor acting on behalf of a public body – if the person to whom the information is required or permitted to be presented or for whom it is required or permitted to be retained consents to the information being presented or retained in that form.

[4–40] The somewhat complex formulation of (d) and (e) are to ensure that public authorities do not arbitrarily adopt or delay adoption of technology. There are concerns about the 'digital divide' between those who have easy access to information technology and those who do not; the latter would be unable to access public services if public bodies could simply use whatever technology they chose. Alternatively, other public bodies may be reluctant to use a particular technology which is fit-for-purpose for no good reason, and therefore the legislation requires them to accept anything which meets their previously communicated requirements.

[4–41] Section 18 makes similar provision for information that is required to be retained or presented in paper or written form.

[4–42] Under s 19, 'An electronic contract shall not be denied legal effect, validity or enforceability solely on the grounds that it is wholly or partly in electronic form, or has been concluded wholly or partly by way of an electronic communication',[44] and any communication relating to the formation of a contract may be conducted electronically.[45] Section 20 allows for electronic communication which requires acknowledgment by electronic communications, unless otherwise specified,[46] and essentially dis-applies the 'postal rule' (already discussed at [4–19]) to such communications, requiring that they must be received by the originator of the original communication before they are to be treated as sent.[47] Under s 21, unless it is otherwise agreed, an electronic communication is regarded as sent when it enters the first electronic communication system outside of the control of the sender, and regarded as received when it enters the information system designated by the recipient.

[4–43] However, this has been largely superseded by the European Communities (Directive 2000/31/EC) Regulations 2003,[48] which apply to the placing of online orders through interactive services (such as the World Wide Web). The 2003 Regulations do not use the traditional terminology of 'offer' and 'acceptance', but instead refers to 'order' and 'acknowledgement'; these may not correspond, depending on how the online ordering process operates.[49] Paragraph 14 specifies that 'the order and the acknowledgement of receipt are deemed to be received when the parties to whom they are addressed are able to access them', which may produce a slightly different result; a message may enter a corporate information system before it is available to the final recipient to access, due to slow internal

---

44 Electronic Commerce Act 2000, s 19(1).
45 Electronic Commerce Act 2000, s 19(2).
46 Electronic Commerce Act 2000, s 20(1).
47 Electronic Commerce Act 2000, s 20(2).
48 European Communities (Directive 2000/31/EC) Regulations 2003, SI 2003/68.
49 Robert Clark, *Contract Law in Ireland* (8th edn, Round Hall 2016) 33.

communications, technical failures, or other issues. The 2003 Regulations apply to both business-to-business and business-to-consumer transactions, but can be contracted out of in the former.

Section 22 of the ECA 2000 makes electronic communications admissible in legal proceedings. Section 25 makes it an offence to commit fraud or to knowingly misuse certificates or electronic signatures. Section 28 clarifies that nothing in the Act requires the disclosure of passwords, cryptographic keys, or other information 'that may be necessary to render information or an electronic communication intelligible'. Part III of the ECA 2000 (ss 29 and 30) authorises the relevant Minister (at the time the Minister for Public Enterprise, now the Minister for Communications, Climate Action and Environment) to establish a scheme for accreditation and supervision of certification service providers.[50]

[4–44]

Consumer Protection Legislation

Consumers who purchase goods and services online are, of course, entitled to all of the protections provided by the Sales of Goods Act 1893, the Sale of Goods and Supply of Services Act 1980, and the European Communities (Certain Aspects of the Sale of Consumer Goods and Associated Guarantees) Regulations 2003.[51] As these are already discussed in detail in other textbooks, they will not be explored further here.

[4–45]

There is specific legislation that deals with the rights of consumers online. The most recent and most important is the Consumer Rights Directive (CRD).[52] It was implemented in Irish law by the European Union (Consumer Information, Cancellation and Other Rights) Regulations 2013,[53] which came into force in 2014. Under paragraph 3(1) of the regulations, these apply to contracts for the sale of goods (including digital content in a tangible medium, such as on a CD or DVD), services, digital content not in a tangible medium (direct downloads), utilities contracts, and district heating. Under paragraph 3(2), they do not apply to contracts for social services, healthcare, gambling, financial services, immovable property, residential accommodation, package travel, timeshares, routine deliveries of food or drink, automated vending machines, use of public telephones, or once-off usage of telecommunications services.

[4–46]

Part 3 of the regulations require that particular information is made available to consumers before a contract is concluded for sale of goods, supply of services, supply of digital content not supplied on a tangible medium, ongoing supply of water, gas or electricity not put up for sale in a limited volume or set quantity, and district heating. This must be in plain and intelligible language. The information to be provided includes

[4–47]

(a)   the main characteristics of the goods or services;
(b)   the identity of the trader, including the trader's trading name;

---

[50]   This has been done by the Electronic Commerce (Certification Service Providers Supervision Scheme) Regulations 2010, SI 2010/233.
[51]   European Communities (Certain Aspects of the Sale of Consumer Goods and Associated Guarantees) Regulations 2003, SI 2003/11.
[52]   Parliament and Council Directive (EU) 2011/83 on Consumer Rights [2011] OJ L304/64.
[53]   European Union (Consumer Information, Cancellation and Other Rights) Regulations 2013, SI 2013/484.

(c) if the trader is acting on behalf of another trader, the geographical address and identity of that trader;

(d) the geographical address at which the trader is established, and the trader's contact information;

(e) the geographical address to which the consumer can address complaints;

(f) the total price of the goods or services inclusive of taxes, or the manner in which the price is to be calculated;

(g) where applicable, any additional costs (such as delivery), or at least an indication that these may be payable.

[4–48] Paragraph 12 further requires a trader who concludes a distance contract to provide the consumer with 'confirmation of the concluded contract on a durable medium' (which is defined sufficiently broadly to include paper and email). The regulations also give consumers the right to cancel off-premises and distance contracts, subject to some restrictions[54] but without incurring costs other than returning the goods, diminution in value, and so on,[55] within 14 days of the delivery of the goods for sales contracts and 14 days of the conclusion of the contract for service contracts.[56]

[4–49] In addition, the regulation limits the fees charged by traders in respect of the use of a given means of payment, the cost of calls by consumers to customer helplines, and payments by consumers additional to the remuneration agreed for the trader's main obligation under the contract.[57]

[4–50] The European Communities (Directive 2000/31/EC) Regulations 2003[58] are also relevant. These apply specifically to online and distance contracts. Under paragraph 7, a service provider must provide certain information to consumers 'in a manner which is easily, directly and permanently accessible'. This includes:

(a) the name of the service provider,

(b) the geographic address at which the service provider is established,

(c) the details of the service provider, including his or her electronic mail address,

(d) details of how natural persons can register their choice regarding unsolicited commercial communications;

(e) where the service provider is registered in a trade or similar public register, the trade or other such register in which the service provider is entered and his or her registration number, or equivalent means of identification in that register,

(f) where the activity is subject to an authorisation scheme, the particulars of the relevant supervisory authority,

(g) where the service provider is a member of a regulated profession –

    (i) any professional body or similar institution with which the service provider is registered,

---

54 para 13.

55 para 14(2).

56 para 15.

57 Part 5 of the Regulations.

58 European Communities (Directive 2000/31/EC) Regulations 2003, SI 2003/68.

      (ii)   the professional title of the provider and the Member State where it has been granted, and

      (iii)   a reference to the applicable professional rules in the Member State of establishment and the means to access them,

   (h)   where the service provider undertakes an activity that is subject to value-added tax, the registration number assigned to that provider,

   (i)   where the relevant service refers to prices, those prices are to be indicated clearly and unambiguously and, in particular, must indicate whether they are inclusive of tax and delivery costs.

There are other items of consumer protection legislation which are not specifically aimed **[4–51]** at the online environment but may nonetheless be relevant when considering online contracts, such as the Unfair Terms in Consumer Contracts Directive 1993,[59] implemented in Ireland by the European Communities (Unfair Terms in Consumer Contracts) Regulations, 1995 (as amended).[60] If a term of a contract is found by a court to be unfair, it will not be binding on the consumer, although the contract as a whole may still stand. A term will be regarded as unfair if, contrary to the requirement of good faith, it causes a significant imbalance in the parties' rights and obligations under the contract to the detriment of the consumer, taking into account the nature of the goods or services for which the contract was concluded and all circumstances attending the conclusion of the contract and all other terms of the contract or of another contract on which it is dependent.[61] The UK courts have applied the equivalent law there to invalidate a clause in the terms and conditions for an online betting website as being unfair to the consumer.[62] The Annex to the Directive contains an indicative list of terms that may be considered unfair. Paragraph 1(i) of this 'grey list' refers to a clause that 'irrevocably binds the consumer to terms with which he had no real opportunity of becoming acquainted before the conclusion of the contract'. This could include 'browse-wrap' methods of presentation of terms, already discussed above.

Financial Transactions Online

	E-money	**Virtual currency**	**Crypto-currency**
Examples	Smart cards, online payments	Frequent flyer miles, online games, meal points	Online transactions and trading
Requirements	'A claim on the issuer'	Not issued by central bank	Cryptographic software
Central Authority	Central bank	Service provider	Community of users

Table 1   *Types of Electronic Money*

---

[59] Council Directive (EEC) 13/1993 on Unfair Terms in Consumer Contracts [1993] OJ L95/29.

[60] European Communities (Unfair Terms in Consumer Contracts) Regulations 1995, SI 1995/27, amended by SI 2000/307, SI 2013/160, and SI 2014/336. For further discussion, see Marco Loos, 'Wanted: A Bigger Stick. On Unfair Terms in Consumer Contracts with Online Service Providers' (2016) 39 Journal of Consumer Policy 63.

[61] SI 1995/27, art 3(1).

[62] *Spreadex Ltd v Cochran* [2012] EWHC 1290 (Ch).

[4–52]   The volume of transactions conducted through electronic means increases significantly year-on-year. Many of these involve payment through credit or debit cards, which are relatively well-established methods of transferring funds, and are managed by conventional financial institutions. However, with the increasing use of digital tools as part of the infrastructure of the business world, the private sector has focused its attention on developing financial technology (often known as 'FinTech'), while governments consider how best to regulate this new field. This has led to the development of virtual and crypto-currencies.

[4–53]   There is some European legislation in this area, primarily the Electronic Money directive (EMD).[63] Under this, only Electronic Money Institutions (which are a subset of credit institutions) can issue 'electronic money', defined as

> electronically, including magnetically, stored monetary value as represented by a claim on the issuer which is issued on receipt of funds for the purpose of making payment transactions as defined in point 5 of Article 4 of Directive 2007/64/EC, and which is accepted by a natural or legal person other than the electronic money issuer[.][64]

[4–54]   This definition covers systems which are based on software-only implementations, smart card-style schemes (such as VisaCash or Mondex), and account-based systems (such as the well-known PayPal). These types of systems are implemented in practice, and certainly have their advantages, such as low transaction costs, suitability for micro-payments (the transfer of amounts so small that using conventional bank transfers or credit cards would be prohibitively costly), and the possibility of offering low transaction costs to small merchants). However, the EMD only applies to sources of value that are in some way based on 'real money', as it only covers balances in units which are issued on receipt of funds, and not the 'virtual currencies' discussed below.[65] The growth in FinTech in recent years has been in mediums of exchange which operate in parallel to, but are not built upon, the conventional currencies.

[4–55]   The Payment Services Directive (PSD)[66] is also relevant. It seeks to create a single internal European payments area. However, it relies on the EMD definition of electronic money,[67] limiting its applicability to virtual and crypto-currencies.

Virtual Currencies

[4–56]   However real the money in your pocket may seem to you, it is fundamentally something which is socially constructed: in other words, it only has value and use because you and others agree that it can be used as a medium of exchange. The notes and coins that we use

---

[63] Parliament and Council Directive (EC) 110/2009 on the Taking Up, Pursuit and Prudential Supervision of the Business of Electronic Money Institutions [2009] OJ L267/7.

[64] Directive 2009/110, art 2(2).

[65] Niels Vandezande, 'Between Bitcoins and Mobile Payments: Will the European Commission's New Proposal Provide More Legal Certainty?' (2014) 22 International Journal of Law and Information Technology 295, 298–301.

[66] Parliament and Council Directive (EC) 64/2007 on Payment Services in the Internal Market [2007] OJ L319/1

[67] Directive 64/2007, art 4.15.

on a day-to-day basis are a physical manifestation of the institution of money, most of which exists only in virtual form as entries in bank databases. Other mediums of exchange have acquired money-like status over time, such as frequent flyer miles, currencies used in online games, and credits purchased for specific purposes (such as meal points or public transport). These are all examples of 'virtual currencies',[68] which the European Central Bank defines as

> a digital representation of value, not issued by a central bank, credit institution or e-money institution, which, in some circumstances, can be used as an alternative to money[.][69]

The International Monetary Fund (IMF) nevertheless went on to define these as 'digital representations of value issued by private developers and denominated in their own unit of account'.[70] However, the Court of Justice of the European Union has ruled that a service for exchanging Bitcoin (a type of crypto-currency, to be explained below) was not subject to VAT as it was engaging in currency transactions, which are exempt.[71] **[4–57]**

Crypto-Currencies

Innovation in recent years has been in currencies that rely on cryptography rather than government backing as their source of authority. A particular type of virtual currency that has increased significantly in popularity and value in recent years is the *crypto-currency*. Essentially, these use very sophisticated mathematics as a way to be certain (or at least as certain as is possible on the global internet) about the ownership, transfer, and security of value. Prominent examples include Bitcoin, Ethereum, and Litecoin, which are discussed further in paragraphs [4–72] to [4–75]. **[4–58]**

As the name implies, these rely on encryption as a core technology in an overall architecture which seeks to leverage the development of a widely distributed and decentralised network of computing power to create a means of exchange which does not depend on government backing or approval. These all use a de-centralised network of computers as a means to circulate and record information about transactions in a particular currency. They rely on a *blockchain*, which is a method for recording information in a way that is difficult to fake or to tamper with. **[4–59]**

Before considering what these may mean for law and the regulatory issues that they raise, it is useful to briefly consider what encryption means, and how it is used in these new forms of 'money', particularly in a *blockchain*. **[4–60]**

---

[68] Benjamin Geva, 'Disintermediating Electronic Payments: Digital Cash and Virtual Currencies' (2016) 31 Journal of International Banking Law and Regulation 661, 664–66.

[69] European Central Bank/Eurosystem, 'Virtual Currency Schemes' (October 2012) <www.ecb. europa.eu/pub/pdf/other/virtualcurrencyschemes201210en.pdf> accessed 13 June 2017, 25.

[70] See IMF Staff Discussion, 'Virtual Currencies and Beyond: Initial Considerations' (20 January 2016) <www.imf.org/en/Publications/Staff-Discussion-Notes/Issues/2016/12/31/Virtual-Currencies-and-Beyond-Initial-Considerations-43618> accessed 13 June 2017, 7.

[71] Case C–264/14 *Skatteverket v Hedqvist* ECLI:EU:C:2015:718.

Encryption

[4–61]   At its most basic form, encryption involves taking information (for example, a sentence such as 'Meet Thursday at five thirty pm') and substituting for each letter one that is a certain number of positions away in the alphabet. This is often known as a 'Caesar cipher', after Julius Caesar, who used such a scheme to make his messages difficult to read if they were intercepted. If we shift each letter by 13 positions, the letter a becomes n, b becomes o, and so on. This particular application of the Caeser cipher is known as ROT13, for rotate by 13 places, and is often used online for very simple information hiding. Applying this to our example sentence, the message becomes 'Zrrg Guhefqnl ng svir guvegl cz'.

[4–62]   This encrypted message is not easy to read on first glance, but it is not very secure. Anyone who knows that the shift applied is 13 letters can quickly decode it. Even if the shift is not known, it can be guessed relatively quickly if the language of the original sentence is known, as there are regular patterns in the frequency and location of letters which can help to identify what the most likely shifts are. For example, in English, the most common letter is e. A modern computer can try a variety of different letter shifts until the message is intelligible in very little time.

[4–63]   Therefore, modern encryption schemes will apply much more complex shifting algorithms. These will take some information (often called 'plaintext') and a 'key' (usually a random number) and combine the plaintext and key through mathematical transformations to generate encoded information (often called 'ciphertext'). (In the ROT13 example above, the key is 13.) It is difficult or impossible to recreate the original plaintext from the ciphertext without knowing the transformations and the key.

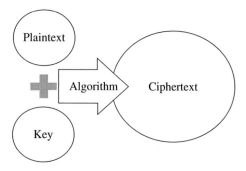

Figure 2   *Encryption Process*

[4–64]   Key-based encryption schemes use either private (symmetric) or public keys. In a private key scheme, the encryption and decryption key are the same, and must be known to both parties to the communication. As this encryption has significant weaknesses, and there is a practical issue involved in sharing the private key, it is not often used for secure messages. However, it is often used for cryptographic hashing, which applies a particular type of algorithm to generate a short piece of text which is unique (it can only be generated from the input) but cannot be decrypted in a reasonable or realistic amount of time. Even a very small change to the plaintext will produce a very different ciphertext. The one-way output (sometimes known as the hash, hash value, message digest, or digest) is more useful than it might seem; it can be used to prove that one person has a piece of information without revealing that information until later. It is essentially a fingerprint for another piece of information and is difficult to fake or counterfeit.

In a public key scheme, one key is made public and easily accessible. The other is kept private. These are generally used in two ways: for encryption and for authentication. First, if Alice wants to send a secure message to Bob, she will use Bob's public key to encrypt. Only Bob's private key will decrypt the message. However, anyone can access and use Bob's public key, and therefore Bob cannot be certain that Alice sent the message. Therefore, for the second method, Alice can also encrypt the message using both her private key and Bob's public key. Only Bob can decrypt the message, using both his private key and Alice's public key. He can be certain that Alice sent the message. The effectiveness of these schemes depend on the private keys remaining secret, and on the mathematical transformations used being so complex that it is not feasible to work out what the private keys are. They are commonly used for public key encryption messaging schemes and for digital signatures. These are often supported by public key infrastructures (PKI) in which central authorities guarantee that the authenticity of public keys. (It is difficult to decentralise the availability of public keys.) [4–65]

Blockchain Technology

Fundamentally, a blockchain is a distributed consensus algorithm. This means that it relies on a loose network of computers, which are not centrally controlled, as a means of agreeing a particular set of facts, and does so by using complex mathematical techniques. It records information in a *distributed* ledger – a record of transactions which anyone can read and write to. (Some implementations of blockchain use a *permissioned ledger*, which can only be accessed by certain pre-authorised individuals. This is not that different to a conventional database.) A blockchain can be used to record almost any type of information but is usually used to keep track of financial transactions. Ultimately, the data on a particular blockchain is no more or less 'real' than the numbers that represent the balance in your bank account. [4–66]

A particular blockchain, such as the blockchain that underpins Bitcoin, is a sequence of transaction records, encoded as 'blocks' in a long 'chain'. Those who wish to make a new transaction, such as the transfer of units from Alice to Bob, will submit a record of this event to the network. If enough other members of the network accept that this is a valid transaction (checking that Alice has at least the required number of units, that she is not trying to double-spend, that Bob's address on the network is a valid destination for units, and so on), then it will be encoded into a new block. In order for this block to be definitively (and irrevocably) written to the master blockchain, certain key members of the network must perform sophisticated mathematical operations and write the results on the chain for others to verify. This is known as 'mining a block'; the first to mine a block is rewarded by fees from the network and from those whose transactions are recorded in the block. This aims to ensure the honesty of participants, particularly miners, as the mathematical problems become more and more difficult and therefore subverting the network to record false transactions requires the application of more and more computing power. For the popular crypto-currencies, mining has become an expensive operation, requiring significant investment. [4–67]

[4–68] It is important to understand the difference between such a system and a conventional database or ledger. Many internal records, such as a bank's list of accounts and balances, or a business's financial management system, can achieve similar possibilities ('affordances', in technical jargon), allowing for value to transferred from Alice to Bob in a secure and verifiable fashion. However, these systems depend on being closed; if an attacker can gain access to a bank's internal processes, she can transfer funds between accounts and falsify transaction records, often without being detected or leaving a trace. A blockchain system assumes that it is public and under attack from the outset; therefore, considerable effort is put into verifying transactions. Traditional databases and ledgers also require a central authority to manage and verify information; this trusted entity (a bank, a financial controller, or government agency) is (in principle) the only definitive authority on the current state of 'facts' within that system, such as what the balance on a particular account at a particular point in time is. A blockchain has no central authority; the current state of the network can be determined by any participant by studying the transactions that it records and calculating account balances and so on, on a case-by-case basis.

Smart Contracts

[4–69] Some crypto-currencies offer scripting or programming languages, which enable users to ask the network to run (or 'execute') programs. Some of these are sufficiently sophisticated to be full programming environments; these are commonly known as 'Turing-complete'. A 'Turing machine' (named after the British cryptographer and key developer of information technology, Alan Turing) is a computing device which is flexible enough to be re-programmed into any other type of computing device. A blockchain-based scripting language that is Turing-complete allows the creation of quite complex programs, which can manipulate financial information and respond to external events in a variety of ways. These are often known as *smart contracts*.

[4–70] It is theoretically possible, and has often been claimed by crypto-currency enthusiasts, that these could (and perhaps even should) replace conventional written contracts. This would remove a great deal of the ambiguity that surrounds a contract written in a human language. It would also greatly reduce the amount of bureaucracy and administration that is required to run a business, government, or other complex organisation. In such entities, a great deal of time is spent verifying identities, confirming balances and other threshold requirements (such as examination results for progression from one year to the next), and granting access to resources. This takes time and may not be perfectly enforced. It also requires a trusted central authority.

[4–71] The vision of smart contracts is one in which businesses can provide goods and services knowing that as soon as items are delivered, payment will be automatically made, without any need to issue invoices, statements, and reminders; where infrastructure (such as buildings or public transport) will grant or deny access based on electronic tokens; and where decision-making and co-ordination can take place within a distributed group without the need for a central manager. Whether or not this vision will come to pass, and the extent to which smart contracts will displace conventional legal agreements, is as yet unclear. Contracts operate in a human and social context that allows for accidents and mistakes, and permits common law and statute to intervene to add or vary terms for a variety of reasons. The ambiguity of human language is sometimes useful as a way to achieving agreement and leaving details to be worked out later.[72] It is very difficult to write software which predicts all situations that may arise between the parties, and blockchain technology has a long way to go in terms of simplicity, speed, and reliability. It is, nonetheless, an area those involved in law and ICT should observe with interest over the coming years.

Examples of Crypto-Currencies

There are dozens of crypto-currencies in circulation. Some are much more active than others. The field is very dynamic and it is therefore impossible to provide an up-to-date or comprehensive overview of all blockchain-based stores of value. However, it is useful to provide a thumbnail sketch of three of the most well known and widely used of these. [4–72]

Bitcoin is the original and most widely accepted crypto-currency. It was originally developed by 'Satoshi Nakamoto', which may be a pseudonym or a group of collaborators. It is decentralised and has a somewhat libertarian ethos. Units of Bitcoin have become very valuable, reaching $1000 at the time of writing, but as there have been crashes in the past, it is not a stable store of value. It is often associated, particularly in the popular media, with drugs and crime, as it has been used as the medium of exchange on underground sites such as the Silk Road website, but is also accepted by legitimate businesses. [4–73]

Ethereum is an attempt to create a decentralised infrastructure that is capable of running smart contracts (which is not possible on Bitcoin). While it has had considerable successes, it has also encountered some challenges, particularly an incident known as the 'DAO Hack' in June 2016, in which an unknown individual was able to exploit a weakness in the smart contract that underpinned the Distributed Autonomous Organisation (DAO) to take control of a significant amount of units of Ethereum.[73] The Ethereum community responded with a 'hard fork' (forcing a change to another chain of blocks that did not record this transfer of value).[74] This highlights the potential for human error undermining the grand vision of smoothly running smart contracts that operate without outside intervention, and the continued importance of social, rather than computational, consensus as the final arbiter of 'facts'. [4–74]

Litecoin is based on Bitcoin but tries to operate much more quickly. A Bitcoin block is created every 10 minutes, whereas Litecoin blocks are generated every two and half minutes. [4–75]

Regulation of Crypto-Currencies

It is as yet unclear whether or not crypto-currencies have a long-term future. How they are regulated will doubtless be an important factor in this. As has already been discussed, crypto-currencies fall outside the current European regulatory framework for electronic money. However, the European Banking Authority has issued an opinion stating that there is a need to regulate these types of medium of exchange in order to mitigate the [4–76]

---

[72] Karen EC Levy, 'Book-Smart, Not Street-Smart: Blockchain-Based Smart Contracts and the Social Workings of Law' (2017) 3 Engaging Science, Technology, and Society 1, 6–7.

[73] David Seigel, 'Understanding the DAO Attack' (CoinDesk, 25 June 2016) <www.coindesk.com/understanding-dao-hack-journalists/> accessed 13 June 2017.

[74] Michael del Castillo, 'Ethereum Executes Blockchain Hard Fork to Return DAO Funds' (*CoinDesk*, 20 July 2016) <www.coindesk.com/ethereum-executes-blockchain-hard-fork-return-dao-investor-funds/> accessed 13 June 2017.

associated risks.[75] The Commission has recently released an 'Action Plan for strengthening the fight against terrorist financing',[76] which proposes to introduce money-laundering controls for virtual currency exchanges (although another Commission strategy paper calls for a more hands-off approach[77]). Germany has created local regulatory requirements for those trading in Bitcoin on a commercial scale.[78] There is no clear Irish position as of yet, although it does seem that their use for payments or in currency speculation could create tax liabilities.[79] Although the regulation of crypto-currency is still in its infancy, that does not mean that there is none. Some countries, such as Thailand, China, and Iceland, have banned or restricted the use of crypto-currencies,[80] while Brazil has been more supportive, changing the law in order to make crypto-currencies acceptable as legal tender.[81] In addition, ignoring or violating rules can have consequences: in 2015, Ripple Labs, a virtual currency start-up, was fined $700,000 for violating US banking law.[82]

Further Reading

- Robert Clark, 'Incorporation of Terms – Important Irish Developments' (2015) 22 Commercial Law Practitioner 272
- Frederic Debussere, 'International Jurisdiction over E-Consumer Contracts in the European Union: Quid Novi Sub Sole?' (2002) 10 International Journal of Law and Information Technology 344
- Jos Dumortier and Niels Vandezande, 'Critical Observations on the Proposed Regulation for Electronic Identification and Trust Services for Electronic Transactions in the Internal Market' (2012) ICRI Research Paper 9 <https://ssrn.com/abstract=2152583> accessed 8 July 2017
- Joshua Fairfield, 'Smart Contracts, Bitcoin Bots, and Consumer Protection' (2014) 71 Washington and Lee Law Review Online 35
- Youseph Farah, 'Allocation of Jurisdiction and the Internet in EU Law' (2008) 33 European Law Review 257
- Youseph Farah, 'Electronic Contracts and Information Society Services Under the E-Commerce Directive' (2009) 12 Journal of Internet Law 3
- Caterina Gardiner, 'Scheme of Consumer Rights Bill 2015: Paving the Way for Digital Consumers. Part 1 – Background and Scope' (2015) 22 Commercial Law Practitioner 222
- Caterina Gardiner, 'Scheme of Consumer Rights Bill 2015: Paving the Way for Digital Consumers. Part 2 – Rights and Remedies' (2015) 22 Commercial Law Practitioner 243

---

[75] European Banking Authority, 'EBA Opinion on "Virtual Currencies"' (EBA/Op/2014/08, 4 July 2014).

[76] European Commission, 'Communication from the Commission to the European Parliament and the Council on an Action Plan for strengthening the fight against terrorist financing' COM(2016) 050 final.

[77] Robert Madelin and David Ringrose, 'Opportunity Now: Europe's Mission to Innovate' (5 July 2016) <ec.europa.eu/epsc/publications/strategic-notes/opportunity-now-europe%E2%80%99s-mission-innovate_en> accessed 13 June 2017.

[78] BaFin, 'Virtual Currency' (undated) <www.bafin.de/EN/Aufsicht/FinTech/VirtualCurrency/virtual_currency_node_en.html> accessed 13 June 2017.

[79] Dáil Deb 10 December 2013, vol 824 cols 133–34; Dáil Deb 15 January 2014, vol 826 cols 177–78.

[80] Andrea Borroni, 'Bitcoins: Regulatory Patterns' (2016) 32 Banking & Finance Law Review 47, 56.

[81] Tara Mandjee, 'Bitcoin, Its Legal Classification and Its Regulatory Framework' (2014) 15 Journal of Business & Securities Law 157, 208.

[82] FinCEN, 'FinCEN Fines Ripple Labs Inc. in First Civil Enforcement Action Against a Virtual Currency Exchanger' (FinCen, 5 May 2015) <https://www.fincen.gov/sites/default/files/shared/20150505.pdf> accessed 8 July 2017.

- Daniel Garrie, 'Encryption for Lawyers' (2016) Business Law Today 1
- Benjamin Geva, 'Disintermediating Electronic Payments: Digital Cash and Virtual Currencies' (2016) 31 Journal of International Banking Law and Regulation 661
- Lorna E Gillies, 'Addressing the Cyberspace Fallacy: Targeting the Jurisdiction of an Electronic Consumer Contract' (2008) 16 International Journal of Law and Information Technology 242
- Stuart Hoegner (ed), The Law of Bitcoin (iUniverse 2015)
- Phillip Johnson, 'All Wrapped Up? A Review of the Enforceability of "Shrink-Wrap" and "Click-Wrap" Licences in the UK and the US' (2003) 25 European Intellectual Property Review 98
- Aonghus McClafferty, 'Effective Protection for the E-Consumer in Light of the Consumer Rights Directive?' (2012) 11 Hibernian Law Journal 85
- Maeve McDonagh and Fidelma White, 'Electronic Signatures: The Legal Framework and the Market Reality in Ireland' (2003) 10 Commercial Law Practitioner 228
- Elizabeth Macdonald, 'Incorporation of Standard Terms in Website Contracting – Clicking "I Agree"' (2011) 27 Journal of Contract Law 198
- Elizabeth Macdonald, 'When is a Contract formed by the Browse-Wrap Process?' (2011) 19 International Journal of Law and Information Technology 285
- Christiana Markou, 'Advanced Automated Contracting and the Problem with the Pre-Contractual Information Duty of the Consumer Rights Directive' (2017) 20 Journal of Internet Law 3
- Joakim ST Oren, 'International Jurisdiction over E-Consumer Contracts in E-Europe' (2003) 52 International Comparative Law Quarterly 665
- Sergii Shcherbak, 'How Should Bitcoin Be Regulated?' (2014) 7 European Journal of Legal Studies 45
- George Walker, 'Financial Technology Law: A New Beginning And A New Future' (2017) 50 International Lawyer 137
- Fidelma White, 'Selling Online: Complying with the New Consumer Protection Regime – Cancellation and Other Rights' (2015) 22 Commercial Law Practitioner 63

CHAPTER 5
Data Protection

'At birth, your data trail began.'[1]

The average individual going about their life today generates more data in 24 hours than **[5–01]** their near ancestors would have generated in their entire lives. The grandparent of today's undergraduate student may have had their date of birth, name, and parentage recorded soon after their birth. If a photograph was taken of the newborn, however, it certainly would not have been shared with an openly accessible repository. While the sharing of baby photographs – sometimes with location information attached – is now common practice on social media sites, it is not even necessary to factor in the Web 2.0 implications of modern life to demonstrate the data-rich nature of the world we live in. In fact, the risks of digitising records and storing personal information in large databases have been clear for many decades.[2] Concerns about the effect such technologies could have on individual privacy led to the early adoption of data protection legislation in Sweden and Germany and the development of non-binding recommendations by the Organization for

---

[1] Martin Enserink and Gilbert Chin, 'Introduction to Special Issue: The End of Privacy' (2015) 347 (6221) Science 491.

[2] See, for example, Alan Westin, *Privacy and Freedom* (Atheneum 1967).

Economic Cooperation and Development (OECD) in 1980.[3] Due to the desire to facilitate the free flow of data, a need for cooperation and collaboration between states on such issues became evident.

History of European Data Protection Rules

[5–02]   While the legislative efforts of the European Union in this area have been the focus of much recent debate, it is important to note the early role of another supranational organisation of states – the Council of Europe – in the development of European data protection standards. Following significant developments in information and communications technology, the Council of Europe developed the Convention for the Protection of Individuals with regard to Automatic Processing of Personal Data (Convention No 108). As the first legally binding international instrument concerning data protection, Convention No 108 includes 'many of the rights, obligations and safeguards that are still visible in the EU's current regime'.[4] The Convention imposes duties on those who process data, sets out rights for the people whose data is processed, and provides special protection for certain categories of data.[5] Subsequent to its inception in 1981, 50 states have ratified the Convention, including a number of non-European states.[6] Ireland gave effect to the Convention domestically by passing the Data Protection Act 1988.

[5–03]   Anticipating the importance of harmonised data protection rules in the Single Market, the EU Parliament[7] continually appealed to the European Commission to address the issue throughout the 1970s and early 1980s.[8] The Commission resisted legislative action but

---

[3] Datalagen (Data Act), SFS 1973:289; Hessicsches Datenschutzgesetz (Data Protection Act of the State of Hesse) vom 7–Oktober 1970; Eleni Kosta, *Consent in European Data Protection Law* (Martinus Nijhoff Publishers 2013) 13; Recommendations of the Council Concerning Guidelines Governing the Protection of Privacy and Trans-Border Flows of Personal Data. The OECD recommendations laid down seven principles for the protection of personal data: 1. Notice, 2. Purpose, 3. Consent, 4. Security, 5. Disclosure, 6. Access, 7. Accountability.

[4] Serge Gutwirth, Ronald Leenes, Paul de Hert, and Yves Poullet, *European Data Protection: Coming of Age* (Springer 2012) 61.

[5] ibid.

[6] In addition to the Council of Europe Members, Convention No 108 has been signed by Cabo Verde, Mauritius, Morocco, Senegal, Tunisia, Uruguay: <www.coe.int/en/web/conventions/full-list/-/conventions/treaty/108/signatures> accessed 7 March 2017.

[7] To avoid confusion, this chapter refers to the European Economic Community and the European Community as the European Union in reflection of the fact that these bodies and their functions have subsequently been absorbed under the EU framework.

[8] Resolution of the European Parliament on the protection of the rights of the individual in the face of developing technical progress in the field of automatic data processing [1975] OJ C60/48; Resolution of the European Parliament of 8 April 1976 on the protection of the right of the individual in the face of developing technical progress in the field of automatic data processing [1976] OJ C100/27. Resolution of the European Parliament on the protection of the rights of the individual in the face of technical developments in data processing [1979] OJ C140/34; Resolution of the European Parliament on the protection of the rights of the individual in the face of technical developments in data processing [1982] OJ C87/39.

instead recommended that all EU Member States ratify Convention No 108.[9] While there is potential for Convention No 108 to continue to influence the global data protection landscape, this is likely, for the time being at least, to be in a minor supporting role to the EU.[10]

In an effort to bring about further harmonisation of data protection regulation within **[5–04]** the internal market, the EU adopted Directive 95/46/EC on the protection of individuals with regard to the processing of personal data and on the free movement of such data. The Data Protection Directive aims to both protect the rights of individuals with respect to the processing of personal data and to protect the free flow of personal data between Member States. In order to meet the new standards, Ireland amended the existing data protection law and passed the Data Protection (Amendment) Act 2003. While these laws are still operative, this chapter focuses on the General Data Protection Regulation (GDPR) which is set to apply from May 2018. As the GDPR is a Regulation as opposed to a Directive, it will be directly applicable in Ireland from May 2018 without the need for implementing legislation.[11] The proximity of the legislation's direct application across Europe means that data users should already be working towards the updated standards.

Relationship of Data Protection to Privacy

While the precise nature of the relationship between privacy and data protection is still open **[5–05]** to debate, the two rights are clearly connected.[12] In some ways, data protection could be seen as a subsection of privacy law, but in other respects, data protection principles provide for broader protection than is traditionally provided under privacy law. For example, among the rights afforded to individuals under data protection law is the right of access to personal information relating to that person.[13]

---

[9] While the subsequent efforts of the EU have dominated discussion in the field of data protection, it is important to note that Convention No 108 is currently undergoing its own reform process. Council of Europe, 'Modernisation of the Data Protection "Convention 108"' <www.coe.int/en/web/portal/28-january-data-protection-day-factsheet> accessed 7 March 2017; Cécile de Terwangne, 'The Work of Revision of the Council of Europe Convention 108 for the Protection of Individuals as Regards the Automatic Processing of Personal Data" (2014) 28(2) International Review Of Law, Computers & Technology. Graham Greenleaf, '"Modernising" Data Protection Convention 108: A Safe Basis for a Global Privacy Treaty?' (2013) 29(4) Computer Law & Security Review; Graham Greenleaf, 'Renewing Data Protection Convention 108: The COE's "GDPR Lite" Initiatives' (2016) 142 Privacy Laws & Business International Report 14–17.

[10] Graham Greenleaf, 'Balancing Globalisation's Benefits and Commitments: Accession to Data Protection Convention 108 by Countries Outside Europe' [2016] University of New South Wales Faculty of Law Research Series 52.

[11] While the GDPR is a directly applicable Regulation, certain provisions of the GDPR will still require national implementing measures. Accordingly, the Heads of a Data Protection Bill are currently being finalised with the aim to give full effect to the GDPR (and to transpose the EU Directive 2016/680). Government Legislation Programme Spring/Summer session 2017 <www.taoiseach.gov.ie/eng/Taoiseach_and_Government/Government_Legislation_Programme/> accessed 7 March 2017.

[12] Nadezhda Purtova, 'Private Law Solutions in European Data Protection: Relationship to Privacy, and Waiver of Data Protection Rights' (2010) 28(2) Netherlands Quarterly of Human Rights 179.

[13] These rights are discussed in more detail below.

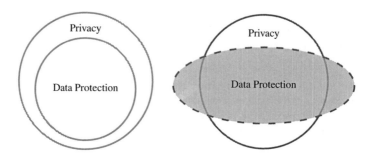

Figure 1   *Scope of Protection Provided by Privacy and Data Protection.*

[5–06]   For the purposes of EU law, however, it is important to point out that privacy and data protection are distinct legal rights. This is made clear by the Charter of Fundamental Rights which recognises the rights separately under Articles 7 and 8 of the Charter. According to Borghi, the rights 'derive their normative force from values that – although at times coincidental and interacting in a variety of ways – may be conceptualized independently'.[14] While the classical conception of the right to privacy tends to centre around the desire to be 'left alone', data protection law is not designed to obscure data but to control – and indeed enable – the sharing of data. In spite of this distinction, data protection law is inherently informed by traditional notions of privacy and the Court of Justice of the European Union (CJEU) has referred to both Article 7 and Article 8 in its interpretation of European Union data protection rules.[15]

Key Principles of Data Protection Law

[5–07]   Article 1 of the GDPR recognises the 'right to the protection of personal data', but also states that the 'free movement of personal data within the Union shall be neither restricted nor prohibited for reasons connected with the protection of natural persons with regard to the processing of personal data'. This reflects the dual mandate of data protection, which aims to facilitate the sharing of data within the EU while also ensuring that the data is shared in a manner that respects privacy. While the human rights functions of the EU have expanded in recent years, it is important to keep in mind the fact that the 1995 Data Protection Directive was introduced under the Union's competency to facilitate the development of the free internal market.[16] While the GDPR has been hailed as a major change in the data protection landscape, Recital 9 of the GDPR states that the 'objectives and principles of Directive 95/46/EC remain sound' and instead highlights the remaining fragmentation of data protection law across the EU as a key motivation for the Regulation. Accordingly, in spite of the

---

[14] Maurizio Borghi, Federico Ferretti, and Stavroula Karapapa, 'Online Data Processing Consent under EU Law: A Theoretical Framework and Empirical Evidence from the UK' (2013) 21(2) International Journal of Law and Information Technology 109, 113–14.

[15] Case C-131/12 *Mario Costeja Gonzalez v Google Spain and Google* ECLI:EU:C:2014:317, 69.

[16] Case C-465/00 *Osterreichischer Rundfunk & Ors* ECLI:EU:C:2003:294.

increased focus on the language of rights, the importance of free movement remains a key influence on EU data protection law.

Data protection is not about protecting 'data' as some abstract concept, but protecting peo- **[5–08]** ple and facilitating the appropriate use of their data. As a result, data protection law only applies to 'personal data' concerning 'natural persons'.[17] In the GDPR, 'personal data' is defined as 'any information relating to an identified or identifiable natural person ("Data Subject")'. According to the Regulation an identifiable natural person is 'one who can be identified, directly or indirectly, in particular by reference to an identifier' such as a name, an identification number or 'to one or more factors specific to the physical, physiological, genetic, mental, economic, cultural or social identity of that natural person'.[18] As we all produce much data relating to ourselves, we are all 'Data Subjects'. It is important to understand the other actors who come into play as our data flows through the world. Indeed, at different points in time, we may assume alternative roles in relation to the personal data of other individuals.

Key Players in Data Protection Law

We have already identified the 'Data Subject' as a central player in the data protection **[5–09]** sphere. Without the Data Subject, there would be no personal data to process. While Data Subjects are granted many rights under data protection law, and may often be asked to consent to certain types of processing, 'Controllers' exert a significant amount of influence over how the personal data of individuals is used. Article 4 of the GDPR defines a 'Controller' as a 'natural or legal person, public authority, agency or other body which, alone or jointly with others, determines the purposes and means of the processing of personal data'.[19] This is a broad definition that captures a wide range of individuals and institutions – from the small town general practitioner who stores records locally on their PC to global social media corporations that process enormous amounts of information in unexpected ways.

Data protection law imposes many obligations on Controllers and as a result, all **[5–10]** Controllers should continually examine their data flow in order to assess whether they are processing data in a compliant manner. The CJEU has interpreted the territorial scope of the Data Protection Directive broadly,[20] but the GDPR states explicitly that data protection rules apply to the processing of personal data in the context of the activities of an establishment based in the Union, regardless of whether the processing takes place in

---

[17] GDPR, art 1(1). Legal persons do not fall within the scope of 'Data Subject' under the GDPR but do receive some protection under the ePrivacy Directive discussed below. It should be noted that the ePrivacy Directive is also being updated.

[18] GDPR, art 4(1).

[19] The definition goes on to state that 'where the purposes and means of such processing are determined by Union or Member State law, the Controller or the specific criteria for its nomination may be provided for by Union or Member State law'.

[20] Case C-230/14 *Weltimmo v Nemzeti Adatvédelmi és Információszabadság Hatóság* ECLI:EU:C:2015:639, 25; Case C-131/12 *Mario Costeja Gonzalez v Google Spain and Google* ECLI:EU:C:2014:317, 53.

the Union or not. The GDPR further expands the scope of European data protection with the assertion that the

> Regulation applies to the processing of personal data of data subjects who are in the Union by a controller or processor not established in the Union, where the processing activities are related to:
> (a) the offering of goods or services, irrespective of whether a payment of the data subject is required, to such data subjects in the Union; or
> (b) the monitoring of their behaviour as far as their behaviour takes place within the Union.[21]

[5–11] As a result of this expansion, the targeting of EU citizens via online services will now trigger the application of the GDPR, irrespective of whether any money is exchanged or where the Controller is established. This highlights the continued importance of data protection law in the modern information-driven business model. While many global internet companies maintain establishments in Europe – often in Ireland – this new extension clarifies the fact that internet companies without a European presence but that target the lucrative European market will be subject to data protection law.

[5–12] In some, but not all, cases, a Data Subject's personal data may not only be processed by a Controller, but also by a 'Processor'. While a Controller determines the purposes and means of data processing, a Processor processes personal data on the Controller's behalf.[22] A large company may engage the services of many Processors that are contracted to process data in the manner dictated by the Controller. For example, a Controller may send the personal data of employees to an external payroll company or may store personal data on a cloud-based service. In both cases, the Controller retains their responsibilities under data protection law, but additional – less onerous – responsibilities will attach to the pay roll company and cloud services provider as Processor. While Processors are currently only required to follow their contractual agreements with Controllers and to maintain adequate security,[23] it is important to note that the GDPR will increase the compliance requirements for Processors. For example, in addition to implementing appropriate technical and organisational measures, Processors will be obliged to evaluate the risks before engaging in data processing and to take appropriate steps to mitigate those risks.[24] Once the contractual relationship with the Controller has expired, Processors must delete or return all the personal data to the Controller.[25] While it is important to be aware of the additional responsibilities that apply to Processors under the GDPR, this chapter focuses on the obligations of Controllers.

[5–13] We have established that data protection law provides Data Subjects with rights and imposes obligations on Controllers and Processors. Another crucial figure on the data protection

---

[21] GDPR, art 3. In terms of employee monitoring issues, see case of *Barbulescu v Romania* ECHR, Case No 61496/08, 12 January 2016; also commentary on the case in Paul Lambert, *Data Protection Law in Ireland, Sources and Issues* (Clarus Press 2016) 444–446.

[22] GDPR, art 4(7)(8).

[23] Directive 95/46/EC, arts 16 and 17.

[24] GDPR, art 28(3); recitals 81, 82, and 83.

[25] GDPR, art 28(3).

landscape – the domestic supervisory authority – aims to ensure that Data Subject rights are realised and that Controllers' and Processors' responsibilities are fulfilled in practice.

Article 8 of the EU Charter of Fundamental Rights states: **[5–14]**

1. Everyone has the right to the protection of personal data concerning him or her.
2. Such data must be processed fairly for specified purposes and on the basis of the consent of the person concerned or some other legitimate basis laid down by law. Everyone has the right of access to data which has been collected concerning him or her, and the right to have it rectified.
3. Compliance with these rules shall be subject to control by an independent authority.

It is notable how the Article explicitly requires the appointment of an independent super-   **[5–15]**
visory authority empowered to enforce compliance with the right. The GDPR fleshes this out by requiring each Member State to provide for a data protection authority that is tasked to monitor the application of the law and to protect data protection rights.[26] Independence is highlighted as a central value in Article 52, which states that supervisory authorities must 'act with complete independence'. The practical side of independence is provided for in Article 52(4), which requires Member States to ensure that their domestic supervisory authority 'is provided with the human, technical and financial resources, premises and infrastructure necessary for the effective performance of its tasks and exercise of its powers'. The financial control of supervisory authorities must not affect its independence.[27]

The Office of the Data Protection Commissioner (ODPC) will continue as the Irish super-   **[5–16]**
visory authority following the implementation of the GDPR.[28] The differences across the EU are perhaps most notable in the various approaches to enforcement adopted by the different domestic supervisory authorities. The ODPC, for example, has been the subject of some criticism.[29] It has been argued that the Irish authority's enforcement of data protection law – particularly its emphasis on a collaborative rather than confrontational approach – is weak and ineffective.[30]

---

[26] A state may provide for one or more independent public authorities. GDPR, art 51(1). For example, it may be that three Commissioners are appointed to a new Office of Data Protection, as opposed to the present single Commissioner. This would not be wholly dissimilar to the three individuals heading up ComReg which deals with telecommunications, communications and communications providers regulatory issues.
[27] See also GDPR, arts 53 and 54. It is interesting to note that the Irish Data Protection authority has been the subject of a legal action on the contention that the authority lacks true independence as required under EU law. Digital Rights Ireland 'DRI Challenges Independence of Ireland's Data Protection Authority' (28 January 2016) Digital Rights Ireland <www.digitalrights.ie/dri-challenges-idependence-of-irelands-data-protection-commissioner/> accessed 7 March 2017.
[28] The ODPC was originally established under the 1988 Data Protection Act, which sought to implement Convention No 108. The governing legislation for the ODPC was subsequently updated with the passage of the Data Protection Amendment Act 2003, which implemented Directive 95/46/EC. The Heads of a new Data Protection Bill are in the process of being finalised.
[29] Duncan Robinson, 'US Tech Groups Spawn a Fight between Europe's Data Regulators' *Financial Times* (London, 28 April 2015) <www.ft.com/content/99eea7a2-e282-11e4-aa1d-00144feab7de> accessed 7 March 2017.
[30] ibid.

[5–17]   The ODPC meets and works with the other supervisory authorities through the mechanism of the Article 29 Working Party established by the Data Protection Directive. The Article 29 Working Party has been very influential in the development and interpretation of data protection law across Europe – particularly as regards the uniform interpretation of rules and the response to new technologies. The European Data Protection Board (EDPB) will replace the Article 29 Working Party under the GDPR. The powers and duties of domestic supervisory authorities are discussed further later in this chapter. For now, it is important to note that Data Subjects have the right to complain to the ODPC if they believe that their data protection rights have been infringed and the ODPC has a duty to investigate such complaints.[31] The ODPC maintains a useful website at www.dataprotection.ie.

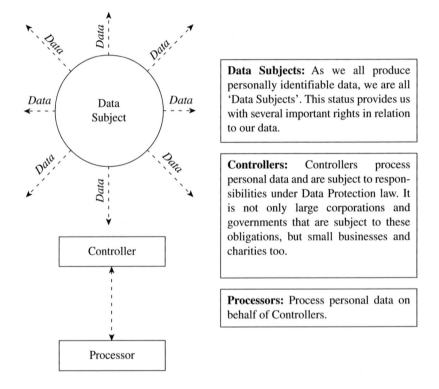

Data Subjects: As we all produce personally identifiable data, we are all 'Data Subjects'. This status provides us with several important rights in relation to our data.

Controllers: Controllers process personal data and are subject to responsibilities under Data Protection law. It is not only large corporations and governments that are subject to these obligations, but small businesses and charities too.

Processors: Process personal data on behalf of Controllers.

Figure 2   *Key Players in Data Protection Law.*

---

[31] Unless the complaint is frivolous or vexatious: Data Protection Acts 1988 and 2003, s 10. This was the view originally taken by the previous Data Protection Commissioner in relation to some or all of Max Schrems original complaints. The Court of Justice took a different view. The subsequent case (pursued following the decision of the Data Protection Commissioner) is discussed at [5–64] *Schrems v Data Protection Commissioner* [2014] IEHC 310.

Duties of Controllers

As mentioned earlier, the GDPR asserts that the 'objectives and principles of Directive 95/46/   **[5–18]**
EC remain sound'.[32] As a result, it is not surprising that the GDPR operates in a similar manner
to the 1995 Directive. Like the Data Protection Directive, the GDPR distinguishes between the
processing of sensitive data (or 'special categories of personal data') and non-sensitive data.[33]

Sensitive data includes
genetic and biometric data
and data concerning:

- Health
- Racial or ethnic origin
- Political opinions
- Religious or philosophical
  beliefs
- Trade union membership
- A person's sex life or
  sexual orientation

Figure 3   *Categories of Sensitive Data.*

Even though Article 9(1) states that the processing of such data is prohibited, the exceptions   **[5–19]**
detailed in paragraph 2 of that Article clarify that the prohibition is not nearly as broad as
it may first appear. In fact, the GDPR permits the processing of sensitive personal data in
a wide range of situations.[34] While it is important to be aware of the types of data that are
considered sensitive and what restrictions are imposed on the processing of such data, this

---

[32] GDPR, recital 9.

[33] See GDPR, arts 9 and 10.

[34] The circumstances in which the processing of sensitive personal data is permitted can be sum-
marised as where: (a) the Data Subject has given explicit consent to the processing of their personal
data; (b) processing is necessary for the purposes of employment, social security and social protection law in so far as it is authorised by law; (c) processing is necessary to protect the vital interests
of the Data Subject or of another natural person where the Data Subject is physically or legally
incapable of giving consent; (d) processing is carried out in the course of its legitimate activities
with appropriate safeguards by a not-for-profit body with a political, philosophical, religious or trade
union aim and on condition that the processing relates solely to the members of the body; (e) processing relates to personal data which are manifestly made public by the Data Subject; (f) processing
is necessary for the establishment, exercise or defence of legal claims; (g) processing is necessary
for reasons of substantial public interest which is proportionate to the aim pursued and safeguards
the rights of the Data Subject; (h) processing is necessary for the purposes of preventive or occu-
pational medicine; (i) processing is necessary for reasons of public interest in the area of public
health; (j) processing is necessary for archiving purposes in the public interest, scientific or historical
research purposes or statistical purposes in accordance with Article 89(1) GDPR. It is important to
note that this is a summary of the circumstances and the text of the GDPR should be referred to for

chapter provides more detail on the general criteria that apply to the processing of non-sensitive personal data.[35]

[5–20]   In order to process non-sensitive personal data, a Controller must meet two primary requirements. First, the Controller must identify an adequate legal basis for the processing, and second, the Controller must act in accordance with the data protection principles at all times. Related to the Controller's obligations to process personal data in accordance with the data protection principles is the obligation on Controllers to respect the rights of Data Subjects.

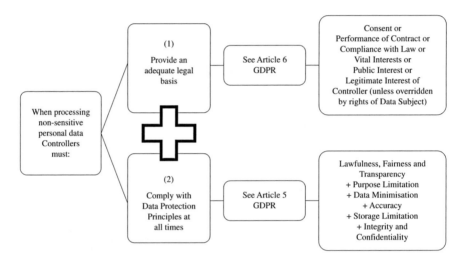

Figure 4   *Obligations of Controller.*

[5–21]   Controllers may only 'process' 'personal data' where it is done with a lawful legal basis. Due to its broad definition, virtually any use of personal data – including collection, erasure, and even anonymisation – will constitute 'processing' under the GDPR.[36]

---

more detail. For example, these legal bases often require grounding in EU or domestic law and must be proportionate to the rights of Data Subjects. See GDPR, art 9.

[35] It has been argued that the singling out of special categories of personal data is no longer meaningful. Moerel and Prins posit that 'with the advent of new analytical techniques, the debate about which categories of data are or are not sensitive is becoming increasingly irrelevant. (…) [I]t is the context in which data are used that is sensitive, more than the data themselves.'. Lokke Moerel and Corien Prins, 'Privacy for the Homo Digitalis: Proposal for a New Regulatory Framework for Data Protection in the Light of Big Data and the Internet of Things' (2016) Tilburg Institute for Law, Technology, and Society <www.papers.ssrn.com/abstract=2784123> accessed 7 March 2017, 11, 57.

[36] The GDPR defines 'processing' as 'any operation or set of operations which is performed on personal data or on sets of personal data, whether or not by automated means, such as collection, recording, organisation, structuring, storage, adaptation or alteration, retrieval, consultation, use, disclosure

Article 6 GDPR states that processing will only be lawful if one of the following conditions [5–22] applies:

(a) the data subject has given consent to the processing of his or her personal data for one or more specific purposes;

(b) processing is necessary for the performance of a contract to which the data subject is party or in order to take steps at the request of the data subject prior to entering into a contract;

(c) processing is necessary for compliance with a legal obligation to which the controller is subject;

(d) processing is necessary in order to protect the vital interests of the data subject or of another natural person;

(e) processing is necessary for the performance of a task carried out in the public interest or in the exercise of official authority vested in the controller;

(f) processing is necessary for the purposes of the legitimate interests pursued by the controller or by a third party, except where such interests are overridden by the interests or fundamental rights and freedoms of the data subject which require protection of personal data, in particular where the data subject is a child.

Crucially, only one of these legal bases needs to be present in order to constitute an adequate legal basis.

While consent is not the only legal basis for lawful data processing, it is frequently relied [5–23] upon by Controllers. The granting of consent will often involve reading and agreeing to a privacy policy or terms and conditions. The GDPR places significant limitations on consent as a legal basis that Controllers need to be mindful of when relying on it. Controllers will need to demonstrate that consent was specific, informed, and freely given and that it was unambiguously obtained on the basis of a statement or clear affirmative action.[37] Narrowing this further, consent may not be considered 'freely given' where consent is a precondition for the provision of a service that is not necessary for the performance of that contract.[38] Moreover, Data Subjects have the right to withdraw consent at any time.[39] In recognition of concerns about child privacy online, those offering information society services directly to children must obtain consent from legal guardians.[40]

Obtaining meaningful consent can be a particular challenge in the modern world. Not [5–24] only do consumers value a 'seamless' experience when using applications and browsing the internet, but with the growing 'internet of everything', many daily interactions and activities are monitored by a multitude of interconnected devices and ubiquitous computing. The embeddedness of these technologies challenges the obtaining of consent.

---

by transmission, dissemination or otherwise making available, alignment or combination, restriction, erasure or destruction': GDPR, art 4(2).

[37] GDPR, art 4(11); GDPR, recital 32; GDPR, art 7.

[38] GDPR, recital 32; GDPR, art 7.

[39] GDPR, art 7(3).

[40] The Regulation accepts that consent is a valid legal ground for the processing of the personal data of a child where the child is at least 16 years old. The GDPR also allows Member States to legislate for a lower age not below 13 years: GDPR, art 8.

With the GDPR requiring that consent be as easy to take away as it is to give, the option to renounce certain consents from an 'Internet of Things' smart device may be a more 'theoretical concept than a real alternative'.[41] While technological solutions – such as the 'tagging' of personal data with metadata describing the relevant consents – can be beneficial, the difficulty of obtaining 'meaningful consent' is likely to remain a significant challenge for all those operating an information-driven business. In fact, some have argued that consent should be abandoned as a basis for legal processing and a 'responsible use framework' should be adopted instead.[42]

In addition to providing an adequate legal basis for the processing of non-sensitive personal data, Controllers must also abide by the 'Data Protection Principles', which state that data must be

(a) processed lawfully, fairly and in a transparent manner in relation to the data subject

(b) collected for specified, explicit and legitimate purposes and not further processed in a manner that is incompatible with those purposes;

(c) adequate, relevant and limited to what is necessary in relation to the purposes for which they are processed

(d) accurate and, where necessary, kept up to date; every reasonable step must be taken to ensure that personal data that are inaccurate, having regard to the purposes for which they are processed, are erased or rectified without delay

(e) kept in a form which permits identification of data subjects for no longer than is necessary for the purposes for which the personal data are processed;

(f) processed in a manner that ensures appropriate security of the personal data, including protection against unauthorised or unlawful processing and against accidental loss, destruction or damage, using appropriate technical or organisational measures.[43]

[5–25] It is important to note that the data protection principles are interlinked. Notably, purpose limitation (discussed below) has been described as 'a prerequisite for applying other data quality requirements'.[44] Furthermore, the purpose limitation requirement is supported by the transparent processing principle. Crucially, if a Controller wishes to process the data for a separate purpose, the Controller must communicate with the Data Subject first and provide all necessary information.[45] In spite of the interconnection of the principles, it is beneficial to consider each of the requirements in turn.

---

[41] Article 29 Working Party Opinion 8/2014 on the on Recent Developments on the Internet of Things Adopted on 16 September 2014 14/EN WP 223, 7.

[42] Executive Office of the President, 'Big Data: Seizing Opportunities, Preserving Values' (2014) White House <www.whitehouse.gov/sites/default/files/docs/big_data_privacy_report_may_1_2014.pdf> accessed 7 March 2017, 56; Lilian Edwards, 'Privacy, Security and Data Protection in Smart Cities: A Critical EU Law Perspective' (2016) 2(1) European Data Protection Law Review 28.

[43] GDPR, art 5.

[44] Article 29 Working Party Opinion 03/2013 on Purpose Limitation Adopted on 2 April 2013 00569/13/EN WP 203.

[45] GDPR, recital 61.

'Transparent Processing': Data Must Be Processed Fairly and Transparently

In accordance with the principle of transparency, Data Subjects should be provided with several pieces of information, including: [5–26]

- the identity of the Controller;
- the purposes of the processing;
- notice of the risks, rules, safeguards, and rights relevant to the processing of personal data;
- how to exercise the relevant rights.

Where the personal data is collected directly from the Data Subject, this information should be provided at the point of collection and the Controller should also communicate whether or not the Data Subject is obliged to provide the data and what the consequences are of not providing the data. This information should be easily accessible and communicated through clear and plain language.[46] The GDPR suggests that the use of standardised icons may be beneficial in some circumstances.[47] Where the information is collected from a source other than the Data Subject, the subject should be informed of the processing within a reasonable period.[48] [5–27]

'Purpose Limitation': Data Must Be Collected for Specified, Explicit and Legitimate Purposes

Once data is collected for a specific purpose, it should not be processed for purposes incompatible with that original purpose. The purpose limitation principle is an essential feature of European data protection law yet some have criticised the principle as unworkable due to the unpredictability of much modern data use. Indeed, purpose limitation has been described as 'antithetical to the rationale of big data and the functioning of data markets which seek to hoard data in case they have possible future value'.[49] In spite of this, the importance of transparency and informational self-determination mean that Controllers should not process personal data for additional purposes unless the processing is compatible with the purposes for which the data was initially collected.[50] [5–28]

---

[46] GDPR, recitals 60, 39, 58.

[47] GDPR, recital 60.

[48] In such cases, the Controller should inform the Data Subject of the origin of the information and, where that cannot be provided (for example, where various sources have been used), general information should be provided: GDPR, recital 61. Recital 62 clarifies, however, that it is not always necessary to inform Data Subjects in all circumstances. For example, where a Data Subject already possesses the information or where the provision of information would involve a disproportionate effort. The processing of information for archiving purposes in the public interest is presented as a possible example of a situation where the information requirement would be disproportionate. When making this assessment, a Controller should consider the number of Data Subjects, the age of the data and any appropriate safeguards.

[49] Rob Kitchin, *The Data Revolution: Big Data, Open Data, Data Infrastructures and their Consequences* (Sage 2014) 178; Viktor Mayer-Schonberger and Kenneth Cukier, *Big Data: A Revolution That Will Transform How We Live, Work, and Think* (John Murray 2013) 15.

[50] GDPR, recital 50.

[5–29] If interested in how the principle of purpose specification may be applied in practice, it is worth exploring the Data Protection Commissioner's website where there is an archive of case studies.[51] While these case studies concern the application of the Data Protection Acts, they can provide a useful indication of how these data protection issues can be reasoned out in practice. An interesting example of a Controller using data for incompatible purposes is provided by Case Study 8/99 where a telecommunications company published its subscriber database in electronic format in addition to the established paper format.[52] The Data Protection Commissioner considered two key questions:

1. Was publication of the telephone directory in electronic format (in addition to the traditional publication in paper format) an incompatible purpose?
2. Was the availability of new search capabilities in the electronic version an incompatible purpose?[53]

[5–30] The Data Protection Commissioner set out a useful question to ask when determining whether a purpose is compatible with the purpose for which the data was originally obtained: 'What would a Data Subject have reasonably expected to happen to his or her data at the time the data were obtained?' The DPC concluded that making the information available in electronic format was not an incompatible purpose where appropriate safeguards were in place. In contrast, however, the DPC concluded that the novel capabilities associated with electronic publication did raise questions of compatibility. Specifically, the new capability to look up telephone numbers without entering a name but on the basis of address was deemed incompatible. The company agreed to modify the electronic version of its directory.

[5–31] In 2013, the Article 29 Working Party adopted an Opinion on purpose limitation that provides further examples of how the principle is applied in practice.[54] The Opinion also provides guidance on the key factors to be considered when determining compatibility with the original purpose.[55] These factors are closely reflected in Recital 50 of the GDPR, which directs those assessing whether a further purpose is compatible with the original purpose to consider:

- the context in which the data was collected and the reasonable expectations of the Data Subjects at the time of collection;
- the nature of the personal data;
- the consequences of the further processing;
- whether there is any link between the new and original purposes; and
- the existence of appropriate safeguards.[56]

---

[51] <www.dataprotection.ie/docs/Case-Studies/> accessed 7 March 2017.

[52] Initially on a CD-ROM and subsequently on the internet.

[53] In assessing the case, the Office of the Data Protection Commissioner applied s 2(1)(c)(ii) of the Data Protection Act.

[54] Article 29 Working Party Opinion 03/2013 on Purpose Limitation Adopted on 2 April 2013 00569/13/EN WP 203.

[55] Article 29 Working Party Opinion 03/2013 on Purpose Limitation Adopted on 2 April 2013 00569/13/EN WP 203, 23–36.

[56] GDPR, recital 50. Recital 50 states that 'further processing for archiving purposes in the public interest, scientific or historical research purposes or statistical purposes should be considered to be compatible lawful processing operations'.

Exceptions to the purpose specification limitation exist where the processing is necessary for the performance of a task carried out in the public interest or in the exercise of official authority vested in the Controller.[57]

'Minimisation Requirement': Data Must Be Adequate, Relevant and Limited

The collection of personal data should be limited to what is 'adequate, relevant and limited to what is necessary for the purposes for which they are processed'.[58] The principle requires Controllers to consider – at the point of collection – what data is actually required in order to pursue the legitimate purposes.[59] It is not acceptable to simply vacuum up all available data and to figure out what to do with it at a later date. As the collection of personal information increases, data protection risks – from information breaches to data misuse – rise. As a result, the consideration of the minimisation requirement from the outset is essential for the protection of personal data.   [5–32]

Like the purpose limitation requirement, the data minimisation requirement creates difficulties for big data business models. While there are technical and organisational solutions that can facilitate data minimisation, such solutions do inevitably result in the collection and storing of less data. While this is a positive from a privacy perspective, big data advocates speak forcefully about the cumulative potential of mass data collection and the unforeseen benefits of drawing new connections and developing unpredicted uses from data sets. It seems clear that we are at a turning point on this issue, where the great – but unproven – promise of big data appears to be in conflict with increased interest in data protection.   [5–33]

'Accuracy Requirement': Data Must Be Accurate and Up-To-Date

Data Controllers must take every reasonable step to ensure that personal data is accurate and up to date. This obligation is closely tied with the Data Subject's right to have inaccurate data rectified and, in certain circumstances, even erased.[60] To facilitate these rights, Controllers must provide 'modalities' to facilitate the exercise of these rights.[61] Accordingly, Data Subjects should have access to mechanisms to request the rectification or erasure of personal data.   [5–34]

'Storage Limitation': Data Must Be Identifiable for No Longer than is Necessary

The storage limitation further supports the purpose limitation and data minimisation principles by prohibiting the storing of personal data once storage is no longer necessary for the purposes for which the personal data was processed. With reduced data storage costs and the availability of Cloud storage, some Controllers may determine that it would be more cost effective to store all data rather than spend time and resources reviewing and deleting unnecessary data. The storage limitation principle works against such reasoning and states that personal data should only be stored for the period of time required to achieve the   [5–35]

---

[57] GDPR, recital 50.
[58] GDPR, recital 39.
[59] GDPR, recital 39.
[60] GDPR, arts 16 and 17.
[61] GDPR, recital 59.

legitimate purpose.[62] As with all the data protection principles, Controllers must consider the data protection implications at all stages of the data life cycle. In addition to applying the data minimisation principle at the point of collection, Controllers should have procedures for the periodic review of data and should establish time limits for the erasure of unnecessary data.[63]

[5–36] While Article 5 of the GDPR states that the principle applies only where personal data is 'kept in a form which permits identification of Data Subjects', there is some ongoing confusion about data identifiability. Limiting the application of the storage limitation to data 'which permits identification' appears redundant as the very definition of personal data is any information relating to an identifiable natural person.[64] It is possible that this language was chosen to acknowledge the potential role for anonymisation in the pursuit of data protection compliance. In principle, anonymised data can be stored indefinitely as it does not constitute 'personal data' for the purposes of the GDPR. It should be noted, however, that with the development of sophisticated data mining techniques and increasing access to multiple databases, it is incredibly difficult to fully anonymise data. Crucially, the GDPR also clarifies that pseudonymised data is still personal data.[65] Pseudonymised data is data that has been processed in such a manner that

> the personal data can no longer be attributed to a specific data subject without the use of additional information, provided that such additional information is kept separately and is subject to technical and organisational measures to ensure that the personal data are not attributed to an identified or identifiable natural person.[66]

[5–37] The application of the storage limitation can be modified where the data will be processed solely for archiving purposes in the public interest, scientific or historical research purposes or statistical purposes. Where data is processed for such purposes, it can be stored for extended periods as long as the appropriate safeguards are provided.[67]

'Integrity Requirement': Data Must Be Stored Securely

[5–38] While information security does not solve all data protection issues, data protection is impossible in the absence of adequate security. The GDPR acknowledges this simple fact by requiring that personal data be processed in a manner 'that ensures appropriate security of the personal data, including protection against unauthorised or unlawful processing and against accidental loss, destruction or damage' using appropriate technical or organisational measures.[68] Due to the connection between the integrity requirement, the principle of 'privacy by design', and other related measures in the GDPR, the final data protection principle is considered in more detail in the following section.

---

[62] GDPR, recital 39.
[63] GDPR, recital 39.
[64] GDPR, art 4(1).
[65] GDPR, recital 26.
[66] GDPR, art 4(5).
[67] See GDPR, art 89.
[68] GDPR, art 5.

'Baking-in' Data Protection

While the effective application of data protection law has always required Controllers to **[5–39]** consider data protection implications at all stages of data processing, the GDPR provides more explicit direction on what is required at each stage of the data flow. A key way in which the GDPR attempts to encourage the 'building-in' of data protection compliance is through the 'Data protection by design and by default' mandate contained in Article 25 GDPR. The first paragraph of that Article requires Controllers to implement appropriate technical and organisational measures which are designed to implement data protection principles in an effective manner and to integrate the necessary safeguards into data processing. Crucially, Controllers are required to do this 'both at the time of the determination of the means for processing and at the time of the processing itself'. Moreover, Controllers are required to implement measures to ensure that 'by default' only the personal data that is necessary to achieve the designated legal purpose is processed.

Once the Controller has evaluated the risks of the processing, the Controller must imple- **[5–40]** ment measures to mitigate those risks. One measure suggested by the GDPR is the use of encryption.[69] While the GDPR places significance emphasis on the importance of security measures, the Regulation attempts to avoid imposing unfeasible requirements by permitting Controllers to take the state of the art and the costs of implementation of security measures into account. When assessing the level of risk, Controllers must consider the data protection risks, with particular consideration of the risks which may cause physical, material, or non-material damage.[70]

These are not entirely new requirements and the Article clearly builds on the Article 17 **[5–41]** Data Protection Directive requirement to adopt appropriate technical and organisational data security measures.[71] The GDPR's increased emphasis on embedded technological and organisational solutions takes inspiration from the principles of 'privacy by design' which encourage the adoption of a 'privacy by design mindset' and the consideration of privacy issues from the outset.[72] Reflecting this approach, Recital 78 GDPR encourages

---

[69] GDPR, recital 83.

[70] GDPR, recital 83.

[71] Ian Brown, 'Britain's Smart Meter Programme: A Case Study in Privacy by Design' (2014) International Review of Law, Computers & Technology 176. Note in contrast that there was significant controversy in relation to various Irish Water issues, which included data protection. Initially, there was not even a Data Protection Officer appointed within Irish Water when these issues were raised. Maria Helen Murphy, 'The Introduction of Smart Meters in Ireland: Privacy Implications and the Role of Privacy by Design' (2015) 38(1) Dublin University Law Journal 191.

[72] Ann Cavoukian, 'Privacy by Design' (2009) Information and Privacy Commissioner <www.ipc. on.ca/images/resources/privacybydesign.pdf> accessed 7 March 2017. A key principle of privacy by design is 'full functionality – positive-sum, not zero-sum'. According to the '7 Foundational Principles', Privacy by Design 'seeks to accommodate all legitimate interests and objectives in a positive-sum "win-win" manner, not through a dated, zero-sum approach, where unnecessary trade-offs are made. Privacy by Design avoids the pretence of false dichotomies, such as privacy vs security, demonstrating that it is possible to have both': Ann Cavoukian, 'The 7 Foundational Principles' (2009) Information and Privacy Commissioner <www.ipc.on.ca/images/Resources/7foundationalprinciples.pdf> accessed 7 March 2017. Also see "Chapter 32 Privacy by Design" in Paul Lambert, *Social Networking, Law, Rights and Policy* (Clarus Press 2014) 471–483.

those involved in the development of products and services that process personal data to 'take into account the right to data protection when developing and designing' such products and services. The GDPR goes beyond simple aspiration and requires Controllers to be able to demonstrate compliance by adopting internal policies and implementing measures designed to meet the principles of data protection by design and by default. The GDPR suggests the minimisation of data processing and the use of pseudonymisation as two examples of privacy enhancing measures.[73]

[5–42]   In further recognition of building data protection compliance in from the outset, Article 35 GDPR mandates the carrying out of 'data protection impact assessments' where processing 'is likely to result in a high risk to the rights and freedoms of natural persons'. An impact assessment evaluates the origin, nature, and severity of any data protection risk. The conclusions of the assessment must inform the selection of compliance measures.[74]

[5–43]   The GDPR recognises the risk of unintended consequences and indicates that data protection impact assessments will be particularly important where new technologies are being introduced.[75] The Regulation provides a non-exhaustive list of situations which will require the completion of an impact assessment.[76] For example, an impact assessment will be required where profiling is used to make decisions that have legal – or similarly significant – effects on a Data Subject.[77]

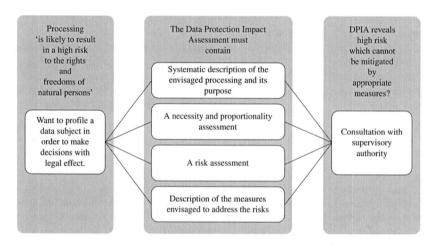

Figure 5   *Data Protection Impact Assessment.*

---

[73] GDPR, recital 78.
[74] GDPR, recital 84.
[75] GDPR, art 35(1).
[76] GDPR, art 35(3).
[77] GDPR, art 35(3)(a).

While a Data Protection Impact Assessment will be a mandatory requirement in many instances, it also offers benefits to Controllers as a useful tool – not just for compliance – but for data governance.   [5–44]

Tied to the emphasis placed on information security is the new requirement for Controllers to report any data breach to their domestic supervisory authority 'without undue delay and, where feasible, not later than 72 hours after having become aware of it'.[78] A notable limitation of this requirement, however, is that the notification duty can be discharged where the Controller is able to demonstrate that the data breach is 'unlikely to result in a risk to the rights and freedoms of natural persons'.[79] It is likely that Controllers may attempt to avoid notification where the relevant data has been pseudonymised. For example, if the key that would enable the data to be reidentified was not part of the breach and remains secure, there is an argument that there is minimal risk to the rights of Data Subjects. While a conscientious Controller is likely to take a precautionary approach and still notify the relevant supervisory authority, such a Controller will have a legitimate case against notifying Data Subjects due to the reduced privacy risk associated with pseudonymised data.[80] With increased public awareness of data protection issues, data breaches can result in significant loss of trust and customer confidence. As a result, the provisions on data breach notification further underscore the necessity of robust data security.   [5–45]

Exemptions from Data Protection Law and the Household Exemption

It is important to note that certain activities fall outside the scope of the GDPR. The Regulation does not apply to the processing of personal data   [5–46]

- in the course of an activity which falls outside the scope of Union law;
- Conducted by Member States when carrying out activities which fall within the scope of Chapter 2 of Title V of the TEU;[81]
- by a natural person as part of a 'purely personal or household activity';[82]
- conducted by Member States for the purpose of the prevention, investigation, detection or prosecution of criminal offences or the execution of criminal penalties.

---

[78] GDPR, art 33. While the data breach notification requirement is a new addition in the general data protection sphere, see the notification requirements under Directive 2009/136/EC of the European Parliament and of the Council of 25 November 2009 amending Directive 2002/22/EC on universal service and users' rights relating to electronic communications networks and services, Directive 2002/58/EC concerning the processing of personal data and the protection of privacy in the electronic communications sector and Regulation (EC) No 2006/2004 on cooperation between national authorities responsible for the enforcement of consumer protection laws (Text with EEA relevance). Please also note the Code of Practice approved by the ODPC in 2011. Data Protection Commissioner, 'Personal Data Security Breach Code of Practice' (*dataprotection.ie*, 29 July 2011) <https://www.dataprotection.ie/docs/Data_Security_Breach_Code_of_Practice/1082.htm> accessed 7 March 2017.

[79] See also GDPR, recital 85.

[80] Article 34 states that Data Subjects need not be notified if 'appropriate technical and organisational protection measures' have been implemented that 'render the personal data unintelligible to any person who is not authorised to access it': GDPR, art 34(3); GDPR, art 34(1)(4).

[81] Concerning the EU's common foreign and security policy.

[82] Please note that Regulation (EC) No 45/2001 applies to 'the processing of personal data by the Union institutions, bodies, offices and agencies' but that No 45/2001 will be adapted to the principles and rules of the GDPR: GDPR, art 2(3). Moreover, the GDPR shall be without prejudice to the application of Directive 2000/31/EC, in particular of the liability rules of intermediary service providers in Articles 12 to 15 of that Directive: GDPR, art 2(4).

[5–47]   The household activity exemption which states that the Regulation does not apply to the processing of personal data 'by a natural person in the course of a purely personal or household activity' is particularly interesting.[83] While even micro-businesses are subject to the requirements of data protection law, the GDPR continues with the position that certain types of small-scale processing should be excluded from the scope of the Regulation. While this exemption may, at first glance, suggest that private individuals are free to process data without regard to data protection law, the CJEU has interpreted the exemption narrowly.[84]

[5–48]   *Bodil Lindqvist* is a notable decision of the CJEU in the data protection context.[85] Lindqvist was a volunteer at a church and had posted personal data concerning her church colleagues on a website. The Swedish Data Protection Authority fined Lindqvist and the appeal court referred a question to the CJEU. The CJEU found that the exception for processing carried out by a natural person 'in the exercise of activities which are exclusively personal or domestic' could not apply to the situation where the personal data is published 'on the internet so that those data are made accessible to an indefinite number of people'.[86]

[5–49]   While the case of *Bodil Lindqvist* clarified that a private individual posting personal information on the internet constitutes processing under European data protection law, the manner in which individuals share on the internet changed remarkably in subsequent years. The year that the case was decided – 2003 – also happened to be the year that the social networking service, *myspace*, was founded. *Facebook* came in 2004, followed by *Bebo* in 2005, *Twitter* in 2006, and *Instagram* in 2010. Many other social networks have been created and currently it is *Snapchat* that appears to best represent the zeitgeist. The role of personal website services – such as the now defunct *GeoCities* – in the publication of personal information online has been supplanted in large part by social networking services. This raises interesting questions about whether data protection law applies to your Facebook page and whether posting photographs of your friends on your personal page constitutes processing.

[5–50]   The GDPR appears to address this modern conundrum in Recital 18 where it is clarified that the Regulation does not apply to

> the processing of personal data by a natural person in the course of a purely personal or household activity and thus with no connection to a professional or commercial activity. *Personal or household activities could include* correspondence and the holding of addresses, or *social networking and online activity undertaken within the context of such activities.* However, this Regulation applies to Controllers or processors which provide the means for processing personal data for such personal or household activities (emphasis added).

---

[83] GDPR, art 2(2)(c). This mirrors Article 3(2) of Directive 95/46/EC.
[84] The household exemption under the GDPR is similar to the exemption provided for in the Data Protection Directive: see Directive 95/46/EC, art 3(2).
[85] Case C-101/01 *Bodil Lindqvist* ECLI:EU:C:2003:596.
[86] Case C-101/01 *Bodil Lindqvist* ECLI:EU:C:2003:596, 46–48.

Clearly the GDPR considers certain types of social network use to fall within the house-   **[5–51]**
hold exception.[87] The specific mentioning of social networking should not, however, be
interpreted as excusing all social network use from the scope of data protection law.
Crucially, the recital also requires the processing to be conducted in 'purely personal or
household' context and without any 'connection to a professional or commercial activity'. This clarification could have implications for the growing band of social media
'influencers' that are such prominent users of social networking services. As pointed out
by the Article 29 Working Party in a 2009 report, there has been a 'shift from "Web 2.0
for fun" to Web 2.0 for productivity and services where the activities of some SNS users
may extend beyond a purely personal or household activity'. According to the Article 29
Working Party, if an individual uses a social network 'mainly as a platform to advance
commercial, political or charitable goals, the exception does not apply'.[88] If anything,
this trend has accelerated since 2009 and it is now commonplace for many individuals
to blend the personal with the professional on their social media accounts. Accordingly,
a rather large cohort of social media users may find their activities subject to the rules of
the GDPR, and the interpretation of the CJEU of 'purely personal or household' will be
important.

Assuming the CJEU will continue with the interpretation of 'purely' that it adopted when   **[5–52]**
considering the use of the term in the context of the Directive, the breadth of the household
exemption is much narrower than a cursory reading would suggest. In *František Ryneš v
Úřad pro ochranu osobních údajů*,[89] the CJEU construed the household exemption rigidly.
Even though Ryneš had installed CCTV cameras primarily to protect his home and family,
the fact that the cameras also captured footage of a public space meant that the processing could not be considered to have been conducted for a 'purely personal or household
activity'. This strict interpretation has clear implications for the many recording devices
that have proliferated in recent years – from wearable devices like *Go-Pro* cameras and
Google Glass to dashboard cameras and camera-enabled drones. The fact that the use of
such devices in public places is unlikely to benefit from the household exemption does not,
of course, mean that such devices cannot be used in a compliant manner in accordance with
data protection principles.

While the GDPR should bring increased uniformity across Europe on matters of data   **[5–53]**
protection, the Regulation retains the possibility for Member States to avail of additional
derogations. These can apply with regard to restricting data protection rights and obligations[90] and with regard to 'specific processing situations'.[91] It is important to note, however, that Member States can only introduce derogations from data protection obligations
and rights where the measure is introduced 'by way of a legislative measure' and 'respects

---

[87] While also clarifying that this does not influence the data protection obligations of the social networks themselves.
[88] Article 29 Data Protection Working Party Opinion 5/2009 on Online Social Networking Adopted on
12 June 2009 01189/09/EN WP 163, 6.
[89] C-212/13 *František Ryneš v Úřad pro ochranu osobních údajů* ECLI:EU:C:2014:2428.
[90] GDPR, art 23.
[91] GDPR, arts 85–91.

the essence of the fundamental rights and freedoms'. Domestic derogations may be valid where the derogation is a necessary and proportionate measure needed to safeguard one of the following interests:

    (a) national security;

    (b) defence;

    (c) public security;

    (d) the prevention, investigation, detection or prosecution of criminal offences or the execution of criminal penalties, including the safeguarding against and the prevention of threats to public security;

    (e) other important objectives of general public interest of the Union or of a Member State, in particular an important economic or financial interest of the Union or of a Member State, including monetary, budgetary and taxation matters, public health and social security;

    (f) the protection of judicial independence and judicial proceedings;

    (g) the prevention, investigation, detection and prosecution of breaches of ethics for regulated professions;

    (h) a monitoring, inspection or regulatory function connected, even occasionally, to the exercise of official authority in the cases referred to in points (a) to (e) and (g);

    (i) the protection of the data subject or the rights and freedoms of others;

    (j) the enforcement of civil law claims.[92]

[5–54]   Furthermore, Chapter IX of the GDPR describes specific data processing situations where additional derogations and exemptions are possible at the domestic level. Crucially, Article 85 mandates that Member States provide for exemptions from many data protection duties where exemptions are necessary to reconcile the right to the protection of personal data with the freedom of expression and information. Chapter IX also allows for domestic modifications of data protection obligations in the context of:

– public access to official documents;

– national identification numbers;

– employee data;

– scientific and historical research purposes or statistical purposes;

– obligations of secrecy;

– churches and religious associations.

Of course, Member States can only implement additional restrictions in certain circumstances and various conditions and safeguards will still apply. Those interested in the specific provisions should examine Chapter IX GDPR in more detail.

---

[92] GDPR, art 23(1).

Rights of the Data Subject

In addition to imposing obligations on Controllers to process data in accordance with the   **[5–55]**
data protection principles and only with an adequate legal basis, the GDPR also confers
specific data protection rights on Data Subjects. Across ten Articles of the GDPR,[93] the
rights contained in the 1995 Directive are reiterated; new rights – such as the right to data
portability – are provided for; and the 'right to erasure', more commonly known as the
'right to be forgotten', is explicitly acknowledged. The table below summarises the various
Data Subject rights that are provided for in the Regulation.

Data Subject Rights

Right to Transparency (Article 12 GDPR)	Information and communications to Data Subjects must be concise, transparent, intelligible, and in an easily accessible form. Communications should be written using clear and plain language, in particular where the information is addressed to children.
Right to Information (Article 13 GDPR)	At the time when personal data is obtained, the Controller must provide a variety of information, including: the identity and contact details of the Controller; the purposes and legal basis of the processing; any recipients of the personal data; whether the data will be transferred to a third country; and the period for which the personal data will be stored. The Controller must also inform the Data Subject about their data protection rights.[94]
Access Rights[95] (Article 15 GDPR)	Data Subjects have a right to obtain confirmation as to whether personal data concerning him or her is being processed and, if so, for what purpose and in what manner. Moreover, Controllers must provide a copy of the personal data undergoing processing where requested. This information must be provided without undue delay and in any event within one month.[96]
Right to Rectification, Erasure, and Restriction (Articles 16, 17, 18, 19 GDPR)	Controllers must rectify inaccurate personal data without undue delay. Data Subjects are entitled to erasure of their data in a number of circumstances including where it is not necessary in relation to the purposes for which it was collected and where the data was unlawfully processed. Controllers must also take reasonable steps to communicate rectifications/erasures/restrictions to relevant third parties. Erasure rights are limited in certain circumstances, eg where the interest is outweighed by free expression considerations.

---

[93] From GDPR, arts 12-22.

[94] See GDPR, art 14 for rules governing situations where the personal data have not been obtained from the Data Subject.

[95] In a significant change, the GDPR now requires Controllers to provide a copy of personal data undergoing processing where requested free of charge where the Directive had permitted the imposition of a nominal charge at the domestic level. The GDPR retains the entitlement for Controllers to charge for further copies of such information where reasonably based on administrative costs.

[96] Article 12 states that the one-month period applies in a number of circumstances. Controllers must respond to information requests under Articles 15 to 22 'without undue delay and in any event within one month of receipt of the request'. That period, however, may be extended by two further months where necessary but the Data Subject must be informed of the reasons for the delay. Where the request is made via electronic means, the information shall be provided by electronic means where possible, unless otherwise requested.

Right to Data Portability (Article 20 GDPR)	Entitles Data Subjects to receive their personal data in a structured, commonly used and machine-readable format and to have the right to transmit their data to another Controller without hindrance where technically feasible. The right does not apply where the processing was necessary for the performance of a task carried out in the public interest or in the exercise of official authority vested in the Controller and should not adversely affect the rights and freedoms of others.
Right to Object (Article 21 GDPR)	Data Subjects have the right to object to processing and, if certain circumstances exist, Controllers must cease processing the data unless they can demonstrate compelling legitimate grounds for the processing which override the rights and interests of the Data Subject. The right to object is absolute in the direct marketing context.
Right to not be Subject to Solely Automated Decision Making (Article 22 GDPR)	Data Subjects have the right to not be subject to decisions based solely on automated processing that have legal or similarly significantly effects on him or her, eg profiling. However, this right will not apply in a number of circumstances, including where the decision is necessary for a contract between the Data Subject and Controller and where the subject gives explicit consent. Controllers using such techniques must take suitable measures to safeguard Data Subject rights and interests.

Figure 6   Data Subject Rights.

[5–56]   The above table summarises the various rights, but it is a worthwhile exercise to read the various Articles to pick apart the nuance. As the CJEU has been crucial in determining the scope of Data Subject rights under the Data Protection Directive, it is likely to play an essential role interpreting the rights provided for by the GDPR also. As a result, it will be necessary to watch for developments in the CJEU jurisprudence over the coming years.

Role of the Data Protection Commissioner

[5–57]   As mentioned above, EU Data Protection law provides for the establishment of a domestic supervisory authority in each Member State.[97] The GDPR describes the extensive powers and duties of these independent authorities in Chapter VI of the Regulation. Some of the key duties of the domestic supervisory authorities include the requirement to:

– monitor and enforce the application of the GDPR;
– promote public awareness of data protection rules;
– advise national authorities on measures concerning data protection;
– investigate data protection complaints and inform the complainant of the progress and the outcome of the investigation within a reasonable period;
– cooperate with, including sharing information and provide mutual assistance to, other supervisory authorities with a view to ensuring the consistency of application and enforcement of the GDPR;
– adopt standard contractual clauses and approve binding corporate rules;

---

[97] Charter of Fundamental Rights of the European Union, art 8; Charter of Fundamental Rights of the European Union, art 51(1).

- establish and maintain a list in relation to the requirement for data protection impact assessments;
- give advice regarding processing operations that pose a high data protection risk.[98]

In order to be meaningful, these duties must be backed up by the appropriate authority to investigate and enforce. The strengthening of the domestic supervisory authorities is a central plank of the GDPR reforms. The core investigative powers include the authority to **[5–58]**

- order the provision of any information it requires for the performance of its tasks;
- carry out data protection audits;
- obtain access to relevant premises.

The core corrective powers include the right to **[5–59]**

- issue reprimands where processing operations have infringed data protection law;
- order a controller or processor to bring processing operations into compliance with the provisions of the GDPR in a specified manner and within a specified period;
- order the rectification or erasure of personal data or restriction of processing;
- impose an administrative fine;
- order the suspension of data flows to a recipient in a third country or to an international organisation.[99]

While the GDPR maintains a similar suite of powers as those set out under the Data Protection Directive,[100] the augmented force behind these powers has been highlighted as a key improvement of the Regulation. Most notable are the increased fines that supervisory authorities have been empowered to issue. The GDPR adopts a two-tiered structure to fining levels. The Regulation allows for the issuing of fines for the most serious breaches of up to €20,000,000 or 4 per cent of the total worldwide annual turnover,[101] whichever is higher.[102] Breaches of the law that do not fall into this category are still subject to far higher fines than previously possible with the GDPR allowing for fines of up to €10,000,000 or up to 2 per cent of annual turnover. Domestic authorities must ensure that the fines are 'effective, proportionate and dissuasive'.[103] The fact that the GDPR allows for the imposition of such significant fines should encourage all Controllers to carefully consider their data protection compliance and should address concerns that data protection law is a 'paper tiger'. The increased focus on fines as a tool of enforcement will be particularly significant in Ireland where the ODPC is not currently empowered to issue fines directly but must take enforcement action through the courts.[104] Of course, domestic supervisory authorities are still likely to take different views regarding the appropriate severity of any specific fine. As a result, consistency of enforcement will remain a challenge. **[5–60]**

---

[98] As concluded by a data protection impact assessment conducted in accordance with Article 35 GDPR. GDPR, art 57.

[99] GDPR, art 58.

[100] With some modifications and notable additions, such as the power to order the communication of a personal data breach to the Data Subject: GDPR, art 58.

[101] Of the preceding financial year.

[102] For more detail on which activities attract which fining maximum refer to Article 83(4)(5)(6) GDPR.

[103] GDPR, art 83(1).

[104] Denis Kelleher, *Privacy and Data Protection Law in Ireland* (Bloomsbury 2015) 344. Paul Lambert, *Data Protection Law in Ireland, Sources and Issues* (Clarus Press, 2016) 139 *et seq.*

[5–61]   From the early discussions of data protection reform, the need for increased uniformity across the EU was considered a major priority. While the Directive left significant discretion to States to implement and integrate data protection law into their domestic regimes as deemed appropriate, the resultant patchwork of laws in an apparently unified system has led to inconsistencies and inefficiencies in application. Increased harmonisation under the GDPR was seen as an important benefit for large companies targeting consumers across the European Union. The cost of compliance with many different regimes was a noted source of discontent and increased uniformity was touted as a benefit that would compensate Controllers for the strengthened data protection regime. A key aspect of early proposals was the introduction of a 'One Stop Shop' (OSS) Mechanism. When OSS was initially proposed, it was expected to allow Controllers to manage all of their EU data protection obligations in one jurisdiction under one domestic authority.[105] In response to concerns that a rigid OSS system would encourage forum shopping and hinder the effective pursuit of a remedy for Data Subjects outside of the chosen jurisdiction, the final text of the GDPR provides for a significantly diluted version of OSS.

[5–62]   To determine the implications of OSS for a particular company, several questions must be answered. It should first be considered whether 'cross-border processing of personal data' is involved.[106] As cross-border processing is defined to include the activities of a single establishment which substantially affects or is likely to substantially affect Data Subjects in more than one Member State, OSS is likely to affect a significant number of companies operating within the EU, especially companies with online operations. Once it has been determined that there is cross-border processing as defined by the GDPR,[107] it is necessary to identify the lead supervisory authority which will have the 'primary responsibility for dealing with a cross-border data processing activity'.[108] The GDPR states that the supervisory authority of the main establishment 'shall be competent to act as lead supervisory authority for the cross-border processing carried out'.[109] Once identified, the lead supervisory authority

---

[105] The CJEU in *Weltimmo* confirmed that data protection authorities do not have the authority under the Data Protection Directive to take coercive action against Controllers where the applicable law is that of another Member State. In spite of this, the CJEU's conclusion that domestic law applies wherever the 'controller exercises, through stable arrangements in the territory of that Member State, a real and effective activity – even a minimal one – in the context of which that processing is carried out' means that many companies – particularly those that operate on the internet – must be mindful of the data protection laws in each jurisdiction they target: Case C-230/14 *Weltimmo sro v Nemzeti Adatvédelmi és Információszabadság Hatóság* ECLI:EU:C:2015:639, 59–60, 66.

[106] Cross-border processing occurs where data is processed in the context of the activities of establishments in more than one Member State in the Union where the Controller and where the data is processed in the context of the activities of a single establishment of a Controller or processor in the Union but which substantially affects or is likely to substantially affect Data Subjects in more than one Member State: GDPR, art 4(23). Article 29 Data Protection Working Party Guidelines for Identifying a Controller or Processor's Lead Supervisory Authority Adopted on 13 December 2016 16/EN WP 244, 3.

[107] See Article 29 Working Party for more detail on how this question will be decided. Article 29 Data Protection Working Party Guidelines for Identifying a Controller or Processor's Lead Supervisory Authority Adopted on 13 December 2016 16/EN WP 244, 3–4.

[108] Article 29 Data Protection Working Party Guidelines for Identifying a Controller or Processor's Lead Supervisory Authority Adopted on 13 December 2016 16/EN WP 244, 4.

[109] GDPR, art 56; Article 29 Data Protection Working Party Guidelines for Identifying a Controller or Processor's Lead Supervisory Authority Adopted on 13 December 2016 16/EN WP 244, 4–5. Main establishment is defined as 'the place of its central administration in the Union, unless the decisions

'will coordinate any investigation, involving other "concerned" supervisory authorities'.[110] The GDPR lays out procedures for cooperation between the lead authority and other concerned supervisory authorities but it is likely to be some time before the operation of the system in practice is fully settled.[111] In light of the number of internet companies operating in Ireland, it will certainly be a major issue for the ODPC in the coming years.

International Data Transfer

The EU acknowledges that the flow of personal data to and from countries outside the Union has benefits for international trade and cooperation.[112] The EU also recognises that the 'increase in such flows has raised new challenges and concerns with regard to the protection of personal data'.[113] As it would be self-defeating to create a data protection framework and then permit the unrestricted transfer of data to third countries outside of the EEA,[114] the GDPR sets out rules governing the transfer of personal data outside of the EEA.[115] A number of options are provided for Controllers who wish to send data outside of the EEA.

[5–63]

Transfer on the basis of an adequacy decision (Article 45 GDPR)	If the EU Commission decides that a third country ensures an 'adequate level of protection', data can be transferred to that country without any specific authorisation.
Transfer subject to appropriate safeguards (Article 46 GDPR)	In the absence of an adequacy decision, personal data may be transferred to a third country where the Controller has provided appropriate safeguards and where enforceable Data Subject rights and effective legal remedies for Data Subjects are available.[116] The safeguards can be provided in a number of ways, including by binding corporate rules (as governed by Article 47).
Derogations for specific situations (Article 49 GDPR)	In the absence of an adequacy decision (Article 45) or appropriate safeguards (Article 46), personal data transfer is still possible in a limited number of circumstances, such as where the Data Subject has explicitly consented to the proposed transfer (after having been informed of the risks) and where the transfer is necessary for the purposes of a contract, for important reasons of public interest, the exercise of legal claims, or to protect vital interests.[117]

on the purposes and means of the processing of personal data are taken in another establishment of the Controller in the Union and the latter establishment has the power to have such decisions implemented, in which case the establishment having taken such decisions is to be considered to be the main establishment': GDPR, art 4(16).

[110] Article 29 Data Protection Working Party Guidelines for Identifying a Controller or Processor's Lead Supervisory Authority Adopted on 13 December 2016 16/EN WP 244, 4.

[111] GDPR, art 57.

[112] GDPR, recital 101.

[113] GDPR, recital 101.

[114] Third countries or international organisations.

[115] These rules are comparable to the rules set out in the Data Protection Directive.

[116] Recital 108 of the GDPR states that 'safeguards should ensure compliance with data protection requirements and the rights of the Data Subjects appropriate to processing within the Union, including the availability of enforceable Data Subject rights and of effective legal remedies, including to obtain effective administrative or judicial redress and to claim compensation, in the Union or in a third country'.

[117] There are limitations to these conditions in practice. For example, as consent must be explicit and informed, it will not be able to be relied upon in certain circumstances.

Residual option where non-repetitive transfer is in the compelling legitimate interest of the Controller (Article 49 GDPR)	As a final residual option, a non-repetitive transfer may take place where it concerns a limited number of Data Subjects and it is in the compelling legitimate interests pursued by the Controller, when those interests are not overridden by the interests or rights and freedoms of the Data Subject and when the Controller has assessed all the circumstances surrounding the data transfer. In such circumstances, the Controller must inform the supervisory authority and the Data Subject.[118]

Figure 7 *International Data Transfer.*

[5–64] Ireland – and the Irish ODPC – has found itself at the centre of an international data transfer debate. Ireland's central role can be explained by the choice of many of the world's largest internet companies – including Facebook – to use Ireland as its European base. Due to the importance of trade between the United States and the EU, a streamlined system – dubbed 'Safe Harbour' – was developed in order to facilitate data transfers. The system operated on a voluntary basis, where US companies self-certified as being compliant with the safe harbour system. In a judgment in response to a preliminary ruling request from the Irish High Court,[119] the CJEU found the safe harbour regime to be invalid in 2015.[120] The responses to the ruling – including the development of a new EU–US 'Privacy Shield' agreement – continue to be debated in the Irish courts and globally.[121] While the Privacy Shield agreement provides for greater protection of European data in the US,[122] the European Data Protection Supervisor maintains that the new EU–US data transfer programme does not adequately include 'all appropriate safeguards to protect the EU rights of the individual to privacy and data protection'.[123] The ODPC has also raised concerns in relation to some of the other transfer legitimising mechanisms, as highlighted in a recent yet to be decided High Court case.[124]

ePrivacy

[5–65] While data protection law is of general application, additional rules apply in the telecommunications sector. Due to the specific privacy risks posed by telecommunications, it was deemed

---

[118] GDPR, art 49(1) and GDPR, recital 113.

[119] TFEU, art 267.

[120] *Maximillian Schrems v Data Protection Commissioner* [2016] 2 CMLR 2; *Schrems v Data Protection Commissioner* [2014] IEHC 310.

[121] Elaine Edwards, 'Major Privacy Case to Open before High Court in Dublin' *The Irish Times* (Dublin, 5 February 2017) <www.irishtimes.com/business/technology/major-privacy-case-to-open-before-high-court-in-dublin-1.2964424> accessed 7 March 2017.

[122] Including possibilities for redress.

[123] European Data Protection Supervisor, 'European Data Protection Supervisor Opinion on the EU–US Privacy Shield Draft Adequacy Decision' Opinion 4/2016 (30 May 2016) <www.edps.europa.eu/sites/edp/files/publication/16-05-30_privacy_shield_en.pdf> accessed 7 March 2017, 22.

[124] See for example Mary Carolan, "US data 'blanket protection' defended in High Court" *Irish Times* (7 March 2017) <www.irishtimes.com/business/technology/us-data-blanket-protection-defended-in-high-court-1.3001646> accessed 7 March 2017.

necessary to 'particularise and complement' the general data protection rules.[125] As a result of this, the EU introduced additional rules for the processing of personal data in the telecommunications sector in 1997.[126] Reflecting the rapid adoption and development of internet and mobile communication services, the rules were replaced by the ePrivacy Directive[127] just five years later. Subsequently, the ePrivacy Directive was amended by Directive 2009/136/EC. The ePrivacy rules are implemented in Ireland via the European Communities (Electronic Communications Networks and Services) (Privacy and Electronic Communications) Regulations 2011.[128]

The ePrivacy rules apply to 'the processing of personal data in connection with the provision of publicly available electronic communications services in public communications networks'. Processing that comes within that definition must still meet the standards set out in general data protection law, but must also comply with some additional requirements. As modern communication almost inevitably results in the processing of personal data – from telephone numbers, to email addresses, to IP addresses – a large range of activities will trigger the application of the ePrivacy rules. The ePrivacy Directive places restrictions on a number of activities that interfere with individual privacy, such as: **[5–66]**

- – Restrictions on the use of traffic data by the service provider;[129]
- – Restrictions on unsolicited communications;[130] and
- – Restrictions on the interception of communications.[131]

Notably, the ePrivacy Directive also imposes a notification requirement similar to the rules set out more recently in the GDPR. A controversial requirement is contained in Article 5(3) of the ePrivacy Directive, where it states that: **[5–67]**

> Member States shall ensure that the use of electronic communications networks to store information or to gain access to information stored in the terminal equipment of a subscriber or user is only allowed on condition that the subscriber or user concerned is provided with clear and comprehensive information in accordance with Directive 95/46/EC, inter alia about the purposes of the processing, and is offered the right to refuse such processing by the data controller.

As 'cookies' are units of information sent from a website and stored on a user's computer in order to allow certain functionality,[132] actions taken by many websites fall within the scope   **[5–68]**

---

[125] Parliament and Council Directive (EC) 66/1997 concerning the processing of personal data and the protection of privacy in the telecommunications sector [1998] OJ L 24/01. Ian Lloyd, *Information Technology Law* (Oxford University Press 2011) 163.

[126] Parliament and Council Directive (EC) 66/1997 concerning the processing of personal data and the protection of privacy in the telecommunications sector [1998] OJ L 24/01. This was implemented domestically by the European Communities (Data Protection and Privacy in Telecommunications) Regulations 2002, SI 2002/192.

[127] Parliament and Council Directive (EC) 58/2002 concerning the processing of personal data and the protection of privacy in the electronic communications sector (ePrivacy Directive) [2002] OJ L201 37.

[128] SI No 336 of 2011.

[129] ePrivacy Directive, art 6.

[130] ePrivacy Directive, art 13.

[131] ePrivacy Directive, art 5. See investigative exceptions in Article 15 of the ePrivacy Directive and discussion of the Data Retention Directive in 15. Chapter Six.

[132] Recital 25 of the ePrivacy Directive recognises that 'cookies' can be a 'legitimate and useful tool, for example, in analysing the effectiveness of website design and advertising, and in verifying the

of this restriction. Even though the ePrivacy Directive excludes certain types of cookies – for example those that are 'strictly necessary in order to provide an information society service explicitly requested by the subscriber' – the breadth of the requirement means that almost all websites now display cookie notices in order to comply.[133] The ubiquity of cookie notices – which can be ignored or clicked away with ease – can be criticised as an illustration of 'transparency theatre' that some believe has led to 'notification fatigue'.[134]

[5–69] It is important to note that the ePrivacy Directive is currently under review in order to 'adapt the current rules which apply to electronic communications services to the new General Data Protection Regulation'.[135] The Commission has ambitious plans to replace the existing ePrivacy Directive with a new Regulation by May 2018 in order to coincide with the implementation of the GDPR.[136] In line with increased penalties under the GDPR, the proposed ePrivacy Regulation will increase potential fines to 4 per cent of annual worldwide turnover. Efforts have also been made to address criticisms regarding the cookie rules. For example, the proposed Regulation exempts cookies used for the purpose of analytics from the cookie consent requirement. Moreover, in an attempt to tackle notice fatigue, the proposed ePrivacy Regulation places increased emphasis on browsers as opposed to individual websites. In recognition of data protection by design and by default, internet browsers should offer various options to consumers to regulate what classes of cookie can be received. For example, browsers could provide users with the option to:

– never accept cookies;
– never accept third party cookies;
– always accept cookies.[137]

[5–70] One of the most significant changes under the proposed Regulation is the application of some of the specific rules governing traditional telecommunications operators to 'over-the-top' communications service providers, such as Whatsapp, Facebook Messenger, and Skype. According to the Commission, this change is necessary to fill the 'void of protection

---

identity of users engaged in on-line transactions'.

[133] The Data Protection Commissioner has suggested that consent can be by explicit action – eg ticking a box that says: 'I accept cookies from this site' – or by implication – eg by displaying a banner that reads: 'By continuing to use this site you consent to the use of cookies in accordance with our cookie policy.' Data Protection Commissioner, 'Storing and Accessing Information on Terminal Equipment' DataProtection.ie <www.dataprotection.ie/docs/Cookies/1416.htm> accessed 7 March 2017.

[134] Jan Philipp Albrecht, 'ePrivacy Regulation is a Good First Step' *The Parliament* (Brussels, 17 March 2017) <www.theparliamentmagazine.eu/articles/opinion/eprivacy-regulation-good-first-step> accessed 7 March 2017.

[135] Jennifer Baker, 'ePrivacy Leaked Draft: The "Good," the "Bad" and the "Missing"' (*IAPP*, 13 December 2016) <iapp.org/news/a/eprivacy-leaked-draft-the-good-the-bad-and-the-missing/> accessed 7 March 2017; European Commission, 'Proposal for an ePrivacy Regulation' (12 June 2017) <ec.europa.eu/digital-single-market/en/proposal-eprivacy-regulation> accessed 7 March 2017.

[136] Proposal for a Regulation of the European Parliament and of the Council concerning the respect for private life and the protection of personal data in electronic communications and repealing Directive 2002/58/EC (Regulation on Privacy and Electronic Communications) 2017/0003 (COD), art 27.

[137] Proposal for a Regulation of the European Parliament and of the Council concerning the respect for private life and the protection of personal data in electronic communications and repealing Directive 2002/58/EC (Regulation on Privacy and Electronic Communications) 2017/0003 (COD), recitals 20–24.

of communications conveyed through new services'.[138] The proposed reforms are not entirely privacy positive, however, as there are indications that the rules regarding the use of communications data may be made more flexible. As the proposed ePrivacy Regulation will almost certainly undergo some amendment as it makes its way through the EU legislative process, you can keep abreast of developments on the Commission's website.[139]

Conclusion

Modern life and interaction is often driven by information and this can have significant implications for the protection of personal data. New technologies are developed, adopted, and adapted at a pace that can be challenging not only for law-makers, but for society in general. 'Internet of Things' devices, for example, are sometimes hailed as the 'next big thing' that will foster increased economic growth and human welfare; yet they are also frequently condemned as an inherently insecure technology that creates new and potentially devastating vulnerabilities. **[5–71]**

It has been argued that data protection law is outdated and unsuited to address the challenges of the modern environment. In fact, the GDPR was designed as an update that would respond to the 'rapid technological developments and globalisation' that 'brought new challenges for the protection of personal data'.[140] In spite of this intent, the GDPR continues in the tradition of the Data Protection Directive as it was maintained that the 'core principles of the Directive' remained valid and that its technologically neutral character was worth preserving.[141] While EU representatives continue to endorse this view, some academics have already condemned the GDPR as failing to respond to the current challenges. The true test of the GDPR will occur over time and its success will depend on its interpretation and enforcement throughout the EU. **[5–72]**

Further Reading

- Orla Lynskey, *The Foundations of EU Data Protection Law* (Oxford University Press 2015).
- Paul Lambert, *Data Protection Law in Ireland: Sources and Issues* (Clarus Press 2016).
- Denis Kelleher, *Privacy and Data Protection Law in Ireland* (Bloomsbury 2015).
- Rosemary Jay, *Data Protection Law and Practice* (Sweet and Maxwell 2014).
- Paul Bernal, *Internet Privacy Rights: Rights to Protect Autonomy* (Cambridge University Press 2014).
- Maria Helen Murphy, 'The Introduction of Smart Meters in Ireland: Privacy Implications and the Role of Privacy by Design' (2015) 38(1) Dublin University Law Journal 191

---

[138] European Commission, Proposal for a Regulation of the European Parliament and of the Council concerning the respect for private life and the protection of personal data in electronic communications and repealing Directive 2002/58/EC (Regulation on Privacy and Electronic Communications) COM(2017) 10 final 2017/0003.

[139] European Commission, 'Proposal for an ePrivacy Regulation' <ec.europa.eu/digital-single-market/en/proposal-eprivacy-regulation#Article> accessed 7 March 2017.

[140] European Commission, 'A Comprehensive Approach on Personal Data Protection in the European Union' Final Communication from the Commission to the European Parliament, the Council, the Economic and Social Committee and the Committee of the Regions Brussels 4.11.2010 Com(2010) 609 <ec.europa.eu/justice/news/consulting_public/0006/com_2010_609_en.pdf> accessed 7 March 2017, 3.

[141] ibid.

- Bert-Jaap Koops, 'Privacy Regulation cannot be Hardcoded. A Critical Comment on the "Privacy by Design" Provision in Data Protection Law' (2014) 28(2) International Review of Law, Computers & Technology 159.
- Lilian Edwards, 'Privacy, Security and Data Protection in Smart Cities: A Critical EU Law Perspective' (2016) 2(1) European Data Protection Law Review 28.
- Christopher Kuner et al, 'The Global Data Protection Implications of "Brexit"' (2016) 6(3) International Data Privacy Law 167.
- Paul Lambert, *Social Networking, Law, Rights and Policy* (Clarus Press 2014).
- Paul Lambert, *International Handbook of Social Media Laws* (Bloomsbury 2014).
- Paul Lambert, *The Data Protection Officer, Profession, Rules and Role* (Routledge, Taylor and Francis, 2017).
- Michelle Dennedy, Jonathan Fox and Tom Finneran, *The Privacy Engineer's Manifesto* (Apress 2014).

PART 3

ICT and Public Law

CHAPTER 6
Privacy

'Each small extension of surveillance can shift the balance between the liberties and rights of individuals and the state and relations among the three branches of government.'[1]

Privacy in the Modern World

Privacy is threatened by many actors – including surveillance agencies conducting investi-   **[6–01]**
gations, companies tracking your actions online, and nosy neighbours directing their CCTV
camera at your private property. The policy of the East German Stasi to 'know everything
about everyone' provides a pertinent historical example of the harm caused by excessive
surveillance.[2] Indeed, the former US President Barack Obama has remarked that the East
German experience is a 'cautionary tale of what could happen when vast, unchecked surveillance turned citizens into informers and persecuted people for what they said in the

---

[1]   Gary Marx, *Undercover: Police Surveillance in America* (University of California Press 1988) 230.
[2]   Anna Funder, *Stasiland: Stories from Behind the Berlin Wall* (Granta Books 2011).

privacy of their own homes'.[3] While a need for privacy has been recognised for thousands of years,[4] the technological realities of the present have propelled the right to heightened levels of prominence. The reduced cost of data storage has led to more data being stored for longer periods of time. The rapid advances in data-processing capabilities mean that more insight and value can be drawn from data sets. When this processing capacity is used in conjunction with large and multiple data sets, it is possible to identify linkages between data that would previously have been impossible. Modern surveillance practices have greater pervasiveness, intensity, and speed.[5]

[6–02]   Adding to these technological advances is the reality that we are all producing more data all of the time. We also tend to communicate this data through insecure systems and store our data on cloud servers – leaving our personal data open to the possibility of data breach. It is clear that many of these changes also have data protection implications, further illustrating the close connection between the right to privacy and the right to protection of personal data. As a result of this overlap, this chapter will focus on the issue of government surveillance. Of course, as a key source of information for government agencies, private companies such as Facebook and Google are now seen as a crucial part of the overall 'surveillant assemblage'.[6] Accordingly, even though there are data protection implications in the surveillance context – see the *Schrems*[7] case for a clear example of this – privacy provides the best framework to analyse the practice of state surveillance.

[6–03]   While there is an elegance to the description of privacy as simply being the right to be 'let alone', the scope of the right raises complex questions of interpretation.[8] Commentators have variously described privacy as a 'canopy'[9] or an 'umbrella'[10] descriptor covering a number of different situations and a 'miscellany of rights or rules which combine to protect various aspects of privacy'.[11] As this book is designed to tackle the legal issues raised by information technology, the definition of 'information privacy' set forth by Alan Westin in 1967 provides a useful starting point. Westin defines information privacy as 'the claim of individuals, groups or institutions to determine for themselves when, how and to what

---

[3] Andrew Curry, 'No, the NSA Isn't like the Stasi – and Comparing them is Treacherous' (*Wired*, 14 January 2015) <www.wired.com/2015/01/nsa-stasi-comparison/> accessed 9 June 2017.

[4] Jan Holvast, 'History of Privacy' in Vashek Matyáš and others (eds), *The Future of Identity in the Information Society* (Springer 2009) 15.

[5] Select Committee on the Constitution, *Surveillance: Citizens and the State* (HL Paper 18-II) 22–25.

[6] Kevin Haggerty and Richard Ericson, 'The Surveillant Assemblage' (2000) 51(4) The British Journal of Sociology 605.

[7] *Maximillian Schrems v Data Protection Commissioner* [2016] 2 CMLR 2; *Maximillian Schrems v Data Protection Commissioner* [2014] IEHC 310.

[8] Samuel Warren and Louis Brandeis, 'The Right to Privacy' (1890) 4(5) Harvard Law Review 193.

[9] Ti-liang Yang, 'Privacy: A Comparative Study of English and American Law' (1966) 15 International and Comparative Law Quarterly 175, 177.

[10] Stanley Benn, 'Privacy, Freedom, and Respect for Persons' in Ferdinand Schoeman (ed), *Philosophical Dimensions of Privacy* (Cambridge University Press 1984) 223, 226.

[11] Jacques Velu, 'The European Convention on Human Rights and the Right to Respect for Private Life, the Home and Communications' in Arthur Robertson (ed), *Privacy and Human Rights – Reports and Communications Presented at the Third International Colloquy about the European Convention on Human Rights* (Manchester University Press 1973) 31–32.

extent information about them is communicated to others'.[12] This definition mirrors some of the key ideas behind the related concept of data protection as discussed in Chapter 5. While this book focuses on the implications for privacy in the connected world, the broader scope of the right remains relevant, particularly when discussing the jurisprudence.

In spite of its fluidity, the right to privacy is widely recognised in national and interna- **[6–04]** tional constitutional instruments. In some cases, such as in the International Covenant on Civil and Political Rights, the European Convention on Human Rights (ECHR), and the EU Charter of Fundamental Rights, the right is explicitly acknowledged. In the case of the US Constitution, the right is protected in a number of ways, most notably by the Fourth Amendment prohibition against unreasonable searches and seizures. While the Irish Constitution does not explicitly acknowledge a right to privacy, Irish courts have identified an unenumerated privacy right.[13] In spite of this legal recognition, privacy has been crit-icised as a moribund right of little value in modern society. In a world where 'data is the new oil' and where we all live connected lives, some would argue the fight for privacy is not worth fighting. Indeed, the former CEO of Sun Microsystems Scott Nealy famously articulated this position when he stated that 'You already have zero privacy. Get over it.'[14] This statement was made in 1999. Considering that 1999 was before smart phones – not to mention today's broad array of smart devices – achieved widespread adoption, it is clear that the privacy challenge has only steepened.

Instead of focusing on practicality, some commentators target the nature of the right, **[6–05]** arguing that privacy is a 'cult' that 'rests on an individualist conception of society'.[15] This position, however, ignores the broad societal benefits associated with privacy protection. While privacy may often be represented as an individual interest, hindering economic progress, seamless interaction, and criminal investigation, the restriction of privacy has broad societal effects. When privacy is threatened, individuals may be hesitant to explore their feelings and share any thoughts that do not reflect the perceived norm. This is known as the chilling effect. To consider how restricted privacy might hinder an individual's personal development, consider how you might alter your behaviour if the terms you typed into an online search engine were publically available for anyone to read. As a plurality of opinions is an essential element of democratic societies, it is vital that individuals maintain sufficient personal space to develop their personalities and rela-tionship with the outside world. Furthermore, the protection of privacy is also beneficial for the private entities who we entrust with our most sensitive data. The loss of trust and reputation that can come with a publicised data breach can harm a company in tangible ways and discourage consumers from using services from which they would otherwise receive a benefit.

---

[12] Alan Westin, *Privacy and Freedom* (Atheneum 1967) 7.

[13] Discussed further at [6–13] to [6–16].

[14] Polly Sprenger 'Sun on Privacy: "Get Over It"' (*Wired,* 26 January 1999) <https://www.wired.com/1999/01/sun-on-privacy-get-over-it/> accessed 9 June 2017.

[15] Heinz Arndt, 'The Cult of Privacy' (1949) 21 Australian Quarterly 68, 70–71.

Surveillance and the Right to Privacy

[6–06]   The practice of surveillance – defined as 'any collection and processing of personal data, whether identifiable or not, for the purposes of influencing or managing those whose data have been garnered' is in clear tension with the protection of privacy.[16] This does not of course render all surveillance invalid, as all organised societies need some means to monitor their citizens in order to enforce their laws. Examples of such means throughout history have included

> simple observation, watching, listening and following, both from law enforcement and private individuals; the use of human spies, undercover operatives and informers by police and security services; a whole range of medical, social security, financial and recruitment procedures based on face-to-face interviews; and the keeping of records on paper files.[17]

[6–07]   Modern communications technology has, of course, increased the capability and invasiveness of surveillance measures. With the increased importance of communications technology, we all create much more data about ourselves. With the reduced cost of storing that data, the data remains in existence for longer – often indefinite – periods of time. With increased connectivity, our data is more accessible and more linkable than previously possible. Moreover, with increased processing power and algorithmic search capabilities, investigative agencies are increasingly interested in large data sets. The rapid increase in storage capacity and computing power in recent years 'has made it easier for large volumes of communications and communications data to be sifted and analysed'.[18] The term 'data mining' is used to describe the 'computerized analysis of extensive electronic databases about private individuals for patterns of suspicious activity'.[19] The technique combines data from multiple sources (often including publicly available sources) and processes that data in order to create profiles that can then be used to target individuals for further scrutiny.

[6–08]   The Snowden revelations[20] clarified and confirmed the vast capabilities of modern intelligence agencies. Not only did the revelations lead to a widespread re-evaluation of modern surveillance measures internationally, but also resulted in careful consideration of the issues in the domestic context in *Schrems v Data Protection Commissioner*.[21] Hogan J set the scene for his judgment by asserting that:

> [T]he Snowden revelations demonstrate a massive overreach on the part of the security authorities, with an almost studied indifference to the privacy interests of ordinary

---

[16] David Lyon (ed), *Surveillance as Social Sorting* (Routledge 2002).

[17] Surveillance Studies Network, 'A Report on the Surveillance Society for the Information Commissioner' (September 2006) <www.ico.gov.uk/upload/documents/library/data_protection/practical_application/surveillance_society_full_report_2006.pdf> accessed 9 June 2017.

[18] Ian Brown, 'Regulation of Converged Communications Surveillance' in Daniel Neyland and Benjamin Goold (eds), *New Directions in Surveillance Privacy* (Willan 2009) 39–73.

[19] David Cole, 'Uncle Sam Is Watching You' *New York Review of Books* (New York, 18 November 2004) 56.

[20] In 2013, a former US government security contractor, Edward Snowden, leaked classified National Security Agency (NSA) documents regarding global surveillance operations. Glenn Greenwald, *No Place to Hide* (Metropolitan Books 2014).

[21] *Schrems v Data Protection Commissioner* [2014] IEHC 310.

citizens. Their data protection rights have been seriously compromised by mass and largely unsupervised surveillance programmes.[22]

Of course, 'privacy is not an absolute value and does not trump all other rights or concerns **[6–09]** for the common good'.[23] In the national security context – where surveillance measures are defended on the grounds that such measures protect the safety of citizens – the privacy argument can seem trivial and out of touch with reality. Opposition to surveillance can be viewed as unpatriotic and even as pandering to terrorists and criminals. In spite of its frequent dismissal by privacy experts, the refrain 'if you have nothing to hide you have nothing to fear' still holds weight in public debates.[24]

It is a mistake, of course, to ignore the benefits of surveillance. While government surveil- **[6–10]** lance is a clear restriction of privacy, the right does not grant absolute 'privacy from the law'.[25] Considering that intelligence is 'one of the crucial ingredients for the prevention of terrorism', it should be clear that government surveillance can play a crucial role in the prevention and prosecution of serious crime and terrorism.[26] In spite of recognising that states should be able to counter such threats with the use of secret surveillance, the European Court of Human Rights (ECtHR) has highlighted the risk of surveillance activities undermining democracy on the ground of defending it.[27] Without careful limitations, surveillance measures are prone to be employed in unenvisaged contexts, expanding in scope, and being exploited by government insiders to protect particular interests. The effectiveness of certain surveillance techniques also raises questions.

In the post-Snowden environment, there has been a reinvigoration of the privacy debate.[28] **[6–11]** This is evidenced in part by the increased visibility of consumer products that advertise their privacy credentials as a key selling point.[29] Apple, for example, has attempted to distinguish itself as a producer of secure devices.[30] According to Apple's CEO, Tim Cook, this is made possible by developing Apple's business model to not rely on the commercialisation of personal data.[31] This of course differentiates Apple from many of its competitors, most

---

[22] *Schrems v Data Protection Commissioner* [2014] IEHC 310, para 8.

[23] Amitai Etzioni, *The Limits of Privacy* (Basic Books 1999) 38.

[24] Daniel Solove, '"I've got Nothing to Hide" and other Misunderstandings of Privacy' (2007) 44 San Diego Law Review 745.

[25] Alan Westin, *Privacy and Freedom* (Atheneum 1967) 60.

[26] Stefan Sottiaux, *Terrorism and the Limitation of Rights* (Hart Publishing 2008) 274.

[27] *Klass v Germany* (1979–80) 2 EHRR 214, paras 48–49.

[28] Maria Helen Murphy, 'The Pendulum Effect: Comparisons between the Snowden Revelations and the Church Committee: What Are the Potential Implications for Europe?' (2014) 23(2) Information and Communications Technology Law 192.

[29] Chris Johnston, 'DuckDuckGo Traffic Soars in Wake of Snowden Revelations' *The Guardian* (London, 17 June 2015).

[30] According to Apple's Tim Cook, the strengthening of device level encryption on iPhones provided an 'engineering solution to a legal quandary'. Jay McGregor, 'Apple Beefs Up iOS8 Security with Unbreakable Passcode' (*Forbes*, 18 September 2014) <www.forbescom/sites/jaymcgregor/2014/09/18/ios8-beefs-up-security-with-unbreakablepasscode/> accessed 9 June 2017.

[31] Although privacy implications remain. See, for example, Theo Priestley, 'Apple Privacy May Not Be as Private as You Think' (*Forbes*, 24 August 2015) <www.forbes.com/sites/theopriestley/2015/08/24/did-apple-lie-about-your-privacy/#5e4032cd2b09> accessed 10 June 2017.

prominently Google. While increased consumer interest in security tools should enhance the privacy of those consumers, important questions remain regarding the role law has to play in this context.

Protection of Privacy in the Irish Legal System

[6–12]   In Ireland, several sources of law provide for some protection of privacy:

1. The courts have recognised a Constitutional right to privacy.
2. As discussed previously, the EU Charter includes a right to respect for private life.
3. The Irish State is bound by the ECHR to ensure the right to respect for private life.
4. Various pieces of legislation protect certain aspects of the right to privacy.[32]
5. The Common Law also provides for some protection although its significance has diminished.

[6–13]   The diagram below depicts the most important sources of human rights protection of privacy in the Irish legal system. Note that the ECHR is not included in the standard hierarchy. While the ECHR is binding in international law, and everyone resident in Ireland has the right to complain to the Council of Europe's European Court of Human Rights (ECtHR) through the individual petition procedure, the Convention does not have the same domestic force as the Constitution. In spite of this, the ECHR has long played a notable 'persuasive' role in Irish decision-making. Furthermore, since 2003, the Convention's status has been enhanced domestically through the introduction of the ECHR Act. Under the ECHR Act, Irish courts are now required to interpret law in accordance with the Convention where possible, to take 'judicial notice' of the case law of the ECtHR, and to declare laws to be incompatible with the Convention as a remedy of law resort. The ECtHR case law concerning the Article 8 ECHR 'right to respect for private life' provides an extensive corpus for consideration.

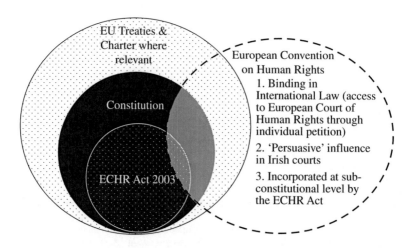

Figure 1   *Protection of the Right to Privacy in Irish Law (Key Sources)*

---

[32] Although it is notable that a Privacy Bill has been tabled and set aside on numerous occasions.

Protection of Privacy Under the Constitution

Irish courts have continually recognised that Article 40.3.1° of the Constitution includes **[6–14]** an unenumerated right to privacy.[33] The special role of privacy in a democratic society was recognised in the case of *Kennedy v Ireland* where the government was found to have intercepted the communications of political journalists without due cause. In the case, Hamilton P described privacy as an essential protector of dignity and freedom.[34] These values are undermined if private communications are 'deliberately, consciously and unjustifiably intruded upon and interfered with'.[35]

While the protection of Article 40.3.1° is frequently invoked, various facets of pri- **[6–15]** vacy receive additional protection from different provisions of the Constitution.[36] The Constitution's protection of the home, for example, will often be relevant.[37] In the case of *Schrems*, Hogan J confirmed that 'the accessing by State authorities of private communications generated within the home – whether this involves the accessing of telephone calls, internet use or private mail – also directly engages the inviolability of the dwelling as guaranteed by Article 40.5 of the Constitution'.[38]

While the Court in *Kennedy* upheld the Constitutional right to privacy and awarded substan- **[6–16]** tial damages against the State,[39] Hamilton P clarified that privacy is limited by the 'exigencies of the common good'.[40] While this position has been confirmed in subsequent cases,[41] intrusions must be in accordance with fair procedures and the principles of constitutional justice.[42] As MacMenamin J set out in *People v Idah*:

> There can be no doubt that the State may make incursions into the right of privacy in accordance with law. This is particularly the case in circumstances where the State is seeking to provide in relation to 'the investigation of arrestable offences, the prevention of suspected arrestable offences and the safeguarding of the State against subversive and terrorist threats'. Nevertheless that law must be sufficiently clear in its terms to give individuals an adequate indication as to the circumstances in which public authorities are entitled to resort to such covert measures and it must provide necessary safeguards for the rights of individuals potentially affected.[43]

---

[33] Which obliges the State to defend and vindicate the personal rights of the citizen as far as practicable. *McGee v Attorney General* [1974] IR 284 (SC); *Kennedy v Ireland* [1987] IR 587 (HC); *Foy v An t-Ard Chlaraitheoir* [2002] IEHC 116.

[34] *Kennedy v Ireland* [1987] IR 587 (HC).

[35] *Kennedy v Ireland* [1987] IR 587 (HC) 593.

[36] Other protections include the privacy of the ballot and the inviolability of the dwelling: Denis Kelleher, *Privacy and Data Protection Law in Ireland* (Bloomsbury 2015) 7.

[37] *DPP v Timothy (Ted) Cunningham* [2012] IECCA 64.

[38] *Schrems v Data Protection Commissioner* [2014] IEHC 310 [48].

[39] *Kennedy v Ireland* [1987] IR 587 (HC).

[40] *Kennedy v Ireland* [1987] IR 587 (HC) 593; *Bailey v Flood* (SC, 14 April 2000); *Haughey v Moriarty* [1999] 3 IR 1 (HC) 59; *Redmond v Flood* [1999] 3 IR 79 (SC) 88.

[41] *Bailey v Flood* [2000] IESC 11; *Haughey v Moriarty* [1999] 3 IR 1 (HC, SC); *Redmond v Flood* [1993] 3 IR 79 (SC).

[42] *Redmond v Flood* [1993] 3 IR 79 (SC); *O'Callaghan v Judge Alan Mahon and Ors* [2005] IESC 9. See discussion in Denis Kelleher, *Privacy and Data Protection Law in Ireland* (Bloomsbury 2015) 14. *Damache v DPP* [2012] 2 ILRM 153 (SC) 51.

[43] *People v Idah* [2014] IECCA 3, 11; *Schrems v Data Protection Commissioner* [2014] IEHC 310 [37].

In the case of *Schrems*, Hogan J pointed out that generalised surveillance could only be valid under the Constitution where the surveillance is 'objectively justified in the interests of the suppression of crime and national security' and 'attended by appropriate and verifiable safeguards'.[44]

Protection of Privacy Under the ECHR

[6–17]   Article 8 ECHR provides explicit protection for privacy rights. While the Article protects a wide range of rights[45] – and has been expansively interpreted to provide protection in unforeseen circumstances – government surveillance practices fall squarely within the Article's remit:

> Article 8 – Right to respect for private and family life
> 1.   Everyone has the right to respect for his private and family life, his home and his correspondence.
> 2.   There shall be no interference by a public authority with the exercise of this right except such as is in accordance with the law and is necessary in a democratic society in the interests of national security, public safety or the economic well-being of the country, for the prevention of disorder or crime, for the protection of health or morals, or for the protection of the rights and freedoms of others.

[6–18]   As mentioned earlier, unlike the Constitution, the ECHR is binding on the Irish State in international, but not domestic law.[46] Notwithstanding this, individuals are entitled to complain about suspected Irish violations of their Convention rights to the ECtHR.[47] Article 1 of the ECHR obliges state parties to secure 'to everyone within their jurisdiction the rights and freedoms' of the Convention. As the ECtHR is the designated interpretive body of the Convention, the governments of signatory states must be cognisant of relevant Strasbourg rulings.[48]

[6–19]   While the Irish government has not yet been the subject of a negative judgment in the surveillance sphere, the ECtHR has been influential in the introduction and substance of Irish rules on surveillance.[49] In an extensive body of case law – famously beginning with *Klass v Germany*[50] – the ECtHR provides useful guidance to domestic authorities attempting to reconcile their interest in detecting and investigating illicit activities with their obligation to respect the privacy rights of their citizens. As mentioned above, the incorporation of the ECHR into the Irish legal system at a sub-constitutional level further enhances the

---

[44] *Schrems v Data Protection Commissioner* [2014] IEHC 310 [55].

[45] Nicole Moreham, 'Privacy Rights' in Mark Warby and others (eds), *Tugendhat and Christie's Law of Privacy and the Media* (OUP 2010) 60. Article 8 provides protection for physical and psychological integrity, autonomy, and identity. See *X v Iceland* [1976] 5 DR 86, 87.

[46] See Figure 1 above.

[47] State Parties agree 'to guarantee the rights enshrined in the ECHR' and declare that they 'will comply with the judgments of the European Court': ECHR, art 41.

[48] ECHR, art 1. Costas Paraskeva, *The Relationship between the Domestic Implementation of the European Convention on Human Rights and the Ongoing Reforms of the European Court of Human Rights (with a Case Study on Cyprus and Turkey)* (Intersentia 2010) 9.

[49] Maria Helen Murphy, 'The Relationship between the European Court of Human Rights and National Legislative Bodies: Considering the Merits and the Risks of the Approach of the Court in Surveillance Cases' (2013) 3(2) Irish Journal of Legal Studies 65.

[50] *Klass v Germany* (1979–80) 2 EHRR 214.

domestic status of the Convention.[51] With the case law of the ECtHR serving to 'elucidate, safeguard, and develop the rules instituted by the ECHR', this chapter now considers the key lessons that can be learned from the surveillance opinions delivered by the ECtHR.[52]

Article 34 of the ECHR requires complainants to claim that they are victims of a violation of the Convention by a Party State. This victimhood requirement could have posed a significant challenge in the secretive world of covert surveillance, but the ECtHR has been flexible in its application of the rule. As the ECtHR endorses the practical effectiveness of the Convention, surveillance legislation can be challenged based on its 'mere existence'.[53] This is an illustration of the commitment of the ECtHR to make rights practical and effective rather than simply theoretical and illusory. **[6–20]**

The ECtHR has also demonstrated flexibility in its interpretation of the scope of Article 8 ECHR, describing 'private life' as a 'broad term not susceptible to exhaustive definition'.[54] Unsurprisingly a wide range of surveillance technologies have been found to interfere with the right to respect to private life, including telephone interception,[55] email and internet usage monitoring,[56] covert video and audio recording devices,[57] GPS tracking,[58] generalised collection and searching of communications,[59] and transmission of intercepted data and its 'use by other authorities'.[60] This list demonstrates how the simple language of the Convention has capably addressed many technological advances since its inception. Notable has been the ECtHR's recognition that further uses of information that has already been collected constitutes additional separate interferences with the right to respect for private life. In a world of data retention and data mining, such a position is vital to ensure the protection of privacy rights. **[6–21]**

An important position in light of the modern abundance of databases is the ECtHR's stance that 'once any systematic or permanent record comes into existence of such material from **[6–22]**

---

[51] European Convention on Human Rights Act 2003 (ECHR Act). A key provision of the Act now requires Irish courts to 'in so far as is possible' interpret and apply the law in a manner compatible with the ECHR: ECHR Act, s 2(1). In addition, the Superior Courts may also make a 'declaration of incompatibility': ECHR Act, s 5. While such a declaration will not affect the ongoing applicability of the relevant law, it does oblige the Taoiseach to bring the declaration before the Oireachtas within 21 days of the order: ECHR Act, s 5(3).

[52] *Ireland v The United Kingdom* [1978] ECHR 1, 239–40; *Karner v Austria* (2004) 38 EHRR 24, 26.

[53] *Klass v Germany* (1979–80) 2 EHRR 214, para 34 and, more recently, *Roman Zakharov v Russia* [2015] ECHR 1065, para 171 and *Szabó and Vissy v Hungary* App no 37138/14 (ECtHR, 12 January 2016) para 171. If an individual's complaint is based on a claim that 'measures of surveillance were actually applied' to him or her, the complainant must demonstrate a 'reasonable likelihood' of this claim. In cases where a complainant asserts that the mere existence of surveillance measures amounts to an interference with their Article 8 rights, no 'proof that an actual interception of communications has taken place' will be required: *Halford v The United Kingdom* (1997) 24 EHRR 523, para 57; *Iliya Stefanov v Bulgaria* [2008] ECHR 42, para 49.

[54] *Peck v The United Kingdom* (2003) 36 EHRR 41, para 57.

[55] *Huvig v France* (1990) 12 EHRR 528, para 32; *Kruslin v France* (1990) 12 EHRR 547.

[56] *Copland v The United Kingdom* (2007) 45 EHRR 37, para 44.

[57] *Khan v The United Kingdom* [2000] Crim LR 684, para 24.

[58] *Uzun v Germany* App no 35623/05 (ECtHR, 2 September 2010).

[59] *Weber and Saravia v Germany* [2006] ECHR 1173.

[60] *Weber and Saravia v Germany* [2006] ECHR 1173, para 79. The ECtHR pointed out that transmission 'enlarges the group of persons with knowledge of the personal data intercepted' and that this can 'lead to investigations being instituted' against the persons concerned.

the public domain', private life considerations are relevant.[61] This position has enabled the ECtHR to identify Article 8 ECHR interferences associated with 'the mere storing of data relating to the private life of an individual' including photographs, DNA data, and fingerprints[62] 'even where the information has not been gathered by any intrusive or covert method'.[63] While some may argue that we waive our right to privacy when we step out in public, the ECtHR rejects that perspective.[64]

[6–23]   The concept of privacy has been described as 'too vague to guide adjudication and law-making',[65] but Article 8 ECHR 'gives form to the obligation'.[66] The tension between the right to privacy and other competing interests is explicitly recognised in the structure of the Article, with the first paragraph acknowledging a 'right to respect for private life' and the second paragraph laying out the criteria that must be met in order to interfere with that right. Due to the broad approach taken to the scope of a private life interference under the ECHR, almost any conceivable means of surveillance or surveillance-related processing will have to be justified in accordance with the terms of the second paragraph of Article 8 ECHR. Accordingly, any surveillance measure will have to be 'in accordance with the law' and 'necessary in a democratic society' in the pursuit of a 'legitimate aim'.

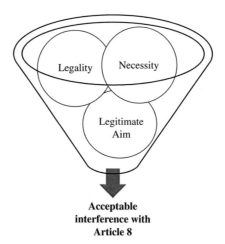

Figure 2   *Steps to Justify Interference with Article 8 ECHR*

---

[61] The arrival at this position appears to have been influenced by the adoption of the principles of Convention No 108: *PG and JH v The United Kingdom* [2001] ECHR 550, para 57.

[62] *S and Marper v The United Kingdom* [2008] ECHR 1581, para 67.

[63] *PG and JH v The United Kingdom* [2001] ECHR 550, para 57.

[64] Elizabeth Paton-Simpson, 'Privacy and the Reasonable Paranoid: The Protection of Privacy in Public Places' (2000) 50(3) University of Toronto Journal 311, 311.

[65] Daniel Solove, 'A Taxonomy of Privacy' (2006) 154(3) University of Pennsylvania Law Review 477, 481.

[66] Jacques Velu, 'The European Convention on Human Rights and the Right to Respect for Private Life, the Home and Communications' in Arthur Robertson (ed), *Privacy and Human Rights – Reports and Communications Presented at the Third International Colloquy about the European Convention on Human Rights* (Manchester University Press 1973) 92.

Is there a 'Legitimate Aim' for the Surveillance Measure?

While the ECtHR considers a wide range of activities to constitute intrusions under the first **[6–24]** paragraph of Article 8 ECHR, the Court also tends to be deferential to government claims that a particular surveillance measure was adopted in pursuit of a legitimate aim. Article 8 ECHR lists potential legitimate aims as including: national security, public safety, the economic well-being of the country, the prevention of disorder or crime, the protection of health or morals, and the protection of the rights and freedoms of others. As a result, the identification of a legitimate aim will not be a serious obstacle in most cases. While the ECtHR has not always scrutinised the legitimate aim of surveillance measures 'as vigorously as it might', it is important to note that the legitimate aim of an action becomes relevant again when the Court considers whether the measure is necessary in a democratic society.[67]

Is the Surveillance Measure 'in Accordance with the Law'?

Once a legitimate aim has been identified, it is necessary to consider whether the inter- **[6–25]** ference with Article 8 ECHR is 'in accordance with the law'. At the most basic level, the requirement of legality obliges governments to provide a legal basis for intrusive actions and to act in accordance with the relevant law. While it should be a straightforward matter to legislate for surveillance measures, a significant amount of surveillance cases that have come before the ECtHR have involved measures conducted without an adequate legal basis.[68] This reflects both the secrecy that is prevalent in this area and the difficulty of ensuring that regulations keep pace with technological developments.

In addition to requiring 'some basis in domestic law', intrusive measures should also be **[6–26]** set out in law that is adequately accessible and foreseeable.[69] Crucially, the legality test does not merely refer back to domestic law but 'also relates to the quality of the law'.[70] Interference with an individual's rights should be subject to effective control and domestic surveillance laws must protect against 'arbitrary interference' by public authorities. This is particularly important in the covert surveillance context as the inherent lack of transparency increases the risk of arbitrary action.

The requirement of foreseeability poses a clear challenge in the secret context of surveil- **[6–27]** lance. The ECtHR clarified in the case of *Malone v The United Kingdom* that 'the requirement of foreseeability cannot mean that an individual should be enabled to foresee when the authorities are likely to intercept his communications so that he can adapt his conduct accordingly'.[71] Importantly, however, the ECtHR also recognises the dangerous implications of opacity and requires laws to indicate the scope of the discretion allowed to surveillance authorities.[72] Accordingly, surveillance legislation should be:

> sufficiently clear in its terms to give citizens an adequate indication as to the circumstances in which and the conditions on which public authorities are empowered to resort

---

[67] David Harris and others, *Law of the European Convention on Human Rights* (OUP 2009) 348.

[68] *Malone v The United Kingdom* [1984] ECHR 10, para 79; *Khan v The United Kingdom* (2000) 31 EHRR 45, paras 27–28; *Copland v The United Kingdom* (2007) 45 EHRR 37, para 48.

[69] *Silver v The United Kingdom* [1983] ECHR 5, 86.

[70] *Malone v The United Kingdom* [1984] ECHR 10, para 67.

[71] *Malone v The United Kingdom* [1984] ECHR 10, para 67.

[72] *Malone v The United Kingdom* [1984] ECHR 10, para 68.

to this secret and potentially dangerous interference with the right to respect for private life and correspondence.[73]

[6–28]   The ECtHR imposes a more stringent test of legality where the Court considers the infringement to be 'particularly serious'. Due to the serious privacy intrusion caused by telephone tapping, for example, it must be 'based on a "law" that is particularly precise'. In the seminal surveillance cases of *Huvig v France* and *Kruslin v France*, the ECtHR set out a series of safeguards that are required to prevent abuses of power.[74] Reiterating the conclusions of the joined French cases, the ECtHR stated in *Valenzuela Contreras v Spain* that the following 'minimum safeguards' should be set out in statute:

(1)   A definition of the categories of people liable to have their telephones tapped by judicial order

(2)   The nature of the offences which may give rise to such an order

(3)   A limit on the duration of telephone tapping

(4)   The procedure for drawing up the summary reports containing intercepted conversations

(5)   The precautions to be taken in order to communicate the recordings intact and in their entirety for possible inspection by the judge and by the defence

(6)   The circumstances in which recordings may or must be erased or the tapes destroyed, in particular where an accused has been discharged by an investigating judge or acquitted by a court.[75]

[6–29]   It should be recalled that these enhanced 'in accordance with the law' safeguards will only be required for the use of surveillance measures that the ECtHR views on a level comparable to the 'particularly serious' interference caused by telephone tapping. The ECtHR has stated that '[w]hat is required by way of safeguard will depend, to some extent at least, on the nature and extent of the interference in question'.[76] The ECtHR has found several surveillance measures to meet this seriousness threshold, including the monitoring of an individual's email or internet usage[77] and the installation of covert listening devices in the home of an individual.[78] In a more recent ruling, the ECtHR has recognised that continued advances in surveillance technologies – particularly compilation and analysis capabilities – may require the ECtHR to further 'scrutinise the question as to whether the development of surveillance methods resulting in masses of data collected has been accompanied by a simultaneous development of legal safeguards securing respect for citizens' Convention rights'.[79] The ECtHR has previously commented in the bulk surveillance context that legislation should also detail the procedure to be followed when examining, using, storing, and

---

[73] *Malone v The United Kingdom* [1984] ECHR 10.

[74] *Huvig v France* (1990) 12 EHRR 528; *Kruslin v France* (1990) 12 EHRR 547.

[75] *Valenzuela Contreras v Spain* (1999) 28 EHRR 483, para 46.

[76] *PG and JH v The United Kingdom* [2001] ECHR 550, para 46.

[77] *Copland v The United Kingdom* (2007) 45 EHRR 37, para 44.

[78] *Khan v The United Kingdom* [2000] Crim LR 684, para 24.

[79] *Szabó and Vissy v Hungary* App no 37138/14 (ECtHR, 12 January 2016) paras 68–70; Maria Helen Murphy, 'Algorithmic Surveillance: The Collection Conundrum' (2017) 31(2) International Review of Law, Computers & Technology 225.

communicating the data to other parties.[80] However, the decision of the Grand Chamber of the ECtHR in *Roman Zakharov v Russia* can be interpreted to deem the practice of mass surveillance as inherently incompatible with the Convention due to the complete absence of 'reasonable suspicion'.[81] Due to the continued emphasis placed by many governments on the importance of mass surveillance programmes for their national security strategies, this is a potential area of contention to monitor in the future.

The safeguards laid out by the ECtHR in *Valenzuela Contreras v Spain* – and other surveil- **[6–30]** lance cases – are prescriptive and it is notable that a supranational court felt empowered to provide such explicit instructions regarding the contents of domestic legislation. On the other hand, the ECtHR has designated several intrusive measures as constituting less seri- ous intrusions. An early example was in the case of *Malone* where the practice of metering phone calls was found to constitute an interference, but a less serious one.[82] A more recent example was found in the case of *Uzun v Germany*, where a GPS tracking device was attached to the car of a terrorist suspect. When assessing the seriousness of the interference with Article 8 ECHR caused by the use of GPS tracking, the ECtHR relied on the conten- tion that location data discloses less information regarding an individual's 'conduct, opin- ions or feelings' than other surveillance measures. While the ECtHR did not bar 'gaining inspiration' from the enhanced 'in accordance with the law' safeguards laid out above, the ECtHR stated that the stricter standards were not applicable. The reasoning can be criticised for underestimating the threat that tracking and analysing location data poses to privacy. Even if the individual may be comfortable with being seen while driving on a public road, the character of that interaction changes when a log is maintained and combined with other information.[83]

Is the Surveillance Measure 'Necessary for Safeguarding Democratic Institutions'?

If a surveillance measure is found not to satisfy the 'in accordance with the law' standards, **[6–31]** the ECtHR often ceases its inquiry there and does not continue on to consider whether the measure was necessary in a democratic society. Where the extensive legality require- ments applicable in the surveillance context have been met, however, the necessity of the measures must be considered. In the surveillance context, the ECtHR has approached the necessity test in a practical manner, stating that it will consider secret surveillance 'strictly necessary for safeguarding democratic institutions' where there are 'adequate and effective safeguards against abuse'.[84] This assessment

> depends on all the circumstances of the case, such as the nature, scope and duration of the possible measures, the grounds required for ordering such measures, the authorities competent to permit, carry out and supervise such measures, and the kind of remedy provided by the national law.[85]

---

[80] *Weber and Saravia v Germany* [2006] ECHR 1173, para 95.

[81] *Roman Zakharov v Russia* [2015] ECHR 1065, para 264.

[82] *Malone v The United Kingdom* [1984] ECHR 10, para 56.

[83] This issue is discussed further in [6–54] to [6–71] dealing with the Criminal Justice (Surveillance) Act 2009.

[84] *Kennedy v The United Kingdom* [2010] ECHR 682, para 153.

[85] *Klass v Germany* (1979–80) 2 EHRR 214, para 50.

The reasoning appears to be that if you impose procedural requirements on surveillance measures, the authorities will be more likely to act in a manner that is necessary in a democratic society. If there is a robust authorisation process, independent supervision, and availability of remedies the likelihood of abuse is reduced.

Protection of Privacy under the EU Charter

[6–32] The more recent Charter of Fundamental Rights of the European Union (EU Charter) has further supplemented the protections of the Constitution and the ECHR. While the institutions of the European Union (EU) have long held that fundamental rights form an 'integral part of the general principles of law' and have recognised an obligation to respect fundamental rights,[86] the EU Charter is the document that codifies the protection of a range of rights for EU citizens and residents. Reflecting its later drafting, the EU Charter separates the right to 'respect for private and family life' and the right to 'protection of personal data'. In spite of this separation, the rights are likely to interact and overlap in many situations.

Article 7 EU Charter	**Article 8 EU Charter**
Respect for private and family life	Protection of personal data
Everyone has the right to respect for his or her private and family life, home and communications.	1. Everyone has the right to the protection of personal data concerning him or her.
	2. Such data must be processed fairly for specified purposes and on the basis of the consent of the person concerned or some other legitimate basis laid down by law. Everyone has the right of access to data which has been collected concerning him or her, and the right to have it rectified.
	3. Compliance with these rules shall be subject to control by an independent authority.

[6–33] The EU Charter gained legal status equivalent to the EU treaties following the entry into force of the Lisbon Treaty in 2009. Accordingly, the EU and its institutions must act in accordance with the EU Charter and Member States must comply with the Charter when implementing EU law. Due to the importance of EU law in the field of privacy and data protection, the EU Charter will be relevant in many instances domestically.[87] Crucially, the Court of Justice of the European Union (CJEU) is empowered to strike down legislation that is found to violate the EU Charter. This power proved crucial in a surveillance case with an Irish inception – *Digital Rights Ireland* – that found its way to the CJEU.[88]

---

[86] Case 228/69 *Internationale Handelsgesellschaft mbH v Einfuhr und Vorratsstelle für Getreide und Futtermittel* [1970] ECR 1125; Maastricht Treaty, art F.

[87] EU Charter of Fundamental Rights, art 51.

[88] Joined Cases C–293/12 and C–594/12 *Digital Rights Ireland and Seitlinger and Others* [2014] WLR (D) 164. *Digital Rights Ireland Ltd v Minister for Communications, Marine and Natural Resources, Minister for Justice, Equality and Law Reform, The Commissioner of the Garda Síochána, Ireland and the Attorney General* [2012] OJ C258/11.

The high-profile ruling was delivered in response to preliminary ruling requests from the **[6–34]**
Irish High Court and the Austrian Constitutional Court. The key question was whether the
Data Retention Directive – an EU-wide surveillance measure introduced in the aftermath of
the London bombings – was compatible with the EU Charter.[89] The Irish information rights
group Digital Rights Ireland opposed the general measure, which had, since 2006, mandated
that Member States require the retention of all communications metadata for between six and
24 months.[90] Metadata is the 'who, when, and where' of communications. While it does not
include content data, it can be used to build up an incredibly detailed profile of an individual's activities and associations. The CJEU noted that the data retained under the Directive
had the potential to

> allow very precise conclusions to be drawn concerning the private lives of the persons
> whose data has been retained, such as the habits of everyday life, permanent or tempo-
> rary places of residence, daily or other movements, the activities carried out, the social
> relationships of those persons and the social environments frequented by them.[91]

The Directive required the collection of data on 'all persons and all means of electronic **[6–35]**
communication as well as all traffic data without any differentiation, limitation or exception
being made'. This generalised collection was criticised by the CJEU and the Directive was
found to be a disproportionate interference with the EU Charter. Articles 7 and 8 of the EU
Charter were central to the holding of the Court.[92] The CJEU was particularly critical of the
blanket application of the Directive and the fact that the Directive did 'not require any relationship between the data whose retention is provided for and a threat to public security'.[93]

---

[89] *Digital Rights Ireland Ltd v Minister for Communications, Marine and Natural Resources, Minister
for Justice, Equality and Law Reform, The Commissioner of the Garda Síochána, Ireland and the
Attorney General* [2010] IEHC 221. See *Digital Rights Ireland Ltd v Minister for Communications,
Marine and Natural Resources, Minister for Justice, Equality and Law Reform, The Commissioner of
the Garda Síochána, Ireland and the Attorney General* [2012] OJ C258/11; *Kärntner Landesregierung
and Others* [2013] OJ C79/7.
[90] Parliament and Council Directive (EC) 24/2006 on the retention of data generated or processed in
connection with the provision of publicly available electronic communications services or of public
communications networks and amending Directive 2002/58/EC [2006] OJ L105/54. The Directive
frequently asserted that the 'content' of communications could not be retained under the authority of
the Directive. See art 1(2), art 5(2), and Recital 13 of the Directive. The compulsory retention of data
under the Directive was introduced as a derogation from the privacy protections established by both the
Parliament and Council Directive (EC) 46/1995 on the protection of individuals with regard to the processing of personal data and on the free movement of such data [1995] OJ L281/31 and the Parliament
and Council Directive (EC) 58/2002 concerning the processing of personal data and the protection
of privacy in the electronic communications sector [2002] OJ L201/37; Joined Cases C–293/12 and
C–594/12 *Digital Rights Ireland and Seitlinger and Others* [2014] WLR (D) 164.
[91] Joined Cases C–293/12 and C–594/12 *Digital Rights Ireland and Seitlinger and Others* [2014]
WLR (D) 164 para 27. While the CJEU did find the retention of information under the Directive to
constitute a 'particularly serious interference' with privacy and personal data rights, the CJEU also held
that the Directive did not violate 'the essence' of those rights. The Court justified this distinction by
recognising that the Directive did not permit the retention of content data and the Directive required
respect for 'certain principles of data protection' at paras 39–40.
[92] Joined Cases C–293/12 and C–594/12 *Digital Rights Ireland and Seitlinger and Others* [2014]
WLR (D) 164, paras 29–30.
[93] Joined Cases C–293/12 and C–594/12 *Digital Rights Ireland and Seitlinger and Others* [2014]
WLR (D) 164, para 59.

Some have argued that the ruling in *Digital Rights Ireland* means that the indiscriminate retention of data can never be compatible with the EU Charter.[94] This position appears to be supported by a subsequent ruling where the CJEU stated that:

> while the effectiveness of the fight against serious crime, in particular organised crime and terrorism, may depend to a great extent on the use of modern investigation techniques, such an objective of general interest, however fundamental it may be, cannot in itself justify that national legislation providing for the general and indiscriminate retention of all traffic and location data should be considered to be necessary for the purposes of that fight.[95]

[6–36]   In addition to criticising the unconstrained retention, the CJEU also requires strict safeguards to be implemented in order to limit the access to and subsequent use of retained data by government authorities. In *Digital Rights Ireland* the CJEU referenced the case law of the ECtHR and stated that EU legislation mandating data retention must contain

> clear and precise rules governing the scope and application of the measure in question and imposing minimum safeguards so that the persons whose data have been retained have sufficient guarantees to effectively protect their personal data against the risk of abuse and against any unlawful access and use of that data.[96]

[6–37]   According to the CJEU, independent prior review should be required before data can be accessed by government authorities and specific rules should be set out to ensure the security and protection of retained data. The CJEU directed additional criticism at the Data Retention Directive for not requiring that data be retained within the EU, as this meant that the Directive could not ensure 'compliance with the requirements of protection and security by an independent authority'.[97] This criticism seems somewhat influenced by the preceding Snowden revelations but also indicates the significance of Article 8 of the EU Charter, which explicitly requires that compliance with data protection rules be subject to control by an independent authority.

[6–38]   Subsequent to the ruling in Digital Rights Ireland, the CJEU has delivered several crucial rulings in favour of privacy – most notably in *Maximillian Schrems v Data Protection Commissioner* and in *Tele2 Sverige AB v Post-och telestyrelsen and Secretary of State for*

---

[94] Glyn Moody, 'EU Lawyers Confirm "General and Blanket Data Retention is no Longer Possible" in European Union' (*Techdirt*, 12 August 2014) <www.techdirt.com/articles/20140811/07430928173/ eu-lawyers-confirm-general-blanket-data-retention-is-no-longer-possible-european-union.shtml> accessed 9 June 2017.

[95] Joined Cases C–203/15 and C–698/15 *Tele2 Sverige AB v Post-och telestyrelsen and Secretary of State for the Home Department v Tom Watson and Others* [2017] 2 WLR 1289, para 103.

[96] Joined Cases C–293/12 and C–594/12 *Digital Rights Ireland and Seitlinger and Others* [2014] WLR (D) 164, para 54, citing *Liberty and Others v the United Kingdom* [2008] ECHR 568, paras 62–63; *Rotaru v Romania* [2000] ECHR 192, paras 57–59; and *S and Marper v the United Kingdom* [2008] ECHR 1581, para 99.

[97] In the subsequent ruling in *Maximillian Schrems v Data Protection Commissioner*, the Court found the 'Safe Harbor' data transfer mechanism to be invalid. The mechanism had facilitated the streamlined sharing of data between the EU and self-certified US companies. Case C–362/14 *Maximillian Schrems v Data Protection Commissioner* ECLI:EU:C:2015:650.

the Home Department v Tom Watson and Others.[98] While the CJEU may be the newcomer to privacy rights adjudication in Europe, it has already established itself as a crucial source of rights protection in the face of increased calls for government surveillance.

Surveillance Laws in Ireland

In accordance with basic rule of law principles, the ECHR, the EU Charter, and the Constitution all require the provision of a legal basis for surveillance measures that interfere with the privacy rights of citizens. Historically, the Irish government has not been proactive in providing legal bases for the surveillance carried out by the State, and has even issued secret directives in order to facilitate surveillance contrary to demands of the Data Protection Commissioner.[99] Unlike the comprehensive approach favoured by the United Kingdom,[100] Ireland regulates surveillance measures in a piecemeal fashion. The following section discusses the three major pieces of legislation governing surveillance measures in Ireland: the Interception of Postal Packets and Telecommunications Messages (Regulation) Act 1993 (Interception Act), the Criminal Justice (Surveillance) Act 2009 (Surveillance Act), and the Communications (Retention of Data) Act 2011 (Retention of Data Act). [6–39]

From a process perspective, it makes sense to think about surveillance measures at three separate stages: [6–40]

1. The period before the surveillance
2. The period when surveillance is ongoing
3. The period after the surveillance ceases

While privacy considerations will be relevant at each stage, different procedures may be appropriate at different points in the investigative process. In a democratic society that does not permit arbitrary action, authorities should have conducted investigations that indicate the merit of subjecting a target to surveillance measures before operations commence. Once an active surveillance operation is underway, good practice requires investigating authorities to conduct the measures in compliance with governing legislation and in accordance with any restrictions or guidelines laid out as a condition of the surveillance measures. Once the surveillance has ceased, attention turns to the use made of the data and reflection on whether or not the investigation was carried out appropriately. In a system that values accountability, repercussions must follow for those who act inappropriately and remedies must be available for those who are harmed. While there is a significant risk of abuse occurring during the surveillance period itself, effective independent review is less likely to occur at this point. Due to barriers to scrutiny and operational considerations, safeguards tend to focus on providing accountability and control before and after surveillance measures have been conducted. This is not to say that independent and contemporaneous review is impossible while surveillance operations are ongoing; it merely reflects the reality that such review is rare and resisted by those who exercise surveillance powers. This is another reason why it is so essential to have *post hoc* review and the availability of accessible redress mechanisms. [6–41]

---

[98] Case C–362/14 *Maximillian Schrems v Data Protection Commissioner* ECLI:EU:C:2015:650; Joined Cases C–203/15 and C–698/15 *Tele2 Sverige AB v Post-och telestyrelsen and Secretary of State for the Home Department v Tom Watson and Others* [2017] 2 WLR 1289.

[99] Karlin Lillington, 'Bill to Give Guidelines on Data Has Bizarre Features' *The Irish Times* (Dublin, 13 February 2009).

[100] See, for example, the Investigatory Powers Act 2016 and the Regulation of Investigatory Powers Act 2000.

Interception of Postal Packets and Telecommunications Messages (Regulation) Act 1993 (Interception Act)

[6–42] The Interception Act is central to the legal framework providing for government interception of telecommunications in Ireland. The Postal and Telecommunications Services Act 1983 made it an offence to intercept postal and telecommunication messages.[101] Before this, the government interception of communications was entirely unregulated. The power granted to the Minister for Communications to instruct service providers 'to do (or refrain from doing) anything which he may specify from time to time as necessary in the national interest' was used to justify interception measures.[102] Taken as the sole legal basis for interception measures, the 1983 Act is clearly deficient from a human rights perspective. In spite of the fact that conducting surveillance under this non-conditional provision would clearly fail under an Article 8 ECHR assessment, revelatory political events – as opposed to legal conscientiousness – eventually forced the introduction of specific amending interception legislation. A phone-hacking scandal – where the government of the day illegitimately intercepted the communications of journalists – was the primary motivation for the introduction of the Interception Act. This Act details the procedures that must be followed and the safeguards that must be applied when conducting interception operations in Ireland.

Initially, the Interception Act conferred interception powers on An Garda Síochána and the Defence Forces. Subsequently, interception powers have been extended to the Garda Síochána Ombudsman Commission (GSOC).[103] While the powers granted to each of these bodies is significant, the similarities of the process for each body mean that it is appropriate to concentrate on how the law applies to An Garda Síochána.

The Period Before the Interception

[6–43] Interception may be possible under the Act where it is in the interests of state security, or where it is necessary for the purposes of a criminal investigation.[104] To qualify as an interception for 'the investigation of crime' there must be an investigation being carried out by an authorised agency and the suspected offence must qualify as 'serious'.[105] The Act lays down certain conditions that must be followed when conducting interception operations. In order to carry out interception measures, an interception authorisation warrant must be obtained in accordance with the Interception Act. The process adopted under the Interception Act differs significantly from the process generally taken when obtaining a physical search warrant that typically involves a judge. The authorisation system for interception warrants is conducted entirely within the executive branch with no external involvement. The additional protection afforded to the practice of physical search seems inconsistent given the contents of personal communications and their connection to intimate private and home life.

[6–44] Under the Interception Act, the warrant process requires the submission of a written application for an authorisation by the Commissioner of An Garda Síochána to the Minister for

---

[101] Interception Act 1993, s 98.
[102] Interception Act 1993, s 110.
[103] Garda Síochána (Amendment) Act 2015.
[104] Interception Act, s 6(1)(a).
[105] A 'serious offence' is defined for the purposes of the Act as an offence for which a person may be imprisoned for five years or more. Interception Act 1993, s 1.

Justice and Equality and Defence.[106] The nominated officer – an officer of the Minister – examines applications first, and makes any inquiries that he or she thinks are necessary. The nominated officer then makes a signed submission to the Minister, stating whether he or she believes the application meets the conditions laid out in the Act.[107]

The application made to the Minister requesting authorisation for interception must contain **[6–45]** 'sufficient information' to enable the Minister to determine whether the requested interception is justified, applying the conditions specified in the Act. For example, in the case of an interception for the purpose of a criminal investigation it is necessary that An Garda Síochána be carrying out investigations into a serious offence.[108] The Interception Act also requires that interception should only be used where non-interception investigative techniques have 'failed, or are likely to fail, to produce, or to produce sufficiently quickly' information or evidence relating to a relevant offence.[109] Moreover, there must be 'a reasonable prospect that the interception would be of material assistance' in the investigation.[110]

If the Minister is satisfied that the conditions specified in the Act have been met, he or she **[6–46]** will issue a warrant for the interception.[111] The warrant should contain certain information that delineates the manner in which the warrant can be used. Such information includes basic information such as the date of the authorisation, the target of the interception, and the type of interception involved.[112] While the Act limits the period of authorisation to three months, the Act also makes provision for extensions (not exceeding three months each).[113] While the availability of an extension may be necessary in certain complex investigations, the possibility of perpetual surveillance without any judicial involvement creates a significant risk of abuse.

The Period After the Interception

The Interception Act established two new offices to conduct *post hoc* review of surveillance **[6–47]** measures conducted under the Act. Due to the inherently secretive nature of interceptions it was thought necessary to restrict access to the ordinary courts and instead establish alternative forums of accountability.[114] The first office is the 'Designated Judge', who conducts annual reviews of the application of the Interception Act.

The Designated Judge is a High Court judge who keeps the operation of the Interception Act **[6–48]** under review and is assigned to assess whether the provisions of the Act are complied with. The Designated Judge is required to report on his findings to the Taoiseach, who must in turn cause a copy of the report to be laid before the Oireachtas.[115] The Interception Act empowers

---

[106] Even though the authorisation process under the Interception Act is conducted entirely within the executive branch, the Act permits an exception to the written requirement where there is 'exceptional urgency'. If this is the case, the Minister may authorise an interception or extend an authorisation orally. When this 'exceptional urgency' procedure is used, confirmation by warrant from the Minister is required 'as soon as may be': Interception Act, s 2(2)(b), (c) and 2(6)(b).

[107] Interception Act, ss 4–5.

[108] Or another public authority charged with the investigation of offences of the kind in question.

[109] Interception Act, s 5.

[110] Interception Act, s 4. Slightly modified standards are laid out in s 4 to address cases where a serious offence is apprehended but has not been committed.

[111] Interception Act, s 2(2)(a).

[112] Interception Act, s 2(4).

[113] Interception Act, s 2.

[114] Dáil Deb 19 May 1993, vol 431, no 1.

[115] Interception Act, s 8(1)(2). If the Taoiseach considers, after consultation with the designated judge, that the publication of any matter in a report of the Designated Judge would be prejudicial to the

the Designated Judge to investigate any case where an authorisation has been granted and entitles the judge to access and inspect any official documents relating to an authorisation or the application.[116] Any person who was involved in an application or an authorisation, or was otherwise concerned with an authorisation or an application, must provide the judge with any relevant information in his or her possession that the judge requests.[117]

[6–49] The freedom granted to the Designated Judge to decide what is appropriate to place in the annual report has resulted in very little substantive information being made available to the public. Digital Rights Ireland has carried out invaluable work, collecting and maintaining copies of the annual reports in their online 'Surveillance Library'.[118] As you can see from the entire text of the 2014 Report (included below), the reports are terse and provide minimal transparency. The fact that numerous bodies were visited and inspected regarding their compliance with two pieces of surveillance legislation over the span of three days provides little reassurance regarding the level of scrutiny to which interception measures are being subject.

Report of the Designated Judge Pursuant to Section 8(2) of the Interception of Postal Packets and Telecommunications Messages (Regulation) Act 1993 and Section 12(1)(c) of the Communications (Retention of Data) Act 2011

I am the 'Designated Judge' under the above mentioned Acts. On 24th October, 2014, I attended at the Headquarters of An Garda Síochána at 'the Depot', Phoenix Park, Dublin and later in the afternoon of the same day, at the Headquarters of the Army in McKee Barracks, Blackhorse Avenue, Dublin.

On 31st October, 2013, I attended at the Office of An Garda Síochána Ombudsman Commission, 150 Upper Abbey Street, Dublin and later on the afternoon of the same date at the Office of the Revenue Commissioners, Block D, Ashtown Gate, Dublin 15.

On the morning of 6th November, 2014, I attended at the Office of the Department of Justice and Equality, St. Stephen's Green, Dublin 2.

In each of these locations, such documents and records pertaining to the operation of the above Acts as were requested by me, were made available and were examined by me. I also spoke with the persons with responsibility for and overseeing the operation of the above Acts, in each location and all of my queries were answered to my satisfaction.

I am satisfied that as of the date of this report, the relevant State authorities are in compliance with the provisions of the above Acts.

Figure 3   *2014 Report of the Designated Judge under the Interception Act 1993[119]*

---

prevention or detection of crime or to the security of the State, the Taoiseach may exclude that matter from the copies of the report laid before the Houses of the Oireachtas Interception Act, s 8(8).

[116] Interception Act, s 8(1)(3)(a)(b).

[117] Interception Act, s 8(1)(5).

[118] Digital Rights Ireland, 'Surveillance Library' (undated) <www.digitalrights.ie/irish-surveillance-documents/> accessed 9 June 2017.

[119] A scan of the original report – signed and dated by Mr Justice Paul McDermott – is available in the DRI Surveillance Library: Digital Rights Ireland, 'Surveillance Library' (undated) <https://www. digitalrights.ie/irish-surveillance-documents/> accessed 9 June 2017. Typographical error in original.

In addition to the provision of a supervising Designated Judge, the Interception Act also **[6–50]** provides for the appointment of a 'Complaints Referee' who is empowered to investigate complaints made under the Act.[120] The Complaints Referee may be a Circuit or District Court judge or a practising barrister or solicitor of not less than 10 years' standing. In spite of this flexibility, the Complaints Referees appointed thus far have been judges. The Complaints Referee is appointed for a renewable term of five years. Under the Act, if a person believes that a communication sent to or by him or her has been intercepted in the course of its transmission by a postal or telecommunications service provider, he or she may apply to the Complaints Referee for an investigation into the matter. While the open jurisdiction should in theory provide wide access to the redress mechanism, the absence of any notification provision in the legislation undermines the plausibility of individuals obtaining effective redress under the section.

Where the application is neither frivolous nor vexatious, the Complaints Referee investi- **[6–51]** gates whether a relevant authorisation was in force at the material time and if so, whether there has been a contravention of the Act. The Act grants the Complaints Referee access and inspection rights to 'any official documents relating to a relevant authorisation or the application'. The Act requires individuals to give the Referee any interception-related information in their possession that the Referee requests.[121]

If a contravention is found, the Complaints Referee notifies the applicant in writing and **[6–52]** makes a report to the Taoiseach. If the Complaints Referee 'thinks fit' he or she will:

(i)   quash the relevant authorisation,
(ii) direct the destruction of any copy of the communications intercepted pursuant to the authorisation,
(iii) make a recommendation for the payment to the applicant of such sum by way of compensation as may be specified in the order.[122]

Section 9(12) obliges the Minister for Justice to implement any recommendation for compensation. If the Complaints Referee finds no contravention of the Act, the notice given to the complainant states only that 'there has been no contravention of a provision of sections 2, 6, 7 or 8(6)'.[123]

The ECtHR has stated on several occasions that 'as soon as notification can be made with- **[6–53]** out jeopardising the purpose of the surveillance after its termination, information should be provided to the persons concerned'.[124] The Interception Act does not provide this type of notification, and to obtain any information regarding interception of communications, an individual must first suspect that they have been the subject of authorisation. If an entirely innocent person is surveilled by mistake or for nefarious reasons, they are never likely to learn of that fact or to receive any recompense for the invasion of their privacy. Moreover, even if an individual somehow correctly suspects that they have had their communications

---

[120] Interception Act, s 9.
[121] Interception Act, s 9(10) (11).
[122] Interception Act, s 9(5)(c).
[123] Interception Act, s 9(8).
[124] *Ekimdzhiev v Bulgaria* [2007] ECHR 533, para 90.

wrongfully intercepted, that fact can only be confirmed if the Complaints Referee believes it is not against the public interest. The discretion given to the Complaints Referee is potentially harmful, particularly as there is no appeal system and his or her determination is final. At this time, there is no evidence of any successful complaints under the Complaints Referee mechanism. While there is no official reporting of decisions or statistics, Digital Rights Ireland obtained a copy of a failed complaint that is stored in the DRI Surveillance Library.[125] In his response to the complaint, the Complaints Referee, Judge John Hannan, thanked the complainant for his or her patience and continued:

> I have carried out an investigation into your complaints which has now concluded.
> I have found that there has been no contravention of the provisions of the of the Criminal Justice (Surveillance) Act 2009.
> I have found that there has been no contravention of a provision of section 2, 6, 7 or 8(6) Interception of Postal Packets and Telecommunications Messages (Regulation) Act 1993.

Figure 4   *2016 Complaints Referee Response to Failed Complaint*[126]

Criminal Justice (Surveillance) Act 2009 (Surveillance Act)

[6–54]   The Surveillance Act provides the legal basis for the government use of covert surveillance devices in Irish law. Under the Surveillance Act, An Garda Síochána, the Defence Forces, the Revenue Commissioners, and the Garda Síochána Ombudsman Commission are given a legal basis to carry out covert surveillance in order to combat serious criminal, subversive, or terrorist activity.[127] While the title of the Act might suggest that the legislation provides for a comprehensive surveillance regime, the term 'surveillance' is defined narrowly as 'monitoring, observing, listening to or making a recording' of a particular person, group,[128] place, or thing 'by or with the assistance of surveillance devices'.[129] As a result, the Surveillance Act applies only where a 'surveillance device' is used to monitor, observe, listen to, or record a person, place, or thing. The scope of activities covered by this definition is narrowed further by the definition of 'surveillance device', which excludes some commonly used tools of surveillance such as CCTV[130] and photographic cameras.

[6–55]   While the Interception Act was introduced in large part to respond to a domestic scandal, the Surveillance Act was promoted by the government of the day as facilitating the admission of surveillance material in criminal proceedings. This was seen as a crucial measure to

---

[125] Digital Rights Ireland, 'Surveillance Library' (undated) <www.digitalrights.ie/irish-surveillance-documents/> accessed 9 June 2017.
[126] A scanned copy of the rejected complaint – signed and dated by Judge John Hannan – is stored in the DRI Surveillance Library: Digital Rights Ireland, 'Surveillance Library' (undated) <www.digitalrights.ie/irish-surveillance-documents/> accessed 9 June 2017. Typographical error in original.
[127] Garda Síochána (Amendment) Act 2015, s 13.
[128] Including their movements, activities and communications.
[129] Surveillance Act, s 1.
[130] Within the meaning of s 38 of An Garda Síochána Act 2005 (which governs CCTV).

tackle gangland crime where witness intimidation was a significant concern.[131] In spite of the focus on evidence and admissibility, the Act was actually the first piece of legislation to provide a statutory basis for the use of surveillance devices in Ireland.[132]

The Period Before the Surveillance Measure

A key distinction between authorising procedures for the Interception Act and the Surveillance Act is the involvement of an independent judge at the authorisation stage – before any surveillance has been carried out – under the Surveillance Act. Under the Surveillance Act, a 'Superior Officer'[133] of either An Garda Síochána, the Defence Forces, the Revenue Commissioners, or GSOC[134] must make an application to a District Court judge for an authorisation before using a surveillance device in an investigation.[135]   **[6–56]**

Before applying to the Court, the Superior Officer of An Garda Síochána must have reasonable grounds for believing that the surveillance measure is necessary

> to determine whether or under what circumstances an arrestable offence[136] has been committed or
> for obtaining evidence for the purposes of court proceedings in relation to the offence or for the maintenance of State security.[137]

In the case of the Defence Forces, the grounds should be belief that the surveillance is necessary for the purpose of maintaining the security of the State. In the case of the Revenue Commissioners, the grounds should be belief that the surveillance is necessary for the investigation of a revenue offence or for preventing the commission of revenue offences.[138] Finally, in the case of GSOC, the grounds should be belief that as part of an investigation being conducted by the GSOC, the surveillance is necessary to determine whether or under what circumstances an arrestable offence has been committed or for obtaining evidence for the purposes of court proceedings.[139]   **[6–57]**

Regardless of the government agency involved, the Superior Officer should reasonably believe that the measure is proportionate and that the requested measure is of a reasonable   **[6–58]**

---

[131] Explanatory Memorandum to the Criminal Justice (Surveillance) Bill 2009.

[132] Alisdair Gillespie, 'Covert Surveillance, Human Rights and the Law' (2009) 19(3) Irish Criminal Law Journal 71; Maria Helen Murphy, 'Surveillance and the Right to Privacy: Is an "Effective Remedy" Possible?' in Alice Diver and Jacinta Miller (eds), *Justiciability of Human Rights Law in Domestic Jurisdictions* (Springer 2016).

[133] A 'superior officer' is '(a) in the case of the Garda Síochána, a member of the Garda Síochána not below the rank of superintendent; (b) in the case of the Defence Forces, a member of the Defence Forces not below the rank of colonel; and (c) in the case of the Revenue Commissioners, an officer of the Revenue Commissioners not below the rank of principal officer': Surveillance Act, s 1.

[134] A member of the Ombudsman Commission other than its chairperson: Garda Síochána (Amendment) Act 2015, s 13.

[135] Surveillance Act, s 4(1)(2)(3).

[136] An arrestable offence is an offence that carries a potential sentence of five years or more. The definition includes attempting to commit such an offence: Criminal Law Act, 1997, s 2.

[137] Surveillance Act, s 4(a).

[138] Surveillance Act, s 4.

[139] Garda Síochána (Amendment) Act 2015, s 13.

duration. Furthermore, the Superior Officer must have reasonable grounds for believing that the surveillance measure for which he or she is seeking authorisation is the 'least intrusive means available, having regard to its objectives and other relevant considerations'.[140]

[6–59] With the inclusion of the general category of 'arrestable offences', the Surveillance Act has the potential to apply in a wide variety of circumstances. This fact was not reflected in the Dáil debates, however, which centred on the role of the Surveillance Act in tackling gangland crime. A former Chief Superintendent, Mr John O'Brien, queried this 'generalist approach by seeking to apply this law to the entire population' when '[t]he threats emanate from specific and defined sources, criminal gangs and subversive organisations'.[141] In the Seanad, Senator Ivana Bacik struck a note of caution in her contribution, reminding those present of the history of political bugging and warning that care should be taken to avoid setting 'the scope of legislation such as this Bill overly broad'. She pressed for a more particularised approach to what offences would be relevant under the Act and cited the 'political reason for the legislation's introduction' as supporting a targeted approach. Senator Bacik suggested that surveillance should be confined to situations where it was necessary to 'investigate and–or gather intelligence on organised crime'.[142] Despite the central stage the gangland situation assumed in the debates, the Minister for Justice asserted that he 'never said the Bill was only to deal with gangland crime; it is to deal with all serious crime'.[143] In spite of the Minister's assertion, it is arguable that the emphasis placed on 'the changing nature of crime, particularly the growth of organised and ruthless gangs' skewed the debate and eclipsed broader consideration of human rights issues and implications.[144]

[6–60] As would be expected in the covert context of surveillance measures, the request for surveillance authorisation is *ex parte* and heard otherwise than in public. The District Court judge may issue a surveillance authorisation if he or she finds that there are appropriate and reasonable grounds for the measure and he or she is satisfied that the requested measure is the 'least intrusive means available', 'proportionate … having regard to all the circumstances', and of a reasonable duration.[145] However, the judge shall not issue an authorisation if he or she is satisfied that the proposed surveillance is likely to relate primarily to communications protected by privilege.[146] The judge must produce a written authorisation specifying the particulars of the surveillance device that is authorised to be used; the person, place, or thing that is to be the subject of the surveillance; the name of the superior officer to whom the authorisation is issued; any conditions subject to which the authorisation is issued; and the expiration date of the authorisation.[147]

---

[140] Surveillance Act, s 4(5)(a).

[141] John O'Brien, 'Surveillance Bill Will Fail to Tackle Gangs' *The Irish Times* (Dublin, 8 June 2009).

[142] Seanad Deb 2 July 2009, vol 196, no 9.

[143] Select Committee on Justice, Equality, Defence and Women's Rights Deb 11 June 2009, 3.

[144] Dáil Deb 29 April 2009, vol 681, col 337.

[145] Surveillance Act, s 4(5).

[146] Surveillance Act, s 5(4).

[147] Surveillance Act, s 5(6). Maria Helen Murphy, 'Surveillance and the Right to Privacy: Is an "Effective Remedy" Possible?' in Alice Diver and Jacinta Miller (eds), *Justiciability of Human Rights Law in Domestic Jurisdictions* (Springer 2016).

When compared with the interception regime, the requirement of judicial authorisation for   **[6–61]** the general use of surveillance devices is a notable advance and acts as a welcome safe- guard for the protection of privacy and the prevention of arbitrary action. Significant pow- ers are granted to the authorising judge under the Surveillance Act. The judge may impose any conditions on the surveillance authorisation as he or she 'considers appropriate'.[148] Although the Superior Officer will recommend a duration for the surveillance measure, the authorising judge is free to set a shorter authorisation period if he or she believes it to be reasonable.[149] The maximum duration of a surveillance authorisation is set to three months under the Surveillance Act, although a judge may renew an authorisation for a further period not exceeding three months as the judge deems appropriate.[150] While the Surveillance Act places no explicit restriction on the possibility of perpetual renewals, the essential role of the independent judge at the reauthorisation stage should act as an effective bulwark against such abuse.

Unfortunately, the District Court will not always be able to play this role as the Surveillance   **[6–62]** Act does not require the safeguard of judicial authorisation in every situation. In cases of urgency, surveillance will be possible without judicial authorisation for a period of up to 72 hours, subject to some conditions. A member of An Garda Síochána, the Defence Forces, GSOC, or an officer of the Revenue Commissioners may apply to a Superior Officer for the grant of an approval to carry out surveillance if he or she reasonably believes that the requirements for a standard application are met[151] and that before a judicial authorisation could be issued:

(a)   it is likely that a person would abscond for the purpose of avoiding justice, obstruct the course of justice or commit an arrestable offence or a revenue offence

(b)   information or evidence in relation to the commission of an arrestable offence or a revenue offence ... is likely to be destroyed, lost or otherwise become unavail- able, or

(c)   the security of the State would be likely to be compromised.[152]

In such situations, a Superior Officer may give approval for the emergency surveillance to   **[6–63]** be carried out if he or she believes on reasonable grounds that the conditions necessary to obtain a District Court authorisation are satisfied.[153] The Surveillance Act imposes some procedural obligations in respect of the operation of the emergency approval procedure by requiring the maintenance of written records and the making of reports by the parties involved.[154] The approving Superior Officer must make a report as soon as possible and not later than seven days after the surveillance has been completed. Notably, these reports

---

[148]   Surveillance Act, s 5(5).

[149]   Surveillance Act, s 5(8): 'An authorisation shall expire on the day fixed by the judge that he or she considers reasonable in the circumstances and that is not later than 3 months from the day on which it is issued.'

[150]   Surveillance Act, ss 5(8) and 6.

[151]   That is to say, he or she must reasonably believe that the surveillance is justified having regard to the matters referred to in s 4(5) and that the standards of ss 4(1), 4(2), or 4(3) are met.

[152]   Surveillance Act, s 7(2)(a)(b)(c).

[153]   Surveillance Act, s 7(2).

[154]   Surveillance Act, s 7(11).

are submitted to an in-house superior and not an external independent party. For example, where the report is made by a member of An Garda Síochána, the report is required to be delivered to an Assistant Commissioner; and where it is made by an officer of the Revenue Commissioners it is required to be delivered to an Assistant Secretary.[155] This is a clear weakness in a system that appears to recognise the importance of independent authorisation. If an urgent procedure is required – and even then, the 72-hour window of urgency seems excessive – it would be appropriate to require the internally prepared reports be sent to the Designated Judge (discussed below) at a minimum.

The Special Treatment of Tracking Devices

[6–64]　A tracking device is defined in the Surveillance Act as a device that, once attached to a person, vehicle, or thing, can be used to monitor the location of that person, vehicle, or thing.[156]

[6–65]　Section 8 of the Surveillance Act provides for a separate regime for the use of tracking devices. The separate regime was defended on the grounds that the tracking of location data is a 'less intrusive form of surveillance'.[157] While the ECtHR held in *Uzun v Germany* that GPS tracking is 'by its very nature' less intrusive than other methods of visual or audio surveillance,[158] growing awareness of the richness of location data casts serious doubt on that position.[159] Accordingly, it is disappointing that the much-vaunted safeguard of prior judicial authorisation is bypassed in the case of tracking devices. Instead of making an application to the District Court, a member of a designated agency is merely required to obtain internal approval from a Superior Officer to 'monitor the movements of persons, vehicles or things using a tracking device'. In addition to revoking the requirement for judicial authorisation, the Surveillance Act also allows for an increased maximum surveillance period of four months in the tracking device context.[160]

[6–66]　Minister of State John Curran asserted that a 'stringent system of control', including rules on record keeping and reporting, counterbalanced the reduced protection provided by the approval system.[161] One control measure is the obligation to keep a written record containing information detailing the person/vehicle/thing that is to be monitored, the time of the granting of the approval, and the duration of the monitoring.[162] A further restriction requires the Superior Officer to prepare a report not later than seven days after the use of tracking devices has ended. The report must include the grounds on which the approval was granted, a copy of the written record of approval, and a summary of the results of the surveillance.[163] This report must be made to a senior member of the relevant agency. For example, in the

---

[155] Surveillance Act, s 7(12)(a)(b)(c).

[156] Surveillance Act, s 1. Alisdair Gillespie, 'Covert Surveillance, Human Rights and the Law' (2009) 19(3) Irish Criminal Law Journal 71.

[157] Explanatory Memorandum to the Criminal Justice (Surveillance) Bill 2009.

[158] *Uzun v Germany* App no 35623/05 (ECtHR, 2 September 2010) s 52.

[159] Maria Helen Murphy, 'Algorithmic Surveillance: The Collection Conundrum' (2017) 31(2) International Review of Law, Computers & Technology 225.

[160] Surveillance Act, s 8.

[161] Seanad Deb 30 June 2009, vol 196, col 447.

[162] Surveillance Act, s 8(7)(a)(b)(c)(d)(e)(f).

[163] Surveillance Act, s 8(9).

case of An Garda Síochána, the report must be made to an officer with the rank of Assistant Commissioner. While these reporting requirements may be of use to the Designated Judge when he or she conducts the annual review, the lack of individualised external scrutiny is a significant weakness of s 8 of the Surveillance Act. Even if the system required all reports to receive individual attention from the Designated Judge, the initial harm would have been committed without any external authorisation process.

The inclusion of a separate regime to govern the use of tracking devices appears to be entirely founded on the contention that the use of tracking devices harms privacy less than the other forms of surveillance covered by the Surveillance Act. While location tracking may not capture content data, when it is collected for extended periods of time it can be an incredibly rich source of information. While 'isolated bits of information (as generated, for example, by merely walking around in public spaces and not taking active steps to avoid notice) are not especially revealing, assemblages are capable of exposing people quite profoundly'.[164] As you go about your day, you may visit the doctor, stop by a pharmacy, and attend a political meeting. When your daily movements are recorded and collated over an extended period of time, a nuanced picture of your life can be constructed. This detailed catalogue of data can reveal a lot about your 'preferences, friends, associations, and habits'.[165] Due to the extent of the possible intrusion, there is a strong case to be made for the use of tracking devices to be subject to the same safeguards as other surveillance devices covered by the Surveillance Act.   **[6–67]**

The Period After the Surveillance Measure

In addition to the judicial authorisation procedure,[166] the Surveillance Act also provides for a system of *post hoc* judicial oversight. While the system of review is modelled on the system established under the Interception Act, a different Designated Judge is appointed to review the operation of the Surveillance Act than the judge appointed to review both the Interception Act and the Retention of Data Act. As under the Interception Act, the Designated Judge for the Surveillance Act is obliged to report to the Taoiseach from 'time to time' and at least once every twelve months.[167] The Designated Judge for the Surveillance Act may investigate any case where a District Court judge authorises or renews surveillance and any case where approval is granted for the use of tracking devices or the emergency use of a surveillance device.[168] As is the case under the Interception Act (which grants the judge access and inspection rights in respect of any official documents relating to any interception authorisations)[169] the Designated Judge under the Surveillance Act is also granted extensive access rights.[170]   **[6–68]**

---

[164] Helen Nissenbaum, 'Protecting Privacy in an Information Age: The Problem of Privacy in Public' (1998) 17 Law and Philosophy 559.

[165] April Otterberg, 'GPS Tracking Technology: The Case for Revisiting Knotts and Shifting the Supreme Court's Theory of the Public Space under the Fourth Amendment' (2005) 46(3) Boston College Law Review 663.

[166] That applies outside of the special circumstances of tracking devices and urgent approvals.

[167] Surveillance Act, s 12.

[168] Surveillance Act, s 12(4).

[169] Interception Act, s 8(1), 8(3)(a)(b).

[170] Surveillance Act, s 8(2)(b), 8(5).

[6–69]   Unsurprisingly, similar concerns have been raised regarding the effectiveness of the review procedure provided under the Surveillance Act as those expressed about the procedure under the Interception Act. It is interesting to note that the form and content of the reports of the Designated Judge under the Surveillance Act have been different and more detailed than the reports previously provided under the Interception Act from successive Designated Judges.[171] This is in spite of the lack of any significant difference between the requirements laid out in either Act. The greater detail of the reports provides additional transparency. For example, reports of the Designated Judges under the Surveillance Acts have included more detailed descriptions of the systems for record-keeping in the government agencies and the manner in which the internal systems operate. A striking difference between the content of the reports made under the Surveillance and the Interception Acts is that the reports made to date under the Surveillance Act have provided an indication of the levels of surveillance that are being carried out. While the numbers are kept vague, they are indicative and can be used to examine trends or significant spikes in usage. For an example of how trends are reported, see the following extract from the Designated Judges Report from 2015.[172]

4.8   I am satisfied that the approvals granted were justified and in accordance with the provisions of the Act and that appropriate written records were maintained and available to me. A document on yearly statistics was provided to me which showed a reduction in section 5 authorisations, a substantial reduction in urgent authorisations and a slight reduction in section 8 authorisations for the period. There was also one section 8 refusal.

Figure 5   *Extract from 2015 Report of Designated Judge under the Surveillance Act 2009*

[6–70]   The fact that the report was 13 pages in total clearly illustrates the different nature of reports under the Surveillance Act. In spite of this, it should be noted that other countries provide for more detailed reports and there is a strong case for the publication of detailed statistics. This latter point is discussed in more detail below in the context of the Retention of Data Act.

[6–71]   Complaints under the Surveillance Act are dealt with by the same Complaints Referee appointed to the office under the Interception Act.[173] Similar investigative obligations apply and if the Complaints Referee finds a contravention, he or she will notify the affected party and prepare a report for the Taoiseach. If a material contravention is identified, the Complaints Referee has the power to quash the authorisation, recommend compensation (not exceeding €5,000), and report the matter to the Designated Judge. Where no contravention is identified, the Complaints Referee writes to the complainant stating this fact. As under the Interception Act, the Complaints Referee procedure will only be triggered where

---

[171]   Mark Tighe, 'Judges' Phone Tap Report "Is Laughable"' *The Sunday Times* (Dublin, 23 May 2009).
[172]   Digital Rights Ireland, 'Surveillance Library' (undated) <www.digitalrights.ie/irish-surveillance-documents/> accessed 9 June 2017.
[173]   Surveillance Act, s 11.

a person believes that they may have been subject to surveillance. In light of the covert nature of surveillance measures and the absence of notification in the Irish system, the effectiveness of the procedure is questionable.[174]

Communications (Retention of Data) Act 2011 (Retention of Data Act)

While the ruling of the CJEU in *Digital Rights Ireland* declared the EU Data Retention [6–72] Directive to be invalid, the legislation that implemented the Directive domestically – the Retention of Data Act – remains the governing law on data retention in Ireland.[175] While the Irish authorities have been proponents of data retention for many years, it is interesting to note that the Irish government actually opposed the introduction of the Data Retention Directive by the EU. The opposition was not based on privacy concerns, however, but on a procedural contention that the Directive was introduced under an inappropriate legal basis.[176]

The Period Before the Disclosure Request

The Communications (Retention of Data) Act 2011 obliges service providers to retain [6–73] telephony data for two years and internet data for 12 months.[177] The Act compels service providers to comply with disclosure requests made by An Garda Síochána, the Defence Forces, the Revenue Commissioners, and the Competition and Consumer Protection Commission.[178] While the Retention of Data Act does not identify GSOC as an authority entitled to access telecommunications records, the Garda Síochána Act 2005 confers designated officers of GSOC with the immunities and privileges conferred on An Garda Síochána.[179] Accordingly, GSOC has extensive powers of investigation and is entitled to make disclosure requests to telecommunications service providers. As the Data Retention Directive granted wide scope to Member States to delineate the detail of their domestic regimes, the Retention of Data Act defines a 'serious offence' as an offence 'punishable by imprisonment for a term of 5 years or more'.[180]

---

[174] Maria Helen Murphy, 'Surveillance and the Right to Privacy: Is an "Effective Remedy" Possible?' in Alice Diver and Jacinta Miller (eds), *Justiciability of Human Rights Law in Domestic Jurisdictions* (Springer 2016).

[175] The constitutionality of the law remains in question.

[176] 'The Court notes at the outset that the action brought by Ireland relates solely to the choice of legal basis and not to any possible infringement by the directive of fundamental rights resulting from interference with the exercise of the right to privacy': Press Release No 11/09 (10 February 2009) <europa.eu/rapid/press-release_CJE-09-11_en.htm?locale=en> accessed 9 June 2017; TJ McIntyre, 'Data Retention in Ireland: Privacy, Policy and Proportionality' (2008) 24 Computer Law and Security Review 326, 326–30.

[177] Communications (Retention of Data) Act 2011, s 3.

[178] Communications (Retention of Data) Act 2011, ss 6–7.

[179] Garda Síochána Act 2005, s 98.

[180] In addition, provision was made for a number of additional offences to be included under the definition of serious offence: Communications (Retention of Data) Act 2011, schedule 1.

[6–74]   In the course of an investigation by An Garda Síochána, disclosure requests may be made by a member of An Garda Síochána not below the rank of chief superintendent where that member is satisfied that the data are required for

    (a) the prevention, detection, investigation or prosecution of a serious offence,

    (b) the safeguarding of the security of the State, [or]

    (c) the saving of human life.[181]

[6–75]   In the course of activities of the Defence Forces, disclosure requests may be made by an officer of at least colonel rank in the Permanent Defence Forces where that officer is satisfied that the data are required for the purpose of safeguarding the security of the State.[182] In the course of an investigation by the Revenue Commissioners disclosure requests may be made by an officer of the Revenue Commissioners of at least principal officer rank where that officer is satisfied that the data are required for the prevention, detection, investigation or prosecution of a revenue offence.[183] In the course of an investigation by the Competition and Consumer Protection Commission, disclosure requests may be made by a member of the Competition and Consumer Protection Commission where that member is satisfied that the data are required for the prevention, detection, investigation or prosecution of a competition offence. These systems of internally authorised disclosure requests clearly fail to provide for independent judicial involvement at the point of access. The ECtHR has highlighted the importance of judicial authorisation and the *Digital Rights Ireland* decision made it clear that independent authorisation is necessary in order to ensure that access will only be granted where it is strictly necessary.[184]

The Period After the Disclosure Request

[6–76]   In a continuation of the approach adopted under the Interception and Surveillance Acts, the Retention of Data Act provides for the review of the operation of Act by a Designated Judge. Review of the Retention of Data Act is carried out by the same judge appointed to supervise the operation of the Interception Act and a combined report is produced on a yearly basis.[185] In line with his or her powers under the Interception Act, the Designated Judge may investigate any case in which a disclosure request is made, and may access and inspect any official documents or records relating to the request.

[6–77]   As was discussed above, the Irish record of *post hoc* judicial review of surveillance measures is open to criticism as an ineffective safeguard against abuse. Notwithstanding this, the

---

[181] The disclosure request must be for the purpose of the prevention, detection, investigation and prosecution of serious crime, safeguarding the security of the State and saving human life: Communications (Retention of Data) Act 2011, ss 6–7.

[182] The disclosure request must be for the purpose of safeguarding the security of the State. Communications (Retention of Data) Act 2011, s 6.

[183] The disclosure request must be for the investigation of a 'serious offence' under one of the following pieces of legislation: s 186 of the Customs Consolidation Act 1876; s 1078 of the Taxes Consolidation Act 1997; s 102 of the Finance Act 1999; s 119 of the Finance Act 2001; s 79 (inserted by s 62 of the Finance Act 2005) of the Finance Act 2003; s 78 of the Finance Act 2005: Communications (Retention of Data) Act 2011, s 6.

[184] Joined Cases C–293/12 and C–594/12 *Digital Rights Ireland and Seitlinger and Others* [2014] WLR (D) 164, para 62.

[185] Retention of Data Act, ss 11–12.

Retention of Data Act does have an additional reporting requirement that at least provides for greater transparency than is available under the other Acts.[186] Crucially, the Data Retention Directive required the preparation of reports that include detailed statistics about the number of disclosure requests being made by authorised agencies. The first step of this procedure requires the various authorised agencies to prepare and submit reports to the Minister for Justice, Equality and Law Reform on a yearly basis.[187] The report must include[188]

(a) the number of times when data had been disclosed in response to a disclosure request,

(b) the number of times when a disclosure request could not be met,

(c) the average period of time between the date on which the retained data were first processed and the disclosure request.

The Minister for Justice, Equality and Law Reform must review the information, prepare a report that consolidates the information and submit it to the European Commission. The feasibility of providing far more detailed statistics when European law requires it demonstrates the fact that there is no reason not to provide detailed statistics in relation to the Interception and Surveillance Acts. In addition to offering greater transparency, statistics reported in an anonymised manner pose little threat to operational effectiveness and should increase public trust in the system.[189] **[6–78]**

With its complaints procedure, the Retention of Data Act again follows the basic model adopted in the other pieces of Irish surveillance legislation.[190] Under s 10 of the Retention of Data Act, a person who believes that their data has been accessed via a disclosure request may apply to the Complaints Referee for an investigation into the matter. The Complaints Referee will investigate whether a disclosure request was made and, if so, whether the Retention of Data Act was complied with. If the Retention of Data Act has been contravened the Referee shall notify the applicant of that conclusion, and report his or her findings to the Taoiseach. Moreover, if the Referee thinks fit, he or she may order the destruction of the relevant data and/or recommend the payment of compensation. If, however, the Complaints Referee concludes that the Act was not contravened, the Referee shall notify the applicant in writing to that effect. The opacity of the operation of the Complaints Referee process is a consistent failure across the suite of Irish surveillance legislation. It is argued that where operational success will not be undermined, targets must be informed **[6–79]**

---

[186] The strength of the Designated Judge as a safeguard has been criticised, including in debates of the Oireachtas and in the media: Seanad Deb 5 May 1993, vol 136, col 480; Mark Tighe, 'Judges' Phone Tap Report "Is Laughable"' *The Sunday Times* (Dublin, 23 May 2009). Alisdair Gillespie, 'Covert Surveillance, Human Rights and the Law' (2009) 19(3) Irish Criminal Law Journal 71, 74; Maria Helen Murphy, 'The Relationship between the European Court of Human Rights and National Legislative Bodies: Considering the Merits and the Risks of the Approach of the Court in Surveillance Cases' (2013) 3(2) Irish Journal of Legal Studies 65, 83.

[187] Retention of Data Act, s 9.

[188] Retention of Data Act, s 9(5).

[189] Maria Helen Murphy, 'Surveillance and the Right to Privacy: Is an "Effective Remedy" Possible?' in Alice Diver and Jacinta Miller (eds), *Justiciability of Human Rights Law in Domestic Jurisdictions* (Springer 2016).

[190] Retention of Data Act, s 10.

that their communications have been interfered with by government authorities. Moreover, the outcomes of these proceedings must be reported publically in order to ensure that surveillance authorities are held accountable and that the public has insight into the operations of its government.

Conclusion

[6–80]   We are living in an interesting time for surveillance policy. We all produce and share more data than ever before, yet many of us are seeking new ways to protect our privacy and secure our data as we so do. We have witnessed significant attention being paid to government overreach since the Snowden revelations, yet numerous terrorist attacks in Europe and the US have led to increased legislative support for enhanced surveillance measures in many jurisdictions. The issue of generalised surveillance – where the entire population is subject to scrutiny – is a key point of tension. The profusion of databases, reduced costs of data storage, and new data-mining techniques cause intelligence agencies to argue for the necessity of mass collection and retention. In contrast, the ECtHR and the CJEU have delivered strong judgments against the practice, calling for a return to targeted surveillance directed at those under suspicion.

[6–81]   The privacy of the general public – as opposed to suspected criminals – is also harmed by techniques that undermine the security of the technologies that enable our communications. The Snowden revelations demonstrated the scale of these operations, with government-backed programmes – such as the NSA's 'Bullrun' – being used to target communications encryption.[191] Accordingly, while private individuals – including subversives based in despotic regimes – attempt to secure the privacy of their communications through technological means, government agencies continually attempt to undermine those efforts through 'supercomputers, technical trickery, court orders and behind-the-scenes persuasion'.[192] While such measures are defended on the basis that they are used to target terrorists and serious criminals, the damage caused to the ostensibly secure services and technologies undermines the privacy of everyday communications for all. How this issue plays out in the future will not just depend on how citizens react, but on how the companies who facilitate these communications choose to resist or comply with government demands.

[6–82]   The metaphor of a pendulum can provide a useful illustration of the manner in which public opinion tends to oscillate between favouring greater security and greater privacy. Major events – such as terrorist attacks on home soil – tend to heighten this effect and cause strong shifts in favour of greater surveillance. Some have argued that once the threat has passed, the intrusive measures 'can gradually be rolled back',[193] but the clandestine nature of surveillance and national security operations means that the public will rarely know if a threat has actually passed or even what measures need to be rolled back.

---

[191]   'Project Bullrun – Classification Guide to the NSA's Decryption Program' *The Guardian* (London, 5 September 2013).

[192]   Nicole Perlroth, Jeff Larson, and Scott Shane, 'NSA Able to Foil Basic Safeguards of Privacy on Web' *New York Times* (New York, 5 September 2013).

[193]   Amitai Etzioni, *The Limits of Privacy* (Basic Books 1999) 25.

Instead of relying on leaks, it seems clear that transparency and good procedures are **[6–83]** required if citizens are to exercise adequate control over the actions of their governments. In the Irish context, there is a compelling case for

- the regular reporting of transparent and comprehensive surveillance statistics,
- mandating the provision of detailed reports from the supervising authorities, and
- increased openness of the activities of the Complaints Referees.

Moreover, to ensure the best chance of preventing wrongful surveillance activities, inde- **[6–84]** pendent judicial scrutiny before any surveillance measures have been carried out seems essential.[194] The fact that such a requirement exists under the Surveillance Act negates argu- ments founded on operational concerns. Historically, the Irish government has rarely been proactive in providing safeguards for surveillance measures. As a result, it is likely that recourse to the courts will be an essential part of any reform efforts.

Further Reading

- Paul Bernal, *Internet Privacy Rights: Rights to Protect Autonomy* (Cambridge University Press 2014)
- Denis Kelleher, *Privacy and Data Protection Law in Ireland* (Bloomsbury 2015)
- TJ McIntyre, 'Data Retention in Ireland: Privacy, Policy and Proportionality' (2008) 24(4) Computer Law & Security Report 326
- TJ McIntyre, 'Judicial Oversight of Surveillance: The Case of Ireland in Comparative Perspective' in Martin Scheinin, Helle Krunke, and Marina Aksenova (eds), *Judges as Guardians of Constitutionalism and Human Rights* (Edward Elgar 2016)
- TJ McIntyre, 'Implementing Information Privacy Rights in Ireland' in Suzanne Egan (ed), *Implementing Human Rights in Ireland* (Bloomsbury Academic 2015)
- Maria Helen Murphy, 'Data Retention in the Aftermath of *Digital Rights Ireland* and *Seitlinger*' (2014) 24(4) Irish Criminal Law Journal 105
- Maria Helen Murphy, 'The Pendulum Effect: Comparisons between the Snowden Revelations and the Church Committee. What Are the Potential Implications for Europe?' (2014) 23(2) Information and Communications Technology Law 192
- Maria Helen Murphy, 'The Relationship between the European Court of Human Rights and National Legislative Bodies: Considering the Merits and the Risks of the Approach of the Court in Surveillance Cases' (2013) 3(2) Irish Journal of Legal Studies 65
- Maria Helen Murphy, 'Surveillance and the Right to Privacy: Is an "Effective Remedy" Possible?' in Alice Diver and Jacinta Miller (eds), *Justiciability of Human Rights Law in Domestic Jurisdictions* (Springer 2016)
- Neil Richards, *Intellectual Privacy* (Oxford University Press 2015)
- Marc Rotenberg, Julia Horwitz, and Jeramie Scott (eds), *Privacy in the Modern Age: The Search for Solutions* (New Press 2015)
- Daniel Solove, *Nothing to Hide: The False Tradeoff between Privacy and Security* (Yale University Press 2011)

---

[194] Perhaps with some exception for urgent measures. Urgent measures, however, should be defined much more narrowly. Moreover, even where urgent measures are necessary, judicial scrutiny must be involved as soon as possible.

CHAPTER 7
ICT and the Criminal Law

*'The proliferation and integration of computers into every aspect of economic activity
and society has inevitably resulted in a growth of criminality involving computers'*[1]

Unique Enforcement Challenges on the Internet

From cameras, to photocopiers, to peer-to-peer file sharing, technological advances are **[7–01]** almost inevitably accompanied by new criminal opportunities. Criminal applications of technological development have tended to follow 'legitimate uses with very little time lag'.[2] When discussing the issue of 'computer crime', the involvement of a computer can be incidental, for example where one party assaults another using a keyboard; these are outside of the scope of this chapter. In other circumstances, a crime may be facilitated by computers, for example where a computer is used to commit fraud. Other criminal acts, however, such as the distribution of malware, fundamentally require the use of a computer.

While computer crime predates and does not require the internet, the commission of crimes **[7–02]** over the internet raises additional complications for policy makers and law enforcement. While the law may have always had to respond to new technologies, the development of the internet created entirely new challenges. In the earlier days of the internet's popular adoption, there was a perception that the rules had fundamentally changed and that potentially a cyber Wild West had been created. The vision of the internet as an entirely new sphere is

---

[1] Ian Walden, 'Computer Crime and Information Misuse' in Chris Reed (ed), *Computer Law* (Oxford University Press 2011).

[2] Ian Lloyd, *Information Technology Law* (Oxford University Press 2000) 200; TJ McIntyre, 'Computer Crime in Ireland: a Critical Assessment of the Substantive Law' (2005) 15(1) Irish Criminal Law Journal 13–22.

represented by John Perry-Barlow in *The Declaration of the Independence of Cyberspace* where he stated, 'Your legal concepts of property, expression, identity, movement, and context do not apply to us. They are all based on matter, and there is no matter here.'[3] While the ideology of cyber-libertarianism (discussed in [1–46] to [1–47]) was a significant influence over such views, practical problems of enforcement over the internet posed – and continue to pose – significant challenges to the effective regulation of criminal activities carried out with the aid of the internet.

[7–03] While some may argue that 'there is nothing new under the sun',[4] others contend that the online environment gives rise to a 'new and distinctive form of criminal activity'.[5] As traditional crimes often retain the same basic characteristics when carried out online, it might be expected that such crimes should be adequately addressed by existing laws. Regardless, early attempts to apply general laws in the computer context were criticised by the House of Lords as a 'Procrustean attempt' to force new activities to fit within the language of a legislative Act 'not designed to fit them'.[6] The House of Lords stated that if it was thought desirable to create a new criminal offence covering dishonest access to a databank, then the legislature rather than the courts should take action.[7] Furthermore, there are specific challenges to the enforcement of crime on the internet that require the implementation of new and often targeted legislative measures.[8] Post, for example, suggests that the scale of the internet may require new approaches and opines that it

> would be astonishing if, say, the copyright law created in the early 1970s were able to cope at this new scale; that would be like expecting a bridge built to carry 1000 vehicles an hour to carry 10 billion vehicles an hour. It might work – but I'm not driving over that bridge until the engineers (who do, incidentally, understand a great deal about scale and scaling) tell me that it's OK.[9]

[7–04] Of significant note have been the digital forensic challenges, the difficulties around identification, the weaknesses of law enforcement in this technical area, and thorny jurisdictional issues. To successfully prosecute cybercrimes it is necessary to identify the perpetrator of

---

[3] John Perry Barlow, 'A Declaration of the Independence of Cyberspace' (8 February 1996) <www.eff.org/cyberspace-independence> accessed 13 June 2017. See discussion in Chapter 1.

[4] Of course, some undesirable computer-based activities do not have clear 'real world' analogues, e.g. denial of service attacks and the distribution of malicious software.

[5] TJ McIntyre, 'Cybercrime: Towards a Research Agenda' in Deirdre Healy and others (eds), *The Routledge Handbook of Irish Criminology* (Taylor and Francis 2015) 104, citing Peter Grabosky, 'Virtual Criminality: Old Wine in New Bottles?' (2001) 10 Social & Legal Studies 243, and Majid Yar, 'The Novelty of "Cybercrime": An Assessment in Light of Routine Activity Theory' (2005) 2 European Journal of Criminology 407.

[6] *R v Gold* [1988] 2 WLR 984. TJ McIntyre, 'Computer Crime in Ireland: a Critical Assessment of the Substantive Law' (2005) 15(1) Irish Criminal Law Journal 13.

[7] *R v Gold* [1988] 2 WLR 984. TJ McIntyre, 'Computer Crime in Ireland: a Critical Assessment of the Substantive Law' (2005) 15(1) Irish Criminal Law Journal 13.

[8] TJ McIntyre, 'Cybercrime: Towards a Research Agenda' in Deirdre Healy and others (eds), *The Routledge Handbook of Irish Criminology* (Taylor and Francis 2015) 106.

[9] David Post, *In Search of Jefferson's Moose: Notes on the State of Cyberspace* (Oxford University Press 2009).

the offence and to prove the case against the accused in court on the basis of evidence.[10] Both of these elements will generally require the use of digital forensic techniques. Digital forensic analysis can only be conducted by trained personnel who will need to be knowledgeable in multiple disciplines, including software engineering, cryptography, and data communications.[11] In addition to this resource constraint, perpetrators may also avail themselves of tools – such as encryption and audit disabling – to help evade detection and identification.[12] The relative novelty and anonymity of actions on the internet can not only cause those perpetrating crimes to feel less guilt or societal constraint, but it can also cause those tasked to enforce crimes to take the harm less seriously, and even cause those who are victims of crime on the internet to stay quiet about their experiences.[13]

The problem of jurisdiction is one of the most fundamental challenges to effective regulation on the internet. As a general matter, different laws apply in different jurisdictions and this situation is made possible by the acceptance 'that nation-states exist in autonomous, territorially-distinct, spheres and that activities therefore fall under the legal jurisdiction of only one legal regime at a time'.[14] Traditionally, a government exercises complete authority within the territorial boundaries of its own nation and not beyond it. While jurisdictional rules have become more flexible in recent decades, 'territorial location remains the principal touchstone for assigning legal authority'.[15] In the ostensibly borderless environment of the internet, the jurisdictional issues create not only problems of enforcement but also raise questions of culture, influence, and hegemony.[16]   **[7–05]**

Due to these pervasive problems of jurisdiction, international cooperation would appear to be essential if laws are to be enforced effectively in the age of the internet. This does not necessarily entail the creation and empowerment of international legislators and law enforcers, but does require a degree of compromise as different nations are likely to have different views on a multitude of criminal matters. We have seen examples of successful   **[7–06]**

---

[10] The Criminal Evidence Act 1992 sets out rules that govern the admissibility of documentary evidence in criminal proceedings. Section 2(1) of the Criminal Evidence Act 1992 defines 'document' to include 'reproduction in permanent legible form, by a computer' and 'information in non-legible form'. The Act defines 'information' to include 'any representation of fact, whether in words or otherwise' and 'information in non-legible form' to includes information on microfilm, microfiche, magnetic tape or disk. s 18 of the Criminal Justice Act 2011 provides for certain presumptions to be made regarding the authorship of documents emanating from identifiable accounts. The Criminal Justice Act 2011is discussed in more detail below.

[11] Barbara Etter, 'The Forensic Challenges Of E-Crime' (7th Indo-Pacific Congress on Legal Medicine and Forensic Sciences, Melbourne, 21 September 2001) 5 <pdfs.semanticscholar. org/15c3/5e8721507feee65d5927bf9d909c9ed1497a.pdf> accessed 7 June 2017.

[12] Dorothy Denning and William Baugh, 'Hiding Crimes in Cyberspace' (1999) 2(3) Information, Communication and Society 251; Peter Swire, 'No cop on the Beat: Underenforcement in E-commerce and Cybercrime' (2009) 7(1) Journal on Telecommunications & High Technology Law 107, 116.

[13] Nir Kshetri, *The Global Cybercrime Industry* (2010 Springer) 35–55.

[14] Paul Schiff Berman, *Global Legal Pluralism: A Jurisprudence of Law Beyond Borders* (Cambridge University Press 2012) 4.

[15] Paul Schiff Berman, 'The Globalization of Jurisdiction' (2002) 151 University of Pennsylvania Law Review 311, 427.

[16] Peter Swire, 'No Cop on the Beat: Underenforcement in E-commerce and Cybercrime' (2009) 7(1) Journal on Telecommunications & High Technology Law 107.

international cooperation in others areas of regulation online – notably in technical areas such as the domain name system. In the criminal context, however, more fundamental differences of culture and more sensitive issues of national authority are likely to arise.

[7–07] Due to the inherent challenges of reaching agreement in this typically sovereign area of the law, the Cybercrime Convention (alternatively known as the Budapest Convention) can be seen as a significant achievement in international cooperation. The Cybercrime Convention entered into force in 2004 and, by April 2017, 53 states had acceded and a further four states had signed but not ratified. The Convention represents international agreement in principle on a wide range of cybercrime issues – from system interference, to computer-related fraud, to child-abuse imagery, and also provides a framework for greater cooperation with regards to the sharing of information and enforcement. While the Convention has been criticised by some,[17] it 'holds a central position on the international plane' as 'the most comprehensive instrument in the international fight against cybercrime'.[18]

[7–08] In spite of the challenges posed to the effective enforcement of cybercrime, control of online space was a top government priority as the internet continued to grow in importance and influence. If the internet was to be a source of economic growth, and not a haven for criminality, methods of control would have to be identified. One particularly effective method – that circumvents several of the challenges discussed – is to target intermediaries. Due to the combination of jurisdictional issues, difficulties of identifiability, and in some instances dispersion and ubiquity of offenders (consider the banality of online illegal downloading), individual enforcement of law on the internet is difficult and resource-intensive. In spite of this, individual enforcement is often seen as an essential facet of the pursuit of online crime – particularly when the crime is egregious, such as the distribution of child-abuse material, or interferes with the interests of a powerful actor, such as the hacking of US government cyber-infrastructure. Outside of such areas, individual action is often motivated by a desire to pierce a perception of impunity and potentially 'make an example' of those unlucky enough to be targeted. In 2002, Ross Nadel (former Attorney General for San Francisco) argued that intellectual property rights enforcement was an area where a strong deterrent effect would be caused by 'aggressive and effective criminal prosecution'.[19]

---

[17] The effectiveness of the Convention has been criticised: see, for example, Nancy Marion, 'The Council of Europe's Cyber Crime Treaty: An Exercise in Symbolic Legislation' 4(1&2) International Journal of Cyber Criminology 699. It has also been criticised for continuing with the 'localized, decentralized system of law enforcement we have had for centuries'. See Susan Brenner, 'The Council of Europe's Convention on Cybercrime' in Jack Balkin, *Cybercrime: Digital Cops in a Networked Environment* (New York University Press 2006) 218. The Convention has also been criticised on human rights grounds with criticisms of its implications for privacy and freedom of speech: see Al Aldesco, 'The Demise of Anonymity: A Constitutional Challenge to the Convention on Cybercrime' (2002) 23 Loyola of Los Angeles Entertainment Law Review 81, 110; and Diane Rowland and Elizabeth Macdonald, 'Information Technology Law' (Psychology Press 2005) 485–86.

[18] Maria Kaiafa-Gbandi, 'Criminalizing Attacks against Information Systems in the EU: The Anticipated Impact of the European Legal Instruments on the Greek Legal Order' (2012) 20(1) European Journal of Crime, Criminal Law, and Criminal Justice 59, 61.

[19] Louis Trager, 'Silicon Valley Lawmaker says IP Law Needs Fair-Use Balance' (*Washington Internet Daily*, 31 May 2002). Jack Goldsmith and Tim Wu, *Who Controls the Internet?: Illusions of a Borderless World* (Oxford University Press 2006) 203.

While early attempts at individual enforcement may have deterred some individuals from engaging in criminal activities online, it quickly became clear that intermediaries will provide a useful indirect target in online criminal law enforcement.[20] In their book, *Who Controls the Internet*, Goldsmith and Wu illustrate through the use of examples the logic of targeting intermediaries instead of – or in addition to – individuals in the online environment.[21] They do this by first demonstrating how targeting intermediaries – and cutting off supply – in the offline world can be logical where jurisdictional issues and ubiquity issues render individual enforcement ineffective and inefficient.[22] An example in the Irish context could be the process by which unlicensed fireworks may be distributed in Ireland.[23] If a large number of Irish individuals purchase unlicensed fireworks, An Garda Síochána are likely to want to take enforcement action. However, a large number of people – dispersed throughout the country – with little or no connection to each other do not provide law enforcement with a reasonable target. If individual enforcement is to occur, it is likely to be somewhat arbitrary and in the spirit of 'setting an example' as mentioned earlier.

[7–09]

Alternatively, if the enforcement authorities target those who both import and sell the unlicensed fireworks, they are likely to get more value for their effort and to effectively stifle supply to individuals who may have considered purchasing the items. It is accepted that some individuals are still likely to bring unlicensed fireworks back into the country from trips abroad and some intermediaries are also likely to continue to take their chances and import such products for resale. As Goldsmith and Wu point out, however, the aim is not perfect but adequate compliance. Laws should 'raise the costs of the activity in order to limit that activity to acceptable levels'.[24] Moreover, the costs of enforcement must also be considered.

[7–10]

Due to the heightened challenges of jurisdiction, identification, and ubiquity when enforcing crimes online, it is clear to see how online intermediaries and gatekeepers – such as Internet Service Providers (ISPs), social networking sites, and search engines – are an attractive target for law enforcement. It is important to note that in Ireland,[25] online intermediaries have limited liability for the content that they passively transmit, store, or host under certain circumstances.[26] Liability is limited in different ways depending on whether the online intermediary is classed as a 'mere conduit', 'cache', or 'host'.[27]

[7–11]

---

[20] For discussion of the role of intermediaries in the copyright context, please refer to [2–49] to [2–99].

[21] Jack Goldsmith and Tim Wu, *Who Controls the Internet?: Illusions of a Borderless World* (Oxford University Press 2006) 203.

[22] Jack Goldsmith and Tim Wu, *Who Controls the Internet?: Illusions of a Borderless World* (Oxford University Press 2006) 67–69.

[23] Criminal Justice Act 2006, s 68.

[24] Jack Goldsmith and Tim Wu, *Who Controls the Internet?: Illusions of a Borderless World* (Oxford University Press 2006) 67–69; Lawrence Lessig, 'Symposium: Surveying Law and Borders: The Zones of Cyberspace' (1996) 48 Stanford Law Review 1403, 1405.

[25] Under the European Communities (Directive 2000/31/EC) Regulations 2003, SI 2003/68.

[26] Diane Rowland, Uta Kohl, and Andrew Charlesworth, *Information Technology Law* (Routledge 2017) 72. The European Communities (Directive 2000/31/EC) Regulations 2003, SI 2003/68 give effect to the Parliament and Council Directive (EC) 31/2000 on certain legal aspects of information society services, in particular electronic commerce, in the Internal Market ('Directive on electronic commerce') [2000] OJ L178/1.

[27] See European Communities (Directive 2000/31/EC) Regulations 2003, SI 2003/68, regs 16–18. The widest immunity is granted to 'mere conduits' involved in the transmission of information in a

[7–12]   The 'host' immunity 'comes closest to the boundary with content providers, because here the intermediary takes a greater part in the publishing process, which may undermine its status as a (neutral immunity-deserving) middleman, as opposed to a co-creator.'[28] The 'host' immunity could potentially apply to social networking sites, comment sections, and blogging platforms.[29] If the intermediary is considered a 'host,' they can only avail of limited liability if they do not have 'actual knowledge of the unlawful activity' and must act expeditiously to remove or to disable access to the information upon obtaining such knowledge or awareness.[30] Crucially, regardless of whether an intermediary is classified as a 'host', a 'cache', or a 'mere conduit',[31] the liability 'safe harbour' does not shield intermediaries from injunctions to terminate or prevent an infringement and cooperative obligations remain.[32]

[7–13]   In the online context, as in the offline context, perfect compliance is not a reasonable goal. As we do not conclude from the occurrence of an occasional bank robbery that the laws against theft are ineffective, we should not hold enforcement on the internet to an unrealistic standard in order to be considered effective.[33] There will often be technological and other means by which certain individuals will be able to evade detection online, but that does not mean that enforcement online should be seen as a failure or as a futile endeavour. As a society we often accept that there will minor evasions of the law. While achieving perfect compliance may be possible in theory, it is not only likely to be excessively expensive but is also likely to only be possible in a surveillance-driven police state where civil liberties are dispensable. We will see in our discussion of the substantive law that the challenges of online enforcement regularly require the co-operation

---

communication network where they provide access to that network (ie internet access) or where the information is provided to them by a recipient of a relevant service (eg email) and the intermediary did not initiate the transmission, select the receiver, nor select or modify the information. The narrow delineation of this definition means that the 'mere conduit' protections do not extend to online services such as social network sites or cloud services. Internet Service Providers are the primary target of both the 'mere conduit' immunity and the 'cache' immunity. If an intermediary relies on the 'caching' immunity, they must act expeditiously to remove or disable access to information upon obtaining actual knowledge that a court or an administrative authority has ordered such removal or disablement. Diane Rowland, Uta Kohl, and Andrew Charlesworth, *Information Technology Law* (Routledge 2017) 107.

[28] Diane Rowland, Uta Kohl, and Andrew Charlesworth, *Information Technology Law* (Routledge 2017) 109.

[29] *Kaschke v Gray* [2010] EWHC 690 (QB); *Tamiz v Google* [2012] EWHC 449 (QB); Case C–324/09 *L'Oréal SA v eBay International AG* [2011] OJ C–269/3 and Case C–360/10 *SABAM – Société belge des auteurs, compositeurs et éditeurs SCRL v Netlog NV* [2012] OJ C98/6.

[30] See European Communities (Directive 2000/31/EC) Regulations 2003, SI 2003/68, reg 18.

[31] Or indeed, does not meet the criteria for any of these safe harbour classifications.

[32] See European Communities (Directive 2000/31/EC) Regulations 2003, SI 2003/68, regs 16(3), 17(2), 18(3). European Parliament and Council Directive 2000/31/EC of 8 June 2000 on certain legal aspects of information society services, in particular electronic commerce, in the Internal Market ('Directive on electronic commerce') [2000] OJ L178/1. Eleonora Rosati, 'Why a Reform of Hosting Providers' Safe Harbour is Unnecessary under EU Copyright Law' (2016) 38(11) European Intellectual Property Review 668.

[33] Jack Goldsmith and Tim Wu, *Who Controls the Internet?: Illusions of a Borderless World* (Oxford University Press 2006) 66–69.

of intermediaries. This will often involve enlisting intermediaries as 'voluntary' law enforcers. While the targeting of intermediaries is an essential tool in the online enforcement armoury, there is a risk that such corporate co-option has the potential to be 'too effective' and poses a threat to fair procedures, accountability, and the consideration of human rights.[34]

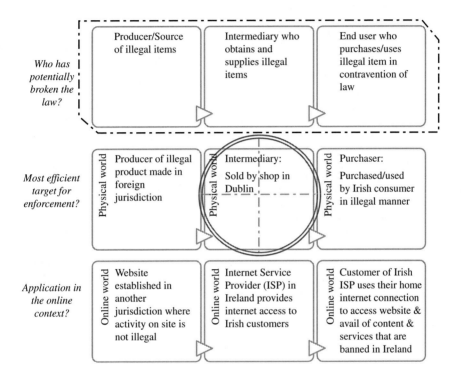

Figure 1   *How Intermediaries May Be Targeted*[35]

---

[34] TJ McIntyre, 'Cybercrime: Towards a Research Agenda' in Deirdre Healy and others (eds), *The Routledge Handbook of Irish Criminology* (Taylor and Francis 2015) 106, citing Majid Yar, 'The Private Policing of Internet Crime' in Yvonne Jewkes and Majid Yar (eds), *Handbook of Internet Crime* (Cullompton Willan 2010).

[35] Bear in mind that the targeting of intermediaries is likely to involve a requirement to prevent access to the illegal content (or identify the perpetrator) and not the attribution of liability as discussed above. See for further discussion Jack Goldsmith and Tim Wu, *Who Controls the Internet?: Illusions of a Borderless World* (Oxford University Press 2006) 66–69. See also the discussion of intermediary co-operation in the context of child-abuse images discussed below.

Computer Crime

[7–14]   In spite of the fact that one might expect the regulation of cybercrime to be a top priority in Ireland – the European home to many of the largest internet companies – Ireland has been described as 'an outlier in having failed to update its cybercrime laws'.[36] Up until May of 2017, two key pieces of cybercrime legislation – the Criminal Damage Act 1991 and Criminal Justice (Theft and Fraud Offences) Act 2001 – were over 25 years and over 15 years old respectively. While the Criminal Justice (Theft and Fraud Offences) Act 2001 remains in force, the computer crime aspects of the Criminal Damage Act 1991 have been repealed following the passage of the Criminal Justice (Offences Relating to Information Systems) Act 2017.[37] The 2017 Act has been described as the 'first piece of legislation in this jurisdiction specifically and solely dedicated to dealing with cybercrime'.[38] In spite of the fact that it may be theoretically possible to fashion technologically neutral laws that continue to function effectively in spite of new innovations, in practice, a continued need for reform seems more likely. It is notable that the primary purpose of the 2017 Act was to give effect to provisions of EU Directive 2013/40/EU on attacks against information systems.[39]

[7–15]   The Cybercrime Convention was highlighted earlier as providing an example of notable international co-operation in this field – with powerful global actors like the US signing and ratifying a convention drawn up by the Council of the Europe.[40] The Convention aims to facilitate 'a common criminal policy aimed at the protection of society against cybercrime, inter alia, by adopting appropriate legislation and fostering international co-operation'. The Convention divides its treatment of different areas of cybercrime into four Titles: (1) offences against confidentiality, integrity, and availability of computer systems and data; (2) computer-related crimes; (3) content-related offences; and (4) offences related to infringements of copyright and related rights. Even though the table below demonstrates that certain parts of the Irish cybercrime regime respond to elements of the Cybercrime Convention, discrepancies remain.

---

[36] TJ McIntyre, 'Cybercrime: Towards a Research Agenda' in Deirdre Healy and others (eds), *The Routledge Handbook of Irish Criminology* (Taylor and Francis 2015) 105. See also TJ McIntyre, 'Computer Crime in Ireland: A Critical Assessment of the Substantive Law' (2005) 15(1) Irish Criminal Law Journal 13.

[37] Criminal Justice (Offences Relating to Information Systems) Act 2017, s 13.

[38] Department of Justice and Equality, 'Tánaiste Welcomes Passage of New Legislation to Deal with Cybercrime through Oireachtas' (18 May 2017) <www.justice.ie/en/JELR/Pages/PR17000167> accessed 7 June 2017.

[39] Department of Justice and Equality, 'Tánaiste Welcomes Passage of New Legislation to Deal with Cybercrime through Oireachtas' (18 May 2017) <www.justice.ie/en/JELR/Pages/PR17000167> accessed 7 June 2017.

[40] Convention on Cybercrime Budapest, 23.XI.2001.

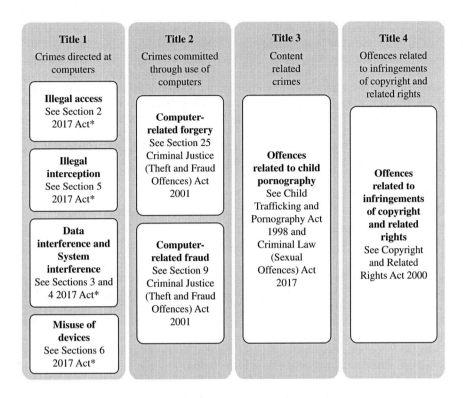

Figure 2   Relevant Irish Law Compared to Cybercrime Convention (*Criminal Justice (Offences Relating to Information Systems) Act 2017)[41]

While Ireland has signed the Convention, it has not as of yet ratified – leaving it as one of only two EU states who have failed to do so.[42] In spite of the fact that Ireland has not ratified – and thus is not yet bound by – the Convention,   **[7–16]**

> key parts of the Convention are reflected in two European [Union] instruments – the 2005 Framework Decision on Attacks Against Information Systems (which should have been transposed by March 2007) and the 2013 Directive on Attacks Against Information Systems (which should have been transposed by September 2015).[43]

---

[41] Please note that this chapter focuses on crimes directed at computers, crimes committed through use of computers, and content-related crimes. Please refer to Chapter 2 for further information on Irish copyright law.

[42] 'Chart of signatures and ratifications of Treaty 185 Status as of 07/06/2017' (7 June 2017) <www.coe.int/en/web/conventions/full-list/-/conventions/treaty/185/signatures> accessed 7 June 2017.

[43] TJ McIntyre, 'Cybercrime: Towards a Research Agenda' in Deirdre Healy and others (eds), *The Routledge Handbook of Irish Criminology* (Taylor and Francis 2015) 111.

[7–17]   Ireland has implemented the Directive on Attacks Against Information Systems by passing the Criminal Justice (Offences Relating to Information Systems) Act in May 2017. The 2017 Act (discussed in detail below) brings Ireland into greater uniformity with other EU Member States but its effectiveness in practice can only be assessed over time. Drawing from the structure of the Cybercrime Convention, this chapter considers the following categories of cybercrime in turn (1) offences against confidentiality, integrity, and availability of computer systems and data [or crimes directed at computers]; (2) computer-related crimes [or crimes conducted using computers as tools]; and (3) content-related offences [or offences involving the viewing, collection, or distribution of illegal content online]. While there is overlap between the categories, it provides a useful structure to examine the extant law in Ireland.[44]

Offences against Confidentiality, Integrity, and Availability of Computer Systems and Data [or Crimes Directed at Computers]

[7–18]   In May 2017, the Criminal Justice (Offences Relating to Information Systems) Act 2017 became the first piece of Irish legislation to specifically and solely address the issue of cybercrime.[45] Its standalone nature is quite a contrast to the first cybercrime offences introduced in Irish law which 'were shoehorned in at a late stage' of the drafting of the Criminal Damage Act 1991 (CDA).[46] When introducing the Criminal Justice (Offences Relating to Information Systems) Bill, the Minister for Justice, Frances Fitzgerald, highlighted the importance of protecting citizens, businesses, and government structures from cyber-attack. Information security is an essential aspect of this goal. When the security of an information system is compromised, potential outcomes can include

- intrusions that alter the operation of a computer or its applications,
- unauthorised access to proprietary or confidential information,
- unauthorised loss of information, and
- service failures.[47]

[7–19]   A key motivation for the originating EU Cybercrime Directive (Directive 2013/40/EU) was the emergence of new cyber threats, and the EU Commission specifically highlighted

---

[44] For a similar organisational approach see Ian Walden, 'Computer Crime and Information Misuse' in Chris Reed (ed) *Computer Law* (Oxford University Press 2011); Maeve McDonagh and Michael O'Dowd, *Cyber Law in Ireland* (International Encyclopaedia of Laws Series, Kluwer Law 2015) 357; and TJ McIntyre, 'Cybercrime: Towards a Research Agenda' in Deirdre Healy and others (eds), *The Routledge Handbook of Irish Criminology* (Taylor and Francis 2015) 111.

[45] Department of Justice and Equality, 'Tánaiste Welcomes Passage of New Legislation to Deal with Cybercrime through Oireachtas' (18 May 2017) <www.justice.ie/en/JELR/Pages/PR17000167> accessed 7 June 2017.

[46] The computer crime offences included in the Criminal Damage Act 1991 have been repealed by the Criminal Justice (Offences Relating to Information Systems) Act 2017. TJ McIntyre, 'Cybercrime: Towards a Research Agenda' in Deirdre Healy and others (eds), *The Routledge Handbook of Irish Criminology* (Taylor and Francis 2015) 112; TJ McIntyre, 'Computer Crime in Ireland: A Critical Assessment of the Substantive Law' (2005) 15(1) Irish Criminal Law Journal 13.

[47] Pedro Freitas and Nuno Gonçalves, 'Illegal Access to Information Systems and the Directive 2013/40/EU' 29(1) International Review of Law, Computers & Technology 50, 54.

the 'emergence of large-scale simultaneous attacks against information systems and the increased criminal use of the so-called "botnets"'.[48] According to the Minister for Justice, the passage of the Criminal Justice (Offences Relating to Information Systems) Act contributes to the goal of enhanced security by better defining the relevant criminal offences and by establishing 'effective, proportionate and dissuasive penalties for such offences'.[49]

In addition to repealing the computer crime elements of the CDA, the Criminal Justice (Offences Relating to Information Systems) Act creates five main offences of   **[7–20]**

– intentionally accessing an information system without lawful authority by infringing a security measure (Section 2)[50]
– intentionally interfering with an information system without lawful authority so as to hinder or interrupt its functioning (Section 3)[51]
– intentionally interfering with data without lawful authority on an information system (Section 4)
– intentionally intercepting the transmission of data to, from, or within an information system without lawful authority (Section 5)
– intentionally producing, selling, procuring for use, importing, distributing, or otherwise making available, a device, computer programme, password, code or data for the purpose of the commission of an offence under Sections 2, 3, 4 or 5 without lawful authority (Section 6).[52]

The Criminal Justice (Offences Relating to Information Systems) Act provides new definitions for a number of key terms. Notably, 'information system' is defined to mean

(a)   a device or group of interconnected or related devices, one or more than one of which performs automatic processing of data pursuant to a programme, and

---

[48] Commission, 'Proposal for a Directive of the European Parliament and of the Council on Attacks against Information Systems and Repealing Council Framework Decision 2005/222/JHA' COM (2010) 517 final 2.

[49] Irish Government News Service, 'Minister Fitzgerald Announces Publication of Legislation on Offences Relating to Information Systems' (19 January 2016) <www.merrionstreet.ie/en/News-Room/Releases/Minister_Fitzgerald_announces_publication_of_legislation_on_offences_relating_to_information_systems_.html> accessed 7 June 2017. Another notable EU law is the Parliament and Council Directive (EU) 1148/2016 concerning measures for a high common level of security of network and information systems across the Union [2016] OJ L194. This Directive entered into force in August 2016 and has a transposition deadline of 9 May 2018.

[50] The intentional accessing of a computer system without lawful authority is very often a precursor to other cybercrime offences. The absence of a definition for a 'security measure' in either the Act or the originating Directive is regrettable and the resultant ambiguity could lead to an excessively narrow application of the unauthorised access offence. The Directive's introduction of a violation of a security measure as an element of the crime of unauthorised access has been described as 'too hasty'. Freitas and Gonçalves point out that 'if the goal is to increase the resilience of information systems (Recital 26) by enforcing the adoption of adequate measures to protect them in a more efficient way against cyber-attacks, then such a goal may not be achieved due to the uncertainty on what constitutes a security measure': Pedro Freitas and Nuno Gonçalves, 'Illegal Access to Information Systems and the Directive 2013/40/EU' 29(1) International Review of Law, Computers & Technology 50, 60.

[51] Criminal Justice (Offences Relating to Information Systems) Act 2017, s 3.

[52] s 15 amends Schedule 1 of the Criminal Justice Act 2011.

(b) data stored, processed, retrieved or transmitted by such a device or group of devices for the purposes of the operation, use, protection or maintenance of the device or group of devices, as the case may be[.][53]

[7–21] According to Deputy David Stanton, who introduced the Bill at second stage, the 'term "information system", rather than "computer", is used in order to enable the Bill to have the widest possible application, taking account of rapidly evolving technology in this area'.[54] For similar reasons 'data' was broadly defined as 'any representation of facts, information or concepts in a form capable of being processed in an information system' and includes a programme capable of causing an information system to perform a function.[55] Both of these definitions are derived from the EU Cybercrime Directive definitions.[56] In addition, 'lawful authority' in relation to an information system is defined to mean

(a) with the authority of the owner of the system,
(b) with the authority of a right holder of the system, or
(c) as permitted by law.[57]

[7–22] The requirement that an offence be committed without 'lawful authority' is designed to avoid criminalising the legitimate activities of those authorised to access information systems or possess a computer programme for the purpose of maintaining, testing or protecting information systems. In spite of this, the precise delineation of the term and its application to a specific set of facts is likely to be a key issue of contention in practice.[58]

[7–23] The s 2 unlawful access offence occurs where a person 'without lawful authority or reasonable excuse, intentionally accesses an information system by infringing a security measure'. The Act considers the s 3 offence of *interfering* with an information system without lawful authority to be a particularly serious offence.[59] Under the 2017 Act, a person will commit this offence where he or she without lawful authority

intentionally hinders or interrupts the functioning of an information system by—
(a) inputting data on the system,
(b) transmitting, damaging, deleting, altering or suppressing, or causing the deterioration of, data on the system, or
(c) rendering data on the system inaccessible.

---

[53] Criminal Justice (Offences Relating to Information Systems) Act 2017, s 1(1).

[54] Dáil Deb 25 January 2017, vol 936, no 1.

[55] Criminal Justice (Offences Relating to Information Systems) Act 2017, s 1(1).

[56] Parliament and Council Directive (EU) 40/2013 on attacks against information systems and replacing Council Framework Decision 2005/222/JHA [2013] OJ L218/8, art 2.

[57] Criminal Justice (Offences Relating to Information Systems) Act s 1. The definition section defines a 'right holder' as a person who is not the owner of the system but who has the right to access the system (including the right to access the system for the purposes of maintaining, testing or protecting the system).

[58] Pearse Ryan, Tom Browne, and Sarah McDermott, 'Cybercrime: Legislative Developments in Ireland' (*Arthur Cox*, March 2016) <www.arthurcox.com/wp-content/uploads/2016/03/Cybercrime-Legislative-Developments-In-Ireland-March-2016.pdf> accessed 7 June 2017.

[59] Criminal Justice (Offences Relating to Information Systems) Act, s 3.

Notably, the introduction of the s 3 offence provides a clear legal basis for the prosecution of denial-of-service attacks.[60]   **[7–24]**

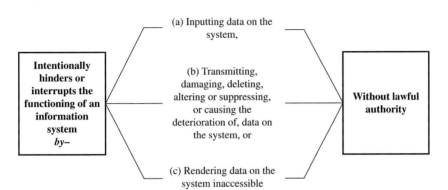

Figure 3   *The Offence of Interfering with an Information System*

Section 4 of the 2017 Act criminalises the act of deleting, damaging, altering, suppressing, rendering inaccessible, or causing the deterioration of data on an information system without lawful authority. Section 5 makes it an offence to intentionally intercept any transmission of data[61] to, from or within an information system without lawful authority.

The s 6 offence of intentionally producing or making available items that facilitate the com-   **[7–25]**
mission of the primary offences recognises the proliferation of tools online that facilitate the commission of cyber offences by both sophisticated hackers and relative novices known as 'script kiddies'.[62] While the corresponding provision in the Cybercrime Directive targets the malicious use of software and passwords, Recital 16 of the Directive acknowledges that there is a risk of criminalising tools produced for a legitimate purpose, notably tools designed to test the security of systems. Accordingly, Section 6 of the Criminal Justice (Offences Relating to Information Systems) Act limits criminalisation to situations where the person makes a computer programme available that 'is primarily designed or adapted for use' in connection with an offence or makes available 'any device, computer password, unencryption key or … similar data, by which an information system is capable of being accessed' without lawful authority.

Section 8 of the Criminal Justice (Offences Relating to Information Systems) Act states   **[7–26]**
that a person convicted of one of the new offences set out in Sections 2, 4, 5, and 6 of

---

[60] See discussion of the prior legal position in Maeve McDonagh and Michael O'Dowd, *Cyber Law in Ireland* (International Encyclopaedia of Laws Series, Kluwer Law 2015) 359 and in TJ McIntyre, 'Cybercrime: Towards a Research Agenda' in Deirdre Healy and others (eds), *The Routledge Handbook of Irish Criminology* (Taylor and Francis 2015) 113–14.

[61] Other than a public transmission.

[62] The term 'script kiddies' tends to refer to individuals who lack sophisticated hacking skills but know enough to run scripts prepared by others with more expertise.

the Act shall be liable to a fine and/or imprisonment for a term not exceeding 12 months on summary conviction.[63] If convicted on indictment a person may be subject to a fine and/or imprisonment for a term not exceeding five years or both. The seriousness of interfering with an information system without lawful authority is acknowledged with higher penalties for those convicted under s 3. If summarily convicted under s 3, a person shall be liable to a class A fine (≤ €5,000) or imprisonment for a term not exceeding 12 months or both. If convicted on indictment, a person shall be liable to a fine or imprisonment for a term not exceeding 10 years or both.[64] Where an individual interferes with information systems or data without lawful authority,[65] an intention to misuse any obtained personal data to commit identity theft will be considered an aggravating factor in sentencing.[66]

[7–27]   Third parties can also be liable under the Criminal Justice (Offences Relating to Information Systems) Act. A person who obstructs or attempts to obstruct government authorities acting under the authority of a search warrant issued under s 7 of the Act can be liable to a class A fine and/or up to 12 months imprisonment.[67] Bodies corporate can also be prosecuted under the proposed legislation. Section 9 of the Act states that where an offence under the Act is committed by a body corporate

> and it is proved that the offence was committed with the consent or connivance, or was attributable to any wilful neglect, of a person who was a director, manager, secretary or other officer of the body corporate, or a person purporting to act in that capacity, that person shall, as well as the body corporate, be guilty of an offence and shall be liable to be proceeded against and punished as if he or she were guilty of the first-mentioned offence.[68]

[7–28]   Even though the passage of the Criminal Justice (Offences Relating to Information Systems) Act brings Ireland closer to compliance with its international obligations, it will be interesting to monitor its effectiveness in practice. It is often the case that even where applicable laws exist 'on the books', significant practical obstacles to the enforcement of cybercrime persist. The many challenges include the risk of underreporting due to potential reputational harm, evidential difficulties, and limited resources. As part of its aim is to facilitate more effective and efficient investigation of white collar crime, the Criminal Justice Act 2011 – discussed in more detail later in this chapter – has some notable implications in the cybercrime context.

---

[63] s 2 prohibits 'accessing information systems without lawful authority'. Section 4 prohibits 'interference with data without lawful authority'. s 5 prohibits 'intercepting transmission of data without lawful authority' and s 6 prohibits the 'use of computer programme, password, code or data for purposes of section 2, 3, 4 or 5': Criminal Justice (Offences Relating to Information Systems) Act, s 8(1).

[64] Criminal Justice (Offences Relating to Information Systems) Act, s 8(2).

[65] The offences laid out in ss 3 and 4 respectively.

[66] Criminal Justice (Offences Relating to Information Systems) Act, s 8(4). Although the sentence imposed shall not be greater than the maximum sentences generally permissible under s 8.

[67] Criminal Justice (Offences Relating to Information Systems) Act, s 7(7).

[68] Criminal Justice (Offences Relating to Information Systems) Act, s 9(3).

Computer-Related Crimes [or Crimes Conducted using Computers as Tools]

As a society, we often share common conceptions of what constitutes a wrongful act in the physical world. It is also the case that as a society we may be able to extrapolate from that common understanding in order to identify an online activity as being of a similar nature. Such intuitive understanding is not sufficient in the criminal law context, however, where the rule of law requires a high standard of certainty. Two reports in the early 1990s concluded that the laws on larceny and fraud required modernisation to clearly account for computer crime.[69] Nearly 10 years later, the government introduced the Criminal Justice (Theft and Fraud Offences) Act 2001 (Theft and Fraud Offences Act), which followed a similar approach to that adopted in the Criminal Damage Act 1991 mentioned above. In addition to creating a computer-specific offence,[70] the Theft and Fraud Offences Act modified some definitions to clearly bring relevant crimes conducted through the use of a computer within the scope of the Act.[71] **[7–29]**

Section 4 of the Theft and Fraud Offences Act states that an individual is guilty of theft if he or she 'dishonestly appropriates property without the consent of its owner and with the intention of depriving its owner of it'. While it is clear how this would apply to someone who has stolen your car and sold it for parts, it is less clear how it would apply in the online world. Fortunately, the section provides that 'appropriates' in this context means to usurp or adversely interfere with an individual's proprietary rights and 'depriving' means temporarily or permanently depriving.[72] If found guilty of theft, an individual is liable to a fine and imprisonment for a term not exceeding 10 years. **[7–30]**

Definitions were designed to address the challenges of computer crime in the forgery context also. According to s 25 of the Act, a person is guilty of forgery if he or she 'makes a false instrument with the intention that it shall be used to induce another person to accept it as genuine and, by reason of so accepting it, to do some act, or to make some omission, to the prejudice of that person or any other person'. False instrument is the ambiguous term here and s 24 provides a long list of items that constitute an instrument under the Act. Crucially for our purposes, 'instrument' is defined to include any document, whether of a formal or informal character, and includes any 'disk, tape, sound track or other device on or in which information is recorded or stored by mechanical, electronic or other means'.[73] **[7–31]**

---

[69] Law Reform Commission, *Report on the Law Relating to Dishonesty* (LRC 43–1992); Government Advisory Committee on Fraud, *Report of the Government's Advisory Committee on Fraud* (PI9409–1992).

[70] The CDA also created a computer-specific offence with the s 5 offence of unauthorised access. This offence has now been replaced by the Criminal Justice (Offences Relating to Information Systems) Act 2017.

[71] The CDA also modified definitions for the purpose of extending its remit to cybercrime. For example, it modified the definition of damage to include damage to data. As mentioned previously, the computer crime aspects of the CDA have been repealed by the Criminal Justice (Offences Relating to Information Systems) Act 2017.

[72] Theft and Fraud Offences Act, s 4(5).

[73] Section 2 defines 'document' as including – (a) a map, plan, graph, drawing, photograph, or record, or (b) a reproduction in permanent legible form, by a computer or other means (including enlarging), of information in non-legible form.

While these changes to the law clarified the application of the general crimes of theft and forgery in the cybercrime context, the Theft and Fraud Offences Act 2001 also introduced an offence of 'unlawful use of computer'.

[7–32]   Section 9 of the Theft and Fraud Offences Act 2001 states that a person who 'dishonestly ... operates or causes to be operated a computer ... with the intention of making a gain for himself or herself or another, or of causing loss to another, is guilty of an offence'. Section 2 of the Act clarifies that 'to make a gain' or 'cause a loss' is to be construed as extending only to gains or losses in money or other property, whether any such gain or loss is temporary or permanent.[74]

Figure 4   *Elements of the Unlawful Use of a Computer*

[7–33]   While there are only two elements to the unlawful use of a computer, interpretation of the offence and its definitions has been the cause of debate and the precise scope of the offence is somewhat uncertain. Section 9 appears to mean that the requirement to act dishonestly only applies to the operation of a computer and not to the intention to make a gain or cause a loss.[75] Others have argued that the offence could be interpreted to apply to the use of a computer for a dishonest purpose, for example to 'somebody who dishonestly sells pirated music over the Internet using a computer'.[76] McIntyre makes a compelling argument against this interpretation, however, pointing out that the 'section does not refer to use of a computer for a dishonest purpose: it applies to a person who "dishonestly operates or causes to be operated" a computer'. As 'dishonestly' is defined in the Interpretation Section as meaning 'without a claim of right made in good faith', the offence should only apply where someone operates a computer 'without a belief that they were entitled to do so'.[77]

[7–34]   Even though the drafting is ambiguous and different interpretations are possible, the necessity to interpret criminal law statutes strictly means that a broader application of the legislation could be problematic. McIntyre has pointed out that this interpretation means that

---

[74] Theft and Fraud Offences Act, s 2(3). The Section further clarifies that '"gain" includes a gain by keeping what one has, as well as a gain by getting what one has not' and that '"loss" includes a loss by not getting what one might get, as well as a loss by parting with what one has'.

[75] Maeve McDonagh and Michael O'Dowd, *Cyber Law in Ireland* (Kluwer Law 2015) 369. This formulation appears to allow for the prosecution of persons who have used a computer without proper authorisation in pursuit of legitimate gains.

[76] TJ McIntyre, 'Computer Crime in Ireland: A Critical Assessment of the Substantive Law' (2005) 15(1) Irish Criminal Law Journal 13. See also Denis Kelleher, 'Cracking Down on the Hack-pack' *The Irish Times* (Dublin, 23 October 2000).

[77] TJ McIntyre, 'Cybercrime: Towards a Research Agenda' in Deirdre Healy and others (eds), *The Routledge Handbook of Irish Criminology* (Taylor and Francis 2015) 115.

the unlawful use of a computer is effectively the 'same basic offence' as the now repealed 'unauthorised access' offence previously found in s 5 of the CDA with the added require-ment of 'intention to make a gain or cause a loss'.[78] While this may have seemed like unnecessary duplication at the time, the fact that the 2001 Act's computer-specific offence can be tried on indictment means that much more severe penalties could be imposed under the 2001 Act than were possible under s 5 of the CDA. Indeed, under the Theft and Fraud Offences Act an offender may be subject to an unlimited fine and/or a maximum sentence of 10 years' imprisonment. Even though the newly introduced approximate offence of access-ing an information system without lawful authority under the Criminal Justice (Offences Relating to Information Systems) Act 2017 is triable on indictment, the new offence is still subject to a lower maximum penalty of five years' imprisonment than that possible under the Theft and Fraud Offences Act.[79]

Criminal Justice Act 2011

The Criminal Justice Act 2011 is a procedural law that applies to a large number of 'relevant offences', some of which are clearly associated with the description 'white collar crime', but many more of which might be thought of as 'mainstream' crimes.[80] Among the offences we have discussed from a cybercrime perspective, the Criminal Justice Act 2011 applies to Sections 4 and 25 of the Criminal Justice (Theft and Fraud Offences) Act 2001,[81] to the offence of dishonest operation of a computer with the intention of making a gain or causing a loss to another,[82] and also applies to the numerous offences provided for in Sections 2, 3, 4, 5 and 6 of the Criminal Justice (Offences Relating to Information Systems) Act 2017.[83] Where an offence was committed before the commencement of s 15 of the Criminal Justice (Offences Relating to Information Systems) Act 2017 – and thus before the repeal of the CDA – the Criminal Justice Act 2011 will continue to apply to the investigation of the

[7–35]

---

[78] TJ McIntyre, 'Computer Crime in Ireland: A Critical Assessment of the Substantive Law' (2005) 15(1) Irish Criminal Law Journal 13.

[79] Criminal Justice (Offences Relating to Information Systems) Act, s 2.

[80] Mark Byrne, 'The Criminal Justice Act 2011: A Boon to Investigators' (2012) 17(1) The Bar Review 14, 15. The fact that the Criminal Justice (Theft and Fraud Offences) Act 2001 falls within the remit of the 2011 Act means that the 2011 Act extends 'well into the everyday life of ordinary law abiding citi-zens': Arthur Cox, 'Litigation & Dispute Resolution Briefing Criminal Justice Act 2011' (*Arthur Cox*, September 2011) 2 <www.arthurcox.com/wp-content/uploads/2014/01/Arthur-Cox-The-Criminal-Justice-Act-2011-September-2011.pdf> accessed 7 June 2017.

[81] Criminal Justice (Theft and Fraud Offences) Act 2001, ss 4 and 25. As discussed earlier, the defini-tions in the 2001 Act enable the prosecution of theft and fraud offences conducted through the use of computers.

[82] As prohibited by s 9 of the Criminal Justice (Theft and Fraud Offences) Act 2001.

[83] As discussed earlier, s 2 prohibits the intentional accessing of information systems without lawful authority; s 3 prohibits the intentional interference with an information system without lawful authority so as to hinder or interrupt its functioning; s 4 prohibits the intentional interference with data without lawful authority on an information system; s 5 prohibits the intentional interception of transmissions of data without lawful authority; and s 6 prohibits the intentional production, sale, or otherwise making available of devices etc for the purpose of the commission of an offence under ss 2, 3, 4 or 5 without lawful authority: Criminal Justice (Offences Relating to Information Systems) Act 2017, s 15.

CDA offences of damaging property, threatening to damage property, and possessing any-thing for use in damaging property.[84]

[7–36] One of the more notable features of the 2011 Act from the perspective of cybercrime is contained in s 15 of the Act, which empowers members of An Garda Síochána to apply to the District Court for an order to compel an individual to make available any docu-ments of a particular description, or to provide specific information.[85] In addition, if the documents are not in legible form – for example if they are encrypted – the District Court can make an order compelling the relevant individual to give An Garda Síochána 'any password necessary to make the documents legible and comprehensible' or to otherwise enable access to or production of the documents for An Garda Síochána in a form in which they can be removed and made comprehensible.[86] This compelled disclosure provision is a significant power that provides the authorities with leverage when faced with encrypted documents that are believed to be pertinent to an investigation. Where a person fails to comply with an order without reasonable excuse, they shall be liable to a class A fine and/or imprisonment for a maximum of 12 months if convicted summarily. If a person is tried on indictment, they may be subject to a fine and/or imprisonment for a maximum of two years.[87] While there are likely to be instances where a criminal will chose to accept such a penalty in lieu of incriminating themselves regarding a more egregious offence, the 2011 Act makes it a more costly calculation than previously the case under Irish law. A similar provision in the Criminal Justice (Theft and Fraud Offences) Act 2001 Act only provided for penalties of a £500 fine and/or six months' imprisonment for failure to disclose pass-words.[88]

[7–37] A controversial element of the Criminal Justice Act 2011 is contained in s 19(1), where it states that

> 19.— (1) A person shall be guilty of an offence if he or she has information which he or she knows or believes might be of material assistance in—
> (a) preventing the commission by any other person of a relevant offence, or
> (b) securing the apprehension, prosecution or conviction of any other person for a relevant offence,
> and fails without reasonable excuse to disclose that information as soon as it is practicable to do so to a member of the Garda Síochána.

The broad scope of this reporting obligation has led to accounts of a surge in precautionary reports being made to An Garda Síochána.[89] Instead of assisting An Garda Síochána in their investigation of serious offences, there have been claims that the legislation has led to a deluge

---

[84] As laid out in ss 2, 3, and 4 of the Criminal Damage Act 1991 respectively.
[85] Criminal Justice Act 2011, s 15.
[86] Criminal Justice Act 2011, s 15(6).
[87] Criminal Justice Act 2011, s 15(15).
[88] Pearse Ryan, Claire O'Brien, and Andy Harbison, 'Cybercrime in Ireland – Recent Legislative Developments' (*Society of Computers and Law*, 2013) <www.tjmcintyre.com/2013/02/impact-of-criminal-justice-act-2011-on.html> accessed 7 June 2017.
[89] TJ McIntyre, 'Cybercrime: Towards a Research Agenda' in Deirdre Healy and others (eds), *The Routledge Handbook of Irish Criminology* (Taylor and Francis 2015) 180; Dearbhail McDonald,

of reports leaving the authorities 'swamped'.[90] While this offence is of general application, it raises particular problems in the cybercrime context as it has implications for information security researchers.[91] If convicted of failing to report information of material assistance, a person shall be liable to a class A fine and/or a maximum prison term of 12 months (on summary conviction), or to a fine and/or a maximum prison term of five years (on indictment).

Content-Related Offences [or Offences Involving the Viewing, Collection, or Distribution of Illegal Content Online]

Throughout history, governments have exerted various degrees of control over content production and distribution. In different cultures, the boundaries of what is acceptable or appropriate vary. The enforceability of those different standards has been threatened by the blurred borders of the internet. While an Irish person living in the 1980s may have had to travel abroad to purchase a copy of *Playboy*, an Irish person can now access pornographic content stored on a UK website without even noticing its country of origin.[92] The blocking of websites deemed undesirable by government authorities is, of course, not impossible, as evidenced by censorship tactics in less democratic regimes. Even those technical measures, however, are often circumvented by users with sufficient motivation to access illegal content. Depending on constitutional background, many democratic nations still impose some limitations on what is considered acceptable content, particularly as regards the appropriate age to view such content. While Title 3 of the Cybercrime Convention requires Party States to adopt legislation to address offences related to child-abuse material, similar issues are raised in the context of hate speech, 'revenge pornography', and online harassment. As a result, these offences are also addressed below.

[7–38]

Child Abuse Material

The creation, collection, and distribution of child-abuse material is not a new phenomenon.[93] Notwithstanding this, the internet – with its relative anonymity and niche online communities – has fostered the development of networks of like-minded individuals with criminal interests and has provided a market for those who wish to sell, purchase, or swap such materials. The Child Trafficking and Pornography Act was introduced in 1998 to address the problem and was 'viewed as forward looking for its time' as it adopted technology-neutral definitions and avoided the use of subjective terms like 'obscene', 'indecent', and 'offensive'.[94] Some of the gaps in the Child Trafficking and Pornography Act that became apparent over time – largely due to technological developments and chang-

[7–39]

'There's Never Been a Better Time for White-Collar Crime, Warns Lawyer' *Irish Independent* (Dublin, 18 April 2017).

[90] Dearbhail McDonald, 'There's Never Been a Better Time for White-Collar Crime, Warns Lawyer' *Irish Independent* (Dublin, 18 April 2017).

[91] TJ McIntyre, 'Cybercrime: Towards a Research Agenda' in Deirdre Healy and others (eds), *The Routledge Handbook of Irish Criminology* (Taylor and Francis 2015) 180.

[92] Editorial, 'Top Shelf: The Day Playboy Went Legit' *Irish Independent* (Dublin, 20 September 2015).

[93] For example, some paintings from ancient Greece depict adults engaged in sexual activities with children. Kenneth Dover, *Greek Homosexuality* (Duckworth 1978). See also Ian O'Donnell and Clare Milner, *Child Pornography: Crime, Computers and Society* (Taylor and Francis 2012) 240.

[94] TJ McIntyre, 'Cybercrime: Towards a Research Agenda' in Deirdre Healy and others (eds), *The Routledge Handbook of Irish Criminology* (Taylor and Francis 2015) 115.

ing modes of internet use – have been addressed by the Criminal Law (Sexual Offences) Act 2017.[95] While the 2017 Act is a wide-ranging piece of legislation, covering many sexual offences, a key aim of the Act is to implement the criminal law provisions of the EU Directive on combating child abuse, child exploitation and child pornography, and related international legal instruments.[96] Relevant offences in Irish law include

- the possession of child pornography[97]
- the production, distribution, etc of child pornography[98]
- knowingly attending (including by means of information and communication technology) a pornographic performance involving children[99]
- the use of information technology to send sexually explicit material to children.[100]

[7–40] As is often the case when interpreting statutes – but particularly the case when interpreting cybercrime statutes – definitions are crucial to understanding the scope of the legislation. While 'child-abuse image' is seen by many as a preferable term, both the 1998 and the 2017 Acts use the term 'child pornography'. Due to its central importance to the scope of the offence, the definition of 'child pornography' is included in full below with some key terms emphasised by the authors.

> *'child pornography'* means—
>
> (a) any *visual* representation—
>
>   (i) that shows or, in the case of a document, relates to a person *who is or is depicted as being a child* and who *is engaged in or is depicted as being engaged in explicit sexual activity,*
>
>   (ii) that shows or, in the case of a document, relates to a person who is or is *depicted as being a child* and *who is or is depicted as witnessing any such activity* by any person or persons, or
>
>   (iii) that *shows, for a sexual purpose, the genital or anal region of a child or of a person depicted as being a child,*

---

[95] Previously, the Child Trafficking and Pornography Act 1998 was amended in a minor way by the Child Trafficking and Pornography (Amendment) Act 2004. This amendment facilitated members of the Oireachtas to lawfully possess, print, and distribute otherwise unlawful material that was the subject of impeachment proceedings against a judge.

[96] Department of Justice and Equality, 'Tánaiste Welcomes Passage of the Criminal Law (Sexual Offences) Bill 2015 through Oireachtas' (14 February 2017) <www.justice.ie/en/JELR/Pages/PR17000056> accessed 7 June 2017.

[97] Child Trafficking and Pornography Act 1998, s 6. Section 6 was amended by s 14 of the Criminal Law (Sexual Offences) Act 2017. Please note that s 9 of the Criminal Law (Sexual Offences) Act 2017 modified the definitions of 'child' and 'child pornography' that are contained in s 2 of the Child Trafficking and Pornography Act.

[98] Child Trafficking and Pornography Act 1998, s 5. Section 5 was amended by s 12 of the Criminal Law (Sexual Offences) Act 2017.

[99] Child Trafficking and Pornography Act 1998, s 5A. Please note s 5A also criminalises anyone who 'causes, incites, compels or coerces, or (b) recruits, invites or induces, a child to participate in a pornographic performance, or gains from such participation': Child Trafficking and Pornography Act 1998, ss 3 and 5. The Criminal Law (Sexual Offences) (Amendment) Act 2007 amended s 3 of the 1998 Act, and s 13 of the Criminal Law (Sexual Offences) Act 2017 made an addition to s 5 of the 1998 Act.

[100] Criminal Law (Sexual Offences) Act 2017, s 8.

(b)　any *audio* representation of a person *who is or is represented as being a child* and who is *engaged in or is represented as being engaged in explicit sexual activity,*

(c)　any visual or audio representation that *advocates, encourages or counsels any sexual activity with children* which is an offence under any enactment, or

(d)　*any visual representation or description of, or information relating to, a child that indicates or implies that the child is available to be used for the purpose of sexual exploitation* within the meaning of section 3

irrespective of how or through what medium the representation, description or information has been produced, transmitted or conveyed and, without prejudice to the generality of the foregoing, includes any representation, description or information produced by or from computer-graphics or by any other electronic or mechanical means but does not include—

(I)　any book or periodical publication which has been examined by the Censorship of Publications Board and in respect of which a prohibition order under the Censorship of Publications Acts, 1929 to 1967, is not for the time being in force,

(II)　any film in respect of which a general certificate or a limited certificate under the Censorship of Films Acts, 1923 to 1992, is in force, or

(III)　any video work in respect of which a supply certificate under the Video Recordings Acts, 1989 and 1992, is in force.[101]

One change brought about by the Criminal Law (Sexual Offences) Act 2017 is that a 'child'　**[7–41]** is now defined as being under 18 when assessing whether an image constitutes child pornography or not. Previously, the age was 17, which mirrored the age of sexual consent in Irish law. Notably, the broad definition of child pornography means that representations of adults depicted as children can still constitute 'child pornography'. Equally, the definition also includes material where sexual activity has not actually occurred but where it is depicted as having occurred. Interestingly, this means it is likely that computer-generated images – where no child is involved in the generation of the images – constitute 'child pornography' under Irish law.[102] In a case decided in 2012, an Irish man was convicted for the possession of animated depictions of child pornography. The images were described as 'lifelike and very graphic in terms of what they depicted' and according to a detective who testified in Court, speech bubbles in the animations made it clear that the images

---

[101] As an aside, it would seem clear that the statutory definition of 'child pornography' extends further than how a layperson may describe the material. The extension of the definition to include 'any visual or audio representation that advocates, encourages or counsels any sexual activity with children' would certainly be viewed by most as something worthy of criminalisation, but would be unlikely to be perceived as 'child pornography'.

[102] Maeve McDonagh and Michael O'Dowd, *Cyber Law in Ireland* (Kluwer Law 2015) 371. While the term has been used differently in varying contexts, 'virtual child pornography' is a term generally used to describe computer generated images that depict 'virtual' children in a sexual manner but do not involve the direct exploitation of real children. In some instances, these images can be almost indistinguishable to images involving real children. Brian Slocum, 'Virtual Child Pornography: Does it mean the End of the Child Pornography Exception to the First Amendment?' (2004) 14 Albany Law Journal of Science and Technology 637.

depicted were of children. Reflecting the complexities of regulating this area, the defendant in the case expressed the opinion that 'computerised images were a safe way of getting gratification without involving real children'.[103]

[7–42] The offence of possession of child-abuse images is provided for in s 6 of the Child Trafficking and Pornography Act.[104] According to the Act, it is illegal to knowingly acquire or possess child pornography, or to knowingly obtain access to child pornography by means of information and communication technology.[105] Section 6 provides an essential exception for those who possess child-abuse images for 'the purpose of the prevention, investigation or prosecution of offences' under the Child Trafficking and Pornography Act.[106] A person found guilty of this offence will be liable on summary conviction to a €5,000 fine or imprisonment for a term not exceeding 12 months or both. If found guilty on indictment, a person will be liable to a fine or imprisonment for a term not exceeding five years or both.

[7–43] The law clearly distinguishes between those who merely view or collect child pornography and those who produce or profit from child pornography. The logic of this is that while there is harm caused in all circumstances, the harm is more direct when the offender moves beyond the act of possession. The difference in culpability is reflected in the differences in sentencing scales. The sentencing ranges set out in the Child Trafficking and Pornography Act indicate acknowledgement that the possession of child-abuse images is a less serious offence than the production of child-abuse images. The criminalisation of simple possession, however, demonstrates the belief that possession for personal use is not a victimless crime. Further to the argument that the subsequent viewing of child-abuse images by third parties can cause additional and cumulative harm to the original victim;[107] the relationship between the producers of child-abuse images and the consumers of such material has been likened to the relationship between receivers and thieves. Without the receivers to take

---

[103] 'Man Pleads Guilty to Possessing Animated Child Porn Images' *Irish Examiner* (Cork, 12 July 2012).

[104] As amended by ss 12–14 of the Criminal Law (Sexual Offences) Act 2017.

[105] There had previously been some uncertainty about whether the offence of possession would apply where an individual downloads and deletes material that is later recovered in a criminal investigation. The amendments made to the possession offence by the Criminal Law (Sexual Offences) Act address this issue by adding the offences of 'acquiring' and 'knowingly obtaining access'. According to the Children's Rights Alliance, this addition brings Irish law into compliance with the requirements of the European Parliament and Council Directive 2011/93/EU of 13 December 2011 on combating sexual abuse and sexual exploitation of children, and child pornography, replacing the Council Framework-Decision 2004/68/JHA [2011] OJ L335: Children's Rights Alliance, 'Advancing Children's Rights through the Criminal Law (Sexual Offences) Bill 2015' (November 2016) 10 <www.childrensrights.ie/sites/default/files/press_materials/files/Advancing%20children%27s%20rights%20through%20the%20Criminal%20Law%20%28Sexual%20Offences%29%20Bill%202015.pdf> accessed 7 June 2017.

[106] In addition, the offence does not apply to 'a person who possesses or obtains access to child pornography – (a) in the exercise of functions under the Censorship of Films Acts 1923 to 1992, the Censorship of Publications Acts 1929 to 1967, or the Video Recordings Acts 1989 and 1992', and a defence exists for those who possess the material for the 'purposes of bona fide research.'

[107] Eric Posner, 'The Puzzle of Paying Amy' *Slate* (New York, 25 April 2015) <www.slate.com/articles/news_and_politics/view_from_chicago/2014/04/the_supreme_court_and_restitution_for_child_pornography_victims_like_amy.html> accessed 7 June 2017.

the goods off the thieves' hands, the incentive to steal is greatly reduced.[108] The Special Rapporteur on Child Protection has reported that prohibitions on both the production and possession of child-abuse images help to prevent 'children from being used and thereby sexually abused, in the making of child pornography'.[109]

Section 5 of the Child Trafficking and Pornography Act[110] makes it an offence if a person: **[7–44]**

    (a) knowingly produces any child pornography,

    (b) knowingly distributes, transmits, disseminates, prints or publishes any child pornography,

    (c) knowingly imports, exports, sells or shows any child pornography,

    (d) knowingly supplies or makes available any child pornography to another person,

    (e) knowingly publishes, distributes, transmits or disseminates any advertisement likely to be understood as conveying that the advertiser or any other person produces, distributes, transmits, disseminates, prints, publishes, imports, exports, sells, shows, supplies or makes available any child pornography,

    (f) encourages, knowingly causes or facilitates any activity mentioned in paragraphs (a) to (e), or

    (g) knowingly possesses any child pornography for the purpose of distributing, transmitting, disseminating, publishing, exporting, selling or showing it[.]

If a person is tried on indictment and found guilty under s 5, they will liable to a fine or imprisonment for a term not exceeding 14 years, or both.[111]

Developments in the means and manner of accessing child-abuse images have occurred   **[7–45]**
since the passage of the Child Trafficking and Pornography Act in 1998. Many of the developments in usage reflect the changes in how society now consumes *legal* forms of media online. There is a move away from downloading and collecting material and a move towards the streaming of video.[112] In recognition of how the consumption of child-abuse images has evolved on the internet, the Criminal Law (Sexual Offences) Act added a new

---

[108] See the statements made by Judge Keenan Johnson in the Circuit Court: 'Former US Lawyer Sentenced to Two Years and Nine Months for Child Pornography' *The Irish Times* (Dublin, 1 October 2015).

[109] Geoffrey Shannon, 'Report of the Special Rapporteur on Child Protection: A Report Submitted to the Oireachtas' (November 2007) 40 <www.dcya.gov.ie/documents/child_welfare_protection/ Report_of_Special_Rapporteur_on_Child_Protection_Geoffrey_Shannon.PDF> accessed 7 June 2017; Cian Ó Concubhair, 'The Role of Policing in Contemporary Child Protection' (2016) 56 The Irish Jurist 66, 76.

[110] As amended by ss 12–14 of the Criminal Law (Sexual Offences) Act 2017.

[111] For a case study on how a sample of judges approach sentencing in child-abuse images cases, refer to Ian O'Donnell and Clare Milner, *Child Pornography: Crime, Computers and Society* (Taylor and Francis 2012) 128.

[112] TJ McIntyre, 'Cybercrime: Towards a Research Agenda' in Deirdre Healy and others (eds), *The Routledge Handbook of Irish Criminology* (Taylor and Francis 2015) 116. See the Council of Europe Convention for the Protection of Children against Sexual Exploitation and Sexual Abuse, CETS No 201 and the Parliament and Council Directive (EU) 93/2011 on combating sexual abuse and sexual exploitation of children, and child pornography, replacing the Council Framework-Decision 2004/68/ JHA [2011] OJ L335.

Subsection 5A to the Child Trafficking and Pornography Act. This new offence criminalises anyone who 'knowingly attends a pornographic performance' where a child is 'engaged in real or simulated sexually explicit activity' or where the sexual organs of a child are displayed 'for primarily sexual purposes'. Crucially, this offence is defined to include viewing the performance by means of information and communication technology and as a result should close the gap left where it was unclear whether those who viewed such performances could be prosecuted for possession.[113] Now, if found guilty under this part of Section 5A, a person could be subject to a maximum fine of €5,000 and 12 months in prison (on summary conviction) or to a fine and ten years' imprisonment (if tried on indictment).

[7–46] The Criminal Law (Sexual Offences) Act not only amends the Child Trafficking and Pornography Act, but also introduces new offences under s 8. In addition to criminalising any person who uses information technology to communicate with others for the purpose of facilitating the sexual exploitation of a child,[114] Section 8 also criminalises any person who uses information technology to send sexually explicit material to children. Due to a child's vulnerability, and relative freedom, on social media, this type of interaction is perceived as an increasing problem. In addition to exposing a child to inappropriate imagery, sexual images may be sent to a child as a form of grooming or as an inducement to convince the child to return an intimate image of themselves.[115] If found guilty of sending sexually explicit materials to a child, an individual can be tried summarily and be subject to a maximum fine of €5,000 or to a prison sentence of 12 months or both. If tried on indictment, an individual can be subject to a prison term not exceeding five years. In light of reports that it has become increasingly common for underage teenagers to consensually share private sexual images with other teenagers, it is notable that s 8 states that no proceedings shall be brought against a child under the age of 17 years except by, or with the consent of, the Director of Public Prosecutions. Furthermore, a 'child' is defined as meaning a person under the age of 17 years as opposed to a person under the age of 18 years as it is defined in the contexts we have discussed previously.

Sentencing in Child Abuse Material Cases

[7–47] While the maximum possible sentence for the various child-abuse image offences have been noted where relevant above,[116] the broad range of punishments possible within the statutory instructions leaves significant discretion to the District and Circuit Court judges who will be sentencing offenders. In wider society, it may be difficult to reconcile the community's 'disgust at the nature of the crime with a recognition that there are degrees of culpability'.[117] In the courtroom, however, a judge must look for objective facts to guide his

---

[113] Section 5A also criminalises anyone who 'causes, incites, compels or coerces, or (b) recruits, invites or induces, a child to participate in a pornographic performance, or gains from such participation'.

[114] A person convicted under this offence would be liable to imprisonment for a term not exceeding 14 years.

[115] For example, a child might be deceived into believing they are trading intimate images with a person of their own age: Andrew Murray, *Information Technology Law: The Law and Society* (Oxford University Press 2016) 435.

[116] Whether tried summarily or on indictment.

[117] Brian Conroy, 'Sentencing under the Child Pornography and Trafficking Act 1998' (2004) 14(2) Irish Criminal Law Journal 8, 8.

or her sentencing decisions in order to ensure fair and proportionate treatment. While the courts have been criticised for inconsistency in sentencing,[118] useful guidance was set out by Fennelly J in the case of *The People (DPP) v Carl Loving*.[119] Initially, the offender was convicted of possession under the Child Trafficking and Pornography Act and sentenced to five years in prison – the maximum penalty possible for that offence. At the Court of Criminal Appeal, it was pointed out that it 'is unusual to impose the maximum sentence allowed by the law for any offence. Such a decision implies that the actual offence is at the highest level of seriousness.'

The Court of Criminal Appeal reduced the sentence to one year. In making this adjustment,   **[7–48]**
Fennelly J stated that

> Any court imposing a sentence for possession of child pornography will have regard to two of the basic mitigating factors in sentencing. They are: firstly whether the accused accepts responsibility for the offence, including his plea of guilty. Secondly, the previous character of the accused with particular reference to the offence in question.[120]

According to Fennelly J, it is also necessary to consider the individual offence. When   **[7–49]**
assessing its seriousness, a court should consider how serious and numerous were the images involved.[121] The circumstances and the duration of time where the offender committed offences under the Act will also be relevant.[122] Furthermore, Fennelly J stated that it would be relevant whether the commission of the offence had a link with any other sexual

---

[118] Charleton and Scott demonstrate the lack of a pattern in sentencing with the comparison of two cases. As Charleton and Scott lay out, in one case the offender had downloaded 13,845 images of children aged between one and six over a three-year period. One Garda described the material as the worst content he had ever seen and a suspended sentence was given. In another case, the offender had downloaded 22 child pornography files of children aged between six and twelve over three weeks. He was assessed as posing a low risk of re-offending and was sentenced to one year in prison. Peter Charleton and Lisa Scott, 'Throw Away the Key: Public and Judicial Approaches to Sentencing – Towards Reconciliation' (The Martin Tansey Memorial Lecture, Dublin, 10 April 2013) 21 <www.acjrd.ie/files/Throw_Away_the_ Key._Public_and_Judicial_Approaches_to_Sentencing_-_Towards_Reconcilliation_3.pdf> accessed 7 June 2017.

[119] *The People (DPP) v Carl Loving* [2006] 3 IR 355. Peter Charleton and Lisa Scott, 'Throw Away the Key: Public and Judicial Approaches to Sentencing – Towards Reconciliation' (The Martin Tansey Memorial Lecture, Dublin, 10 April 2013) 2–3 <www.acjrd.ie/files/Throw_Away_the_Key._Public_ and_Judicial_Approaches_to_Sentencing_-_Towards_Reconcilliation_3.pdf> accessed 7 June 2017.

[120] *The People (DPP) v Carl Loving* [2006] 3 IR 355 (CCA).

[121] In the English case of *R v Oliver*, the Court of Appeal opined that judges should personally examine the relevant images in order to make an assessment of seriousness. According to the Court, different examples of child-abuse imagery can be categorised on a scale of seriousness from one to five: '(1) images depicting erotic posing with no sexual activity; (2) sexual activity between children, or solo masturbation by a child; (3) non-penetrative sexual activity between adults and children; (4) penetrative sexual activity between children and adults; (5) sadism or bestiality': *R v Oliver* [2002] EWCA Crim 2766. This categorisation has subsequently been used in Irish courts, notably in *DPP v GMcC* [2003] 3 IR 609 (CCA).

[122] For example, if it can be demonstrated that the images were downloaded over a comparatively short period of time, that could lead to a lesser sentence being imposed. It may also be relevant whether the individual paid for the images.

offence or improper relations with children. In spite of the guidance laid out by the Court of Criminal Appeal, not all judges have 'internalised the idea that some structure can and should be placed on sentencing'.[123]

The Role of Intermediaries and Child Abuse Material

[7–50]   While limiting the core offences under the Child Trafficking and Pornography Act to situations where the possessor 'knowingly' carries out the relevant act provides important protection for intermediaries, duties can still arise. For example, s 8 of the Child Trafficking and Pornography Act can be used to impose criminal liability on bodies corporate and corporate directors for offences under the Act.[124] To be found guilty, an offence must have been committed under the Child Trafficking and Pornography Act with the consent, connivance, or neglect of the relevant secondary party. If found guilty, the secondary party is punishable as if he or she were guilty of the original offence.

[7–51]   Earlier in this chapter, we discussed how the challenges of ubiquity, anonymity, and jurisdiction in the online context mean that intermediaries are often targeted by government authorities. The formation and maintenance of child-abuse image markets, rings, and communities depends on services provided by ISPs and increasingly Social Media Networks. The gatekeeper role of ISPs was soon recognised and the Internet Service Providers' Association of Ireland (ISPAI) responded by establishing a voluntary code of practice.[125] The Code 'mandates the development of acceptable use policies (AUPs) for participating ISPs which clearly set out guidelines for customers/users, including prohibitions on customers using ISP services to create, host, transmit material which is unlawful/libellous/abusive/offensive/vulgar/obscene/calculated to cause unreasonable offence'.

[7–52]   A central part of the industry's voluntary effort was the provision of a website for the reporting of illegal content, Hotline.ie. The primary roles of Hotline.ie are

- Ensuring that child abuse material is removed from ISPAI Members' facilities by providing the ISPs with qualified Notice for Takedown
- Ensuring international reach against child abuse material originating from outside of the jurisdiction by working in conjunction with 51 other Internet Hotlines worldwide
- Working with relevant national and international stakeholders in order to understand and identify solutions that could be applied to address emerging challenges
- In addition to taking action against child abuse material, Hotline can also take action if the reported online content is assessed as illegal under the Prohibition of Incitement to Hatred Act 1989 (which is discussed in [7–57] to [7–62]).[126]

---

[123] Niamh Maguire, 'Consistency in Sentencing' (2010) 2 Judicial Studies Institute Journal 14, 26–28, as referenced in Paul Hughes, 'A Proposed Sentencing Council for Ireland' (2015) 25(3) Irish Criminal Law Journal 65, 67. A 2007 case study of judicial attitudes to sentencing in child-abuse material cases published by O'Donnell and Milner provides helpful insight. Ian O'Donnell and Clare Milner, *Child Pornography: Crime, Computers and Society* (Taylor and Francis 2012) 99.

[124] And other similar officers.

[125] ISPAI, 'The Code of Practice and Ethics for Internet Service Providers' (undated) <www.ispai.ie/code-of-practice/> accessed 7 June 2017.

[126] ISPAI, 'ISPAI Hotline.ie Service Annual Report 2016' (2016) 2–3 <www.hotline.ie/library/annual-reports/2016/report-for-2016.pdf> accessed 7 June 2017.

The system operates on a 'notice and take down' basis. Members of the public who see content that they believe is illegal can report it to the Hotline.ie team, who then assess the content to determine if it is illegal. The ISPAI code of practice requires ISPs to set in place communication structures with Hotline.ie and An Garda Síochána in order to facilitate the removal of suspect material.[127] In addition to removing the material, if the Hotline.ie analysts determine that the material is likely to be in breach of the Child Trafficking and Pornography Act, they will report the matter to the Paedophile Investigation Unit of the Garda National Protective Services Unit.[128]

[7–53]

A step beyond the notice and takedown system is the blocking of entire websites. Mobile phone operators have blocked websites alleged to host child-abuse images since 2008.[129] In 2014, an ISP, UPC (now Virgin), agreed to block domains or URLs deemed to contain child-abuse material according to a list provided by An Garda Síochána.[130] A benefit of this system is that it avoids the difficult enforcement problems that can occur when a website is based outside of the jurisdiction. For the purposes of blocking access to the material, the location of the originating website is immaterial. McIntyre questions the legality of such a blocking system as blocking occurs without 'any prior notice, judicial involvement or legislative basis'.[131]

[7–54]

According to McIntyre, the UPC blocking agreement – which appears to provide for the blocking of material at the domain level – does not meet the requirements of Directive 2011/93/EU on combating the sexual abuse and sexual exploitation of children and child pornography. Article 25 of that Directive permits the use of blocking, but only where transparent procedures and adequate safeguards are in place to ensure that the restriction is limited to what is necessary and proportionate and that users are informed of the reason for the restriction. Article 25 explicitly states that the possibility of judicial redress is a required safeguard. McIntyre acknowledges, however, that if the UPC agreement is classed as 'voluntary industry action' it may fall outside the scope of the Directive.

[7–55]

---

[127] ISPAI, 'ISPAI Hotline.ie Service Annual Report 2016' 2–3 (2016) <www.hotline.ie/library/annual-reports/2016/report-for-2016.pdf> accessed 7 June 2017.

[128] ISPAI, 'ISPAI Hotline.ie Service Annual Report 2016' 2–3 (2016) <www.hotline.ie/library/annual-reports/2016/report-for-2016.pdf> accessed 7 June 2017.

[129] TJ McIntyre, 'Cybercrime: Towards a Research Agenda' in Deirdre Healy and others (eds), *The Routledge Handbook of Irish Criminology* (Taylor and Francis 2015) 110; GSMA Mobile Alliance Against Child Sexual Abuse Content, 'Implementation of Filtering of Child Sexual Abuse Images in Operator Networks' (November 2008) <www.gsmworld.com/documents/GSMA_Child_Tech_Doc.pdf> accessed 7 June 2017; Jillian van Turnhout, 'Online Child Abuse Material: Effective Strategies to Tackle Online Child Abuse Material' (18 September 2013) <www.jillianvanturnhout.ie/online-cam/> accessed 7 June 2017.

[130] Christine Bohan, 'In a First for Ireland, UPC is to Ban Access to Child Sex Abuse Websites' *The Journal* (Dublin, 10 November 2014) <www.thejournal.ie/upc-ban-child-sex-abuse-1772439-Nov2014/> accessed 7 June 2017; Pamela Duncan, 'Garda and UPC Agreement Will Restrict Access to Sites with Child Porn Images' *The Irish Times* (Dublin, 11 November 2014).

[131] TJ McIntyre, 'Cybercrime: Towards a Research Agenda' in Deirdre Healy and others (eds), *The Routledge Handbook of Irish Criminology* (Taylor and Francis 2015) 110.

Enforcement of the Child Trafficking and Pornography Act

[7–56] A number of bodies are relevant to the investigation and enforcement of cybercrime in Ireland. The Computer Crimes Investigation Unit has the primary responsibility, but the Paedophile Investigation Unit is also relevant in the context of child-abuse images. Due to the fragmentary nature of enforcement under the split system, there have been proposals for the creation of a National Cybercrime Unit but there has been no restructuring at this time.[132] More critically, there is evidence of severe resourcing issues within these organisations. In 2016, the lack of investment in the Garda Computer Crime Investigation Unit was robustly criticised by Judge Seán Ó Donnabháin when hearing a case taken under the Child Trafficking and Pornography Act. Judge Ó Donnabháin described the delays – of up to five years – in examining computer equipment by experts as 'inexcusable'.[133]

Online Hate Speech

[7–57] As the internet creates new ways for individuals to interact, it also provides new ways for individuals to harm each other with their communications. With the ubiquity of smart phone use, the pervasiveness of internet communications has increased and harmful communications can now intrude into intimate personal spaces at all times of the day. Politicians have called for legislative change[134] and a Law Reform Commission Report proposes amendments of existing law and the introduction of new offences to address the current challenges.[135] For now, there are three pieces of legislation that are relevant to the issue of online harassment and related offences: the Non-Fatal Offences Against the Person Act, 1997; the Post Office Amendment Act 1951; and the Prohibition of Incitement to Hatred Act 1989.

[7–58] There is a general perception that the internet has provided those with racist and xenophobic beliefs an 'unlimited platform in which they can air their views'.[136] Multiple factors make the internet an attractive mechanism to disseminate hate speech. In light of its 'cheap, instantaneous and decentralized distribution, numerous points of access, no necessary ties to geography, no simple system to identify content, as well as sophisticated encryption tools', the internet 'has become an asset for hate groups to transmit propaganda and provide information about their aims, allow an exchange between like-minded individuals, vindicate the use of violence, raise cash, and legitimize their actions while demoralizing and de-legitimizing others'.[137]

---

[132] TJ McIntyre, 'Cybercrime: Towards a Research Agenda' in Deirdre Healy and others (eds), *The Routledge Handbook of Irish Criminology* (Taylor and Francis 2015) 108.

[133] Barry Roche, 'Judge Criticises "Inexcusable" Five-Year Delays in Child Porn Cases' *The Irish Times* (Dublin, 29 October 2016).

[134] Lorraine Higgins, 'Lorraine Higgins: New Laws Must Tackle Abusive, Threatening Trolls' *The Irish Times* (Dublin, 23 July 2015); Daniel McConnell, 'Labour Brings Two Separate Bills Targeting Online Bullying' *Irish Independent* (Dublin, 17 April 2015).

[135] Law Reform Commission, *Report: Harmful Communications and Digital Safety* (LRC 116–2016).

[136] Jennifer Schweppe and Dermot Walsh, 'Combating Racism and Xenophobia through the Criminal Law' (2008) 154 <www.integration.ie/website/omi/omiwebv6.nsf/page/AXBN-7UPE6D1121207-en/$File/Combating%20Racism%20with%20the%20Criminal%20Law.pdf> accessed 7 June 2017.

[137] Raphael Cohen-Almagor, 'Fighting Hate and Bigotry on the Internet' (2011) 3(3) Policy & Internet 1.

Sections 2 and 3 of the Prohibition of the Incitement to Hatred Act outlaw the distribu-   **[7–59]**
tion, display, and broadcasting of material of a threatening, abusive or insulting nature
that is intended or is likely to stir up hatred.[138] 'Hatred' is defined in the Act as meaning
'hatred against a group of persons in the State or elsewhere on account of their race, colour,
nationality, religion, ethnic or national origins, membership of the travelling community,
or sexual orientation'. As the Act applies to words used and written material displayed 'in
any place other than inside a private residence', the offence applies to material posted on
the internet.[139]

Section 4 of the Prohibition of Incitement to Hatred Act also criminalises the preparation   **[7–60]**
and possession of written material likely to stir up hatred. To be convicted of the offence,
the individual must have:

1. prepared or possessed material
2. that is threatening, abusive or insulting and is intended or is likely 'to stir up hatred'
3. with a view to distributing, displaying, or otherwise publishing that material

As 'written material' is defined to include 'any sign or other visual representation', it appears
to apply to material in electronic form.[140] If found guilty of an offence under the Act, a person is liable on summary conviction to a fine not exceeding €1,270 and/or imprisonment
for a term not exceeding six months. If tried on indictment, a person is liable to a fine not
exceeding €12,700 and/or imprisonment for a term not exceeding two years.

While the Prohibition of Incitement to Hatred Act can be applied in the online context,   **[7–61]**
the effectiveness of the Act in practice can be doubted when the results of a 2011 case
involving a Facebook page are considered. In the District Court, Judge James O'Connor
dismissed a case against a man who had admitted to setting up a Facebook page that was
highly disparaging towards members of the Travelling community. While Judge O'Connor
recognised that the defendant's actions were 'obnoxious and revolting', he maintained that
there was reasonable doubt about the defendant's intent to incite hatred towards members
of the Travelling community.[141]

---

[138] The Act criminalises the publication/distribution of such written material, the use of words or display of such written material 'in any place other than inside a private residence' or 'inside a private
residence so that the words, behaviour or material are heard or seen by persons outside the residence'
and the distribution, showing, or playing of a recording of visual images or sounds of such material. The Prohibition of the Incitement to Hatred Act introduced three separate incitement to hatred
offences, which can be distinguished by 'the manner in which the offensive words, material or behaviour are communicated or processed'. s 2 is the general offence and s 3 provides for a 'separate,
narrower offence' that criminalises broadcasts likely to stir up hatred. It has been noted that 'it is likely
that broadcasting the offensive material would probably be covered by the general offence anyway':
Jennifer Schweppe and Dermot Walsh, 'Combating Racism and Xenophobia through the Criminal
Law' (2008) 61, 64 <www.integration.ie/website/omi/omiwebv6.nsf/page/AXBN-7UPE6D1121207-
en/$File/Combating%20Racism%20with%20the%20Criminal%20Law.pdf> accessed 7 June 2017.
[139] Law Reform Commission, *Report: Harmful Communications and Digital Safety* (LRC 116–2016) 9.
[140] Maeve McDonagh and Michael O'Dowd, *Cyber Law in Ireland* (Kluwer Law 2015) 993–95.
[141] John O'Mahony, 'Man Cleared of Online Hatred against Travellers' *Irish Examiner* (Cork, 1
October 2011).

[7–62]   While acknowledging that the Prohibition of the Incitement to Hatred Act can be used to combat the distribution of hate speech on the internet, Schweppe and Walsh argue that in order to comply with best international practice and standards Ireland needs to sign and ratify the Additional Protocol to the Convention on Cybercrime, concerning the criminalisation of acts of a racist and xenophobic nature committed through computer systems.[142] As Ireland is also obliged to implement the EU Framework Decision on combating racism and xenophobia, significant reform of the law against hate speech may be necessary.[143]

Online Harassment

[7–63]   In their submission to the Law Reform Commission (LRC) on Cyberbullying and Harassment, Digital Rights Ireland posited that 'two offences exist which are tailor-made, without any amendment, for use in respect of online communication'.[144] These most pertinent offences are both contained in the Non-Fatal Offences Against the Person Act 1997. Under s 10 of the Non-Fatal Offences Against the Person Act

> any person who, without lawful authority or reasonable excuse, by any means including by use of the telephone, harasses another by persistently following, watching, pestering, besetting or communicating with him or her, shall be guilty of an offence.

[7–64]   A person 'harasses' another person under this section where he or she 'intentionally or recklessly, seriously interferes with the other's peace and privacy or causes alarm, distress or harm to the other', and 'his or her acts are such that a reasonable person would realise that the acts would seriously interfere with the other's peace and privacy or cause alarm, distress or harm to the other'. If convicted summarily, an offender can be subject to a maximum prison sentence of 12 months and/or a maximum fine of €1875. If convicted on indictment, an offender can be subject to an unlimited fine and a maximum prison sentence of seven years.[145]

[7–65]   Even though the section mentions the use of a telephone, it is clear that it has general applicability and will apply where other technologies are used to commit the offence. In spite of its apparent general applicability, the Law Reform Commission has recommended that

---

[142] 'Chart of Signatures and Ratifications of Treaty 189: Additional Protocol to the Convention on Cybercrime, Concerning the Criminalisation of Acts of a Racist and Xenophobic Nature Committed through Computer Systems Status as of 07/06/2017' (7 June 2017) <www.coe.int/en/web/conventions/full-list/-/conventions/treaty/189/signatures> accessed 7 June 2017; Jennifer Schweppe and Dermot Walsh, 'Combating Racism and Xenophobia through the Criminal Law' 61, 64 (2008) <www.integration.ie/website/omi/omiwebv6.nsf/page/AXBN-7UPE6D1121207-en/$File/Combating%20Racism%20with%20the%20Criminal%20Law.pdf> accessed 7 June 2017.

[143] Due to the scale of the needed reforms, the Law Reform Commission did not believe it would be appropriate to address the issue of online hate speech within its 2016 report: Law Reform Commission, *Report: Harmful Communications and Digital Safety* (LRC 116–2016) 9.

[144] Digital Rights Ireland, 'Submissions of Digital Rights Ireland to Issues Paper on Cyber-crime Affecting Personal Safety, Privacy and Reputation Including Cyber-bullying' <www.digitalrights.ie/dri/wp-content/uploads/2015/03/DRI-Submissions-to-LRC-re-cyberbullying.pdf> accessed 7 June 2017.

[145] The section also empowers a court to order 'in addition to or as an alternative to any other penalty' an offender to refrain from communicating by any means with the other person for such a period as the court may specify.

s 10 should be amended to explicitly address other forms of online harassment, including the posting of fake social media profiles. According to the Commission, this could be done by amending the offence of harassment 'to include a specific reference to harassment of or about a person by online or digital means'. Even if such actions could theoretically come within the offence as currently articulated, the Law Reform Commission maintains that such a change 'would offer important clarification'.[146] Setting aside any uncertainties about the scope of the section, the requirement that the harassment be persistent also prevents the applicability of the offence to a number of serious scenarios. According to the Law Reform Commission 'features of the online and digital environment mean that even a single communication has the capacity to interfere seriously with a person's peace and privacy or cause alarm, distress or harm, particularly as internet communications are also difficult to erase completely'.[147]

Section 5 of the Non-Fatal Offences Against the Person Act makes it an offence to threaten to kill or cause serious harm with the intention that the target of the threat believes that it will be carried out. As the threat can be delivered by any means, threats delivered via electronic communications clearly fall within the scope of the offence. If summarily convicted of this offence, an individual can be sentenced to a maximum prison term of 12 months. If convicted on indictment, a person can be sentenced to a maximum of 10 years in prison. [7–66]

Reform Proposals and the Non-Consensual Distribution of Intimate Images ('Revenge Pornography')

In September 2016, the LRC published a report on harmful communications and digital safety.[148] A key goal of the report was to investigate appropriate legal responses that would address the 'tendency for some online and digital users to engage in communications that cause significant harm to others'. The scope of the report specifically included the act of posting intimate images online without consent, commonly known as 'revenge pornography'.[149] While the LRC report acknowledges that existing laws address some of the issues raised, it concludes that there are gaps in protection. To address these gaps, the LRC has drafted a Bill that could provide a model for future legislation in this area. [7–67]

The Justice Minister, Frances Fitzgerald, has described the LRC report as 'very useful' and has committed the government to legislating on the matter in a way that strikes 'the correct balance between the right to freedom of expression and the right to privacy'.[150] The Legislation Programme for the Spring/Summer Session 2017 indicates that work is underway on a Non-Fatal Offences against the Person (Amendment) Bill designed to address the criminal law aspects of the LRC report. It has been reported that Fitzgerald [7–68]

---

[146] Law Reform Commission, *Report: Harmful Communications and Digital Safety* (LRC 116–2016) 5. The Law Reform Commission recommends that such amendments be implemented through the introduction of a single piece of legislation that also includes additional offences recommended to address undesirable online behaviour.

[147] Law Reform Commission, *Report: Harmful Communications and Digital Safety* (LRC 116–2016) 6.

[148] Law Reform Commission, *Report: Harmful Communications and Digital Safety* (LRC 116–2016).

[149] Law Reform Commission, *Report: Harmful Communications and Digital Safety* (LRC 116–2016) 1.

[150] Shane Phelan, 'Minister Gets Green Light to Implement Laws to Combat "Revenge Porn"' *Irish Independent* (Dublin, 1 December 2016).

plans to publish the Bill in the near future.[151] While not yet published, a reform Bill is likely to extend the offence of harassment, to introduce a specific offence of non-consensual distribution of intimate images, and to extend the offence of sending threatening or indecent messages to all online communications.[152] It is uncertain whether the recommendations of the LRC regarding the establishment of a Digital Safety Commissioner – with regulatory authority over digital service providers – will be reflected in the proposed legislation.[153]

Conclusion

[7–69] The law has continually had to respond to the evolving threat of cybercrime. In spite of this, the computer crime offences contained in the Criminal Damage Act 1991 stood for over 25 years before the passage of the Criminal Justice (Offences Relating to Information Systems) Act in 2017. This chapter has identified many reform proposals – such as the Non-Fatal Offences against the Person (Amendment) Bill – that aim to better address the harms of cybercrime. The provisions on child-abuse material in the Criminal Law (Sexual Offences) Act 2017 illustrate how even when legislation is progressive and relatively technologically neutral, amendments are likely to be required due to the unpredictability of how society chooses to interact and access information. Due to the importance of cross-jurisdictional cooperation and consistency, cybercrime law in Ireland is heavily influenced by both European Union legislation and international agreements. The importance of international collaboration makes Ireland's failure to ratify the Cybercrime Convention all the more surprising. It should, however, be noted that a Cybercrime Bill – designed to give full effect to the Cybercrime Convention and to enable its ratification – is described as being in the preparatory stages by the Government Legislation Programme.[154]

---

[151] Sarah Bardon, '"Upskirting", Cyberstalking, and Revenge Porn to Be Criminal Offences' *The Irish Times* (Dublin, 15 May 2017).

[152] These align with the main recommendations for criminal law reform made by the LRC: Law Reform Commission, *Report: Harmful Communications and Digital Safety* (LRC 116–2016) 155–57; Shane Phelan, 'Minister Gets Green Light to Implement Laws to Combat 'Revenge Porn'' *Irish Independent* (Dublin, 1 December 2016).

[153] On introducing a Private Member's Bill – the *Harassment, Harmful Communications and Related Offences Bill* – designed 'to consolidate and reform the criminal law concerning harmful communications', Brendan Howlin acknowledged that the LRC Report contained provision for a Digital Safety Commissioner, but pointed out that the creation of 'a new statutory agency is outside the remit of a Dáil Private Member's Bill'. While the government would, of course, face no such limitation, the establishment of a new regulatory body would be a costly and complicated exercise. In spite of this, however, the Minister for Communications, Denis Naughten, has expressed an intention to create a new State office to carry out such a role: Brendan Howlin, 'Howlin Speech at Launch of Harassment, Harmful Communications and Related Offences Bill 2017' (4 April 2017) <www.labour.ie/news/2017/04/04/howlin-speech-at-launch-of-harassment-harmful-comm/> accessed 7 June 2017; Hugh Linehan, 'Digital Safety Watchdog Could Prove a Milestone Online' *The Irish Times* (Dublin, 8 February 2017).

[154] 'Government Legislation Programme Spring/Summer Session 2017' <www.taoiseach.gov.ie/eng/Taoiseach_and_Government/Government_Legislation_Programme/> accessed 7 June 2017. Inclusion on the legislative programme does not, of course, guarantee the passage of the Bill, or even its introduction to the Oireachtas.

Further Reading

- Alisdair Gillespie, *Child Pornography: Law and Policy* (Routledge 2011)
- Jack Goldsmith and Tim Wu, *Who Controls the Internet?: Illusions of a Borderless World* (Oxford University Press 2006)
- Maeve McDonagh and Michael O'Dowd, *Cyber Law in Ireland* (Kluwer Law 2015)
- TJ McIntyre, 'Computer Crime in Ireland: A Critical Assessment of the Substantive Law' (2005) 15(1) Irish Criminal Law Journal 13
- TJ McIntyre, 'Cybercrime: Towards a Research Agenda' in Deirdre Healy, Claire Hamilton, Yvonne Daly, and Michelle Butler (eds), *The Routledge Handbook of Irish Criminology* (Taylor and Francis 2015)
- Andrew Murray, *Information Technology Law* (Oxford University Press 2016)
- David Post, *In Search of Jefferson's Moose: Notes on the State of Cyberspace* (Oxford University Press 2009)
- Majid Yar, *Cybercrime and Society* (Sage 2013)
- Ian O'Donnell and Claire Milner, *Child Pornography: Crime, Computers and Society* (Willan 2007)

CHAPTER 8
Freedom of Speech Online

> *'The risk of harm posed by content and communications on the Internet to the exercise and enjoyment of human rights and freedoms, particularly the right to respect for private life, is certainly higher than that posed by the press.'*[1]

Freedom of expression is widely recognised as a fundamental right with a central role in democratic society. At an instrumental level, the ability to access information about how our society is being run, and the facility to develop, debate, and discuss our views with others, supports informed electoral choices. While the protection of free expression is essential to the operation of a democratic society, there is also a need to protect the right for reasons more concerned with the individual and their autonomy.　**[8–01]**

> Holding an opinion, stating an argument, expressing one's agreement or disagreement with a societal, technological or any other development is always a communication of personality. The protection of freedom of speech then is part of the protection of personality and thus of great importance to the development and existence of individuality itself.[2]

Many use the internet to express themselves and to educate themselves politically. This is unsurprising as the internet facilitates easy communication and speedy access to information for little expense of time or money. Individuals proclaim their political affiliations in their Twitter bios, announce that they voted on Facebook, and seek out like-minded individuals in online chat rooms. The internet enables a greater immediacy of expressive action and can also be used to facilitate real-world political actions and effects as well. In 2008, the social media driven campaign for Barack Obama's presidential candidacy was widely hailed for disrupting the traditional model of top-down political campaigning. Through the Obama campaign's use of social media and other Web 2.0　**[8–02]**

---

[1] *Editorial Board of Pravoye Delo and Shtekel v Ukraine* (2014) 58 EHRR 28, para 63.
[2] Indra Spiecker genannt Döhmann, 'The Difference between Online and Offline' in Clive Walker and Russell Weaver (eds), *Free Speech in an Internet Era: Papers from the Free Speech Discussion Forum* (Carolina Academic Press 2013) 92.

tools, a new way to 'organize supporters, advertise to voters, defend against attacks and communicate with constituents' was shown to be effective.[3] Many perceive the presidential election of 2016 as being notable for different reasons, including being the campaign in which so-called 'fake news' reached the mainstream through the unfiltered distribution networks and echo chambers of social media.[4] While the 2017 Women's March on Washington was described as illustrating that '21st century protest is still about bodies, not tweets', the organisation of the protest was initiated on Facebook where logistical communication and rallying also took place.[5] There is a much darker side to social media organisation too, of course. The Islamic State of Iraq and Syria, for example, uses social media sites to

> spread its message and encourage others, particularly young people, to support the organization, to travel to the Middle East to engage in combat. (...) The terrorist group has even directed sympathizers to commit acts of violence wherever they are when traveling to the Middle East isn't possible.[6]

[8–03]   A related use of modern technologies that receives significant attention from politicians and government agencies is the use of internet communication tools – particularly those that offer end-to-end encryption. The restriction of encryption tools is discussed in more detail later in this chapter but it is important to note that terrorist attacks have an understandably powerful influence over public opinion, and advocates of government interference recognise that terrorism tragedies can be utilised in order to gain popular support for intrusive measures. In 2015, the terrorist attacks in Paris were described as a 'wake-up call' and Senator John McCain called for encryption-restricting legislation.[7] These arguments were made in spite of the uncertainty about whether restricting encryption would have prevented the attacks.[8]

---

[3]   Claire Cain Miller, 'How Obama's Internet Campaign Changed Politics' *New York Times* (New York, 7 November 2008).
[4]   Hunt Allcott and Matthew Gentzkow, 'Social Media and Fake News in the 2016 Election' (2017) 31(2) Election Journal of Economic Perspectives 211.
[5]   Kaitlyn Tiffany, 'The Women's March Proves that 21st Century Protest is Still About Bodies, not Tweets' (*The Verge*, 23 January 2017) <www.theverge.com/2017/1/23/14354434/womens-march-on-washington-social-media-twitter-app> accessed 8 June 2017. While the Washington March was the first planned protest, it inspired hundreds of sister events and worldwide participation reached millions of protesters. Sister Marches <www.womensmarch.com/sisters> accessed 8 June 2017; Anemona Hartocollis and Yamiche Alcindor, 'Women's March Highlights as Huge Crowds Protest Trump: "We're Not Going Away"' *The New York Times* (New York, 21 January 2017).
[6]   Lisa Blaker, 'The Islamic State's Use of Online Social Media' (2015) 1(1) Military Cyber Affairs 4.
[7]   Brendan Sasso, 'Senators Take Aim at Encryption in Wake of Paris Attacks' *The Atlantic* (Boston, 17 November 2015); Ellen Nakashima, 'Officials Seizing the Moment of Paris Attacks to Rekindle Encryption Debate' *Washington Post* (Washington, 18 November 2015).
[8]   Several of the terrorists were known to the authorities and some of the perpetrators had used standard SMS messaging to communicate. Karl Bode, 'After Endless Demonization of Encryption, Police Find Paris Attackers Coordinated Via Unencrypted SMS' (*TechDirt*, 18 November 2015) <www.techdirt.com/articles/20151118/08474732854/after-endless-demonization-encryption-police-find-paris-attackers-coordinated-via-unencrypted-sms.shtml> accessed 8 June 2017.

These examples illustrate both the expressive potential and the accompanying down-sides of the internet. As with other areas of the law, the problems of anonymity, mass infringements, and jurisdictional uncertainties persist in the freedom of expression con-text. The increased dominance of a small number of internet companies – most nota-bly Facebook and Google – raises risks of monopolisation and the privatisation of the online public sphere. The potentially deleterious effects of such domination should be clear when it is noted that an increasing number of individuals are accessing their news through social media.[9]

[8–04]

Legal Protection of the Right to Free Expression

The right to freedom of expression – or free speech as it is sometimes called – receives protection in a wide range of human rights documents, including domestic constitutions and international conventions. A related idea to freedom of expression is freedom of the press. Generally, the freedom of the press is not protected for its own sake, but for the service it provides to the citizenry. Due to the central role of the press in the distribution of information in a democratic society, freedom of expression and freedom of the press can be considered as 'two sides of one coin'.[10] In Ireland, the importance of free expression is acknowledged by a number of important documents. In the Irish Constitution itself, there are in fact two sources of protection for free expression. Article 40.6.1° states that

[8–05]

> The State guarantees liberty for the exercise of the following rights, subject to public order and morality:
> i. The right of the citizens to express freely their convictions and opinions.
> The education of public opinion being, however, a matter of such grave import to the common good, the State shall endeavour to ensure that organs of public opinion, such as the radio, the press, the cinema, while preserving their rightful liberty of expression, including criticism of Government policy, shall not be used to undermine public order or morality or the authority of the State.
> The publication or utterance of blasphemous, seditious, or indecent matter is an offence which shall be punishable in accordance with law.

Article 40.6.1° provides protection for the citizen to freely express their opinions and also acknowledges the instrumental role of the 'organs of public opinion' in educating the pub-lic. Article 40.6.1° explicitly considers the radio and the cinema to constitute 'organs of public opinion' alongside the print media. The non-exhaustive nature of the Article means that the same constitutional protections can also apply in the internet context. Indeed, in the case of *Cornec v Morrice*, the High Court recognised that a 'blogger' was entitled to protection under Article 40.6.1° as even though the blogger was not 'a journalist in the strict sense of the term', he was acting as an organ of public opinion with his coverage of

[8–06]

---

9   Jeffrey Gottfried and Elisa Shearer, 'News Use Across Social Media Platforms 2016' (*Journalism*, 26 May 2016) <www.journalism.org/2016/05/26/news-use-across-social-media-platforms-2016/> accessed 8 June 2017.
10 Indra Spiecker genannt Döhmann, 'The Difference between Online and Offline' in Clive Walker and Russell Weaver (eds), *Free Speech in an Internet Era: Papers from the Free Speech Discussion Forum* (Carolina Academic Press 2013) 92.

religious cults.[11] According to the Court, '[p]art of the problem here is that the traditional distinction between journalists and lay people has broken down in recent decades, not least with the rise of social media.' Specifically, it was accepted that a blogger may have a claim to confidentiality in relation to the identity of his or her sources.[12] Hogan J cited from the opinion he delivered in *Doherty v Referendum Commission*, where he stated that:

> The Constitution envisaged a plebiscitary as well as a parliamentary democracy and, in doing so, it has created a State which can demonstrate – in both word and deed – that it is a true democracy worthy of the name.[13]

[8–07]   While it is positive for the media that Article 40.6.1° recognises their 'rightful liberty of expression, including criticism of Government policy', Article 40.6.1° places emphasis on the State's obligation to endeavour to ensure that organs of public opinion 'shall not be used to undermine public order or morality or the authority of the State'. The protection of free expression is also starkly limited by the statement that the 'publication or utterance of blasphemous, seditious, or indecent matter is an offence which shall be punishable in accordance with law'. The blasphemy laws in Ireland are considered further later in this chapter.

[8–08]   Freedom of expression receives further protection from Article 40.3.1° in which an unenumerated right to communicate was identified. Article 40.3.1° states that:

> The State guarantees in its laws to respect, and, as far as practicable, by its laws to defend and vindicate the personal rights of the citizen.

As put by Costello J in *Attorney General v Paperlink*:

> as the act of communication is the exercise of such a basic human faculty that a right to communicate must inhere in the citizen by virtue of his human personality and must be guaranteed by the Constitution (…) I conclude that the very general and basic human right to communicate which I am considering must be one of those personal unspecified rights of the citizen protected by Article 40.3.1°.[14]

[8–09]   In *Murphy v IRTC*, Barrington J posited that Article 40.6.1° was designed to protect the public activities of the citizen in a democratic society, but Article 40.3.1° was designed to enable the individual to convey 'needs and emotions' and to participate in 'rational

---

[11] *Cornec v Morrice* [2012] 1 IR 804 (HC).

[12] Hogan J noted that the right to free expression as protected by Article 40.6.1° would 'be meaningless if the law could not (or would not) protect the general right of journalists to protect their sources'. According to Hogan J, 'the public interest in ensuring that journalists can protect their sources remains very high, since journalism is central to the free flow of information which is essential in a free society': *Cornec v Morrice* [2012] 1 IR 804 (HC) 819.

[13] *Cornec v Morrice* [2012] 1 IR 804 (HC); *Doherty v Referendum Commission* [2012] 2 IR 594 (HC); Eoin Carolan, 'Constitutionalising Discourse: Democracy, Freedom of Expression and the Future of Press Regulation' (2014) 51(1) Irish Jurist 1.

[14] *AG v Paperlink Ltd* [1983] IEHC 1 [31].

discourse'.[15] While this distinction between Article 40.6.1° and Article 40.3.1° has been praised as providing a 'clear and intellectually coherent mechanism for examining freedom of expression issues' that recognises their roots in 'different philosophical systems',[16] it is important to note that Fennelly J has remarked that Articles 40.3.1° and 40.6.1° are 'inseparable'.[17] Regardless, the rights are likely to overlap significantly in practice.[18]

The European Convention on Human Rights (ECHR) recognises the right to free expression in a more structured way than the Irish Constitution. The first paragraph of Article 10 ECHR clearly enunciates a broad right to free expression:

 [8–10]

> Article 10 – Freedom of expression
> 1. Everyone has the right to freedom of expression. This right shall include freedom to hold opinions and to receive and impart information and ideas without interference by public authority and regardless of frontiers. This article shall not prevent States from requiring the licensing of broadcasting, television or cinema enterprises.

It is notable that the Article 10 ECHR right to free expression includes not only the right to impart information and ideas but to also hold opinions and receive information and ideas without interference by public authorities. The ECtHR recognises that freedom of expression – and particularly freedom of political and public debate – is an essential component of democratic societies. The ECtHR also acknowledges the special importance of freedom of expression for the free press as it is 'incumbent on the press to impart information and ideas' of public interest and the public has a right to receive such information.[19] It is unsurprising that these principles also apply to online expression. The ECtHR has stated that in light of the internet's 'accessibility' and 'capacity to store and communicate vast amounts of information', it plays an important role in 'enhancing the public's access to news and facilitating the dissemination of information generally'.[20] It should also be noted, however, that the ECtHR identifies a particularly high 'risk of harm posed by content and communications on the Internet to the exercise and enjoyment of human rights and freedoms, particularly the right to respect for private life'.[21]

 [8–11]

---

[15] *Murphy v IRTC* [1999] 1 IR 12 (SC) 24; Eoin Carolan and Ailbhe O'Neill, *Media Law in Ireland* (Bloomsbury Professional 2010) 24.

[16] *Murphy v IRTC* [1999] 1 IR 12 (SC) 25; Eoin Carolan and Ailbhe O'Neill, *Media Law in Ireland* (Bloomsbury Professional 2010) 25.

[17] *Mahon v Post Communications* [2007] 3 IR 338 (SC).

[18] *Murphy v IRTC* [1999] 1 IR 12 (SC) 25; Eoin Carolan and Ailbhe O'Neill, *Media Law in Ireland* (Bloomsbury Professional 2010) 372. O'Dell has argued that the identification of the right to communication as a supplement to Article 40.6.1° was 'an unnecessary cure for a non-existent ill' as a 'flexible, purposive approach to Article 40.6.1° would have achieved the same end': Eoin O'Dell, 'The Constitution at 70' (*Cearta*, 7 May 2007) <www.cearta.ie/2007/05/the-constitution-at-70/> accessed 13 June 2017.

[19] *Sunday Times v United Kingdom (No 2)* (1992) 14 EHRR 153, para 50; see also *Sunday Times v United Kingdom (No1)* (1980) 2 EHRR 245, para 59.

[20] *Times Newspapers Ltd (Nos 1 and 2) v United Kingdom* [2009] ECHR 451, para 27.

[21] *Delfi AS v Estonia* (2016) 62 EHRR 6, para 133.

[8–12]   Like the Irish constitutional protection of free expression, the ECHR right is clearly limited, primarily by the second paragraph of Article 10 ECHR, which states:[22]

> 2. The exercise of these freedoms, since it carries with it duties and responsibilities, may be subject to such formalities, conditions, restrictions or penalties as are prescribed by law and are necessary in a democratic society, in the interests of national security, territorial integrity or public safety, for the prevention of disorder or crime, for the protection of health or morals, for the protection of the reputation or rights of others, for preventing the disclosure of information received in confidence, or for maintaining the authority and impartiality of the judiciary.

While the second paragraph of Article 10 ECHR appears to offer a remarkably broad range of exceptions that can be used to justify government interference with the right to free expression, any interference must also be 'prescribed by law' and 'necessary in a democratic society' in the pursuit of the legitimate aim. The European Court of Human Rights (ECtHR) has clarified that while the 'adjective "necessary" is not synonymous with "indispensable", neither has it the flexibility of such expressions as "admissible", "ordinary", "useful", "reasonable" or "desirable" ... it implies the existence of a "pressing social need"'.[23]

[8–13]   The ECtHR recognises that the initial responsibility for securing Convention rights lies with the individual Contracting States, but even though the Convention grants Contracting States a 'margin of appreciation', the Court retains the ultimate supervisory authority. The ECtHR will consider whether the interference was 'proportionate to the legitimate aim pursued' and whether the reasons asserted by the national authorities as justifying the interference are 'relevant and sufficient'.[24]

[8–14]   The importance of the standard of sufficiency was made clear in the case of *Sunday Times v UK (No 2)*, where a newspaper was restrained by means of injunction from publishing information taken from a memoir, *Spycatcher*.[25] The government defended the injunction on the grounds that the book contained confidential information that was a threat to national security. While the ECtHR will generally grant a wide margin of appreciation when considering such matters, the Court did not find that the circumstances constituted a 'sufficient' reason for the purposes of Article 10 ECHR. Crucially, the ECtHR found that a permanent injunction would not have achieved the purported goal as the confidentiality of the material had already been destroyed – irrespective of any further reporting by the *Sunday Times* – as a result of the book's publication in the United States.[26] This decision predates the mass adoption of the internet, but it is clear to see how the reasoning of the Court has implications for the globalised media environment of the internet.[27]

---

[22] Paragraph 1 allows for some government interference where necessary for the licensing of broadcasting, television or cinema enterprises.

[23] *Sunday Times v United Kingdom (No 1)* (1980) 2 EHRR 245, para 59.

[24] *Sunday Times v United Kingdom (No 2)* (1992) 14 EHRR 153, para 50.

[25] *Sunday Times v United Kingdom (No 2)* (1992) 14 EHRR 153.

[26] *Sunday Times v United Kingdom (No 2)* (1992) 14 EHRR 153, paras 54–55.

[27] See also *Éditions Plon v France* (2006) 42 EHRR 36, para 53.

As was discussed in [6–12] to [6–13], the ECHR was incorporated into Irish law at a **[8–15]** sub-constitutional level by the ECHR Act 2003. While Denham J described the constitutional rights under Articles 40.3.1° and 40.6.1° as being 'similar to the right of freedom of expression guaranteed by Article 10 of the European Convention on Human Rights', it seems clear that the ECHR has been a positive influence on the protection of free expression in Irish law.[28] The ECHR Act requirement that the courts interpret laws in accordance with the Convention where possible has 'encouraged increasing citation of and references to Strasbourg case law and an increasing cross-fertilisation of Irish and Strasbourg jurisprudence'.[29]

As might be expected, the European Union Charter of Fundamental Rights also provides **[8–16]** protection for freedom of expression, with Article 11 of the Charter stating that

1. Everyone has the right to freedom of expression. This right shall include freedom to hold opinions and to receive and impart information and ideas without interference by public authority and regardless of frontiers.
2. The freedom and pluralism of the media shall be respected.

While the first paragraph of Article 11 of the Charter clearly draws from Article 10 ECHR, **[8–17]** it is notable that paragraph two of the Charter explicitly acknowledges the need to protect 'the freedom and pluralism of the media'. The Charter has, of course, quite different legal status to the ECHR. On the one hand, the Charter is binding on States 'only when they are implementing Union law'.[30] On the other hand, the greater enforcement power of the Court of Justice of the European Union (CJEU) in comparison to the ECtHR means that the Charter can be a very powerful tool of human rights protection. This has been particularly evident in the contexts of privacy and the protection of personal data,[31] which interestingly are rights that sometimes conflict but also complement the protection of free expression. We have discussed how the Constitution and the ECHR recognise that rights are rarely absolute and the Charter agrees. Article 52 clarifies that

1. Any limitation on the exercise of the rights and freedoms recognised by this Charter must be provided for by law and respect the essence of those rights and freedoms. Subject to the principle of proportionality, limitations may be made only if they are necessary and genuinely meet objectives of general interest recognised by the Union or the need to protect the rights and freedoms of others.
2. Rights recognised by this Charter for which provision is made in the Treaties shall be exercised under the conditions and within the limits defined by those Treaties.

The reduced relevance of national borders on the internet and the globalised consump- **[8–18]** tion of content is a key area of tension in freedom of expression law due to varying

---

[28] *O'Brien v Mirror Group Newspapers Ltd* [2001] 1 IR 1 (SC) 33.

[29] Eoin Carolan and Ailbhe O'Neill, *Media Law in Ireland* (Bloomsbury Professional 2010) 18.

[30] Charter, art 51.

[31] See the landmark cases of Joined Cases C–293/12 and C–594/12 *Digital Rights Ireland and Seitlinger and Others* [2014] WLR (D) 164; and Case C–131/12 *Google Spain v AEPD and Mario Costeja González* [2014] 36 BHRC 589, para 69.

cultural attitudes regarding the nature of the right. The First Amendment of the US Constitution states that

> Congress shall make no law respecting an establishment of religion, or prohibiting the free exercise thereof; or abridging the freedom of speech, or of the press; or the right of the people peaceably to assemble, and to petition the Government for a redress of grievances.

[8–19] US courts have interpreted the right to freedom of speech as protected by the First Amendment as a broad right with minimal restrictions. An emphasis on free speech – and the belief in the 'marketplace of ideas' – has strong cultural resonance in the US and this is particularly true of many who identify with internet culture. With many of the world's largest internet companies being based in the US, a powerful coalition of support for free expression and minimal government intervention is formed.

[8–20] The *LICRA et UEJF v Yahoo! Inc and Yahoo! France* litigation provides an early example of how these differences can play out. Back in 2000, litigation was initiated in French court by the International League against Racism and Anti-Semitism (LICRA) against Yahoo!. LICRA complained that one of Yahoo!'s platforms offered Nazi memorabilia for purchase in breach of French law and a French court ordered Yahoo! to 'take such measures as may be necessary to prevent the exhibition or sale on its Yahoo.com site of Nazi objects throughout the territory of France'. In response to the ruling, the Yahoo! CEO at the time, Jerry Yang, commented, 'We are not going to change the content of our sites in the United States just because someone in France is asking us to do so.'[32] The opposing point was put to Yahoo! that 'French law does not permit racism in writing, on television or on the radio, and I see no reason to have an exception for the Internet.'[33] In response, Yahoo! put forward a defence of 'impossibility', but this was proven to be false following expert investigation into the potential of IP-identification and self-reporting technologies – which were developing techniques at that time.[34]

[8–21] Following the confirming ruling, Yahoo! remained resistant and proceeded to take action in the US courts, asserting that the French court had no authority over Yahoo! as a US company.[35] In spite of this, however, the real-world consequences of continued resistance – including potential asset seizure and legal action against Yahoo! executives when in

---

[32] Janet Kornblum and Leslie Miller, 'Town of Half.com is Halfway Home' *USA Today* (Virginia, 19 June 2000); Jack Goldsmith and Tim Wu, *Who Controls the Internet?: Illusions of a Borderless World* (Oxford University Press 2006) 5.

[33] Lee Dembart, 'Boundaries on Nazi Sites Remain Unsettled in Internet's Global Village' *International Herald Tribune* (Paris, 29 May 2000).

[34] Jack Goldsmith and Tim Wu, *Who Controls the Internet?: Illusions of a Borderless World* (Oxford University Press 2006) 5–7.

[35] After some initial success in the US courts, the Court of Appeals for the Ninth Circuit reversed the lower US court's decision on procedural grounds. As the Supreme Court later denied certiorari, the outcome of the US litigation is somewhat inconclusive. *Yahoo! Inc v La Ligue Contre Le Racisme et L'antisemitisme* 433 F3d 1199 (9th Cir 2006); *Yahoo! Inc v La Ligue Contre Le Racisme et L'antisemitisme* 433 F 3d 1199 (9th Cir 2006) certiorari denied, 126 S Ct 2332 (2006); Yaman Akdeniz, *Racism on the Internet* (Council of Europe 2009) 63–67. See Andrew Murray, *Information*

Europe – became clear. In 2001, Yahoo! announced that it would 'no longer allow items that are associated with groups which promote or glorify hatred and violence, to be listed on any of Yahoo!'s commerce properties'.[36] While Yahoo! maintained that this was not done in response to the French ruling, Goldsmith and Wu point out that 'the timing and threat of French sanctions suggest otherwise'.[37]

Defamation Online

The law on defamation in Ireland is primarily governed by the Defamation Act 2009. **[8–22]** In this Act a 'defamatory statement' is defined as 'one that tends to injure a person's reputation in the eyes of reasonable members of society'. In order to succeed in a defamation action:

- The defamatory statement must have been made to a third party.
- The plaintiff must show that the plaintiff was identified or was capable of being identified by the relevant material, and
- The defendant must not be able to avail of any defence. Crucially, truth is a complete defence to an allegation of defamation.[38]

Defamation – the tort that covers the traditional wrongs of libel and slander – has a long **[8–23]** history in common law. This history has clashed at times with the right to free expression and the freedom of the press. Reflecting the particular risk posed to the media, defamation has been described as

> one of the most serious dangers facing journalists and publishers today. Eighty per cent of all defamation actions are brought against the media – and a libel action can bankrupt a small newspaper or radio station.[39]

Speaking about the UK law on defamation extant in 2010,[40] Lord Lester of Herne Hill QC described the law as 'the enemy of free speech in some respects' and argued that evidence

---

Technology Law (Oxford University Press 2016) 123–24 for more discussion. 'French Judge Orders Web Site Auction of Nazi Goods Blocked' *Chicago Tribune* (Chicago, 21 November 2001).

[36] Jack Goldsmith and Tim Wu, *Who Controls the Internet?: Illusions of a Borderless World* (Oxford University Press 2006) 8; Troy Wolverton and Jeff Pelline, 'Yahoo to Charge Auction Fees, Ban Hate Materials' (*CNET News*, 2 January 2001) <news.com.com/2100-1017-250452.html?legacy=cnet> accessed 8 June 2017.

[37] Jack Goldsmith and Tim Wu, *Who Controls the Internet?: Illusions of a Borderless World* (Oxford University Press 2006) 8. For a discussion of 'cyberspace liberum' see Mireille Hildebrandt, 'Extraterritorial Jurisdiction to Enforce in Cyberspace? Bodin, Schmitt and Grotius in Cyberspace' (2013) 65 University of Toronto Law Journal 163.

[38] Other defences (partial and total) include: fair and reasonable publication on a matter of public interest; absolute privilege; qualified privilege; honest opinion; offer of amends; apology; consent; innocent publication.

[39] Kieron Wood, 'Defamation Legislation in Ireland' (*Lawyer.ie*) <www.lawyer.ie/defamation/> accessed 8 June 2017.

[40] The UK law on defamation was reformed by the Defamation Act 2013.

showed that the existing laws had 'a serious chilling effect on freedom of speech, not only of the press but of any citizen critic, including non-governmental organisations'.[41]

[8–24] As discussed above, neither the constitutionally protected right nor the ECHR protected right to freedom of expression is an unlimited right. Even in the United States – where free speech receives robust protection under the First Amendment – it is theoretically possible, although practically very difficult, to sue based on a defamatory statement.[42] Defamation actions are on a stronger footing in Ireland, in large part due to the recognition of a right to a good name as a constitutional right. Article 40.3.2° of the Irish Constitution states that

> The State shall, in particular, by its laws protect as best it may from unjust attack and, in the case of injustice done, vindicate the life, person, good name, and property rights of every citizen.

[8–25] This Article does not only recognise a right to a 'good name', but also puts a duty on the State to ensure that its laws protect the right from unjust attack and where necessary to vindicate the right. The position of the right to a good name in the Constitution provides some explanation for the past tendency of the Irish courts to favour the protection of a good name in defamation actions over free speech claims. Carolan and O'Neill have noted, however, that in recent decades 'there occurred something of a shift in the legal protection provided to the media's freedom of expression under Irish law'.[43] Carolan and O'Neill explain the evolution as the increasing influence of the Article 10 ECHR jurisprudence of the ECtHR. Of course, the right to freedom of expression as protected by Article 10 ECHR can be restricted where the restriction is prescribed by law and is necessary in a democratic society in pursuit of a legitimate aim, including the 'protection of the reputation or rights of others'. More recently, the ECtHR has also recognised a right to protection of reputation as being encompassed by the Article 8 ECHR right to respect for private life.[44]

[8–26] It is clear that the publication of a defamatory statement on the internet – whether on an online newspaper or on a social media page – can be the subject of a defamation action.[45] This is clear to the general public based on the reporting of notable cases in the mainstream media. In 2017, for example, the controversial *Daily Mail* columnist, Katie Hopkins, was found to have defamed Jack Monroe through the publication of a number of Twitter posts, or 'tweets'.[46] While the so-called 'twibel' case received much attention in the media (both

---

[41] Ian Burrell, 'Lord Lester: "The Law is the Enemy of Free Speech"' *The Independent* (London, 25 August 2010).

[42] Especially difficult for 'public figures'. *New York Times v Sullivan* (1964) 376 US 254.

[43] Eoin Carolan and Ailbhe O'Neill, *Media Law in Ireland* (Bloomsbury Professional 2010) 178–80.

[44] *Pfeifer v Austria* (2007) 48 EHRR 175.

[45] A seminal case in this area of internet law is *Godfrey v Demon Internet Service* [2001] QB 201. In this case, Morland J found that 'every time one of the Defendants' customers accesses "soc culture thai" [an internet newsgroup] and sees that posting defamatory of the Plaintiff there is a publication to that customer'.

[46] Maev Kennedy, 'Jack Monroe Wins Twitter Libel Case against Katie Hopkins' *The Guardian* (London, 10 March 2017). The subject of the tweets, Jack Monroe (@MxJackMonroe) claimed that (i) the first tweet suggested that she had either vandalised a war memorial, which was a criminal act,

traditional and social), David Banks points out – on Twitter – that the result means 'business as usual' as 'Twitter is no different in law from any other medium as far as court is concerned.' He went on to say that if the judge had found otherwise that then 'we would've had to revise the textbooks'.[47] Another high-profile finding concerning defamation on the internet was made by the English courts in *Lord McAlpine of West Green v Sally Bercow*.[48] In this case, Tugendhat J concluded that the inclusion of the text '*innocent face*' at the end of an apparently innocuous question ('Why is Lord McAlpine trending?')[49] was to be read as a 'stage direction'. Tugendhat J found that the reasonable reader would read Bercow's words as insincere and ironical and the tweet was accordingly defamatory in nature.[50]

Digital defamation case law in Ireland includes the case of *Tansey v Gill*,[51] where a solicitor successfully sought a number of interlocutory orders against the website, www.rate–your–solicitor.com. The orders that were granted   **[8–27]**

- required the defendants to remove from the internet the defamatory material complained of and prohibited any further publication of such material
- required the defendants (and other parties with notice) to terminate the operation of the relevant website
- required the defendants to deliver up to the plaintiff the names and addresses of all persons involved in the publication of defamatory material concerning the plaintiff.

In his ruling, Peart J commented that:

> The Internet has facilitated an inexpensive, easy, and instantaneous means whereby unscrupulous persons or ill-motivated malcontents may give vent to their anger and their perceived grievances against any person, where the allegations are patently untrue, or where no right thinking person would consider them to be reasonable or justified.[52]

In the case of *McKeogh v John Doe & Ors*,[53] which involved the publication of a YouTube video and associated defamatory comments, a plaintiff also had success in achieving orders requiring the removal of defamatory material concerning him from the internet. It is interesting to note that in his ruling Peart J criticised the 'vituperative internet chatter and comment on YouTube and on Facebook' and lamented the fact that 'it is impossible to "unring"   **[8–28]**

---

or condoned or approved that vandalisation; and (ii) the second tweet bore a defamatory innuendo meaning that she approved or condoned that vandalisation. She argued that both tweets had caused her serious harm pursuant to s 1 of the Defamation Act 2013.

[47] <https://twitter.com/DBanksy/status/840215294786297856> accessed 8 June 2017.

[48] *Lord McAlpine of West Green v Sally Bercow* [2013] EWHC 1342 (QB).

[49] The plaintiff, Lord McAlpine, was 'trending' due to false accusations that he was a paedophile who had sexually abused children living in care.

[50] Ursula Smartt, *Media & Entertainment Law* (Routledge 2014) 14. It is interesting to note that Lord McAlpine ceased legal action against hundreds of Twitter users who had less than 500 followers in return for a small donation to BBC Children In Need: Josh Halliday, 'Lord McAlpine Drops some Twitter Defamation Cases' *The Guardian* (London, 21 February 2013).

[51] *Tansey v Gill* [2012] IEHC 42.

[52] *Tansey v Gill* [2012] IEHC 42, [25]. See also *Robins v Kordowski* [2011] EWHC 1912, where a permanent injunction was ordered against the website 'solicitorsfromhell.co.uk'.

[53] *McKeogh v John Doe & Ors* [2012] IEHC 95.

the bell that has sounded so loudly'. While the practice of spreading false statements about others is an ancient one, the conditions created by the internet exacerbate the problem. As pointed out by Murray:

> When gossip was passed over pints of beer or glasses of wine in the local pub or exchanged over coffees in Starbucks it was shortlived: in the air for a second and then gone again. Actionable defamation, that is the type of defamatory statement which causes an action to end up before a judge, was a world away from gossip. It tended to be statements published in the press or broadcast on television or radio. This is partly due to the extensive audience such statements could reach and partly due to the fact that a publisher or broadcaster indicated deep pockets which could be called upon to fulfil a damages award.[54]

[8–29] Now, of course, much gossip takes place over the internet: on blogs, in comment sections, in chat groups, and on social media. In a case before the Monaghan Circuit Court, Judge John O'Hagan awarded maximum damages against a man who had posted defamatory statements on Facebook. According to Judge O'Hagan, the award should 'teach people posting messages on the social media site to be very careful'.[55]

[8–30] Even if the defamatory statement was only ever intended to be seen by a select group of insiders with the subject of the statement being none-the-wiser, publication to a third party will have occurred as long as just one person aside from the publisher heard or saw the statement.[56] Moreover, the 'forward-ability' of emails and the 'screenshot-ability' of WhatsApp conversations and social media posts means that the total audience for a defamatory statement can grow exponentially from that intended by the publisher – particularly if the content is salacious or shocking. While the size of the audience will not affect the question of whether a defamatory statement has been published, it can have a significant influence on the size of a damages claim and whether or not an action is actually taken. The opportunity to deny ever making the defamatory statement will also be limited when faced with the type of hard evidence that does not result when gossip is spread through casual in-person conversation.

[8–31] The nature of communication over the internet also creates opportunities for forum shopping, with many claimants initiating actions in favourable regimes – particularly the UK and Ireland – even where those jurisdictions may not have been the primary market for the defamatory statement.[57] Following reform to UK law by the Defamation Act 2013, the jurisdiction of UK courts in defamation cases has been restricted to situations where 'of all the places in which the statement complained of has been published, England and Wales is

---

[54] Andrew Murray, *Information Technology Law* (Oxford University Press 2016) 173.

[55] Similarly, in another Facebook defamation case, Judge James O'Donoghue warned that '[p]eople perhaps with alcohol late at night can post these remarks and injure people's character. It is a highly dangerous activity and can result in long-term hurt.' Maria O'Halloran, 'Damages in Facebook Case a "Wake-up Call"' *The Irish Times* (Dublin, 18 June 2016); Stephen Maguire, 'Couple Awarded €30,000 Over Online Insults' *The Irish Times* (Dublin, 18 January 2017).

[56] Excluding the subject of the statement.

[57] Diane Rowland, *Information Technology Law* (Routledge 2016) 61.

clearly the most appropriate place in which to bring an action in respect of the statement'.[58] According to Rowland,

> This provision suggests that compartmentalising a worldwide publication into a purely local one should no longer be so readily possible, as the provision invites a comparative analysis of the relative significance of different places of the publication.[59]

Since this reform, Ireland is now perceived as a 'more plaintiff-friendly jurisdiction' relative to the UK. McCarthy has argued that the action taken by Jessica Biel and Justin Timberlake against *Heat* magazine in the Irish courts in 2014 is an indication of this.[60] Section 5 of the Defamation Act 2009 requires the Minister for Justice to 'not later than 5 years after the passing of this Act, commence a review of its operation'. The Minister for Justice and Equality, Frances Fitzgerald, called for submissions to assist this review in November 2016. Included in the invitation for submissions was an indicative list of some specific issues which may be considered under the review. Of particular relevance to this textbook is '[w]hether the Act's provisions are adequate and appropriate in the context of defamatory digital or online communications'.[61] Of further relevance, due to the role of intermediaries in the enforcement of law online, is the issue of '[w]hether any change should be made to the defences of truth, absolute privilege, qualified privilege, honest opinion, fair and reasonable publication on a matter of public interest, and innocent publication, as defined by the Act'.

[8–32]

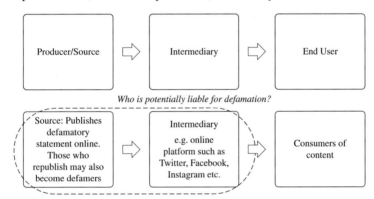

Figure 1   *Intermediaries and Defamation*[62]

---

[58] Defamation Act 2013, s 9(2).

[59] Diane Rowland, *Information Technology Law* (Routledge 2016) 61.

[60] Hugh McCarthy, 'Libel Tourism May Become our Newest Cottage Industry' *The Irish Times* (Dublin, 10 November 2014). O'Dell contends that in spite of the several perceived advantages for complainants in the Irish system, it is likely that 'a libel tourist who presses a case to judgment in Dublin may not find it all that very different from London, after all': Eoin O'Dell, 'Is Dublin Becoming the Defamation Capital of the World, the Libel-Tourism Destination of Choice?' (*Cearta*, 16 November 2015) <www.cearta.ie/2015/11/is-dublin-becoming-the-defamation-capital-of-the-world-the-libel-tourism-destination-of-choice/> accessed 8 June 2017.

[61] Department of Justice and Equality, 'Review of the Defamation Act 2009 – Public Consultation: Invitation for Submissions' <www.justice.ie/en/JELR/Pages/Review_of_the_Defamation_Act_2009_Public_Consultation#_ftn1> accessed 8 June 2017.

[62] An individual may be deemed to have republished a defamatory statement – and be accordingly subject to a defamation action – if they 'share' or 'retweet' defamatory material.

[8–33]   In [7–10] to [7–12], we saw how the liability of intermediaries is limited on the internet. Limiting the liability of intermediaries is often justified on the grounds that a limited liability regime for internet intermediaries is justified by a public interest in the 'growth and innovation of e-commerce and the Internet economy', which is dependent on a 'reliable and expanding Internet infrastructure'.[63] In its simplest sense, you can imagine how permitting defamation actions against Google whenever a defamatory statement is made underneath a YouTube video would result in a chilling effect and make the availability of comment sections impracticable. The tort of defamation has historically provided for a defence of 'innocent dissemination' to protect innocent parties – such as libraries and printers – who may technically be spreading defamatory material, but doing so unintentionally. A statutory version of the defence – known as the defence of 'innocent publication' – is found in the Defamation Act and also provides protection for internet publishers.[64] This defence is discussed in more detail below, but it is first necessary to examine the facts of the case in *Muwema v Facebook Ireland Ltd*.

[8–34]   Mr Muwema was a partner in a Ugandan law firm who claimed that statements made about him on Facebook were 'highly offensive and defamatory'.[65] As is often the case with controversial statements, the defamatory posts had been made using a pseudonymous Facebook account (TVO).[66] Before issuing proceedings, Mr Muwema requested that Facebook remove the defamatory statements made by the pseudonymous third party (TVO), but Facebook Ireland refused. In correspondence with the plaintiff, counsel for Facebook Ireland asserted that:

> To the extent you claim that any content on the Facebook service is defamatory in nature, your complaint should be addressed to the user who created and posted the content, not Facebook. Moreover, Facebook is not in a position to evaluate the truth or falsity of such content and will not remove or block it absent proper service of a valid court order identifying the specific content deemed to be defamatory.

In court, Mr Muwema sought an order under the Defamation Act 2009 requiring Facebook to remove and prevent further publication of the defamatory content. Mr Muwema also sought a *Norwich Pharmacal* order requiring Facebook to provide the plaintiff with any details which it holds relating to the identities and location of the defaming party.

[8–35]   The key issue was not whether the statements were defamatory, but whether Facebook Ireland could be obliged to take action with regard to material posted by third parties on their platform. Facebook Ireland argued that they could avail of the 'host' immunity provided by Regulation 18 of the eCommerce Regulations.[67] You may recall that the 'host' immunity only applies where the intermediary does not have 'actual knowledge of the

---

[63]   OECD, 'The Role of Internet Intermediaries in Advancing Public Policy Objectives' (September 2011) <www.oecd.org/sti/ieconomy/theroleofinternetintermediariesinadvancingpublicpolicyobjectives.htm> accessed 8 June 2017.

[64]   Defamation Act 2009, s 27.

[65]   *Muwema v Facebook Ireland Ltd* [2016] IEHC 519, [2], [3], [7].

[66]   *Muwema v Facebook Ireland Ltd* [2016] IEHC 519.

[67]   See discussion in Chapter 7 about Regulation 18 of the European Communities (Directive 2000/31/EC) Regulations 2003, SI 2003/68.

unlawful activity' and acts expeditiously to remove or to disable access to the information upon obtaining such knowledge or awareness.[68] Facebook Ireland maintained that they did not have 'actual knowledge' of unlawful activity as they did not know whether or not the reported content was unlawful.[69] As pointed out by O'Dell, this is an 'extremely wide submission' and does not address the question of whether the defendants were aware of the 'facts or circumstances from which the defamation was apparent'.[70]

Mr Muwema countered that the immunities provided by the eCommerce Regulations do not shield intermediaries from injunctions to terminate or prevent an infringement.[71] While the Court accepted that the Regulation preserves the power of courts to order the cessation of infringements by intermediaries otherwise immune from action, the Court stated that the 'Regulations themselves do not confer a power upon the Court to make such an order – the power to do so must be derived from elsewhere.'[72] The power to make such an order in the defamation context is found in the Defamation Act where s 33 states that [8–36]

> (1) The High Court, or where a defamation action has been brought, the court in which it was brought, may, upon the application of the plaintiff, make an order prohibiting the publication or further publication of the statement in respect of which the application was made if in its opinion—
>   (a) the statement is defamatory, and
>   (b) the defendant has no defence to the action that is reasonably likely to succeed.
> (2) Where an order is made under this section it shall not operate to prohibit the reporting of the making of that order provided that such reporting does not include the publication of the statement to which the order relates.
> (3) In this section 'order' means—
>   (a) an interim order,
>   (b) an interlocutory order, or
>   (c) a permanent order.

The key part of s 33 for the purposes of the *Muwema* case was whether Facebook Ireland could avail of a 'defence to the action that is reasonably likely to succeed'. This is where the aforementioned defence of 'innocent publication' becomes relevant. Section 27 of the Defamation Act states that [8–37]

> It shall be a defence (to be known as the 'defence of innocent publication') to a defamation action for the defendant to prove that—
>   (a) he or she was not the author, editor or publisher of the statement to which the action relates,
>   (b) he or she took reasonable care in relation to its publication, and

---

[68] See European Communities (Directive 2000/31/EC) Regulations 2003, SI 2003/68, reg 18.
[69] *Muwema v Facebook Ireland Ltd* [2016] IEHC 519 [40].
[70] Eoin O'Dell, 'Reform of the Law of Defamation – The Defence of Innocent Publication (*Muwema v Facebook* Part 2)' (*Cearta*, 27 September 2016) <www.cearta.ie/2016/09/reform-of-the-law-of-defamation-the-defence-of-innocent-publication-muwema-v-facebook-part-2/> accessed 8 June 2017.
[71] *Muwema v Facebook Ireland Ltd* [2016] IEHC 519 [40]. See European Communities (Directive 2000/31/EC) Regulations 2003, SI 2003/68, reg 18(3).
[72] *Muwema v Facebook Ireland Ltd* [2016] IEHC 519 [55].

(c) he or she did not know, and had no reason to believe, that what he or she did caused or contributed to the publication of a statement that would give rise to a cause of action in defamation.

[8–38] A defendant must meet each of these conditions to avail of the defence. While this might seem relatively straightforward, it is necessary to examine the scope of the key terms to understand their application. The first condition to avail of the defence of innocent publication is to show that you are not the 'author, editor or publisher'. Section 27(2)(c) of the Defamation Act clarifies that a person should not be considered to be the 'author, editor or publisher' if in relation to any electronic medium on which the statement is recorded or stored

> he or she was responsible for the processing, copying, distribution or selling *only* of the electronic medium or was responsible for the operation or provision *only* of any equipment, system or service by means of which the statement would be capable of being retrieved, copied, distributed or made available.[73]

[8–39] According to Binchy J, the defendant was reasonably likely to succeed with the defence of 'innocent publication' as laid out above and thus refused the application for takedown and prior restraint orders.[74] Binchy J expressed some unease at this conclusion, voicing concern that

> Persons whose reputations are seriously damaged by anonymous and untrue internet postings may be left without any legal remedy against the site hosting the publication, even in the most flagrant of cases. The reluctance of the courts here and in other jurisdictions to grant prior restraint orders reflects the importance attached by the courts and society at large to freedom of expression. There must be a doubt however about whether an ISP, which disclaims any responsibility for or interest in the material complained about, is entitled to assert in defence of an application such as this, the right to freedom of expression of a party who has chosen to remain anonymous and remains at the time of the hearing of the application unidentified and beyond the jurisdiction of the Court, and who in any event does not have a right to publish defamatory statements.[75]

[8–40] Notably, Binchy J followed these concerns by stating: 'If this is indeed a consequence of s.27 of the Act of 2009, I doubt very much if it is a consequence intended by the Oireachtas.' Bearing these misgivings in mind, it is important to note that O'Dell has questioned the reasoning of Binchy J in *Muwema*. As noted earlier, in order to avail of the defence of innocent publication, a defendant must meet the three components of the defence. While Binchy J appears to emphasise the fact that Facebook Ireland was not an 'author' for the purposes of the defence, O'Dell highlights the ways in which it is questionable whether Facebook Ireland met the second and third elements of the defence. First, O'Dell points

---

[73] Emphasis added.

[74] *Muwema v Facebook Ireland Ltd* [2016] IEHC 519 [64]. Binchy J opined that the application should also be 'refused because it would serve no useful purpose, having regard to the availability of publications containing the same and other damaging allegations about the plaintiff elsewhere on the internet'. The judge did, however, make a 'Norwich Pharmacal' order.

[75] *Muwema v Facebook Ireland Ltd* [2016] IEHC 519 [65].

out that the fact that Facebook Ireland did not act after being put on notice regarding the defamatory content 'could easily have gone to the question of whether they had taken reasonable case, for the purposes of the second condition as stated in section 27(1)(b)'.[76] Second, Facebook Ireland's decision not to act 'could at least as easily have gone to the question of what the defendant had "reason to believe" for the purposes of the third condition as stated in section 27(1)(c)'.[77]

27. — (1) It shall be a defence (to be known as the "defence of innocent publication") to a defamation action for the defendant to prove that—

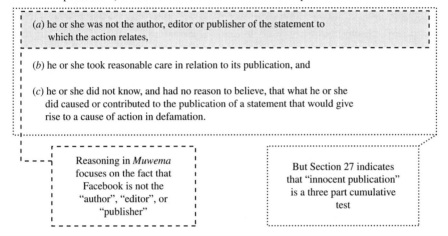

(*a*) he or she was not the author, editor or publisher of the statement to which the action relates,

(*b*) he or she took reasonable care in relation to its publication, and

(*c*) he or she did not know, and had no reason to believe, that what he or she did caused or contributed to the publication of a statement that would give rise to a cause of action in defamation.

Reasoning in *Muwema* focuses on the fact that Facebook is not the "author", "editor", or "publisher"

But Section 27 indicates that "innocent publication" is a three part cumulative test

Figure 2   *There are Three Cumulative Components to the Defence of Innocent Publication*

As the judgment in *Muwema v Facebook* leaves significant uncertainty regarding the application of the defence of innocent publication, it cannot be regarded as 'the last word' on the liability of internet intermediaries for defamatory posts on their platforms.[78] This is especially the case as we have previously seen another High Court judge, Baker J, grant an injunction requiring an intermediary to remove defamatory posts from a blog post hosted on its site.[79] Readers should be mindful of the possibility of a different result being reached   [8–41]

---

[76] Typographical error in original.

[77] Eoin O'Dell, 'Reform of the Law of Defamation – The Defence of Innocent Publication (*Muwema v Facebook* Part 2)' (*Cearta*, 27 September 2016) <www.cearta.ie/2016/09/reform-of-the-law-of-defamation-the-defence-of-innocent-publication-muwema-v-facebook-part-2/> accessed 8 June 2017.

[78] Eoin O'Dell, 'Internet Defamation and the Liability of Intermediaries (*Muwema v Facebook* Part 1)' (*Cearta*, 6 September 2016) <www.cearta.ie/2016/09/internet-defamation-and-the-liability-of-intermediaries-muwema-v-facebook-part-1/> accessed 8 June 2017.

[79] *Petroceltic International plc v Aut O'Mattic A8C Ireland Ltd* (HC, 20 August 2015); Eoin O'Dell, 'Internet Defamation and the Liability of Intermediaries (*Muwema v Facebook* Part 1)' (*Cearta*, 6 September 2016) <www.cearta.ie/2016/09/internet-defamation-and-the-liability-of-intermediaries-muwema-v-facebook-part-1/> accessed 8 June 2017.

in a future case and should keep track of any legislative developments resulting from the review of the Defamation Act initiated by Frances Fitzgerald.

[8–42] In its submission to the Defamation Act 2009 review, the law firm McCann Fitzgerald argue that the breadth of the defence of innocent publication may mean that the Defamation Act is of 'little use to a plaintiff wishing to urgently have harmful content removed online'.[80] As a result of this perceived weakness and the uncertainty the interpretation of the defence creates for defendants, McCann Fitzgerald suggest that the Defamation Act be amended to provide for a procedure similar to the 'Notice of Complaint' process adopted in the UK Defamation Act 2013. Section 5 of the UK Defamation Act is explicitly directed at 'operators of websites' and provides for a defence where the operator can show that it did not post the statement on the website. In a similar manner to how the defence of innocent publication has three necessary components in Irish law, the operators of websites defence in England and Wales is defeated where the claimant shows that

(a) it was not possible for the claimant to identify the person who posted the statement,

(b) the claimant gave the operator a notice of complaint in relation to the statement, and

(c) the operator failed to respond to the notice of complaint in accordance with any provision contained in regulations.[81]

[8–43] While McCann Fitzgerald acknowledge the existence of strict 'notice and takedown' policies on many websites, the lack of uniformity across different platforms and the lack of an easy mechanism to obtain the details of the third party publisher is unsatisfactory.[82] Interestingly, Google also recommends adopting some elements of the UK Defamation Act 2013. Google supports the preclusion of defamation claims against intermediaries where it is 'reasonably practicable' to bring an action directly against the actual author, editor, or publisher.[83] According to Google, such an approach encourages 'individuals to be responsible online citizens, and ensure[s] that citizens who do not act responsibly are held accountable for any online misconduct'.[84]

Blasphemy and Hate Speech

[8–44] It is clear that all online platforms need to be cognisant of many different governing laws. We have already seen in this textbook, for example, how a social network website must be aware of different data protection, copyright, and defamation rules. The internet is the

---

[80] McCann Fitzgerald, 'Submission to the Department of Justice and Equality Review of Defamation Act 2009' 4–5 <www.justice.ie/en/JELR/McCann_FitzGerald.pdf/Files/McCann_FitzGerald.pdf> accessed 8 June 2017.

[81] Defamation Act 2013, s 5(3).

[82] McCann Fitzgerald, 'Submission to the Department of Justice and Equality Review of Defamation Act 2009' 4–5 <www.justice.ie/en/JELR/McCann_FitzGerald.pdf/Files/McCann_FitzGerald.pdf> accessed 8 June 2017.

[83] Defamation Act 2013, s 10.

[84] Google Inc, 'Google Inc's Response to the Tánaiste and Minister for Justice and Equality's Review of the Defamation Act 2009' 5 <www.justice.ie/en/JELR/Google_Inc.pdf/Files/Google_Inc.pdf> accessed 8 June 2017.

world's largest distributor of content and where global standards and mores regarding content vary, challenging questions for multinational service providers can result. Platforms where users can upload information to a large audience with minimal restraint must be particularly wary. In [8–19] to [8–20], we saw how Yahoo! – at the time a burgeoning internet power with Silicon Valley values – had to reckon with Europe's specific historical experience and resulting restrictions on hate speech.

Due to its deep connection with a nation's history and perceived collective character, **[8–45]** approaches to censorship, blasphemy, and hate speech can be one of the most varied and protectively guarded areas of policy distinction. This reality is reflected in the wide discretion (margin of appreciation) granted by the ECtHR to Party States when considering whether a measure is necessary for the protection of morals. As stated by the ECtHR in the seminal case of *Handyside v UK*:

> The Convention leaves to each Contracting State, in the first place, the task of securing the rights and liberties it enshrines (…) These observations apply, notably, to Article 10 para. 2 (art. 10–2). In particular, it is not possible to find in the domestic law of the various Contracting States a uniform European conception of morals. The view taken by their respective laws of the requirements of morals varies from time to time and from place to place, especially in our era which is characterised by a rapid and far-reaching evolution of opinions on the subject. By reason of their direct and continuous contact with the vital forces of their countries, State authorities are in principle in a better position than the international judge to give an opinion on the exact content of these requirements as well as on the 'necessity' of a 'restriction' or 'penalty' intended to meet them.[85]

Of course, the margin of appreciation does not give the Contracting States an 'unlimited power of appreciation' and the ECtHR retains the authority to give the final ruling on whether a restriction is reconcilable with freedom of expression.[86]

In a notable quirk, Article 40.6.1° of the Irish Constitution guarantees the right to free **[8–46]** expression but also criminalises blasphemous, seditious, and indecent utterances. In 1991, the Law Reform Commission expressed the view that

> there is no place for the offence of blasphemous libel in a society which respects freedom of speech. The strongest arguments in its favour are (i) that it causes injury to feelings, which is a rather tenuous basis on which to restrict speech, and (ii) that freedom to insult religion would threaten the stability of society by impairing the harmony between the groups, a matter which is open to question in the absence of a prosecution.[87]

The Irish legislature clarified the scope of the blasphemy offence in statute with s 36 **[8–47]** of the Defamation Act 2009. According to the law, a 'person who publishes or utters blasphemous matter shall be guilty of an offence and shall be liable upon conviction on indictment to a fine not exceeding €25,000'. While historically blasphemy was applied

---

[85] *Handyside v UK* (1979) 1 EHRR 737, para 48.
[86] *Handyside v UK* (1979) 1 EHRR 737, paras 48–49.
[87] Law Reform Commission, *Consultation Paper on the Crime of Libel* (August 1991) 231.

to speech offensive to Christians, the 2009 Act provides that a person who publishes or utters blasphemous matter 'that is grossly abusive or insulting in relation to matters held sacred by *any religion*' may commit the offence of blasphemy where the publication/ utterance causes 'outrage among a substantial number of the adherents of that religion', and 'he or she intends, by the publication or utterance of the matter concerned, to cause such outrage'.[88]

[8–48]   The offence is technologically neutral and one could imagine how the inflammatory and viral nature of much internet communication could result in liabilities. In 2015, for example, Dr Ali Selim commented that he would consider invoking the Act if the Irish media 'retweeted' or reprinted a cartoon of the Prophet Mohammed from the satirical magazine Charlie Hebdo.[89] Interestingly, the former Minister for Justice who introduced the law, Dermot Ahern, recognised the offence as 'arcane' and intended the offence to be unenforceable.[90] The offence requires that a number of hurdles be overcome for a successful prosecution and these render the offence largely ineffectual. In addition to creating ambiguity with the requirement that the publication be '*grossly* abusive or insulting', 'outrage' must be caused to a '*substantial*' number of religious adherents.[91] This latter criterion seemed relevant to the termination of a controversial investigation into comments made by Stephen Fry.[92] Furthermore, the publisher must have intended to cause the outrage and it will be a defence if a reasonable person would find genuine 'literary, artistic, political, scientific, or academic value in the matter to which the offence relates'. In spite of the apparent 'unenforceability by design', there is still potential for the offence to cause a chilling effect harmful to free expression. Evidence of a potential chilling effect can be seen from comments made by the Secretary of the National Union of Journalists, Séamus Dooley, who remarked, '[i]t is a sobering thought that Charlie Hebdo would be in clear breach of Ireland's blasphemy laws.'[93] It is important to note that there are long-running calls for the blasphemy offence to be removed from the Constitution and the statute books. More recently, the Department of Justice has confirmed that preparatory work has begun on a Bill providing for a referendum on the matter.[94]

[8–49]   While blasphemous speech, hate speech, and other offensive speech can occur anywhere, the internet has facilitated the widespread reach – and consumption – of such material.

---

[88] Emphasis added.

[89] These comments were made in the aftermath of the terrorist attacks at the offices of Charlie Hebdo in Paris. Aoife Barry, 'Muslim Scholar Could Seek Legal Advice if Irish Media Republish Mohammed Cartoon' *The Journal* (Dublin, 7 January 2015) <www.thejournal.ie/dr-ali-selim-charlie-hebdo-cartoon-1870437-Jan2015/> accessed 8 June 2017.

[90] Carol Taaffe, 'Its Form and Buttons' *The Dublin Review* (Dublin, Autumn 2009); Paul O'Brien and Senan Hogan, 'Ahern to Press Ahead with "Arcane" Blasphemy Law' *Irish Examiner* (Cork, 21 May 2009); Ryan Nugent, 'We made Blasphemy Law "Almost Impossible to Prosecute" – Former Minister Says about Stephen Fry Garda Investigation' *Irish Independent* (Dublin, 8 May 2017).

[91] Emphasis added.

[92] Cathal McMahon, 'Stephen Fry Blasphemy Probe Dropped after Gardaí Fail to Find "Substantial Number of Outraged People"' *Irish Independent* (Dublin, 8 May 2017).

[93] Colin Gleeson, 'Republic's Blasphemy Laws are "Outdated", NUJ Boss Says' *The Irish Times* (Dublin, 15 December 2016).

[94] Conor Pope, 'Referendum on Blasphemy Being Prepared as Complaint made against Stephen Fry' *The Irish Times* (Dublin, 6 May 2017).

The traditional media provides a filter that prevents the publication of much offensive speech. A 'letter to the editor' containing objectionably offensive speech is unlikely to be printed, at least not without substantial editing. Even where the traditional media wants to publish controversial material – whether for journalistic, ideological, or commercial reasons – they are typically subject to much greater regulation than material distributed on the internet. This is particularly the case for broadcast media, which have historically been considered more influential than print media.[95] In Ireland, for example, the Broadcasting Authority of Ireland monitors and enforces compliance of the licensed broadcasters with broadcasting codes and rules.[96] Even the more resistant print media has largely signed up to a system of self-governance that was statutorily recognised in the Defamation Act 2009.[97]

More 'old-fashioned' methods for spreading ideas – such as distributing newsletters, leaf- **[8–50]** letting, and public speaking – are inherently limited in their ability to reach those outside the established community without the support of – or at least interest in and coverage by – the media. The comparative lack of control – both regulatory and institutional – combined with the relative anonymity and greater reach of the internet, creates the perfect conditions for offensive, racist, extremist, sexist, and trolling speech.[98] How such speech can and should be regulated raises complex questions about the appropriate balance between free expression and other societal interests.

In the aforementioned case of *Handyside*, the ECtHR pointed out that Article 10 ECHR

> is applicable not only to 'information' or 'ideas' that are favourably received or regarded as inoffensive or as a matter of indifference, but also to those that offend, shock or disturb the State or any sector of the population. Such are the demands of that pluralism, tolerance and broadmindedness without which there is no 'democratic society'.

---

[95] For example, in a case involving Ireland, the ECtHR found that the 'State was, in the Court's view, entitled to be particularly wary of the potential for offence in the broadcasting context, such media being accepted by this Court and acknowledged by the applicant, as having a more immediate, invasive and powerful impact including, as the Government and the High Court noted, on the passive recipient. He was consequently free to advertise the same matter in any of the print media (including local and national newspapers) and during public meetings and other assemblies': *Murphy v Ireland* (2004) 38 EHRR 13, para 74.

[96] For example, the Broadcasting Act 2009 requires that in respect of programme material broadcast by a broadcaster that audiences are protected from harmful or offensive material, in particular, that programme material in respect of the portrayal of violence and sexual conduct, shall be presented by a broadcaster (i) with due sensitivity to the convictions or feelings of the audience, and (ii) with due regard to the impact of such programming on the physical, mental or moral development of children: Broadcasting Act 2009, s 42(2)(f).

[97] Press Council, 'Code of Practice' (undated) <www.presscouncil.ie/code-of-practice> accessed 8 June 2017.

[98] '#Gamergate' is a notable recent controversy. The loose movement connected with the term #Gamergate has been associated with online harassment, including the 'doxing' of video game developer, Zoe Quinn ('Doxing' involves posting a target's contact details and personal information online). Proponents of #Gamergate cite concerns with games journalism as the reason for their discontent, but others have described the movement as 'darkly misogynistic': Keith Stuart, 'Zoe Quinn: "All Gamergate Has Done Is Ruin People's Lives"' *The Observer* (London, 3 December 2014).

This means, amongst other things, that every 'formality', 'condition', 'restriction' or 'penalty' imposed in this sphere must be proportionate to the legitimate aim pursued.[99]

[8–51] In certain circumstances, including those where the speaker has expressed views that are xenophobic or anti-Semitic, the ECtHR has tended to invoke Article 17 ECHR in order to preclude purveyors of hateful speech from relying on Article 10 ECHR.[100] For example, in *Glimmerveen & Hagenbeek v Netherlands*, extremist right-wing politicians were precluded from relying on Article 10 ECHR to defend their distribution of leaflets endorsing discrimination based on race.[101]

[8–52] With the increased ease, speed, and versatility with which expression can be disseminated online, the internet is becoming an important tool for those who wish to spread hate speech.[102] McGonagle reports that the internet is now used to distribute hate speech through the

- dissemination of propaganda and other types of (mis-)information
- exchange of information and ideas, including via social media networks, discussion groups, listservs and communities of interest
- attracting of inadvertent users by 'usurping domain names' and 'using misleading metatags'.

[8–53] The internet is also used by hate groups for organisational purposes, commercial ends, trolling, and criminal behaviour.[103] In Chapter 7, we saw how the Prohibition of the Incitement to Hatred Act applies to the distribution of hate speech via the internet. In spite of this, the Irish Immigrant Support Centre (NASC) has opined that not only is the current law inadequate to tackle hate crime, but it is especially inadequate in the tackling of online hate crime.[104] It is particularly challenging to enforce hate crime legislation online for a number of reasons, not least the fact that it is 'common practice for hate websites to be hosted in jurisdictions that are considered to be favourable to, or tolerant of, hate speech'.[105] Even

---

[99] *Handyside v UK* (1979) 1 EHRR 737, para 49. In spite of this strong statement of principle, the ECtHR found that the prosecution of the Applicant for the possession of obscene books for publication for gain was proportionate to the legitimate aim of protecting morals. The margin of appreciation played an important role in this case.

[100] Tarlach McGonagle, 'The Council of Europe against Online Hate Speech: Conundrums and Challenges' (2014) <rm.coe.int/16800c170f> accessed 8 June 2017. Article 17 ECHR reads: 'Nothing in this Convention may be interpreted as implying for any State, group or person any right to engage in any activity or perform any act aimed at the destruction of any of the rights and freedoms set forth herein or at their limitation to a greater extent than is provided for in the Convention.'

[101] *Glimmerveen & Hagenbeek v Netherlands* (1982) 4 EHRR 260.

[102] Tarlach McGonagle, 'The Council of Europe against Online Hate Speech: Conundrums and Challenges' (2014) < rm.coe.int/16800c170f> accessed 8 June 2017, 26–27.

[103] Tarlach McGonagle, 'The Council of Europe against Online Hate Speech: Conundrums and Challenges' (2014) 26–27 < rm.coe.int/16800c170f> accessed 8 June 2017, 26–27.

[104] Jennifer Schweppe, Amanda Haynes, and James Carr, 'A Life Free from Fear' (August 2014) <ulsites.ul.ie/law/sites/default/files//Life%20Free%20From%20Fear%20-%20Reprint%20Aug28%20 2014%20-%20web%20version_2_0.pdf> accessed 8 June 2017.

[105] Tarlach McGonagle, 'The Council of Europe against Online Hate Speech: Conundrums and Challenges' (2014) <rm.coe.int/16800c170f> accessed 8 June 2017, 26–27.

where the perpetrator appears to be based in Ireland and uses a social network or other online platform within the reach of An Garda Síochána, challenges remain as individuals often operate under pseudonyms. Once again, the internet intermediaries have a key role to play.

An interesting case on the issue of online intermediaries was decided by the Grand Chamber of the ECtHR in 2015. In *Delfi AS v Estonia*, a news portal had printed a balanced article, but several of the comments from readers viewable underneath the article were grossly insulting.[106] Like many news sites you may be familiar with, Delfi operated a notice and takedown system for offensive comments and also ran a technical filter that would automatically filter prescribed obscenities. The ECtHR found that Estonia had not violated Article 10 ECHR holding that **[8–54]**

> where third-party user comments are in the form of hate speech and direct threats to the physical integrity of individuals (…), the rights and interests of others and of society as a whole may entitle Contracting States to impose liability on Internet news portals, without contravening Article 10 of the Convention, if they fail to take measures to remove clearly unlawful comments without delay, even without notice from the alleged victim or from third parties.

This opinion – that appears to endorse laws mandating that news sites continually monitor their comment sections[107] – may seem surprising in light of what we know about host immunity under the eCommerce Directive. While the decision has been the subject of significant criticism, it is important to note that the ECtHR accepted the domestic court's interpretation of its own law (including its implementation of EU law) and as a result the case should not be considered as authority for how the EU host immunity should be interpreted.[108] The joint dissenting opinion of Judges Sajó and Tsotsoria demonstrates the risks of targeting intermediaries in this manner by pointing out that **[8–55]**

> Governments may not always be directly censoring expression, but by putting pressure and imposing liability on those who control the technological infrastructure (ISPs, etc.), they create an environment in which collateral or private-party censorship is the inevitable result. Collateral censorship 'occurs when the state holds one private party A liable for the speech of another private party B, and A has the power to block, censor, or otherwise control access to B's speech'. Because A is liable for someone else's speech, A has strong incentives to over-censor, to limit access, and to deny B's ability to communicate using the platform that A controls. In effect, the fear of liability causes A to impose prior restraints on B's speech and to stifle even protected speech.

---

[106] *Delfi AS v Estonia* (2016) 62 EHRR 6.

[107] Such a requirement could prompt some publishers to remove comment sections entirely.

[108] There is some dispute over how the CJEU would have resolved the question. Aleksandra Kuczerawy and Pieter-Jan Ombelet, 'Not so Different After All? Reconciling *Delfi vs Estonia* with EU Rules on Intermediary Liability' (*Media Policy Project Blog*) <blogs.lse.ac.uk/mediapolicyproject/2015/07/01/not-so-different-after-all-reconciling-delfi-vs-estonia-with-eu-rules-on-intermediary-liability/> accessed 8 June 2017.

[8–56]   Even though *Delfi* was a decision from the Grand Chamber of the ECtHR, it appears that subsequent decisions of the ECtHR have tended to 'distinguish' *Delfi* in a manner that may suggest that the Court is reconsidering its approach, at least in circumstances that do not involve hate speech or incitements to violence. Indeed, one commentator has gone so far to suggest that the ECtHR has begun to 'rewrite' the ruling in *Delfi*.[109] It appears that the seriousness of the illegal speech, the size and reach of the online site, and the speed with which the material is removed will all be considered relevant factors in the fair balance between Article 10 ECHR and other competing rights.[110]

[8–57]   Particularly notable language is found in the case of *Magyar Tartalomszolgáltatók Egyesülete and Index.Hu Zrt v Hungary*, where the ECtHR appears to recognise that requiring the advanced filtering of internet comments for legal breaches would require 'excessive and impracticable forethought capable of undermining freedom of the right to impart information on the Internet'.[111] Furthermore, the ECtHR (albeit the Fourth Chamber and not the Grand Chamber) appears to endorse an effective system of notice and takedown as offering a suitable tool for balancing competing rights in this context.[112] In spite of the moderation in approach, there still appears to be a space for domestic governments to defend laws that penalise intermediaries for allowing third parties to post content that amounts to 'clearly unlawful content'[113] – even where effective systems of notice and takedown are in place.[114]

[8–58]   The continued uncertainty of how Article 10 ECHR applies in this context is concerning, particularly in light of proposals to reform the liability of intermediaries at the European Union level.[115] Plans in the Digital Single Market Strategy include the introduction of 'sectorial legislation that would de facto erode liability exemptions for online intermediaries, especially platforms' in an effort to close a '"value gap" between rightholders and online platforms allegedly exploiting protected content'.[116] A number of related proposals – from reform of the Audio-visual Media Services Directive to the encouragement of

---

[109] Sophie Stalla-Bourdillon, '*MTE v Hungary*: Is the ECtHR Rewriting *Delfi v Estonia*?' (*Peep Beep*, 2 February 2016) <peepbeep.wordpress.com/2016/02/02/mte-v-hungary-is-the-ecthr-rewriting-delfi-v-estonia/> accessed 8 June 2017.

[110] *Magyar Tartalomszolgáltatók Egyesülete and Index.Hu Zrt v Hungary* [2016] ECHR 135, para 25.

[111] *Magyar Tartalomszolgáltatók Egyesülete and Index.Hu Zrt v Hungary* [2016] ECHR 135, para 82.

[112] *Magyar Tartalomszolgáltatók Egyesülete and Index.Hu Zrt v Hungary* [2016] ECHR 135, para 91.

[113] Such as illegal hate speech or incitement to violence. Privacy or defamation claims would be less likely to meet this standard.

[114] Dirk Voorhoof, 'ECHR in *Pihl v Sweden*: Blog Operator not Liable for Promptly Removed Defamatory User Comment' (*Media Report*) <www.mediareport.nl/en/press-law/23032017/echr-in-pihl-v-sweden-blog-operator-not-liable-for-promptly-removed-defamatory-user-comment/> accessed 8 June 2017.

[115] European Commission, 'Evidence Gathering on Liability of Online Intermediaries' (4 May 2017) <https://ec.europa.eu/digital-single-market/en/news/evidence-gathering-liability-online-intermediaries> accessed 8 June 2017.

[116] Giancarlo Frosio, 'Reforming Intermediary Liability in the Platform Economy: A European Digital Single Market Strategy' (*Oxford Law*, 2 April 2017) <www.law.ox.ac.uk/business-law-blog/blog/2017/04/reforming-intermediary-liability-platform-economy-european-digital> accessed 8 June 2017.

voluntary intermediary measures – have the potential to turn online intermediaries into 'internet police'.[117]

Following the launch of an online code of conduct – drafted by the EU Commission and agreed to by Facebook, Twitter, YouTube and Microsoft – Věra Jourová, the EU Commissioner for Justice, commented, '[t]he recent terror attacks have reminded us of the urgent need to address illegal online hate speech.' Jourová pointed out that '[s]ocial media is unfortunately one of the tools that terrorist groups use to radicalise young people and racists use to spread violence and hatred.'[118] The voluntary code states that the co-operating internet companies agree to act in accordance with guidelines regarding the manner in which they tackle illegal hate speech online. The desire to create the voluntary agreement appears to stem from the difficulty of taking enforcement action when laws vary in different countries.[119] While the practical advantages of such an approach are clear to see, judges are trained experts in the application of legal standards, including human and constitutional rights. The creation of entirely private decision-making processes on issues as essential to a democracy as free expression poses a significant threat to the core values of transparency and accountability.

[8–59]

The Role of Encryption

Encryption has been discussed in a number of different contexts already in this textbook. Encryption was described in detail in [4–61] to [4–65] and we saw the importance of encryption for data protection and data protection by design in [5–39] to [5–45]. While encryption can be a useful tool to protect information in your possession, it is a particularly important tool in the leaky internet. The commercialisation of the internet – that facilitated its central position in modern society – would not have been possible without the use of encryption tools. Without secure communications and transactions, trust on the internet would not have been possible.[120] Reflecting the mutually reinforcing relationship between privacy and freedom of expression, encryption is not only a privacy enhancing technology, but is also a crucial tool for free expression.[121] This chapter focuses on the importance of encryption for communicating freely in the information age.

[8–60]

---

[117] Giancarlo Frosio, 'Reforming Intermediary Liability in the Platform Economy: A European Digital Single Market Strategy' (*Oxford Law*, 2 April 2017) <www.law.ox.ac.uk/business-law-blog/blog/2017/04/reforming-intermediary-liability-platform-economy-european-digital> accessed 8 June 2017.

[118] European Commission, 'Press Release: European Commission and IT Companies Announce Code of Conduct on Illegal Online Hate Speech' (31 May 2016) <europa.eu/rapid/press-release_IP-16-1937_en.htm> accessed 8 June 2017.

[119] Alex Hern, 'Facebook, YouTube, Twitter and Microsoft Sign EU Hate Speech Code' *The Guardian* (London, 31 May 2016).

[120] Gordon Corera, *Intercept: The Secret History of Computers and Spies* (Weidenfeld & Nicholson 2015) 104–05; Sarah McKune, 'Encryption, Anonymity, and the "Right to Science"' (*Just Security*, 28 April 2015) <justsecurity.org/22505/encryption-anonymity-debates-right-science/> accessed 8 June 2017.

[121] Human Rights Council, *Report of the Special Rapporteur on the Promotion and Protection of the Right to Freedom of Opinion and Expression* (A/HRC/23/40–2013); Daniel Solove, 'A Taxonomy of Privacy' (2006) 154 University of Pennsylvania Law Review 477, 491–99; Edward Long, *The Intruders* (Praeger 1967) viii. As referenced in Stanley Benn, 'Privacy, Freedom, and Respect for Persons' in Ferdinand Schoeman (ed), *Philosophical Dimensions of Privacy* (Cambridge University Press 1984) 304.

[8–61] Encryption can be defined as a 'process of converting messages, information, or data into a form unreadable by anyone except the intended recipient'.[122] A system of encryption facilitates communication with others by protecting the 'confidentiality and integrity' of messages from prying eyes.[123] While encryption can make it difficult for unauthorised third parties to comprehend your information, there is little to justify sending information to others if the encryption also prevents the intended viewers from interpreting the information. Accordingly, a 'key' is needed to 'unlock' the encrypted information and reveal its content in a legible form. This key must, of course, be unknown to unauthorised parties.

[8–62] In the modern world, symmetric-key encryption – which uses the same secret key to encrypt data that is used to decrypt data – is impractical as the need to securely exchange the secret key with the party you wish to communicate with will often require an in-person meeting.[124] Public key encryption is very practical in the internet context. It operates with the use of two keys, one public and one secret.[125] For example, many journalists choose to publicise their public key, for example by putting it in their Twitter bios. They do this to encourage potential sources to contact them with tips and useful information. Once a source sees the public key, they can use the key to encode sensitive data, knowing that data communicated in that manner will be much more secure than data communicated through standard email. The journalist can then decrypt the data using a second private and non-inferable key.[126]

Recent Controversies and a Human Right to Encryption

[8–63] In spite of its many benefits, due to its capacity for opacity, governments have often looked at non-commercial, non-governmental use of encryption with suspicion. This was evident

---

[122] See SANS Institute, 'History of Encryption' (2001) <www.sans.org/reading-room/whitepapers/vpns/history-encryption-730> accessed 8 June 2017; and Human Rights Council, *Report of the Special Rapporteur on the Promotion and Protection of the Right to Freedom of Opinion and Expression* (A/HRC/29/3–2015) 4.

[123] Human Rights Council, *Report of the Special Rapporteur on the Promotion and Protection of the Right to Freedom of Opinion and Expression* (A/HRC/29/3–2015) 4; Susan Landau, 'Under the Radar: NSA's Efforts to Secure Private-sector Telecommunications Infrastructure' (2014) 7 Journal of National Security Law & Policy 411, 411, 419.

[124] John Palfrey, 'Security and the Basics of Encryption in E-Commerce' (*Berkman Center for Internet and Society*, 2001) <http://cyber.law.harvard.edu/ecommerce/encrypt.html> accessed 8 June 2017; Hans Delfs and Helmut Knebl, *Introduction to Cryptography* (Springer 2007) 11–31; Gordon Corera, *Intercept: The Secret History of Computers and Spies* (Weidenfeld & Nicholson 2015) 112; Maria Helen Murphy, 'Technological Solutions to Privacy Questions: What is the Role of Law?' (2016) 25(1) Information and Communications Technology Law 4.

[125] John Palfrey, 'Security and the Basics of Encryption in E-Commerce' (*Berkman Center for Internet and Society*, 2001) <http://cyber.law.harvard.edu/ecommerce/encrypt.html> accessed 8 June 2017; see Whitfield Diffie and Martin Hellman, 'New Directions in Cryptography' (1976) 22 IEEE Transactions on Information Theory 644.

[126] It is non-inferable by reason of the complexity of inverting the encryption method; knowing the public key does not benefit decryption efforts: Susan Landau, 'Under the Radar: NSA's Efforts to Secure Private-Sector Telecommunications Infrastructure' (2014) 7 Journal of National Security Law & Policy 411, 411 and 419; John Palfrey, 'Security and the Basics of Encryption in E-Commerce' (*Berkman Center for Internet and Society*, 2001) <http://cyber.law.harvard.edu/ecommerce/encrypt.html> accessed 8 June 2017.

in the 1990s during what has been dubbed the 'Crypto War' and has become a major issue again in recent years. The victory for encryption and its supporters in the first Crypto War is attributed to the technology's importance for internet security. While the debate went quiet for a time, the resurgence of interest in the topic can be partially explained by the growth in user-friendly encryption solutions. While encryption tools have been considered specialist tools only suitable for the technologically sophisticated user in the past, several companies now market their easy encryption as a key selling point. In September 2014, Apple touted their ability to thwart government data requests by designing their products in a way that denies Apple access to encrypted customer information held on devices.[127] While the FBI's then Director, James Comey, spoke out about this policy change from its inception, criticism of user-friendly encryption gained increased traction following the terrorist attacks in San Bernardino.

The key issue at the heart of the legal dispute dubbed 'Apple v FBI' was whether Apple **[8–64]** could be compelled by a court order to undermine its security systems. A US Magistrate Judge did indeed order Apple to automatically 'push' an update to an iPhone used by one of the San Bernardino attackers containing a specially designed operating system that would enable access to the device.[128] Apple contested the order, arguing that it could undermine security for all of its users. As public support for Apple's position grew, the FBI withdrew its motion to compel and claimed that an alternative solution had been identified to unlock the iPhone.[129] While this was hailed as a victory for encryption, it is clear that government authorities are unwilling to move on from the issue entirely. Since the conclusion of the Apple v FBI saga, legislation was proposed by Senators Diane Feinstein and Richard Burr that would have required 'all persons receiving an authorized judicial order for information or data' to provide 'in a timely manner, responsible, intelligible information or data, or appropriate technical assistance to obtain such information or data'. Such a Bill would have been detrimental to the many companies that aim to offer encryption as a key security measure for their customers and it did not progress much further.[130] Reflecting the cross-jurisdictional concern on this matter, The UK Investigatory Powers Act 2016 requires communications providers to remove 'electronic protection applied … to any communications

---

[127] Craig Timberg, 'Apple will no Longer Unlock Most iPhones, iPads for Police, even with Search Warrants' *Washington Post* (Washington, 18 September 2014).

[128] The update would allow unlimited passcode entry attempts on the targeted device without any time delays. This would enable 'brute force' access: Andrew Blankstein, 'Judge Forces Apple to Help Unlock San Bernardino Shooter iPhone' (*NBC News*, 16 February 2016) <www.nbcnews.com/storyline/san-bernardino-shooting/judge-forces-apple-help-unlock-san-bernardino-shooter-iphone-n519701> accessed 8 June 2017; 'In the Matter of the Search of an Apple iPhone Seized during the Execution of a Search Warrant: Order Compelling Apple to Assist Agents in Search' (16 February 2016) <https://assets.documentcloud.org/documents/2714001/SB-Shooter-Order-Compelling-Apple-Asst-iPhone.pdf> accessed 8 June 2017.

[129] Katie Benner and Eric Lichtblau, 'US Says it Has Unlocked iPhone without Apple' *New York Times* (New York, 28 March 2016).

[130] Tim Bradshaw, 'Barack Obama Warns Over "Fetishising our Phones"' *Financial Times* (London, 12 March 2016); Mark Hosenball and Dustin Volz, 'Exclusive: White House Declines to Support Encryption Legislation – Sources' (*Reuters*, 7 April 2016) <www.reuters.com/article/us-apple-encryption-legislation-idUSKCN0X32M4> accessed 8 June 2017.

or data' under legal authority and anti-encryption measures are also being considered at the European Union level.[131]

[8–65]   The United Nations Special Rapporteur on the Promotion and Protection of the Right to Freedom of Opinion and Expression, David Kaye,[132] recommends that States should only impose restrictions on encryption and anonymity on a case-specific basis.[133] While there is no express right to encryption contained in international texts, the restriction of encryption could clearly constitute interference with both the right to respect for private life and the right to freedom of expression. If you look at how the rights are protected in the ECHR, we can clearly see how the restriction of encryption could be problematic from a human rights perspective.

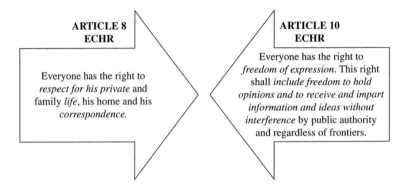

ARTICLE 8 ECHR

Everyone has the right to *respect for his private* and family *life*, his home and his *correspondence*.

ARTICLE 10 ECHR

Everyone has the right to *freedom of expression*. This right shall *include freedom to hold opinions and to receive and impart information and ideas without interference* by public authority and regardless of frontiers.

Figure 3   *The Restriction of Encryption has Implications for Both the Right to Privacy and the Right to Free Expression*

[8–66]   Through the use of encryption communication tools, an individual not only protects their messages from government viewing but also protects their communications from third-party interception. The use of encryption can provide important security for an individual's private life and correspondence.[134] The relevance of Article 10 ECHR is even clearer as the Article explicitly recognises that the right to free expression includes the freedom to impart information and ideas without public authority interference. This is supported by the position of the ECtHR that Article 10 ECHR protects 'the means of transmission or reception'

---

[131] Catherine Stupp, 'EU to Propose New Rules Targeting Encrypted Apps in June' (*EURACTIV. com*, 29 March 2017) <www.euractiv.com/section/data-protection/news/eu-to-propose-new-rules-on-police-access-to-encrypted-data-in-june/> accessed 8 June 2017.

[132] Human Rights Council, *Report of the Special Rapporteur on the Promotion and Protection of the Right to Freedom of Opinion and Expression* (A/HRC/29/3–2015).

[133] Human Rights Council, *Report of the Special Rapporteur on the Promotion and Protection of the Right to Freedom of Opinion and Expression* (A/HRC/29/3–2015) 19.

[134] 'Correspondence' includes electronic communications: *Halford v The United Kingdom* [1997] 24 EHRR 523.

of communications and any restriction on the means of communication 'necessarily interferes with the right to receive and impart information'.[135]

Of course, the second paragraphs of both Article 8 and Article 10 ECHR allow for some restriction of the rights where it is prescribed by (or in accordance with) the law and necessary in a democratic society for the pursuit of a legitimate aim.[136] The key problem with many government interferences with encryption is the generalised nature of the restrictions. Examples of interference have ranged from interfering with products through hacking and attempting to legislate to allow for 'back doors' to encrypted material that can only be opened with 'golden keys'. As Kaye has pointed out, however, 'encroachments on encryption and anonymity will be exploited by the same criminal and terrorist networks that the limitations aim to deter'.[137] The reality is that encryption-restricting measures impact the rights of all users – whether by the criminalisation of certain communication tools or by the creation of security vulnerabilities – with no regard to individual suspicion. This is highly problematic from a Convention perspective where government intrusions must be proportionate to the legitimate aim pursued and blanket measures are considered inherently problematic. Furthermore, the wide-scale restriction of encryption is unlikely to be very suitable for achieving the legitimate aim as those with a criminal incentive are those most likely to circumvent legal restrictions and to continue to use encryption technology – perhaps downloaded over the internet. **[8–67]**

Conclusion

In democratic societies around the globe, freedom of expression receives protection from constitutional and human rights documents. In Ireland, protection is gained from the Constitution, the ECHR (and the ECHR Act 2003), and the EU Charter of Fundamental Rights. Moreover, judges in the various systems recognise the foundational role of the right in democratic society. As the internet is such an efficient and effective communication mechanism, it has incredible power as a tool to receive and impart information. While acknowledging the benefits of the internet, judges have also been wary of the harm such a powerful tool can cause – particularly when other rights are in issue. In addition to the concern that the structure of the internet may hinder the effective pursuit of rights – for example in defamation cases – some express particular disquiet regarding the use of the internet to distribute hate speech, to intimidate, to harass, and to radicalise. **[8–68]**

The appropriate balance between free expression and other rights – including the rights to privacy, a good name, security, and religion – is a complex and disputable question, even **[8–69]**

---

[135] *Autronic AG v Switzerland* [1990] ECHR 12, para 47; Maria Helen Murphy, 'Technological Solutions to Privacy Questions: What Is the Role of Law?' (2016) 25(1) Information and Communications Technology Law 4.

[136] While not concerned with encryption directly, but with the related issue of anonymity, the decisions of the ECtHR in *KU v Finland* and *Delfi AS v Estonia* provide useful guidance on this matter: *KU v Finland* [2008] ECHR 1563, para 49; *Delfi AS v Estonia* [2015] ECHR 586, para 161; Maria Helen Murphy, 'Technological Solutions to Privacy Questions: What is the Role of Law?' (2016) 25(1) Information and Communications Technology Law 4.

[137] Human Rights Council, *Report of the Special Rapporteur on the Promotion and Protection of the Right to Freedom of Opinion and Expression* (A/HRC/29/3–2015) 12.

in the standard 'in real life' context. On the internet, the question is complicated further and greater challenges to enforcement arise. Intermediaries have been central to enforcement efforts thus far and that looks set to remain a feature of this area into the future. In light of this reality, it is all the more important that when intermediaries act in this role that policies must be adopted that are transparent, harm-focused, and open. Of course, an inherent problem remains that intermediaries are generally commercial entities whose interests are not always best served by acting in this way. Regardless, due to the position assumed by intermediaries, there should be forums to express disagreement and opportunities to seek review of decisions made.[138]

Further Reading

- Yaman Akdeniz, *Racism on the Internet* (Council of Europe 2009)
- Eoin Carolan and Ailbhe O'Neill, *Media Law in Ireland* (Bloomsbury Professional 2010)
- Danielle Keats Citron, *Hate Crimes in Cyberspace* (Harvard University Press 2014)
- Danielle Keats Citron and Helen Norton, 'Intermediaries and Hate Speech: Fostering Digital Citizenship for Our Information Age' (2011) 91 Boston University Law Review 1435
- Neville Cox, '*Delfi AS v Estonia*: The Liability of Secondary Internet Publishers for Violation of Reputational Rights under the European Convention on Human Rights' 77(4) Modern Law Review 619
- Human Rights Council, *Report of the Special Rapporteur on the Promotion and Protection of the Right to Freedom of Opinion and Expression* (A/HRC/29/3–2015)
- David Mangan and Lorna Gillies (eds), *The Legal Challenges of Social Media* (Edward Elgar 2017)
- Clive Walker and Russell Weaver (eds), *Free Speech in an Internet Era* (Carolina Academic Press 2013)

---

[138] Danielle Keats Citron and Helen Norton, 'Intermediaries and Hate Speech: Fostering Digital Citizenship for Our Information Age' (2011) 91 Boston University Law Review 1484.

PART 4

ICT in Legal Practice

CHAPTER 9
ICT in Legal Practice

'... it could be said that computers affect almost all regular activities of lawyers'[1]

ICT in the Courts
ICT in Courts Globally

The legal system, and particularly the courts, are very much driven by administrative pro-   **[9–01]**
cesses and procedures – submitting paperwork to initiate a case, arranging dates for preliminary matters, and ensuring that all of the people necessary for a full hearing are available
at the relevant time. These types of routine and structured activities are very amenable to
being assisted or managed by ICT. However, court practices and procedures tend to change
slowly and developing large-scale ICT systems that can operate reliably and consistently
can be a challenge. Therefore, while there is considerable deployment of technology in the
day-to-day working of courts globally, and significant reliance on it for the behind-the-
scenes operation of the civil service, it has not yet reached the level of deep integration that
is visible in other public sector contexts. For all that courts find ICT useful, and that they
would operate with more difficulty and less speed without computer technology, it is not
essential to their functioning. The court system would continue to operate if the computers
were taken away, but at a slower pace.

Video Conferencing

A relatively early application of ICT in the courtroom was the use of video-conferencing.   **[9–02]**
This involves connecting video camera feeds in two or more locations so that an individual

---

[1] Richard L Marcus, 'The Impact of Computers on the Legal Profession: Evolution or Revolution'
(2008) 102 Northwestern University Law Review 1827, 1830.

who is not physically present in the courtroom can nonetheless observe and participate in the proceedings. This is sometimes used for expert witnesses who find it difficult to travel to the court location. It is also used for child witnesses who would be intimidated by the very formal setting and atmosphere of a court hearing. Another use is to allow prisoners to participate in hearings without the risk and expense of transporting them from the prison to the courtroom; this is particularly useful with high-security prisoners whose movements require considerable expense.

Digital Audio Recording

[9–03]   Digital Audio Recording (DAR) provides a straightforward and relatively inexpensive way to record what occurs during a court hearing. Recording onto physical audio tapes is a cumbersome and error-prone process, with significant risk of failure. Having a stenographer present for every single hearing is quite costly. However, DAR systems allow the registrar or court clerk to start a recording whenever the court is in session. This is archived and can be retrieved or transcribed if required at a later date.

Document Management and Display

[9–04]   A considerable amount of court time, particularly in civil cases, is taken up with the reading of documents. These include affidavits, documents exhibited with those, or primary legal materials (such as legislation or case law). While finding a particular document, and a particular page within that document, is not particularly difficult, it can take time, and over the course of a trial, those small delays add up. Given how expensive courtroom time is, saving time and effort in bringing everyone in the court to reading the same text can be very worthwhile. There has therefore been considerable investment worldwide in developing systems that allow lawyers to manage the documents that are submitted as part of a trial process, and displaying them electronically in the courtroom.

CCTV and Audio/Video Recording of Interviews

[9–05]   In criminal investigations and trials, it is well known that eyewitness testimony is not reliable, and that written statements given to the police or transcripts of interviews do not capture all of the nuance of communication. There is therefore considerable use of, and sometimes a legislative requirement for, video recording where possible. In the preliminary stages of an investigation, this will generally involve obtaining closed-circuit television (CCTV) recordings from the time and location of the relevant incident. These can be used both to assist the police in identifying possible suspects and also as evidence in any eventual trial. As the investigation proceeds and individuals are interviewed, these conversations will often be recorded by audio, or if possible, by video. These recordings can become part of the evidence at a trial.

Electronic Filing

[9–06]   The issues involved in reading documents in a courtroom have already been mentioned. What is less obvious to an observer are the logistical issues involved in having all of the relevant documents available for a hearing. The easy availability of ICT seems to have made the generation of paper documents even easier, and the use of online databases for legal research (making it easier to locate a wider range of relevant primary material) also contributes to the volume of paper that is submitted to a court in a particular case. The physical work involved in duplicating and delivering these to all personnel concerned – lawyers for the other side, judge(s), and so on – can be substantial, and storing and distributing them is a significant task for court staff. Courts are therefore beginning to move towards the electronic filing of documents, something which makes electronic retrieval and display much easier.

Case Management

As mentioned in the introduction, a great deal of the work of the court involves arranging [9–07] and scheduling court hearings. It is not surprising, therefore, that the use of database software has considerable potential in assisting with the systematic work that is required in order to track the progress of a case, schedule its next stage, and produce lists and diaries of hearings.

Public Websites

The work of courts is to be carried out in as public a fashion as possible. In addition, court [9–08] users – litigants, practitioners, and others such as journalists – need to be able to find out where and when particular cases are taking place. The use of websites which provide access to information such as lists of scheduled hearings, practical information such as forms and summaries of procedures, and archives of research information such as the text of court judgments, have proved to be quite popular and are seen as saving court staff considerable time and money (as electronic information is easier and cheaper to distribute widely than paper-based means).

ICT in the Irish Courts

The Irish courts did not have any significant investment in ICT until this century. The [9–09] Working Group on the Courts Commission underlined the value of developing appropriate systems during its work in the late 1990s, saying that 'the application of modern technology to the Courts would be of considerable benefit'.[2] Since then, considerable developments have taken place. However, there have been concerns regarding under-funding in more recent years,[3] although these have been partly addressed,[4] and ICT is still somewhat under-utilised in courts in this jurisdiction.

While the use of technology such as electronic display of documents has been a feature [9–10] of specialist tribunals such as the Commercial Court since the beginning of this century,[5] rolling it out across the entire network of courts and court office is still an ongoing process.

The most recent annual report of the Courts Service provides a snapshot of the use of [9–11] ICT in Irish courts. In the courtroom, video viewing facilities are available in 51 courtrooms, in addition to mobile CCTV units. Video conferencing is used in a variety of instances, including mutual assistance cases, criminal cases, and commercial cases, with

---

[2] Working Group on the Courts Commission, 'Second Report: Case Management and Court Management' (1996) 10.
[3] Mark Hilliard, 'Courts Service Boss Fears Collapse of IT System' *The Irish Times* (Dublin, 28 November 2015).
[4] Courts Service, 'Annual Report 2015' 13.
[5] The Hon Mr Justice Peter Kelly, 'The Commercial Court' (2004) Bar Review 4.

links to prisons across the country. Digital audio recording is being extended.[6] Across the service generally, technology is a key priority. A new project, Courts Service Online (CSOL) 'aims to deliver a single civil case management system to provide a common platform for the civil processes of all jurisdictions'.[7] This will allow for electronic filing in the future. The Criminal Case Tracking System (CCTS) is being expanded to take account of changes in the law around fines introduced by the Road Traffic Act 2010 and the Fines (Payment and Recovery) Act 2014.[8] The courts also use ICT to manage the funds that it controls, which are over 1.6 billion. The Courts Service has made wireless network access available in some court buildings.

[9–12] The Courts Service ICT Strategy Statement 2016–2018 provides some insight into how this might develop in the future. Amongst the priorities are providing helpdesk and training facilities to the judiciary,[9] training for staff,[10] expanding use of electronic document display, video linking, and video conferencing,[11] and further development of the CSOL.[12]

Use of ICT by Legal Practitioners
A Very Brief History of Legal Informatics

[9–13] The use of 'information technology' (broadly defined) to store legal information is almost as old as writing. The Code of Hammurabi is a Babylonian law code, almost 4000 years old, and is one of the oldest pieces of deciphered ancient script. Popular representations of the law and lawyers will generally involve written documents, books of laws, and letters. Now, however, many practitioners will work in front of a computer, using online databases of materials, and sending emails rather than letters.

[9–14] A great deal of the vision of information access, inter-connection, and retrieval that we see realised in the global internet and the plethora of research tools that have grown up around that infrastructure is set out in an article from 1945, pre-dating the availability of digital computers, by Vannevar Bush (at the time head of the US Office of Scientific Research and Development), named 'As We May Think'. He described a system based around what was then cutting-edge technology of microfilm viewers, automatic typewriters, and mechanical controls. He proposed a system of instant access to vast volumes of information, the ability to link particular items together (the hyperlink), and systems for recording notes and comments.[13] At the time this was revolutionary but it became a very influential piece of writing.

[9–15] As computers became generally available in the 1950s, simple text databases which would allow Keyword in Context (KWIC) searches were developed. In the 1960s, this was extended to allow the use of logical operators ('and', 'or'), full-text searching, and relevance searching

---

6 Courts Service, 'Annual Report 2015' 22–3.
7 Courts Service, 'Annual Report 2015' 26.
8 Courts Service, 'Annual Report 2015' 27.
9 Courts Service, 'ICT Strategy Statement 2016–2018' 5.
10 Courts Service, 'ICT Strategy Statement 2016–2018' 6
11 Courts Service, 'ICT Strategy Statement 2016–2018' 7.
12 Courts Service, 'ICT Strategy Statement 2016–2018' 7–8.
13 Vannevar Bush, 'As We May Think' (1945) 176(1) The Atlantic Monthly 101.

(adding search terms based on documents that were known to be relevant to the query). In the 1970s, computer-based indexing allowed libraries to keep pace with the explosion in academic and scientific publishing. Commercial online databases were developed, with LEXIS's compilation of court judgments being amongst the first. Through the 1980s, this market developed at a rapid pace, along with CD-ROM technology, which enabled easy distribution of large amounts of data before the internet became widely available.[14]

The use of computer retrieval techniques for legal research became increasingly obvious from the 1950s on. In 1955, Professor John F Horty at the Graduate School of Public Health at the University of Pennsylvania used early IBM computers (one of which used vacuum tubes) to build a text indexing system, first for a specific task (finding instances of particular words in statutes for the purposes of amending legislation) and later (in 1963) the first computerised legal information service, the LITE system of the Air Force Staff Judge Advocate in Denver, Colorado. Similar but more limited and more academically focused projects were developed in Europe through the 1960s. In the 1970s, Germany developed a comprehensive legal information system known as JURIS, with similar systems following in Italy, France, Norway, Sweden and elsewhere. In the US, West launched a competitor to LEXIS known as Westlaw. In the 1990s, the development of the World Wide Web enabled the creation of an international network of Legal Information Institutes (LIIs), open-access repositories of primary legal material generally hosted by third-level institutions.[15] These began in Cornell, extended to Zambia, Australia, and then to many other jurisdictions (including Ireland).[16] **[9–16]**

In other applications of computerisation to legal work, the 1980s saw significant interest in the development of 'expert systems' (the codification of legal thought processes in rules that a computer could apply to new problems). These ultimately failed because they were over-ambitious, misunderstood the complexity of legal reasoning, did not properly investigate the needs of users, and saw law as a static system rather than a dynamic process in which procedure is often more important than argument-based on legal points of detail.[17] Computers were also applied for legal education, through the Center for Computer Aided Legal Instruction (CALI) in the US, and the Law Courseware Consortium in the UK with its IOLIS Courseware. As internet access and broadband became more available, law programmes began to rely much more on online information sources, course websites, and the use of digital content in the classroom.[18] **[9–17]**

ICT in Legal Practice: A Taxonomy

The modern lawyer's office has generally (but not always) moved on from the stereotype of dusty filing cabinets, quill pens, and documents in triplicate. Every legal practice will now **[9–18]**

---

14 Michael Lesk, 'The Seven Ages of Information Retrieval' (1996) UDT Occasional Papers 5.
15 Jon Bing, 'Let There Be LITE: A Brief History of Legal Information Retrieval' (2010) 1 European Journal of Law and Technology.
16 Graham Greenleaf, 'The Global Development of Free Access to Legal Information' (2010) 1 European Journal of Law and Technology.
17 Philip Leith, 'The Rise and Fall of the Legal Expert System' (2010) 1 European Journal of Law and Technology.
18 Abdulla Paliwala, 'Socrates and Confucius: A Long History of Information Technology in Legal Education' (2010) 1 European Journal of Law and Technology.

rely on computer-based information technology for at least some part of its work. However, the level of uptake of technology varies significantly from firm to firm and practitioner to practitioner. Some will use as little as they are required to; others will enthusiastically adopt the freedom and flexibility afforded by mobile devices (particularly tablet computers) and apps, often using these to make productive use of time spent waiting in court. (It is important to note that using the most-up-to-date and sophisticated technology can be quite expensive, something which makes it out of the reach of the smaller or solo firm. This can raise significant issues in terms of basic fairness, as a client who cannot afford a large firm's fees will be even more disadvantaged in the future.) What is presented here, therefore, is a taxonomy of what might be found in law offices, ordered from the most common to the less often found.

Word Processing

[9–19] Practically every law firm will use computer-based word processors to prepare documents. The extent to which this technology is exploited will vary, however: some will use it only as a more convenient typewriter, while more sophisticated firms will have libraries of templates and precedents, and some will assemble common documents automatically through software that asks the user questions or enables the insertion of commonly used paragraphs or clauses into (for example) a letter or contract. Some will also make use of voice recognition software to free secretarial staff from routine dictation typing for more specialised work.

Marketing

[9–20] Solicitors must advertise their presence to potential clients, and most firms will have a website providing at least basic contact information. Others will make use of social networking tools such as Twitter or LinkedIn to establish a more interactive online presence. Some barristers are also users of social media.

Research Databases

[9–21] Many firms will also rely heavily on online legal research databases. Some of these will be the free, open-access services, such as the Court Service's online database of decisions or the British and Irish Legal Information Institute (BAILII). Others may use the commercial providers, such as LexisNexis, Westlaw, or JUSTIS. The latter can be quite expensive and are sometimes out of the reach of smaller firms or sole practitioners.

Research Tools

[9–22] Some lawyers may also use tools such as Juris-M or other software packages to store, manage, and cite the information that they locate using these research databases.

Video Conferencing

[9–23] Many firms, in common with other businesses, will use video conferencing to communicate with clients and collaborators in remote locations. This may involved expensive, dedicated facilities in larger firms, or the use of software such as Skype on off-the-shelf devices.

Electronic Discovery

[9–24] Discovery is an essential stage in litigation, in which each side provides the other with relevant documents and correspondence. As computer technology has made it easier to generate large volumes of text, the burden (and thus the cost) of discovery has increased dramatically. Computer technology is also helping to manage this process, and its associated costs, in two ways: first, by providing discovered documents in electronic rather than paper form (thus reducing transit and storage costs); and second, through the use of software which can automatically locate relevant documents, thus avoiding the significant cost of having trained lawyers read a large number of documents in order to decide if they should be discovered. More recently, machine learning is being applied for this second purpose.

Practice Management

The day-to-day running of a legal practice, particularly a solicitor's firm, is complex, with staffing, appointments, client funds, and regulatory requirements (such as avoiding conflicts of interest) to be kept track of. Specialised software has developed to assist with this. Financial management is an important aspect of these systems, with hourly billing, integration with accounting systems, and online payments as useful features. Some will allow clients to access information, such as uploading and downloading documents. More sophisticated firms will use document scanning, cloud computing, and virtual private networks to create paperless workflows that facilitate remote work. **[9–25]**

Litigation Support

A sub-category of practice management software is litigation support. This is software that will keep track of the various steps involved in litigation, including reminders for impending deadlines, storing and tracking documents (including discovery), and managing correspondence. **[9–26]**

Electronic Contracting, Signatures and Conveyancing

Aspects of electronic contracting and electronic signatures have been touched upon in Chapter 4. While e-commerce has certainly proved very popular, other aspects of electronic transacting that have the potential to radically alter the day-to-day work of practitioners have not achieved the same level of use. As noted in [4–35], electronic signatures cannot yet be used for certain key legal documents, such as wills and deeds. The conveyancing of land is still conducted on paper, despite the publication of a Law Reform Commission report on 'eConveyancing' in 2006.[19] However, the Property Registration Authority is actively seeking to expand its electronic services, and the Government's Construction 2020 strategy document commits to 'review and report on the steps required to deliver a system of eConveyancing in Ireland',[20] while the Law Society has outlined a vision for eConveyancing[21] and launched a project which aims to bring conveyancing online by December 2017.[22] These initiatives have been supported by legislative change: the Land and Conveyancing Law Reform Act 2009 contains some provisions intended to simplify conveyancing in order to facilitate electronic transactions. **[9–27]**

---

[19] LRC 79–2006.
[20] Construction 2020, 'A Strategy for a Renewed Construction Sector' (2014) 57.
[21] Law Society eConveyancing Task Force, 'eConveyancing: Back to Basic Principles ("eVision")' (2008).
[22] Aine McMahon, 'Move to Electronic Transactions Part of Radical Overhaul of Conveyancing' *The Irish Times* (Dublin, 23 March 2015).

The Future of ICT and Law: Computer Lawyers?

[9–28]   It is clear that the use of information technology will remain a key aspect of the work of legal practitioners. The brief history presented above should make it clear that predicting exactly which technologies will be developed to a standard acceptable to the marketplace is not always straightforward. Artificial intelligence (AI), particularly expert systems, has been a failure in the past. However, there is again considerable interest in AI, this time in the form of machine learning (the use of computers to detect and predict patterns in large volumes of data), and newer technologies, such as blockchain (discussed further in [4–66] to [4–68]). Some commentators predict that such systems will bring about significant transformations in the ways in which practitioners carry out transactional and routine work such as discovery, database searches for primary materials, drafting of forms, generation of briefs and memoranda, and the use of legal analytics to try to foresee the likely outcome of a case. This may lead to junior or less-specialised lawyers being replaced by computers.[23]

[9–29]   Richard Susskind has written extensively on the use of ICT by lawyers and attempted to show the path forward. His most recent writings predict radical changes in legal practice, and have focused on what he calls 'disruptive technologies' (which alter the balance of power and income in the legal marketplace), such as automated document assembly, electronic marketplaces, e-learning, and embedded knowledge and rules. These create opportunities for innovation (new types of services) rather than simple automation (doing the same type of work more quickly). Firms will need to become more efficient or to collaborate, or both.

This should lead to greater access to the law and the development of multi-disciplinary partnerships, as expertise is packaged, transactions are decomposed into smaller packages which are more easily outsourced, and law becomes more commodified (routine elements are re-used). He speculates that this will lead to new roles for lawyers, such as 'legal knowledge engineer', 'legal process analyst', or 'online dispute resolution practitioner'. Many of these individuals will be employed in settings other than the traditional law firm, such as accounting firms, legal publishers, and legal management consultancies.[24] Susskind's views on digital technology may lead to deeper changes in the reforms of the legal profession promised by the Legal Services Regulation Act 2015.[25]

[9–30]   There is also a greater reliance on embedded automated decision-making (so-called 'smart devices'), particularly in the built environment, transport. These are likely to create new issues of product liability, privacy and security. There are also rapid developments taking place in machine intelligence and learning (so-called 'smart apps'), which have seen the application of chatbots to provide legal advice and the use of AI to predict the outcome of court cases. This increasing reliance on digital technology may lead to deeper changes in the ways in which legal texts are written and interpreted.[26]

---

[23] John O McGinnis and Russell G Pearce, 'The Great Disruption: How Machine Intelligence Will Transform the Role of Lawyers in the Delivery of Legal Services' (2014) 82 Fordham Law Review 3041, 3047–55.

[24] Richard E Susskind, *Tomorrow's Lawyers: An Introduction to Your Future* (Oxford University Press 2013).

[25] 'Legal Services Regulation' (2015) Annual Review of Irish Law 519.

[26] Peter M Tiersma, *Parchment, Paper, Pixels: Law and the Technologies of Communication* (University of Chicago Press 2010).

Further Reading

- Anthony J Casey and Anthony Niblett, 'Self-Driving Laws' (2016) 66 University of Toronto Law Journal 429
- Iria Giuffrida, 'Legal, Practical and Ethical Implications of the Use of Technology in European Courtrooms' (2004) 12 William and Mary Bill of Rights Journal 745
- Michael E Heintz, 'The Digital Divide and Courtroom Technology: Can David Keep Up with Goliath?' (2002) 54 Federal Communications Law Journal 567
- Fredric I Lederer, 'WIRED: What We've Learned About Courtroom Technology' (2010) 24 Criminal Justice 18
- Richard L Marcus, 'The Impact of Computers on the Legal Profession: Evolution or Revolution' (2008) 102 Northwestern University Law Review 1827
- H Michael O'Brien, 'The Internet of Things' (2016) 19 Journal of Internet Law 1
- Richard Susskind and Daniel Susskind, *The Future of the Professions* (Oxford University Press 2015)
- Harry Surden, 'Machine Learning and Law' (2014) 89 Washington Law Review 87
- Janet Walker and Garry D Watson, 'New Trends in Procedural Law: New Technologies and the Civil Litigation Process' (2008) 31 Hastings International and Comparative Law Review 251
- Elizabeth C Wiggins, 'The Courtroom of the Future Is Here: Introduction to Emerging Technologies in the Legal System' (2006) 28 Law and Policy 182

PART 5

Issues, Trends and the Future

CHAPTER 10
A Dynamic and Unpredictable Future

'... computer law has its share of failed predictions, but this is typical of any attempt to predict technological advances. ... IT law commentators need to keep this in mind when presented with the temptation of making predictions about the legal implications of new advances and perhaps appropriate caveats should be put in place.'[1]

Summarising the current state and importance of information and communications technology law at this point in time is not straightforward. Making predictions for the future is even more challenging. The industry thrives on hype, much of which is unthinkingly repeated, or even expanded upon, by a media that has little real understanding of the underlying technical details. For those who are seeking to understand the relationship between law and ICT, therefore, it is important to remain sceptical and to always ask questions about the veracity of the claims that are being made. Is the current focus on information technology as a significant factor in modern law and policy simply the result of marketing puff pieces, or has this indeed become a key issue for law in the 21st century? **[10–01]**

The answer is probably a bit of both. ICT has considerable promise but also (as outlined in the first chapter) significant limits. This is for two reasons. First, digital measurement and calculation is fundamentally quite a crude device, which can only deal with ones and zeros and which only achieves sophistication through scale. Second, achieving that scale requires huge human effort in developing and engineering increasingly complex infrastructures, something which is still very difficult and challenging to achieve on a consistent and reliable basis. However, as has been explored in the other chapters of the book, various aspects of the law (such as intellectual property, contract law, and data protection, and privacy) are very significant to commerce and industry, while ICT has become a key tool for legal practice. **[10–02]**

Students and practitioners who seek to understand and work with ICT and the law therefore need to bear a number of issues in mind. The two spheres of law and ICT have a close relationship with each other, with law (particularly IP law) enabling the early rapid development of ICT, but also at times constraining it (for example, data protection).[2] In general, the ICT industry depends on law as an important support for its development. At times, law has **[10–03]**

---

[1] Andrés Guadamuz González, 'Attack of the Killer Acronyms: The Future of Information Technology Law' (2004) 18 International Review of Law, Computers & Technology 411, 419.

[2] As discussed in [5–39] to [5–44], the Privacy by Design approach 'seeks to accommodate all legitimate interests and objectives in a positive-sum "win-win" manner, not through a dated, zero-sum

been hugely important in determining who controls the development of a particular industry, and the significant market trends within it. This is particularly obvious when considering the development of the software industry and the music industry, as has been explored in Chapter 2. However, those who seek to wrest control of an industry away from its mainstream will sometimes also rely on elements of the law as an important tool: prominent examples include the Free, Libre and Open Source Software movement, and Creative Commons.

[10–04] Law is, however, not the only factor to be considered. As can be seen from the efforts to curtail online file sharing, strictly legal approaches to widespread social problems often meet with limited results. This leads some to highlight the rapid pace of technological change and the slow pace of legal change. It is true that in some instances, as with the Copyright Review Committee,[3] suggestions for law reform are only progressed very slowly. However, it is not always necessary or appropriate that the law should change at the same pace as ICT. Part of the ICT industry's rhetoric is that it is at the forefront of 'progress'. On closer examination, this can often mask a socially regressive agenda which seeks to minimise democratic oversight while maximising profits. In such situations, law can provide a valuable brake on too-rapid social dislocation.

[10–05] Does the law transform the information technology industry? In some aspects it is clearly very important, but (much to the chagrin of lawyers), law is not always the most important determinant of business plans or business success. Will information technology transform the law? ICT is certainly important in legal practice, which is not surprising given that lawyers are, at their core, knowledge workers who deal with the understanding and application of rules, something which computer technology can do much to facilitate. It is also clear that certain aspects of contracting (whether that be business-to-business or business-to-consumer), policing, and the functioning of bureaucracy are being significantly modified due to the new capabilities that are provided by information technology. Many aspects of modern society would cease to function, in some cases for considerable periods of time, if ICT or electricity were not available. However, ICT is only one tool in a broad constellation of institutional factors and historical accidents that give rise to the modern capitalist economy and the administrative state. ICT is very important, but it is not the sole factor, nor is it the final determiner of outcomes.

Significant Issues

[10–06] There are a number of topics dealt with in this textbook that are likely to continue to be very important for those working with ICT law for the next five to ten years. These include:

- *Privacy*: Modern privacy law is largely the result of concerns regarding the potential negative effects of ICT on individual autonomy and freedom. With the widespread use of online services for so many aspects of our day-to-day lives, these concerns have become even more accentuated in recent years. There are no signs of these dissipating in the near future, and the application of the General Data Protection Regulation in May 2018[4] is likely to create further interesting legal questions and challenges for business and government.

---

approach, where unnecessary trade-offs are made': Ann Cavoukian, 'The 7 Foundational Principles' (2009) <www.ipc.on.ca/wp-content/uploads/Resources/privacybydesign.pdf> accessed 13 June 2017.

3 Discussed in [2–114] to [2–116].

4 May 2018 is also the date by which a new ePrivacy Regulation is intended to be operative.

- *Intellectual Property*: IP has been very important in the development of the information technology industry, and the ways in which the widespread availability of ICT has destabilised IP-based industries (such as music, movie, and television) are well known. While the infringement of audio and video content is no longer attracting the types of mainstream media coverage that it was a number of years ago, the phenomenon continues. In addition, for those who advise commercial clients, other aspects of intellectual property, such as patents, design rights, and trademarks are very important, and often involve significant shareholder value.
- *Electronic Commerce*: The buying and selling of goods and services online has become a significant convenience for consumers and disruptor of existing markets. There has been some legislative reform to address consumer protection online. At present, there is significant interest in the development of open and permissionless ledger systems (commonly known as 'blockchains') which may offer new ways to transfer value and authenticate transactions online. These new online spaces also offer an opportunity to provide truly 'autonomous agents', something which has been a topic of discussion for many years but has never been realised on a sufficiently broad scale to truly capture consumer imagination.
- *Fairness and Equity*: While some have been raising concerns regarding the equality implications of the development of ICT for many years, the recent and relatively rapid development of 'machine learning' tools has brought this issue to the fore. Many are now concerned about the equality implications of decision-making by hidden and sometimes impenetrable algorithms. In addition, the increasing reliance on ICT as a tool for delivery of essential services (such as healthcare, education, and public services) generally gives rise to concerns regarding the 'digital divide', in which those without access to, or the skills to operate, ICT are increasingly disenfranchised and shut out from accessing what they need. These developments raise serious concerns regarding the rule of law in the administrative and regulatory state.
- *Open or Closed Systems*: Much of the early success of ICT was built on open systems and open standards. The Linux software infrastructure is a key example here: with software based on well-known and widely accepted technological standards and easy access to the underlying source code, many were able to get involved and build on what had gone before. However, there are alternative models, such as Apple's App Store, which built their success on being a closed and tightly controlled space in which all software is vetted before being made available to the customer and efforts are made to ensure that it is free from viruses and other malicious elements. For the foreseeable future, such open and closed systems are likely to coexist side-by-side. Time will tell whether one or the other becomes the dominant model.

Significant Trends

The development of these issues will also be influenced by trends in the development of ICT. There are three closely connected trends that will doubtless prove significant in the coming years: [10–07]

- *More of the Same*: The importance of ICT for the day-to-day running of businesses, large organisations, and government will continue apace for the foreseeable future. This will mean that policy decisions about key legal topics such as privacy will be quite important.

245

- *Internet of Things*: ICT is becoming increasingly miniaturised, ubiquitous, and embedded. This is colloquially known as the 'Internet of Things'. Devices are now mobile, can interact with their environment, and are often invisible to the user. This provides significant power and capability, but also creates many security problems, together with significant legal questions around privacy and other legal topics.
- *'Artificial Intelligence'*: This trend has been given different names over the years – big data, machine learning, the algorithm, artificial intelligence – and may have other marketing labels in the future. These all describe the same phenomena: the use of computers to process large volumes of data, seek to identify patterns, and draw conclusions from those. The two other trends described above provide a wealth of input for this type of processing to work with. Computer-based models now drive marketing campaigns, policing, and health-care systems. There are already indications that it is being used in fraud detection, criminal justice decision-making, and even weapon systems. Self-driving cars are now being tested. This raises many questions around privacy, autonomy, and equality.

Predictions

[10–08] Much of the rhetoric which surrounds ICT uses a discourse of discontinuity. This should also be approached with scepticism. Humans and human nature have not (yet) changed in any fundamental way. (More intimate human/computer interfaces, genetic manipulation, and ICT-based social control mechanisms are as yet not significant except in science fiction.) However, although we have not yet arrived at a transformative break from the past, there is no doubt that the world of business and government are quite different to what they were 20 years ago. The rapid development of mobile communications, and now the Internet of Things, also provide a very different technological context. We may see the development of embedded and automated law enforcement, a move from regulating people to regulating machines, or even more focus on regulating people through machines. Any of these options could easily become dystopias. However, we should not lose sight of the fact that a sociotechnical system has a significant social component, and ultimately how the technology develops will be a function of human values and social choices.

We may also see ICT law disappear from university curricula, as it finally overflows its initially quite limited boundaries and discussion of ICT-related issues becomes part of the more mainstream subjects, such as contract, tort, and constitutional law.

Further Reading

- Andrés Guadamuz González, 'Attack of the Killer Acronyms: The Future of Information Technology Law' (2004) 18 International Review of Law, Computers & Technology 411
- Mireille Hildebrandt, *Smart Technologies and the End(s) of Law: Novel Entanglements of Law And Technology* (Edward Elgar Publishing 2015)
- Mireille Hildebrandt and Antoinette Rouvroy (eds), *The Philosophy of Law Meets the Philosophy of Technology* (Routledge 2011)
- Mireille Hildebrandt and Bert-Jaap Koops, 'The Challenges of Ambient Law and Legal Protection in the Profiling Era' (2010) 73 The Modern Law Review 428
- Jaron Lanier, *You are not a Gadget: A Manifesto* (Alfred A Knopf 2010)
- Julia JA Shaw, 'From Homo Economicus to Homo Roboticus: An Exploration of the Transformative Impact of the Technological Imaginary' (2015) 11 International Journal of Law in Context 245
- Jonathan Zittrain, *The Future of the Internet – And How to Stop It* (Yale University Press 2008)

Index